Selections from

RECORDS OF
THE HISTORIAN

Written By Szuma Chien

Translated by
Yang Hsien-yi and Gladys Yang

FOREIGN LANGUAGES PRESS
PEKING

First Edition 1979

Printed in the People's Republic of China

CONTENTS

Preface

Wang Po-hsiang

The *Records of the Historian*, written two thousand years ago by Szuma Chien of the Han Dynasty, is the greatest historical work China has produced. Many parts of it are fine literature. Thanks to Szuma Chien's rich experience of life, his enlightened approach to history and his brilliance as a man of letters, he was able to make a discriminating selection of material and to write a new form of history. His monumental work provides a realistic picture of many different historical figures and aspects of Han society, in addition to much information about earlier times. The excellent organization of this work, and its method of presenting history from various angles, made it a model for later historians from the Han to the Ching Dynasties. In fact, this became the accepted way of recording official history. The rich contents of the *Records*, its remarkable character sketches and its vast panoramic view of complex social life induced later prose writers to imitate its style. In this way it has had a profound influence on Chinese literature.

Szuma Chien was born in 145 B.C. in Hsiayang County, Fengyi, in what is now the province of Shensi. When he was a child of about six his father, Szuma Tan, was appointed the grand historian and took his son with him to the capital Changan (present-day Sian). Szuma Chien began his studies there and by the time he was ten was able to read the classics. After he was twenty he travelled widely and, on his return to the capital, was made a palace attendant. This post afforded him further opportunities for travel, and he went on government missions, accompanying the emperor on his journeys, or touring the country collecting material for his records. Indeed, he travelled so widely that there were few parts of the country he did not visit. He became especially familiar with the lower reaches of the Huai and Yangtse Rivers. This enabled him to make a close study of social conditions in those parts of China most thickly populated and richest in tradition, thus laying the foundation for the writing of the *Records*.

His father Szuma Tan died in 110 B.C., and three years later Szuma Chien, who was then thirty-eight, succeeded his father as grand historian and began to collect materials for his history. He edited and studied the historical documents in the imperial library, consulted many people, and verified facts, supplementing them by his own investigations. In 104 B.C., when he was forty-two, his preparations were complete and he started to write his history in a way which had never been attempted before.

Five years later when he was forty-seven, he offended the emperor by defending General Li Ling who had been defeated in battle and had surrendered to the Huns. For this he was punished by imprisonment and castration. Despite this cruel indignity, he continued his writing in gaol. In 96 B.C. he was pardoned and appointed palace secretary, a post slightly higher than that of grand historian but one usually held by eunuchs. Humiliated and distressed, he nevertheless went on writing the history and completed his work in 91 B.C. when he was fifty-five.

The *Records of the Historian* is divided into: Twelve Basic Annals, Ten Tables, Eight Treatises, Thirty Hereditary Houses and Seventy Lives. It contains one hundred and thirty sections in all, and more than half a million words. Apart from certain minor additions and changes he made later, he finished writing it when he was fifty-six, and we have no reliable information about his closing years. The date of his death is still uncertain.

There had been a great deal of historical writing in China before the time of Szuma Chien. Some of these works are lost, but those that remain include such chronicles as the *Spring and Autumn Annals, Anecdotes of the States, Records of the*

Warring States, political documents like those preserved in the *Shu Ching* (*Book of Documents*), and critical accounts of different schools of thought in some of the writings of such philosophers as Chuang Tzu and Hsun Tzu. There was, however, no systematized and comprehensive history of China. Szuma Chien was able to assemble all the material needed for this great task, and to create a new form of historical writing.

The Twelve Basic Annals contain records of the twelve most important reigns from the legendary Yellow Emperor down to Szuma Chien's own sovereign. Important social changes were included here in chronological order. Historical events which could not be grouped under any definite year were incorporated in the Ten Tables, which clearly present the dynastic successions, the relations between different states, and the appointments of important officials. The Eight Treatises show the development of ceremony, music, law, calendar science, astronomy, sacrifice, water conservancy, and weights and measures. The Thirty Hereditary Houses deal with the most important nobles and princes during the Spring and Autumn Period, the time of the Warring States, and the Chin and early Han Dynasties. The Seventy Lives are biographies, though sometimes several men belonging to the same category are grouped together, even though they may have lived in different periods. There are also accounts of foreign countries and of the minority peoples within China, showing their relations with the Han people. These records usually end with the author's comments and give supplementary facts from Szuma Chien's personal investigations, or refute misconceptions. His comments are balanced and matter-of-fact, unlike those of some later historians who deliberately advanced startling conclusions.

Szuma Chien's outstanding ability is shown not only in his creation of a new historical form, but also in his attitude to his work. He travelled widely in search of the historical materials then available, made a selection from them to draft his basic records, and verified his facts by comparing different versions.

iii

He made use of his travels to carry out investigations all over China, and often corrected mistakes he found in the records. In this way he was able to compile a remarkably accurate history. His aim was to tell the truth, and he fought all his life against falsehood and hypocrisy. The Twelve Basic Annals, for example, deal mainly with the rule of kings and emperors, but during the five years of fighting and confusion which followed the Chin Dynasty, Hsiang Yu was the man who actually led the insurgent forces against Chin. Szuma Chien, therefore, put an account of Hsiang Yu between the records of the First Emperor of Chin and the First Emperor of Han. The First Emperor of Han was succeeded by his son, but because the actual authority was in the hands of the empress dowager, Szuma Chien wrote a record of Empress Dowager Lu. It was contrary to his principles to deny a defeated hero his place in history, or to consider women as less important than men. He made this penetrating comment: "Though the Empress Dowager ruled as a woman from within doors, the empire was at peace, there were few punishments and few criminals, the peasants tilled the land diligently, and there was an abundance of food and clothing."

Similarly, his strong sense of right and wrong made him write frankly about the ugly conduct of rulers. Thus he exposed Emperor Wu's superstition, greed and ambition, the obsequiousness and craftiness of certain ministers, their avarice, cruelty, scheming and backbiting, and the licentiousness of nobles like the Prince of Yen and Prince Li of Chi. He described these vices truthfully, and made his condemnation clear. This attitude offended the ruling class, and some of his contemporaries dubbed his work "a slanderous book." Szuma Chien's fighting spirit made him a champion of justice and a spokesman of the people. He did not discriminate against the different professions and trades of his day, but gave equally fair pictures of scholars, gallant citizens, peasants, merchants, physicians, fortune-tellers, astrologers and others. Those who deserved his sympathy could be sure of getting it, and he was not sparing in his criticism either. His likes and dislikes were so strong that readers of later ages can almost see his characters in the flesh and share the historian's partisan view of them.

After this brief reference to Szuma Chien's achievements as a historian, his great influence on Chinese literature should be noted. His writing is highly realistic. He chooses typical characters and brings them to life, breaking with stultified literary conventions and using the colourful vernacular of his day. He boldly rewrites archaic passages from old books to make them more easily intelligible, interspersing them with colloquialisms and local figures of speech. He deliberately rejects the euphuistic parallelisms popular at the time in favour of a more natural prose, clear, concise and pleasing in style. All the people he describes are very much alive and have strong individuality. Their conversation is authentic and in character, subtly conveying the atmosphere of the occasion. In his choice of episode he shows himself a master of significant detail, one able to make history come alive.

The lively tales from the *Records of the Historian* have been favourites with Chinese in all walks of life throughout the centuries. Many Ming Dynasty prose romances, such as the *Romance of the Warring States* by Yu Shao-yu and the *Romance of the Early Han Dynasty* by Tseng Wei, took their material from Szuma Chien. Folk artists and story-tellers all over China are still performing or relating episodes from these romances. Chinese drama owes a great debt to Szuma Chien too, numerous Yuan and Ming dramas being based on stories from the *Records*. Eleven of the *Selected Yuan Plays* edited during the Ming Dynasty and the *Sixty Dramas* printed at the beginning of the Ching Dynasty owe their plot to Szuma Chien. The same is true of many popular Peking operas and local operas which are being performed today. The modern writer Kuo Mo-jo drew on Szuma Chien for his historical plays *Chu Yuan, The Tiger Tally* and *Cherry Blossom*. This testifies to the fact that, two thousand years after it was written, Szuma Chien's *Records of the Historian* still exercises a great influence on Chinese literature.

In this selection we include two of the Basic Annals, five of the Hereditary Houses, and twenty-four of the Lives rearranged in chronological order starting from the sixth century B.C., the time of Confucius, down to the first century B.C., Szuma Chien's own time.

CONFUCIUS

Confucius was born in Tsou, a village in the district of Chang-ping in the state of Lu. His ancestors came from Sung and one of them, Kung Fang-shu, had a son named Po-hsia, whose son was Shu-liang-heh. In his old age Shu-liang-heh took a daughter of the Yen family, and after he had prayed at the shrine of Nichiu she gave birth to Confucius. That was in the twenty-second year of Duke Hsiang of Lu.* Because he was born with a hollow in the top of his head, he was given the personal name of Chiu, with the courtesy name Chung-ni and the surname Kung.

Soon after his birth Shu-liang-heh died and was buried at Mount Fang in the east of Lu. Later Confucius suspected that his father's grave was there, but his mother hid the truth from him. As a child, Confucius liked to play with sacrificial vessels, setting them out as if for a ceremony. After his mother's death, as a precaution, he had her coffin entombed in Wufu Lane. Then the mother of Wan Fu of Tsou told him the whereabouts of his father's grave, and he had his mother buried with her husband at Mount Fang.

Confucius was still wearing the belt of mourning when he went to a feast for gentlemen given by the Chi clan. Yang Hu turned him away, saying, "The Chi clan is entertaining gentlemen: you are not included." At that Confucius withdrew.

When Confucius was seventeen, Meng Hsi-tzu the minister of Lu fell ill and as he was dying he told his successor Yi-tzu, "Kung Chiu is descended from sages. One of his ancestors was killed in Sung. One of his ancestors, Fu-fu-ho, should have

* 551 B.C.

1

been the ruler of Sung but made over the state to his younger brother Duke Li. And Cheng Kao-fu, his great-grandson who served Duke Tai, Duke Wu and Duke Hsuan, behaved more modestly after each appointment. Thus his tripod inscription reads: 'At the first appointment I inclined my head, at the second I bowed, at the third I bent low. I hug the wall and no one dares insult me. Pap and gruel stay my hunger.' See how unassuming he was! I have heard that even if he does not hold office the descendant of sages is always a wise man. Kung Chiu is young, but he sets such store on the rites that I am sure he is a man of understanding. When I am gone, make him your teacher."

So after Meng Hsi-tzu's death, Yi-tzu and Nankung Ching-shu, another native of Lu, studied the rites with Confucius. That same year Chi Wu-tzu died and Ping-tzu succeeded him.

Confucius was poor and humble. Growing up and working as keeper of the granaries for the Chi clan he measured the grain fairly; when he was keeper of the livestock the animals flourished; and so he was made minister of works. Subsequently he left Lu, was dismissed from Chi, driven out of Sung and Wei and ran into trouble between Chen and Tsai. Finally he returned to Lu.

Well over six feet, Confucius was called the Tall Man and everybody marvelled at his height. He returned to the state of Lu as it had treated him well. Nankung Ching-shu asked the duke of Lu to let him accompany Confucius to Chou, and the duke gave them a carriage, a pair of horses and a page boy. They went to Chou to study rites and there met Lao Tzu.

When Confucius was leaving, Lao Tzu's parting words to him were, "I have heard that the rich and great offer farewell gifts of money while the good offer advice. I am neither rich nor great but, unworthy as I am, have been called good; so let me offer you a few words of advice." Then he said, "A shrewd observer, prone to criticize others, risks his own life. A learned man who exposes the faults of others endangers himself. A filial son must never thrust himself forward, and neither may a good subject."

On his return from Chou to Lu, Confucius began to gather more disciples.

Now the situation at this time was that Duke Ping of Tsin was a dissolute man whose six ministers held the reins of government and were attacking other states in the east, King Ling of Chu was harrying the central states with his powerful armies, and mighty Chi bordered on Lu. Lu was small and weak. If she attached herself to Chu, this would offend Tsin; while if she allied with Tsin, Chu would attack her; if she took no defensive measures, the men of Chi would invade her.

In the twentieth year of Duke Chao of Lu, Confucius reached the age of thirty. Duke Ching of Chi and Yen Ying visited Lu and the duke said to Confucius, "Duke Mu of Chin had only a small, outlying state, yet he became a great conqueror. How was that?"

Confucius replied, "Though Chin was small it aspired to great things. Though outlying, its conduct was correct. With five sheepskins the duke freed a slave from bondage and gave him the rank of a minister. After talking with him for three days he entrusted the affairs of state to him. Judging by this he was worthy to be a king — being a conqueror was not good enough for him."

The duke was pleased with this reply.

When Confucius was thirty-five, Chi Ping-tzu, because of a cockfight between a bird of his and one owned by Hou Chao-po, offended Duke Chao of Lu. The duke led troops against him. Chi Ping-tzu fought back with the support of the houses of Meng-sun and Shu-sun and defeated the duke, who fled to Chi where he settled at Kanhou. After this there was such confusion in Lu that Confucius went to Chi to serve as Kao Chao-tzu's steward in the hope of getting an introduction to Duke Ching. He discussed music with the chief musician of Chi, heard the Shao Music and studied it, and for three months did not know the taste of meat. The men of Chi thought highly of him.

Duke Ching of Chi questioned him about government. His answer was, "Let the prince be a prince, the minister a minister, the father a father and the son a son."

The duke rejoined, "Well said! For indeed when the prince is not a prince, the minister not a minister, the father not a father, the son not a son, even if there were grain I might be unable to eat it."

Another day he asked about government again and Confucius said, "The main thing is economy in the use of wealth."

The duke was pleased and would have given the field of Nihsi to Confucius as his fief had not Yen Ying protested, "These Confucians are such unruly windbags, so arrogant and self-willed that there is no controlling them. They set great store by long mourning and bankrupt themselves for a sumptuous funeral; it would never do if this became the custom. A beggar who roams the land talking is not a man to entrust with affairs of state. Ever since the passing of the great sages and the decline of the Chou Dynasty, the rites and music have fallen into decay. Now Confucius lays such stress on appearance and costume, elaborate etiquette and codes of behaviour that it would take generations to learn his rules — one lifetime would not be enough! To adopt his way of reforming the state would not be putting the common people first."

So when next Duke Ching saw Confucius he did not question him about ceremony. And on another day he told him, "I cannot give you the rank of first minister." He treated him as someone between the first and third rank. The other ministers of Chi conspired to injure Confucius, who learned of their plot. And Duke Ching said, "I am old, I cannot make use of your services." So Confucius left Chi and returned to Lu.

When Confucius was forty-two, Duke Chao of Lu died at Kanhou and Duke Ting succeeded him. In the summer of the fifth year of Duke Ting, Chi Ping-tzu died and Chi Huan-tzu took his place as first minister. While sinking a well, Chi Huan-tzu found an earthenware pot with a creature like a sheep inside it and, although aware of what it was, he told

4

Confucius that it was a dog. "From all I have heard," said Confucius, "it must be a sheep. For *kuei* and *wang-liang* are the spirits of woods and rocks, those of the deep are dragons and *wang-hsiang*, while those of the earth are entombed sheep."

When Wu attacked Yueh and captured Kuaichi, a skeleton was discovered that filled a whole chariot. The king of Wu sent an envoy to ask Confucius, "What has the largest bones?"

Confucius replied, "When Yu* summoned all the gods to Mount Kuaichi, Fang-feng arrived late and Yu killed him as a warning to others. His skeleton filled a whole chariot: that is the largest."

"What gods were those?" asked the envoy.

"Gods of the hills and streams to regulate the world, gods who were local chiefs; and gods of earth and grain who became barons under the sovereign."

"Of what was Fang-feng in charge?"

"He was lord of Wangwang of the Hsi clan, ruling over Mounts Feng and Yu. In the time of King Shun and during the Hsia and Shang Dynasties, the family was called Wangwang; in the Chou Dynasty they were known as the giants of Ti; today we just call them giants."

"What height can men reach?"

"The Chiaoyao pygmies, three feet high, are the smallest. The tallest cannot be more than ten times their height: that is the upper limit."

Then the envoy of Wu commented, "Well spoken, sage!"

Chi Huan-tzu's favourite minister, Chung-liang Huai, was an enemy of Yang Hu, who would have driven him away had not Kungshan Pu-niu dissuaded him. That autumn Chung-liang Huai behaved even more insolently and Yang Hu had him arrested. Because Chi Huan-tzu was angry, Yang Hu imprisoned him too, releasing him after they had reached an agreement. This made Yang Hu despise the Chi clan more than ever. While the Chi clan usurped the duke's authority, their own servants had actual control of the state. In fact, all the

* The legendary pacifier of floods and founder of the Hsia Dynasty.

men of Lu from the ministers down overstepped their right-ful bounds and did not act correctly. This is why Confucius took no official post but edited the *Book of Songs, Book of Documents, Book of Rites* and *Book of Music* in retirement, and more and more pupils came even from distant places to study under him.

In the eighth year of Duke Ting, Kungshan Pu-niu who bore a grudge against the Chi family rebelled with Yang Hu, hoping to overthrow the heirs of the three chief families and set up in their place the concubines' sons befriended by Yang Hu. Chi Huan-tzu was captured but contrived to escape. In the ninth year of Duke Ting, Yang Hu was defeated and fled to Chi. By now Confucius was fifty.

Then Kungshan Pu-niu, who controlled the district of Pi, rebelled against the Chi family and sent for Confucius. Confucius had long been following the true way without being able to put it into practice because no one would employ him. So now he said, "King Wen and King Wu of Chou started from the districts of Feng and Hao and became kings. Though Pi is small, this may be worth trying."

He was planning to go, but Tzu-lu demurred and stopped him.

"He would not send for me without a reason," said Confucius. "By using my services he could make another Chou in the east." However, in the end he did not go.

Later Duke Ting appointed Confucius the magistrate of Chungtu. After one year of his administration, all the neighbouring districts were following his example. He was promoted to be minister of works, then chief justice.

In the spring of the tenth year of Duke Ting, Lu and Chi made peace. That summer Li Tsu, a minister of Chi, warned Duke Ching of Chi, "Lu is employing Kung Chiu. That is dangerous for us." So they invited the duke of Lu to a friendly meeting at Chiaku. He was about to set off by carriage when Confucius, then acting prime minister, interposed, "I have heard that in peace men should prepare for war; in war they should prepare for peace. In the old days a baron never left his territory unless accompanied by military officials. I beg you to take the senior and junior war ministers."

Duke Ting agreed and took these two ministers to meet the duke of Chi at Chiaku. Seats had been placed on an earthen platform with three steps leading up to it and the two dukes met on equal terms, mounting the steps after bowing to each other. When wine had been offered, Chi's master of ceremonies stepped forward to ask, "May we play the Music of the Four Quarters?"

Upon Duke Ching's assenting, men with pennants, feathers, spears, halberds, swords and shields advanced to the roll of drums. At once Confucius stepped forward, rushed up the steps and, raising his sleeves, protested, "Our two rulers are meeting in friendship: what is the meaning of this barbarian music? Let these men be dismissed by the officer in charge!" The master of ceremonies made them step back, but they did not go. The attendants looked at Yen Ying and Duke Ching, and the shamefaced duke waved them away.

Presently Chi's minister of ceremonies came forward again to ask, "May we play palace music?"

When Duke Ching assented, jesters, singers and dwarfs trooped in to perform. At once Confucius stepped forward, rushed up the steps and again protested, "Commoners who beguile their lords deserve to die. Let them be punished!" Then the officer in charge had the players killed.

Aware that he had been in the wrong, Duke Ching was greatly perturbed. He returned to his capital in dismay and reproached his ministers, saying, "In Lu they use the gentleman's way to guide their prince, while all you teach me is the barbarian way. Now we have offended the duke of Lu. What shall we do?"

A minister advanced to reply, "A gentleman who is at fault shows his regret by deeds, while a low man shows it by words. If you are sorry, sir, show your regret by deeds."

So to make amends the duke returned to Lu the lands of Yun, Wenyang and Kueiyin which he had taken.

In the summer of the thirteenth year of Duke Ting, Confucius told him, "A subject should not conceal arms, a noble should not have city walls three thousand feet long."

Chung Yu was appointed steward under Chi Huan-tzu, but before he could demolish the fortified towns of the three chief nobles, the Shu-sun family tore down the walls of Hou. When the Chi clan tried to demolish the wall of Pi, Kungshan Pu-niu and Shu-sun Cheh led the men of Pi against the Lu capital; whereupon the duke and his three noble ministers withdrew to the Chi clan mansion and took refuge in the tower of Chi Wu-tzu. The men of Pi attacked the tower but failed to take it. When they came near the tower, Confucius sent Shen Chu-hsu and Lo Chi to fight back and the men of Pi were put to flight by the forces of Lu at Kumieh. At that Kungshan Pu-niu and Shu-sun Cheh fled to Chi and the city of Pi was demolished.

They were about to tear down the wall of Cheng when Kunglien Chu-fu warned Meng-sun, "If Cheng is demolished, we shall have the men of Chi at our North Gate. Besides, Cheng is the bulwark of the Meng family, without which we must fall. I refuse to destroy it." In the twelfth month the duke besieged Cheng but failed to take it.

In the fourteenth year of Duke Ting, Confucius, now fifty-six, appeared gratified when he was appointed both chief justice and prime minister.

His pupils said, "We have heard that a gentleman would show no fear in the face of calamity, no joy in the face of good fortune."

"True," replied Confucius. "But what of the saying, 'He delights in high position because he can show his humility'?" He executed Shao-cheng Mao, a minister of Lu who had made trouble. After three months of his administration vendors of lamb and pork stopped raising their prices, men and women walked on different sides of the street, no one picked up anything lost on the road, and strangers coming to the city did not have to look for the officers in charge for everyone made them welcome.

When the men of Chi knew this they took fright and said, "With Confucius at the head of the state, Lu is bound to grow powerful; then we who are close to it will be the first to be swallowed up. We had better offer them some land."

But Li Tsu said, "Let us first see if we can't foil them. If that fails, it will not be too late to offer land."

So they chose eighty of the prettiest girls in Chi who could dance to the *kang* music, dressed them in gay costumes and sent them with sixty pairs of dappled horses as a gift to the duke of Lu. The dancers were displayed with the horses outside Kao Gate in the south city, and Chi Huan-tzu who went in disguise several times to see them was tempted to accept. He persuaded the duke to go there by a roundabout way, and they watched all day, neglecting state affairs.

Then Tzu-lu said, "Master, it is time to leave!"

Confucius replied, "The duke will soon be sacrificing to heaven and earth. If he presents portions of the offerings to the ministers, I can stay."

But Chi Huan-tzu accepted the dancers from Chi, for three days no court was held, and no meat was offered to the ministers at the sacrifice. So Confucius left, putting up for one night at Tun. Shih Yi, who had come to see him off, said, "This is not your fault, master."

Confucius retorted, "Shall I sing you a song?" And he chanted:

> A woman's tongue
> Can cost a man his post;
> A woman's words
> Can cost a man his head;
> Then why not retire
> To spend my last years as I please?

Upon Shih Yi's return Chi Huan-tzu asked, "What did Confucius say?" When told, he said with a sigh, "I've offended the master because of a pack of girls."

9

Confucius went to Uei and lived with Tzu-lu's brother-in-law Yen Cho-tsou. Duke Ling of Uei asked, "What stipend had Confucius in Lu?"

He was told, "Sixty thousand measures of grain."

So Uei also gave him sixty thousand measures. Later someone slandered Confucius to Duke Ling, who ordered Kung-sun Yu-chia to set a guard over him. Then Confucius, fearing trouble, left after a stay of ten months.

He was passing Kuang on his way to Chen when Yen Keh, who was accompanying him, pointed to the city wall with his whip and said, "I got in through that gap before."

Some men of Kuang heard this and mistook Confucius for Yang Hu of Lu, who had treated them badly. They had detained him for five days because of his resemblance to Yang Hu, when Yen Hui arrived.

Confucius told him, "I thought you were dead."

Yen Hui answered, "How dare I die when you are still living, master?"

The men of Kuang now behaved in such a threatening way that the followers of Confucius were afraid. But he said, "Since King Wen is no more, who but I can be the standard-bearer of culture? If Heaven had wanted culture to disappear, I should not have possessed it after all this time. And if Heaven does not intend culture to disappear, what can the men of Kuang do to me?" He sent one of his followers to serve Ning Wu-tzu in Uei and was finally able to leave.

Proceeding to Pu, he returned after a month and more to Uei and stayed with Chu Po-yu. There Duke Ling's wife, Nan-tzu, sent Confucius this message, "When gentlemen from other lands honour our lord with their friendship, they always call on his lady. She would like to meet you." Confucius declined at first, then was forced to comply. The lady sat behind a linen curtain to receive him. Confucius, entering, faced north and bowed low. She returned his bow behind the curtain and her jade pendants tinkled.

"I did not want to go," said Confucius later, "but once there I had to conform to etiquette." Since Tzu-lu looked displeased he made an oath: "If what I did was wrong, may Heaven punish me! May Heaven punish me!" He had been over a month in Uei when Duke Ling drove out in a carriage with his lady escorted by the eunuch Yung Chu, and with Confucius as assistant escort. In this fashion they drove openly through the streets.

Confucius commented, "I have yet to see the man who loves virtue as much as he loves feminine beauty." He left Uei in disgust for Tsao. That year Duke Ting of Lu died.

From Tsao Confucius went to Sung. He was expounding the rites to his pupils under a great tree when Huan Tui, the war minister of Sung who wanted to kill him, sent men to fell the tree. Confucius withdrew, and his disciples urged, "Let us hurry away!"

But Confucius said, "Heaven has implanted virtue in me. What can men like Huan Tui do to me?"

Going on to Cheng, Confucius was separated from his followers. He was standing alone at the East Gate when a citizen of Cheng remarked to Tzu-kung, "There is a man at the East Gate with a forehead like Yao, a neck like Kao Yao and shoulders like Tzu-chan, and just three inches shorter below the waist than Yu. Lost as a stray dog he looks!"

When this was repeated to Confucius, he chuckled. "The appearance is unimportant," he said. "But it's true that I'm like a stray dog. That is certainly true!"

Confucius proceeded to Chen and stayed with Ssu-cheng Chen-tzu for a year and more. Then King Fu-cha of Wu attacked Chen and took three towns. Chao Yang attacked Chaoko. The army of Chu invaded Tsai and the capital of Tsai was moved to Wu. The forces of Wu defeated King Kou-chien of Yueh at Kuaichi.

A falcon fell dead in the court of Chen, shot by a thorn arrow eighteen inches long with an arrowhead of stone. Duke Min of Chen was sent to consult Confucius, who said, "This falcon has come a long way. The arrow belongs to the Churchens. When King Wu conquered the Shangs he opened up communications with all the eastern and southern barbarians, ordering them to send in their local products as tribute and not to fail in this duty. The Churchens used to send thorn arrows with stone arrowheads like this, eighteen inches long. And to make known his glory and virtue, the king gave these arrows with the fief of Chen to his eldest daughter when she married Duke Hu of Yu. Precious jade was distributed among his kinsmen to strengthen their bonds, and other clans were given tribute from distant parts that they might not forget their allegiance. This is how these Churchen arrows were given to Chen." The duke looked in the old treasury and actually found similar arrows there.

During the three years Confucius spent in Chen, the state was invaded again and again, now by Tsin, now by Chu, in their contest for supremacy, and also by Wu.

"Let us return!" cried Confucius. "Let us return! We may be ambitious, reckless fellows, but in our quest we do not forget our origin." With that he left Chen.

Kung-shu rebelled in Pu while Confucius was passing through, and the men of Pu detained him. Among his disciples was a certain Kung-liang Ju who had accompanied him with five of his own chariots. A tall and enormously strong man, he said, "I was with the master when we ran into trouble in Kuang, and here we are in trouble again. Well, this must be fate and at least I can die fighting."

He put up such a fight that the men of Pu were afraid and told Confucius, "If you don't go to Uei, you may leave."

He gave them his word and they let him out through the East Gate. He still proceeded to Uei and Tzu-kung asked, "Is it right to break your word?"

Confucius replied, "I gave it under pressure: the gods will not count it."

Delighted to hear that Confucius was back, Duke Ling of Uei welcomed him outside the city and asked, "Can we attack Pu?"

Confucius answered, "Yes."

The duke said, "My ministers are against it because Pu is a buffer between us and Tsin and Chu. Does that not make it wrong to attack it?"

Confucius said, "The men there are ready to die for our state and the women are determined to defend Hsiho. We shall only punish a handful of rebels."

The duke approved but did not attack in the end. Since Duke Ling was old and had lost interest in state affairs, he did not give office to Confucius.

Confucius sighed and said, "To be in office for just one year would satisfy me. In three years real results would show." After that he left.

Pi Hsi was then the steward of Chungmou. When Chien-tzu of the Chao clan attacked the Fan and Chunghang clans he struck at Chungmou too, and Pi Hsi rebelled. He sent for Confucius, who was willing to join him.

But Tzu-lu protested, "I have heard you say, master, 'A gentleman will not enter the house of an evil-doer.' How can you think of going to Pi Hsi who has rebelled in Chungmou?"

"True," replied Confucius. "But is there not also a saying, 'Too hard to be ground thin, too white to be dyed black'? Am I a gourd to hang here and never be eaten?"

One day Confucius was playing the chimes when a man with a wicker crate passed the door and said, "Poor fellow, playing the chimes! He is self-willed but does not know himself. It is useless to talk with him."

Confucius practised playing the lute for ten days without attempting anything new. Shih Hsiang, his tutor, said, "You can go ahead now."

"I have learned the tune but not the technique," said Confucius.

After some time Shih Hsiang said, "You have mastered the measure now, you can go on."

But Confucius replied, "I have not yet caught the spirit."

Some time later the other said, "Now you have caught the spirit, you can go on."

13

"I cannot yet visualize the man behind it," answered Confucius. Later he observed, "This is the work of a man who thought deeply and seriously, one who saw far ahead and had a calm, lofty outlook." He continued, "I see him now. He is dark and tall, with far-seeing eyes that seem to command all the kingdoms around. No one but King Wen could have composed this music."

Shih Hsiang rose from his seat and bowed as he rejoined, "Yes, this is the *Lute-song of King Wen*."

Since Confucius had not been employed in Uei, he decided to go west to see Chao Chien-tzu. But upon reaching the Yellow River he received news of the death of Tou Ming-tu and Shun Hua and, facing the water, said with a sigh, "A grand sweep of water! But I am not fated to cross it."

Tzu-kung stepped forward to ask, "What do you mean?"

Confucius replied, "Tou Ming-tu and Shun Hua were good ministers of Tsin. Before Chao Chien-tzu rose to power he insisted on having these men before he would join the government; but now that he is in power he has killed them. I have heard that when you destroy unborn animals or kill young game, the unicorn will not come to the countryside; when you dredge and empty the ponds while fishing, the dragon will not harmonize the *yin* and *yang*;* when you upset a nest and destroy the eggs, the phoenix will not hover nearby. It follows that a gentleman must take offence if one of his kind is injured. If the very birds and beasts shun the unjust, how much more must I!"

He went back to stay in the village of Tsou, where he composed the *Lute-song of Tsou* to mourn the two men. Then, returning to Uei, he became the guest of Chu Po-yu.

Some time later, Duke Ling consulted him about warfare. "I know something about sacrificial vessels," said Confucius, "but have never studied military science." The next day during a conversation with him, the duke saw some wild geese in the

---

* Positive and negative forces of nature.

sky and looked up at them, ignoring the sage. So Confucius went back to Chen.

That summer Duke Ling of Uei died and his grandson Che succeeded him as Duke Chu. In the sixth month Chao Yang sent the crown prince, Kuai Kuei, to the town of Chi. Yang Hu dressed the prince in deep mourning and made eight other mourners, ostensibly from Uei, welcome him with tears into the town. And there he stayed. That winter Tsai's capital was moved to Choulai. This was the third year of Duke Ai of Lu, when Confucius was sixty years old. Chi helped Uei to besiege the town of Chi because the crown prince was there.

That summer a fire broke out in the temples of Duke Huan and Duke Hsi of Lu, and Nankung Ching-shu put it out. Confucius, then in Chen, heard of this conflagration and said, "It was probably in the temples of Duke Huan and Duke Hsi." And he was proved correct.

That autumn Chi Huan-tzu fell ill. Driven in his carriage to the city wall of Lu, he said with a sigh, "This state could have become great if I had not offended Confucius." Then turning to his heir Chi Kang-tzu, he said, "Once I am dead you will become prime minister of Lu. When that happens, you must ask Confucius to come back."

A few days later he died and Chi Kang-tzu succeeded him. After the funeral the new prime minister wanted to recall Confucius, but Kung-chih Yu said, "Our former lord lost faith in him in the end, so that other states laughed at us. If we have him back and find we cannot put his ideas into practice, we shall only make ourselves ridiculous again."

"In that case, whom shall we get?"

"Recall Jan Chiu."

So Chi Kang-tzu sent for Jan Chiu.

When Jan Chiu was leaving, Confucius said, "The men of Lu cannot be recalling Jan Chiu for any small task, but must mean to entrust important work to him." Later that day he exclaimed, "Let us return! Let us return! My pupils aspire to great things. But although they have certain elegant accomplishments, I do not know how to educate them properly."

15

Tzu-kung knew that Confucius longed to return to Lu, so while seeing Jan Chiu off he said, "If you are in power, make sure the master is recalled."

The year following Jan Chiu's departure, Confucius moved from Chen to Tsai. Duke Chao of Tsai decided to go to Wu after receiving a summons from that state. As the duke had already moved the capital to Choulai without consulting his ministers, now that he wanted to go to Wu they feared he might move the capital again, and Kungsun Pien shot and killed him. Chu invaded Tsai. That autumn Duke Ching of Chi died.

The next year Confucius went from Tsai to Sheh. Asked about government by the duke of Sheh, he replied, "The art lies in attracting the people from far away and winning the hearts of those close by."

Another time the duke of Sheh asked Tzu-lu his opinion of his master, but Tzu-lu did not reply. When Confucius heard this he said, "Why didn't you tell him, 'He is a man who never wearies of studying the truth, never tires of teaching others, but who in his eagerness forgets his hunger and in his joy forgets his bitter lot, not worrying that old age is creeping on'?"

On the road from Sheh to Tsai they met Chang-tsu and Chieh-ni ploughing together. Taking them for recluses, Confucius told Tzu-lu to ask them the way to the ford.

"Who is the man holding the reins of your carriage?" asked Chang-tsu.

Tzu-lu answered, "That is Kung Chiu."

"You mean Kung Chiu of Lu?"

"That's right," said Tzu-lu.

"He should know where the ford is then," retorted Chang-tsu.

Then Chieh-ni asked Tzu-lu, "And who are you?"

He answered, "My name is Chung Yu."

"Are you a disciple of Kung Chiu?"

"Yes, I am."

"The whole world goes its way and who is to change it?" asked Chieh-ni. "Better, surely, to follow those who shun the world than one who only shuns certain men?"

With that they went on covering the seed.

Tzu-lu returned and told Confucius, who commented ruefully, "Birds and beasts are no company for men. If the world were on the right path I should not try to change it."

Another day on the road Tzu-lu met an old man carrying a hoe and asked him, "Sir, have you seen my master?"

The old man retorted, "You who never use your four limbs, who don't know the difference between the five grains — who is your master?" Planting his staff in the ground, he started weeding.

Tzu-lu went and told Confucius, who said, "He must be a recluse." They went back to find him but he had disappeared.

When Confucius had spent three years in Tsai, Wu attacked Chen and Chu sent troops which were stationed at Chengfu to Chen's assistance. Learning that Confucius was living between Chen and Tsai, the men of Chu sent him an invitation. Before he could accept it, however, the ministers of Chen and Tsai discussed the matter and said, "Confucius is an able man who has laid his finger unerringly on the abuses in every state. He has spent a considerable time between Chen and Tsai and disapproves of all our measures and policies. Now powerful Chu has sent for him. If he serves Chu, so much the worse for us!" They sent men to surround Confucius in the country-side, so that he could not leave. His supplies ran out, his followers were too weak to move, but Confucius went on teaching and singing, accompanying himself on the lute.

Tzu-lu went to him and asked indignantly, "Does a gentleman have to put up with privation?"

"A gentleman can stand privation," answered Confucius. "A mean man exposed to privation is prone to do wrong."

As Tzu-kung looked displeased, Confucius asked him, "Do you think me a learned, well-read man?"

"Certainly," replied Tzu-kung. "Aren't you?"

"Not at all," said Confucius. "I have simply grasped one thread which links up the rest."

Knowing that his disciples were in low spirits, Confucius called Tzu-lu and said to him, "The old song runs: 'I am neither rhinoceros nor tiger, yet I go to the wilderness.' Is our way wrong? Is that why we have come to this?"

"Maybe we lack humanity and therefore men do not trust us," replied Tzu-lu. "Or perhaps we are not intelligent enough for them to follow our way."

"Do you really think so?" countered Confucius. "If the humane were always trusted, how do you account for what happened to Po Yi and Shu Chi?* If the intelligent always had their way, how do you explain the case of Prince Pi-kan?"**

After Tzu-lu left, Tzu-kung came and Confucius put the same question to him. "The old song says, 'I am neither rhinoceros nor tiger, yet I go to the wilderness.' Is our way wrong? Is that why we have come to this?"

Tzu-kung answered, "Master, your way is too great for the world to accept. You should modify it a little."

"A good farmer can sow but may not always reap a harvest," said Confucius. "A good craftsman can use his skill but may not be able to please. A gentleman can cultivate his way, draw up principles, recapitulate and reason, but may not be able to make his way accepted. Now your aim is not to cultivate your way but to please others. Your ambition is not high enough."

After Tzu-kung had left, Yen Hui came and Confucius again put the same question to him.

"Master, your way is too great for the world to accept," said Yen Hui. "All the same, you should persist in it. What does it matter if they cannot accept it? That just shows that you are a superior man. We are at fault if we do not cultivate the true way. Yet if we cultivate it fully and it is not adopted, it is the rulers who are at fault. What does it matter if they cannot accept your way? That just shows that you are a superior man."

Confucius smiled with pleasure and exclaimed, "Well

---

* Two Shang nobles who starved to death after the fall of the Shang Dynasty.

** A wise noble who was killed by the last king of Shang.

said, son of Yen! If you had great wealth, I should like to administer it for you."

Then Confucius sent Tzu-kung to Chu. King Chao of Chu dispatched troops to meet him, and he was finally able to get away.

King Chao of Chu was on the point of giving Confucius seven hundred *li* of village communities as his fief, when his chief minister Tzu-hsi asked, "Has Your Majesty any ambassador comparable to Tzu-kung?"

"No," said the king.

"Any minister comparable to Yen Hui?"

Again the answer was, "No."

"Any general comparable to Tzu-lu? Any administrator comparable to Tsai Yu?"

Once again the answer was, "No."

"When the founder of the House of Chu received his fief from the Chou Dynasty, he had a low rank and only fifty *li* of land. Now Confucius is following the ways of the ancient kings to display the virtues of the duke of Chou and the duke of Shao. If you entrust him with authority, sir, Chu will not keep these few thousand *li* for many generations. When King Wen was in Feng and King Wu in Hao, they were only princes with a hundred *li* of territory, but they rose to sovereignty of the whole empire. If Confucius with such able disciples to help him were to have land of his own, that would not be to our advantage." Accordingly King Chao gave up the idea. And that autumn he died in Chengfu.

The eccentric of Chu, Chieh Yu, walked past Confucius singing:

> Ah, phoenix, phoenix,
> How powerless you are!
> Useless to blame what's done,
> Take thought for what's to come.
> Enough, enough!
> Today there is danger
> For those who guide the state.

19

Confucius alighted from his carriage to speak to this man, but the eccentric ran off. Then Confucius went back from Chu to Uei. He was sixty-three this year, the sixth year of Duke Ai of Lu.

The next year the king of Wu and the duke of Lu met at Tseng and the king demanded a hundred oxen. Chancellor Po Pi of Wu summoned Chi Kang-tzu, who sent Tzu-kung in his place. Then Wu dropped its demand.

Confucius said, "The rulers of Lu and Uei are like two brothers."

At this time Duke Cheh-fu of Uei had not succeeded to power but was staying in another state. The other feudal lords regarded him as having abdicated. Since most of Confucius' disciples were serving Uei, the duke wanted him to join the government too.

Tzu-lu asked, "If the duke of Uei urged you to govern his state, what would you do first?"

"I would rectify titles," said Confucius.

"You are very unpractical," said Tzu-lu. "Why are you so set on rectifying titles?"

Confucius retorted, "What a savage you are! If titles are incorrect, orders will not be carried out; and if orders are not carried out, then nothing can be achieved. That means that rites and music will not flourish, laws and punishments will be wide of the mark, and people will not know what to do. A gentleman's actions must be such as he can name; he must promise only what he can perform. A gentleman must keep a careful watch on his speech."

The following year Jan Chiu, given the command of the army by Chi Kang-tzu, defeated Chi at Lang.

"Have you studied the arts of war?" Chi Kang-tzu asked him. "Or are you naturally gifted?"

Jan Chiu replied, "I learned this from Confucius."

"What kind of man is he?"

"He wants his actions to correspond to his principles. In applying his principles to govern the people he tries to carry

20

out the wishes of the gods. This is what he wants, not to possess wealth to the value of a thousand villages."

"Could I ask him back?"

"If you do, you must not let petty-minded men obstruct him."

At that time Kung Wen-tzu of Uei planned to attack Tai-shu and asked Confucius for a plan of campaign, but Confucius declined on the ground that this was beyond him. Upon withdrawing he ordered his carriage, saying, "The bird chooses its tree; the tree cannot choose the bird." However, Kung Wen-tzu prevailed on him to stay. Then Chi Kang-tzu sent Kung-hua, Kung-pin and Kung-lin with gifts to invite Confucius back to Lu. He had been away from the state for fourteen years.

Asked about government by Duke Ai of Lu, he replied, "The art lies in choosing your ministers well."

Asked about government by Chi Kang-tzu, he answered, "If you use the straight in place of the crooked, the crooked will become straight."

Chi Kang-tzu was troubled by some cases of theft. Confucius said, "If you yourself were free from desire, they would not steal even if you paid them to do so." However, as it turned out Lu did not employ him and Confucius did not ask for an official post.

During the time of Confucius the House of Chou had declined, the ancient rites and music were forgotten, and many of the songs and records were missing. He verified the rites of the Three Dynasties and compiled the *Book of Documents,* arranging the records chronologically from the time of Yao and Shun to that of Duke Mu of Chin, marshalling the facts in good order. He said, "I can speak about the rites of Hsia, but the records of Chi are too scanty to verify. I can speak about the rites of Yin,* but the records of Sung are too scanty to verify. Had they been complete, I should have been able to check them." With regard to the differences in the Shang and Hsia cultures, he declared, "Far removed as we are in time, we

---

* Another name for Shang.

can still tell that one culture was elaborate, the other simple. Chou, which learned from both, reached a pinnacle of culture. I follow Chou."

Thus both the *Book of Documents* and the *Book of Rites* were compiled by Confucius.

He told the chief musician of Lu, "As far as we know, music started with strict unison. Then more licence was allowed, but it has remained pure, clear and consistent to the end. Since my return from Uei to Lu, I have set right the music and arranged the odes and hymns in proper order."

There were more than three thousand ancient songs, but Confucius rejected those which were repetitious and retained those which had moral value, beginning with songs about the ancestors of Shang and Chou, going on to descriptions of the good reigns of both dynasties and thence to the misdeeds of King Yu and King Li. He put the poems about daily life first, starting the folk-song section with the *Song of the Dove*, the Lesser Odes with *The Deer Cries*, the Greater Odes with *King Wen* and the Hymns with the *Temple of Purity*. Confucius chose three hundred and five songs in all, and these he set to music and sang, fitting them to the music of Emperor Shun and King Wu. After that the old rites and music became widely known, to the enrichment of the kingly culture, and the Six Classics were established.

In his old age Confucius loved to study the *Book of Change*, the order of the hexagrams, definitions, appendices, interpretations, explanations and commentaries. He studied this book so much that the leather thongs binding the wooden strips wore out three times. "Give me a few years more," he said, "and I shall become quite proficient!"

Confucius taught his pupils the old songs, records, rites and music. In all he had three thousand pupils, seventy-two of whom were versed in all Six Arts.* Many more, like Yen Cho-tsou, also received instruction from him.

In his teaching Confucius laid emphasis on four things: cul-

---

* Ceremony, music, archery, charioteering, writing and mathematics.

ture, conduct, loyalty and honesty. Four things he avoided: foregone conclusions, arbitrary views, obstinacy and egoism. He advocated caution during sacrifice, war and sickness. He rarely spoke of profit, fate or goodness. He would only help those who were in earnest. If he gave one corner of a square and the pupil could not infer the other three corners, he would not repeat his explanation.

In his native village his manner was unassuming, as though he did not trust himself to speak. But in the ancestral temple or at court his speech was ordered, and he chose his words with care. At court he addressed high ministers firmly, low officials affably. Entering the gate of a public office he bowed his head, and advancing in haste he spread his sleeves gracefully. Summoned by a prince to accompany guests, he bore himself gravely; and at a summons from his lord he set off without waiting for his carriage.

He would not eat fish that was not fresh, meat that was high or anything carelessly cut. He would not sit on a mat that was not straight. In the company of a man in mourning he would not eat his fill. On the day that he attended a funeral he would not sing. Deep mourning or blindness, even in a child, always made him grave.

"When three walk together, there must be one who can teach me," said Confucius. "Failure to cultivate virtue, to perfect my knowledge, to change when I hear what is right and to correct my faults — these are the things that worry me."

When he invited men to sing and found the song good, he would ask for a repetition and join in himself. The subjects on which he did not talk were: extraordinary things, feats of strength, political disorders, and the supernatural.

Tzu-kung once said, "We can hear the master's views concerning culture, but he does not tell us anything about Nature and Fate."

And Yen Hui once said with a sigh, "The more I look up, the higher is his teaching above me. The deeper I probe, the harder it becomes. One moment I think I have it, but the next it eludes me again. How skilfully, step by step, the

23

master leads us on! He has broadened me with culture, restrained me with ritual. Even if I wanted to, I could not stop. I go all out, yet just as I think I am achieving something, he is far beyond me again. I want to follow, but cannot find the way."

A villager of Tahsiang remarked, "Confucius is truly great, known for his wide knowledge, but not for any special skill."

When Confucius heard this he asked, "What shall I take up? Charioteering or archery? I choose charioteering."

Chin Lao commented, "The master said he learned many arts because he never held office."

In the spring of the fourteenth year of Duke Ai of Lu there was a great hunt at Tayeh, and Shu-sun's charioteer Tzu Shang caught a creature which he thought was ill-omened. Confucius seeing it exclaimed, "This is a unicorn!" He took it back, saying, "No chart has come out of the Yellow River, no writings from the River Lo.* All is over with me." When Yen Hui died Confucius had cried, "Heaven has forsaken me!" And now that this unicorn was captured in the west, he exclaimed, "My way has come to an end!" Sighing, he lamented, "Nobody understands me."

Tzu-kung asked, "Why does nobody understand you?"

Confucius said, "I bear no grudge against Heaven nor do I blame men. I learn from below and try to reach above, but only Heaven can understand me. Po Yi and Shu Chi held fast by their principles and would not debase themselves, whereas Liuhsia Hui and Shao Lien surrendered their principles and debased themselves. Then there were Yu Chung and Yi Yi who held aloof as recluses and spoke their mind. They would not serve a government unless it was incorrupt and resigned from office whenever expedient. I am not like these men: I have no such scruples."

The master said, "Alas! Alas! What a gentleman dreads is to die before his name is known. My way is not popular. How shall I make myself known to later ages?"

Then he compiled the *Spring and Autumn Annals* based on

---

* Referring to auspicious omens of an earlier age.

the historical records of twelve reigns, from that of Duke Yin down to the fourteenth year of the reign of Duke Ai. In this book Lu is given the predominant position, Chou is considered worthy of respect, Shang is relegated to the past, and the spirit of the Three Dynasties is used as a guiding principle. The language is concise, the content profound. Though the rulers of Wu and Chu had styled themselves kings, the *Spring and Autumn Annals* criticizes them by calling them barons. Although the duke of Tsin actually summoned the king of Chou to a meeting at Chientu, the *Spring and Autumn Annals* records that "the Great King went to hunt at Hoyang". These examples can be used as criteria in any age to criticize or condemn men's actions, and later princes should uphold this tradition and broaden its application. When the principles of the *Spring and Autumn Annals* are carried out, all traitors and evil-doers in the world must tremble. When Confucius as a government official tried a case, he used the common speech and not distinctive language. But in editing the *Spring and Autumn Annals* he recorded certain events and omitted others so that not even men like Tzu-hsia could make any comment. The disciples of Confucius studied the *Spring and Autumn Annals* under him, and he said, "It is these annals by which later men will know me, and it is these annals which will make men condemn me."

The next year Tzu-lu died in Uei and Confucius fell ill. When Tzu-kung went to see him, the master, pacing by the door with a stick, demanded, "Why have you come so late?" Then he sighed and sang:

> Mount Tai crumbles,
> The great beam breaks,
> The wise man withers away.

With tears he told Tzu-kung, "The world has long strayed from the true way and no one can follow me. The men of Hsia mourned the dead by the east steps, the men of Chou by the west steps, while the men of Yin mourned between pillars. Last night I dreamed that I was sitting before offerings between two pillars. It follows that I must be a man of Yin."

He died seven days later at the age of seventy-three, on the *chi-chou* day of the fourth month of the sixteenth year of Duke Ai of Lu.*

Duke Ai, mourning Confucius, said, "Kind Heaven had no pity on me and would not spare this grand old man. I am left alone in the world, full of grief and sorrow. Oh, master, to whom shall I look for guidance now?"

Tzu-kung commented, "The duke shall die in an alien land. The master said that lack of ceremony is folly, the misuse of designations a fault. To abandon your principles is also folly, to forget your place a fault. Not to employ the master during his lifetime but to mourn him after death runs counter to true ceremony, while the description 'alone in the world' does not befit a duke."

Confucius was buried by the River Szu north of the city of Lu, and after his pupils had mourned for him for three years without wearing the customary mourning they bade each other farewell. But then they wept and mourned again, and some stayed longer at the grave. Tzu-kung alone built a hut beside the grave and stayed there for three more years. Because more than a hundred of Confucius' disciples and other men of Lu settled near the grave, the district was named Confucius Village. The custom of sacrificing at the sage's grave during festivals has persisted from generation to generation. Scholars discuss ceremony there, while village feasts and archery contests are held there. His graveyard covers over a hundred *mou*. The house in which he lived was made into a temple by the descendants of some of his disciples, and there his clothes, hat, lute, carriage and books were kept. The place still existed more than two hundred years later, in the Han Dynasty. When the First Emperor of Han passed Lu, he offered a grand sacrifice there. Barons and ministers appointed to posts there pay homage to the shrine of Confucius before taking up their duties.

Confucius' son Li, styled Po-yu, lived to be fifty and died

---

* 479 B.C.

before his father. Po-yu's son Chi styled Tzu-szu, who lived to be sixty-two, once found himself in difficulties in Sung and wrote the *Doctrine of the Mean*. Tzu-szu's son Po, styled Tzu-shang, lived to be forty-seven. His son Chiu, styled Tzu-chia, lived to be forty-five. His son Chi, styled Tzu-ching, lived to be forty-six. His son Chuan, styled Tzu-kao, lived to be fifty-one. His son Tzu-shen, who lived to be fifty-seven, was a minister in Wei. Tzu-shen's son Fu, who lived to be fifty-seven, served as literary adviser to Prince Chen Sheh and died in Chen. Fu's younger brother Tzu-hsiang, who lived to be fifty-seven, served as literary adviser under Emperor Hui and was later appointed governor of Changsha. He was over six feet in height. Tzu-hsiang's son Chung lived to be fifty-seven. Chung's son Wu had two sons, Yen-nien and An-kuo. The latter served as literary adviser to the present emperor and later became governor of Linghuai, but he died long ago. An-kuo's son Chiung had a son named Huan.

The Grand Historian comments: One of the songs says, "The great mountain, I look up to it! The great road, I travel it!" Although I cannot reach him, my heart goes out to him. When I read the works of Confucius, I try to see the man himself. In Lu I visited his temple and saw his carriage, clothes and sacrificial vessels. Scholars go regularly to study ceremony there, and I found it hard to tear myself away. The world has known innumerable princes and worthies who enjoyed fame and honour in their day but were forgotten after death, while Confucius, a commoner, has been looked up to by scholars for ten generations and more. From the emperor, princes and barons downwards, all in China who study the Six Arts take the master as their final authority. Well is he called the Supreme Sage!

SUN WU AND WU CHI

Sun Wu, a native of Chi, gained an audience with King Ho-lu of Wu on the strength of his military theory.

"I have read all thirteen chapters of your book," said the king. "Will you train a few troops as an experiment?"

"Very well," replied Sun Wu.

"Will you try with women?"

"If you wish."

The king sent him one hundred and eighty beauties from the palace, and Sun Wu divided them into two companies with the king's two favourite concubines as their leaders. Having made them take up halberds, he asked, "Do you know the front from back, and your left hand from your right?"

The women assured him that they did.

"When I give the order to advance, go forward. At the order 'Left!' turn towards your left hand, at 'Right!' turn towards your right, at 'Retreat!' turn back."

The women assented.

Having laid down these rules, he had executioners' swords and axes made ready and repeated his instructions a third and yet a fourth time. Then with the roll of a drum he gave the order "Turn right!" The women burst out laughing.

Sun Wu said, "If the rules are not clear and orders are not understood, the commander is to blame." Once more he repeated his instructions a third and a fourth time, then beat drums and gave the order for a left turn. But once more the women burst out laughing.

Then he said, "If the rules are not clear and orders are not understood, the commander is to blame. But when orders are clear yet not carried out, it is the officers who are to blame." He prepared to execute both company leaders.

The king, watching from his stand, was aghast to see that his favourites were about to be executed and hastily sent messengers with orders, saying, "I can see you are an able general. But without these two concubines my food would lose all flavour. I beg you to spare them."

Sun Wu replied, "I have been appointed commander, and a general in the field is not bound by orders from his sovereign." So he had the two leaders killed as an example, and made the next two officers. This time, when he sounded the drums, the women turned left or right, advanced or retreated, and knelt or stood up exactly as they were told, not daring to utter a sound.

Then Sun Wu sent a message to the king, saying, "The troops are in fighting trim, ready for inspection. Your Majesty can do what you please with them — they will go through fire or water."

"You may go back to your hostel and rest," replied the king. "I have no desire to inspect them."

Sun Wu said, "Your Majesty is only interested in the theory, not in the real thing."

King Ho-lu, convinced of Sun Wu's skill as a commander, later made him his general. In the west he defeated mighty Chu, entering Ying.* In the north, he struck awe into Chi and Tsin, and Wu's fame spread through all the states. All this was partly thanks to Sun Wu.

More than a hundred years after Sun Wu's death, a descendant of his named Sun Pin was born in the district between Ngo and Chuan. Sun Pin studied the art of war with Pang Chuan, who later served in Wei as one of King Hui's generals; but Pang Chuan knowing that he was no match for Sun Pin, secretly arranged to have him summoned to the court. After Sun Pin's arrival Pang Chuan, afraid of being outshone, was jealous of him. He had Sun Pin's feet cut off and his face tattooed on a criminal charge in the hope that he would no longer appear in public. When an envoy from Chi came to the capital of Wei, Sun Pin went privately to see him although

---

* The capital of Chu.

he was a mutilated convict. The envoy was so impressed that he smuggled him out in his carriage to Chi. And there General Tien Chi treated him well and became his patron.

Now Tien Chi often bet heavily on races between his chariots and those of the young lords of Chi. Their teams, divided into three classes, were well-matched. Seeing this, Sun Pin advised, "Stake heavily! I shall see that you win."

Taking him at his word, Tien Chi bet a thousand gold pieces with the king and lords. Just before the race started, Sun Pin said, "Run your worst team against their best, your best against their second-best, and your second-best against their worst." Then Tien Chi lost one race but won the two others, getting a thousand gold pieces from the king. After this he recommended Sun Pin to King Wei, who consulted him on military theory and then made him his chief of staff.

Later Wei attacked Chao, and Chao turned in desperation to Chi for aid. King Wei of Chi wished Sun Pin to lead his army, but he declined because he was mutilated. So Tien Chi was made commander with Sun Pin as his chief of staff. Sun Pin accompanied him in a covered carriage to advise him.

Tien Chi wanted to march on Chao but Sun Pin said, "To unravel a knot you must not hold it tight. To settle a quarrel you must not join in the fighting. If we leave what is knotted and attack what is loose, making further entanglement impossible, matters can be sorted out. Since Wei and Chao are at war, their picked troops have all been called out, leaving none at home but the old and infirm. Your best course is to lead your men quickly to Taliang,* cut their lines of communication and attack undefended points, so that Wei's forces have to leave Chao to save their own land. Then at one stroke we shall raise the siege of Chao and harass Wei."

Tien Chi acted on this advice and the army of Wei withdrawing from Hantan** was routed by the men of Chi at Kueiling.

---

* The capital of Wei.

** The capital of Chao.

Thirteen years later Wei and Chao together attacked Hann. Hann turned to Chi for help and Tien Chi was sent out with another army which again marched straight against Taliang. When General Pang Chuan of Wei knew this, he returned from Hann, but by then the forces of Chi had advanced further west.

Then Sun Pin told Tien Chi, "The soldiers of Wei are brave and bellicose, despising our men and considering them cowards. A skilful strategist should make use of this and lure them with the prospect of easy success. According to the military treatise, an army that rushes a hundred *li* after easy success may lose its commander; fifty *li*, and half its troops will fail to arrive. So let us light a hundred thousand camp-fires on the day our troops enter Wei, fifty thousand the second day, and thirty thousand the third."

After pursuing the army of Chi for three days, General Pang Chuan exulted, "I knew the men of Chi were cowards! After only three days in our territory, more than half of them have deserted." Leaving the bulk of his army and taking only lightly-armed crack troops he pressed on at twice the pace in hot pursuit.

Sun Pin reckoned that by dusk the pursuers would reach Maling. The road there was narrow and had boulders on both sides where ambushes could be laid. He stripped the bark from a large tree and wrote on the trunk, "Under this tree shall Pang Chuan die!" That night he placed ten thousand of his finest bowmen in ambush on both sides of the road, with orders to shoot when they saw a flame. And sure enough, when Pang Chuan came to the tree in the dark and glimpsed some writing on the bare trunk, he struck a light. Before he could finish reading, ten thousand crossbows were discharged together and the army of Wei was thrown into confusion. Pang Chuan knew that he was out-generalled, his army doomed.

"I have let that puppy make his name!" he swore, and cut his own throat.

In the flush of victory the men of Chi utterly routed the enemy and returned with Shen, the crown prince of Wei, as their captive. Thus the fame of Sun Pin spread wide, and his military treatise was handed down to later generations.

Wu Chi of Uei was a brilliant soldier. After studying under Tseng Shen, he served the duke of Lu. When the army of Chi attacked Lu, the duke wanted to make him a commander but did not trust him because his wife came from Chi. In his eagerness to make a name, Wu Chi killed his wife to show that Chi meant nothing to him. Then he was made commander and inflicted a crushing defeat on Chi.

Some men of Lu condemned him, saying, "Wu Chi is suspicious and ruthless. When he was young his family was well-to-do, but he ruined it by his vain wanderings in search of official posts. Because his fellow villagers jeered at him, he killed thirty and more of his detractors and left through the East Gate of the capital of Uei. Taking leave of his mother, he bit his arm and swore, 'Unless I become a high minister, I shall never return to Uei!' He went to study under Tseng Shen, but he did not go home when his mother died shortly afterwards, so Tseng Shen despised him and broke with him. Then he came to Lu and studied military science in order to serve our lord, and when our lord suspected him he killed his wife to obtain the post of commander. If a small state like ours makes its name as a conqueror, the other states will all turn against us. Besides, the rulers of Lu and Uei are of the same family, and if our lord employs Wu Chi it will mean that we no longer want Uei's friendship." Then the duke of Lu began to have doubts about Wu Chi and declined his services.

Upon this Wu Chi, hearing good reports of Marquis Wen of Wei, tried to enter his service. The marquis asked Li Keh, "What sort of man is Wu Chi?"

"He is ambitious and debauched," said Li Keh. "But not even Szuma Jang-tsu of old was a better strategist."

Then the marquis gave Wu Chi the command against Chin, and he took five cities.

In the field, Wu Chi ate and dressed like the rank and file. He slept without a mat, marched on foot instead of riding on horseback or in a chariot, carried his own rations and shared all his troops' hardships. When one of his men had a boil, Wu Chi sucked the pus from it. The soldier's mother wept when she heard of this.

"Why do you weep?" someone asked her. "Your son is a common soldier, yet the commander sucked the pus from his boil."

"You don't understand," said the woman. "Some years back Lord Wu did the same for the boy's father, who then fought without giving ground until he fell. Now Lord Wu has cured my son, the boy too will surely die in a strange place. That is why I am weeping."

When the marquis saw that Wu Chi was an able commander, frugal and just and popular with his men, he made him governor of Hsiho to defend his land against Chin and Hann.

Wu Chi, after the death of Marquis Wen, served his son, Marquis Wu. One day they were sailing down the Yellow River, when the marquis turned in mid-stream to remark to Wu Chi, "What magnificent defences these hills and the river make! These are Wei's greatest treasure."

"We must rely on our virtue, not on our strategic position," replied Wu Chi. "Long ago, the San Miao had Tungting Lake on one side and Pengli Lake on the other; but because they did not cultivate virtue and righteousness, Yu overthrew their state. King Chieh of the Hsia Dynasty had the Yellow River and the River Chi on one side and Mount Tai and Mount Hua on the other, with Mount Yichueh on his south and Yangchang Slope on his north; but because he ruled without benevolence, he was sent into exile by Tang of the Shang. King Chou of Yin had Mengmen Mountain on one side and the Taihang Range on the other, with Mount Changshan on his north and the Yellow River on his south; but because he ruled without virtue, he was killed by King Wu of Chou. This shows that success depends on virtue, not on favourable terrain. If Your Lordship did not cultivate virtue, all the men in this boat could turn against you." The marquis, approving this speech, confirmed his appointment as governor of Hsiho, and Wu Chi became yet more famous.

When the marquis made Tien Wen his chief minister, Wu Chi was far from pleased. He asked Tien Wen:

"Shall we compare our achievements?"

Tien Wen said, "As you please."

"How do you compare with me in commanding the army so that the troops gladly lay down their lives and no enemy dare attack?"

"I am no match for you."

"How do you compare with me in running offices of state, ruling the citizens and keeping the treasury filled?"

"I am no match for you."

"How do you compare with me in defending the western frontier so that the army of Chin dares not move east and both Hann and Wei obey us?"

"I am no match for you."

"If in all these respects you are no match for me, how is it you are given the more important post?"

Tien Wen replied, "When the sovereign is young and the state unsettled, when the chief ministers waver in their allegiance and the common people lack confidence, who is better fitted to be in charge — you or I?"

After a considerable silence Wu Chi answered, "You are, sir."

He realized that Tien Wen was the more able man.

After Tien Wen's death, Kung Shu, the new chief minister who had married a daughter of the marquis, feared Wu Chi.

One of Kung Shu's servants said, "You can easily rid yourself of him." When asked how, he replied, "Wu Chi leads a disciplined and simple life, and is proud. Tell the marquis that he is an able man but our state is so small and so close to mighty Chin that you fear that he may not intend to stay. When the marquis asks what you advise, suggest that he test Wu Chi by offering him one of his daughters, for he will accept only if he means to stay. This is a way to find out. Then invite Wu Chi to your house and let the princess who is your lady insult you. When Wu Chi sees with what contempt she treats you, he will decline the offer."

When this happened just as the servant had predicted, the marquis began to have his doubts of Wu Chi, who, to avoid trouble, went to Chu.

As King Tao of Chou had heard of Wu Chi's ability, he made him chief minister. Wu Chi enforced the laws and strengthened discipline, dispensed with sinecures, abolished the privileges of distant relatives of the royal house, and spent the money saved on building up the army. He also refuted the travelling orators who advocated submission or opposition to Chin. Then Chu conquered the tribes of Pai-yueh in the south, annexed Chen and Tsai in the north, repulsed Hann, Chao and Wei* and attacked Chin in the west. All the other states were alarmed by Chu's strength, and the nobles of Chou wanted to kill Wu Chi. As soon as King Tao died, the nobles and ministers rose up and attacked him. Wu Chi took refuge behind the king's corpse, and some of the arrows of his enemies pierced King Tao's body too. After the burial of King Tao, the crown prince ascended the throne. He ordered his chief minister to execute all who had shot Wu Chi and desecrated his father's corpse. More than seventy families were wiped out in connection with this crime.

The Grand Historian comments: When men speak of military strategy, reference is nearly always made to the thirteen chapters of Sun Wu's treatise, while Wu Chi's military treatise is also widely known. For this reason I passed over them to speak only of these men's actions and achievements. The proverb says: Doers are not always talkers, nor talkers doers. Sun Pin showed great intelligence in foreseeing Pang Chuan's moves, yet failed earlier to forestall his own mutilation. Wu Chi, who assured the marquis that virtue was more important than strategy, acted with such cruelty and ruthlessness that finally he brought about his own death. The pity of it!

---

* During the Warring States Period Tsin was split into three states — Hann, Chao and Wei.

WU TZU-HSU

Wu Tzu-hsu, or Wu Yun, was a native of Chu. His father was Wu Sheh, his elder brother Wu Shang. Their ancestor Wu Chu had been noted for his frank advice to King Chuang of Chu, and so his descendants were well-known in that state.

King Ping of Chu appointed Wu Sheh senior guardian to Crown Prince Chien, with Fei Wu-chi as junior guardian. Fei was not loyal to the prince, however. Sent to Chin by the king to bring back a wife for the prince and finding her very lovely, he galloped back to report, "This girl from Chin is a marvellous beauty. Your Majesty had better take her yourself and find another wife for the crown prince."

So King Ping took the girl, who became his favourite and gave birth to a son Chen, while a different bride was found for the crown prince. Since Fei had pleased the king in this matter, he left the crown prince and entered the king's service. But fearing that when the king died and Chien ascended the throne he might be killed, he began to slander Chien. As the king did not love the crown prince's mother, who was from Tsai, he gradually became estranged from Chien, whom he sent to guard the frontier city of Chengfu.

Soon Fei was belittling Chien day and night to the king. "The crown prince naturally resents losing his bride from Chin," he said. "I must beg Your Majesty to be on your guard. Now the prince is in command of an army at Chengfu and in contact with other states, he may make trouble."

King Ping summoned the senior guardian Wu Sheh and asked him about it. Wu Sheh, knowing of Fei's slander, told the king, "Don't let yourself be estranged from your own flesh and blood, sir, by a petty treacherous slanderer."

Fei insisted, "Unless you stop them, they will succeed. And then you will be trapped."

So the king in his anger had Wu Sheh imprisoned. He ordered Fen Yang, the military commander at Chengfu, to kill the crown prince, but instead Fen Yang sent a man to warn Chien, saying, "Fly for your life, or you are lost!" So Prince Chien fled to Sung.

Fei Wu-chi told the king, "Wu Sheh has two sons, both able. If you do not eliminate them they will cause Chu trouble. With their father as hostage you can summon them. Failing this, they will be a menace to our state."

Then the king sent word to Wu Sheh, "Get your two sons here and you shall live. Otherwise you die."

"Shang has a good heart and would come," replied Wu Sheh. "But Tzu-hsu has a hard character, can stand abuse and is capable of great things. When he sees this is a trap, he will not come."

The king paid no attention but sent for both sons, saying, "Come, and your father lives. Otherwise he must die."

Shang wanted to obey the summons but Tzu-hsu reasoned, "The king has no intention of sparing our father but has sent for us because he is afraid of the trouble we may cause if we escape. He is holding our father as hostage in order to trick us. If we go we shall all die together — what good would that do our father? We should simply lose all chance of revenge. No, better escape to another state and enlist support to avenge him. There is no point in perishing together."

"I know I cannot save him by going," Shang rejoined. "But I don't want to be sneered at by the whole world for staying away to save my own skin and perhaps failing later to avenge him." He added, "You leave! You can avenge our father while I die with him."

With Shang in their hands, the messengers tried to seize Tzu-hsu, but he fitted an arrow to his bow and aimed it at them so that they dared not advance. Thus he escaped. Hearing that the crown prince was in Sung, he went there to join him.

37

When Wu Sheh learned of Tzu-hsu's flight he said, "Now the king of Chu and his ministers face military disaster."

As soon as Shang returned, he was put to death with his father.

After Wu Tzu-hsu reached Sung there was a revolt led by Hua Hai, so Wu Tzu-hsu and Prince Chien went on to Cheng, where they were well received. Then Prince Chien visited Tsin.

Duke Ching of Tsin said, "You are a good friend of Cheng and trusted there. If you help from within while I attack from without, I can certainly conquer Cheng and give it to you."

The prince returned to Cheng. But before the plan was carried out he made an attempt on the life of one of his followers against whom he had a grudge, and this man, knowing the plot, informed against him. Then Duke Ting of Cheng and his minister Tzu-chan killed Prince Chien.

The prince had left a son named Sheng, with whom Wu Tzu-hsu fled in alarm to Wu. The guards at the Chao Pass tried to arrest them and, being on foot, they were very nearly caught. With pursuers hot behind them they reached the river, where a fisherman who saw that their case was desperate ferried them across in his boat. On the further shore, Wu Tzu-hsu unbuckled his sword.

"This sword, worth a hundred gold pieces, I leave with you," he said.

The fisherman answered, "A reward of fifty thousand piculs of grain and a noble title has been offered in Chu to the man who captures Wu Tzu-hsu. Why should I take a sword worth only a hundred gold pieces?" And he refused it.

On the way to Wu, Wu Tzu-hsu fell ill and had to stop to beg for food. When he reached Wu, King Liao was on the throne with Lord Kuang as his commander, and through him Wu Tzu-hsu obtained an audience with the king.

Some time later, the women raising silkworms in Wu's frontier town of Piliangshih started fighting about mulberry leaves with those in Chu's frontier town Chungli. King Ping of Chu was so incensed by this that he called out his troops, and the king of Wu sent Lord Kuang to attack Chu. Upon his return after storming Chungli and Chuchao, Wu Tzu-hsu advised the king, "Chu can be defeated if you send Lord Kuang out on another expedition."

But Lord Kuang told the king, "Wu Tzu-hsu's father and brother were killed in Chu. He is advising you to attack because he wants revenge. We cannot defeat Chu."

Wu Tzu-hsu knew that Lord Kuang was plotting to kill the king and take his place, and that therefore it was useless to speak to him about matters outside. So he introduced Chuan Chu to Lord Kuang and went into retirement himself ploughing the fields with Sheng, the son of Prince Chien.

Five years later King Ping of Chu died and Chen, his son by the beauty from Chin, succeeded him as King Chao. King Liao of Wu seized this opportunity to dispatch two lords with troops against Chu, but the army of Chu cut off their retreat so that Wu was left undefended. Then Lord Kuang made Chuan Chu assassinate the king and set himself up as King Ho-lu. His ambition realized, he put Wu Tzu-hsu in charge of relations with other states and consulted him on government affairs.

When the king of Chu killed his ministers Chueh Wan and Po Chou-li, the latter's grandson Po Pi fled to Wu and King Ho-lu made him a minister too.

After the two lords sent to attack Chu found retreat impossible and heard that Lord Kuang had assassinated King Liao and enthroned himself, they surrendered with their forces to Chu and were given the district of Shu as their fief.

Three years after King Ho-lu ascended the throne, he raised an army and with the help of Wu Tzu-hsu and Po Pi attacked Chu, took Shu and captured the two renegades. He wanted to advance on Ying, the capital of Chu, but his commander Sun Wu said, "Our men are tired. The time has not yet come. We had better wait." So they returned.

In the fourth year the army of Wu attacked Chu again and took Lu and Chien. In the fifth year they attacked and defeated Yueh. In the sixth year King Chao of Chu sent Lord Nang with troops against Wu, but Wu Tzu-hsu, who had been dispatched by King Ho-lu to resist, utterly routed him at Yuchang and captured Chuchao from Chu.

In the ninth year of his reign King Ho-lu said to Wu Tzu-hsu and Sun Wu, "Some years ago you told me the time was not ripe to attack the capital of Chu. Is the time now ripe?"

"Chu's commander, Lord Nang, is a grasping man," they replied, "and both Tang and Tsai bear him a grudge. If you want to attack in strength, first win over Tang and Tsai."

The king, acting on their advice, mobilized all his forces and attacked Chu with the help of Tang and Tsai. They took up battle formation facing the army of Chu across the River Han. The king's younger brother Fu-kai wanted to join in with his troops, but the king refused. However, Fu-kai charged with five thousand men and defeated General Kungsun Wa of Chu, who fled to Cheng. Then the men of Wu advanced victoriously and after five more battles reached the capital of Chu. King Chao of Chu fled his capital which the king of Wu entered the next day. King Chao fled to Yunmeng, but being attacked there by rebels escaped to Yun.

Lord Huai, younger brother of the lord of Yun, said, "King Ping killed my father — should I not kill his son?" For fear lest he do so, the lord of Yun escorted King Chao to Sui.

The forces of Wu besieged Sui and told the defenders, "Chu has wiped out all descendants of the House of Chou in the Han Valley." Then the men of Sui would have killed King Chao had not his son Chi hidden him and taken his place. They consulted an oracle to see whether or not they should hand the king over to Wu, but receiving a negative answer they did not surrender him.

Wu Tzu-hsu had been a friend of Shen Pao-hsu and when he fled from Chu had told him, "I mean to overthrow Chu."

Shen had replied, "Then I mean to preserve it."

When the army of Wu entered the capital, Wu Tzu-hsu searched in vain for the king. Then he dug up King Ping's grave, exhumed the corpse and gave it three hundred lashes. Shen fled into the mountains but sent back a message saying, "Are you not overdoing your revenge? I have heard that when they are many, men can overcome Heaven, but that Heaven can break men too. You were King Ping's subject, serving him as your lord, yet now you go so far as to defile the dead. Surely this is utterly counter to the laws of Heaven?"

Wu Tzu-hsu told the messenger, "Take this answer to Shen. Because time is short and I still have far to go, I am forced to act counter to propriety."

Shen Pao-hsu fled to Chin to ask for help. When he was refused, he stood in the court of Chin and wept without ceasing for seven days and seven nights till Duke Ai of Chin took pity on him, saying, "Although the king of Chu did wrong, since they have such a minister we cannot let the state perish." He sent five hundred chariots to aid Chu against Wu, and in the sixth month they defeated Wu at Chi.

King Ho-lu stayed so long in Chu searching for the King that his brother Fu-kai went back and usurped the throne. When Ho-lu knew this, he decided to leave Chu. He returned to attack Fu-kai, who fled to Chu in defeat. King Chao, seeing that Wu was torn by internal strife, went back to his capital and gave Fu-kai the district of Tanghsi as his fief. Thus Fu-kai became lord of Tanghsi. Chu inflicted another defeat upon Wu, whereupon King Ho-lu withdrew.

Two years later the king sent his son Fu-cha with an army against Chu and he took Pan. Afraid that Wu might strike again with a great force, the king of Chu abandoned his capital, Ying, and moved his court to Jo.

So now, thanks to the stratagems of Wu Tzu-hsu and Sun Wu, Wu had defeated powerful Chu in the west, awed Chi and Tsin in the north and subdued Yueh in the south.

Four years later Confucius became prime minister of Lu. Five years later King Ho-lu attacked Yueh. King Kou-chien of Yueh resisted and defeated the army of Wu at Kusu, wounding King Ho-lu in the hand. The Wu forces retreated. King Ho-lu's wound made him mortally ill, and as he lay dying he asked his son Fu-cha, "Will you forget that Kou-chien has killed your father?"

"I shall never forget!" swore Fu-cha.

That night King Ho-lu died and Fu-cha became king. He made Po Pi his chief minister and practised archery and other military arts. Two years later he attacked Yueh and defeated its army at Fuchiao. King Kou-chien withdrew to Mount Kuaichi with the five thousand men remaining to him and sent his minister Chung with rich presents to Po Pi to sue for peace, promising to be Wu's vassal. The king of Wu was willing, but Wu Tzu-hsu advised against it.

"The king of Yueh knows how to bide his time," he said. "If you do not destroy him now, you will live to regret it." King Fu-cha disregarded him, however, and on Po Pi's advice made peace with Yueh.

Five years later King Fu-cha heard that Duke Ching of Chi had died and that the new king was weak, with his ministers contending for power. He raised an army to march north and attack Chi.

Wu Tzu-hsu advised against this expedition, saying, "King Kou-chien eats only one dish at each meal. He mourns his dead subjects and shows concern for the sick. This means that he intends to use his men for some purpose. So long as he lives, he is a menace to us. Today Yueh is like a cancer in our stomach. It is wrong to attack Chi before destroying Yueh."

The king paid no attention but attacked Chi, inflicting a great defeat on its army at Ailing and striking awe into the hearts of the kings of Tsou and Lu. After that he paid even less attention to Wu Tzu-hsu's advice.

Four years later King Fu-cha decided to strike at Chi again. King Kou-chien of Yueh, adopting Tzu-kung's plan, sent troops to help Wu and presented rich gifts to the chief minister Po Pi who, because he had received many bribes from Yueh, liked and trusted Kou-chien and constantly spoke well of him to the king. And the king was influenced by him.

Once more Wu Tzu-hsu warned, "Yueh is a cancer in our

stomach, yet now trusting their empty, deceitful promises you mean to invade Chi. Even if you conquer Chi, it will be as useless to us as a stony field. *The Admonition of Pan-keng* says, 'An unruly and insolent people should be wiped out, leaving no remnants, no seeds of trouble sown in the land.' This was how the Shang Dynasty prospered. I entreat you to give up Chi and deal first with Yueh, before it is too late for anything but regret."

The king, instead of listening to him, sent him on a mission to Chi. Just before he left, he told his son, "The king has turned a deaf ear to all my warnings. I can see that Wu will fall, but there is no need for you to fall with Wu." He entrusted his son to Pao Mu of Chi, after which he returned alone to Wu to report on his mission.

Since Po Pi bore Wu Tzu-hsu a grudge he slandered him to the king, saying, "Wu Tzu-hsu is stubborn, hot-tempered, heartless and suspicious. His resentment may lead to serious trouble. When you decided to attack Chi he was against it, and when your expedition was so successful he felt humiliated at having his advice passed over and became an embittered man. Now that you are going to attack Chi again, Wu Tzu-hsu is so set against it that he is undermining our efforts in the hope that we will fail, and thus prove him right. You are going to lead the campaign in person with all the armed forces of the state, yet Wu Tzu-hsu, because his advice was disregarded, has excused himself from going on the pretext of illness. Be very vigilant, sir! He could easily start a rebellion. Besides, I have sent men to watch his movements. When he went on that mission to Chi, he entrusted his son to a family there named Pao. He is your subject, yet in his dissatisfaction he has found a protector elsewhere. He is always complaining that he was your father's adviser but is now no longer trusted. I hope you will take steps against him in good time."

The king said, "I had my suspicions before you spoke." He sent a messenger to give Wu Tzu-hsu his sword *Shu-lou* with the order, "You may kill yourself with this."

Wu Tzu-hsu cast up his eyes to heaven and sighed. "Ah,

that slanderer Po Pi is plotting treason, but you, my king, are punishing me instead! I made your father a mighty conqueror. Before you came to the throne many princes were contending for it, and had I not fought for you with the last king you would never have been enthroned. After you became king you offered me half your kingdom, but I declined. Now, taken in by the words of a flatterer, you are killing your senior statesman." He instructed his steward, "Plant catalpas over my grave to provide a coffin for the king in time to come. Pluck out my eyes and hang them over the East Gate to see when the Yueh invaders break through and destroy our state." With that he cut his throat.

These words so enraged the king that he had Wu Tzu-hsu's corpse stuffed in a leather sack and thrown into the river. The men of Wu, grieving over Wu Tzu-hsu, built a temple to him by the river and renamed the hill there Mount Tzu-hsu.

After killing Wu Tzu-hsu, King Fu-cha set out on his expedition against Chi. The Pao clan of Chi killed Duke Tao and set up Yang-sheng in his place, but King Fu-cha failed to crush their rebellion and withdrew. Two years later he summoned the princes of Lu and Uei to a conference at Tokao.

The following year he went north and held a great conference with the heads of all the states at Huangchih, posing as the protector of Chou. Then King Kou-chien of Yueh launched a sudden attack, killed the crown prince of Wu and routed Wu's army. When King Fu-cha heard this he went back, sending envoys with rich gifts to sue for peace.

Nine years later King Kou-chien destroyed Wu and killed King Fu-cha. He also put to death the chief minister Po Pi because he had been disloyal to his sovereign, collaborated with another state and considered only his own selfish interests.

Wu Tzu-hsu, at his first coming to Wu, had been accompanied by Sheng, son of Crown Prince Chien, who had also fled from Chu. During the reign of Fu-cha of Wu, King Hui of Chu wanted to recall Sheng, but the lord of Sheh advised against it, saying, "Sheng sets store by military prowess and is quietly assembling men ready to die for him. He may be plotting something." King Hui did not listen to this warning but summoned Sheng back and installed him in the frontier district of Yen with the title lord of Pai. Three years after Sheng's return to Chu, Wu Tzu-hsu was killed.

After the lord of Pai returned to Chu, he nursed a grievance against the state of Cheng for killing his father, and secretly kept armed men to seek revenge. Five years later he asked permission to attack Cheng, and the chief minister Tzu-hsi agreed. But before the expedition set out, Cheng was invaded by Tsin and begged Chu for aid. Then Chu sent Tzu-hsi to the rescue, and he returned after making a pact with Cheng.

The lord of Pai was angry and declared, "It seems Tzu-hsi is my enemy, not Cheng!" He whetted his sword and, when asked the reason, replied, "This is to kill Tzu-hsi!"

When Tzu-hsi heard this he said with a laugh, "That egg-shell Sheng, what can he do to me?"

Four years later the lord of Pai and his follower Shih Chi fell on the Chu chief minister Tzu-hsi and the war minister Tzu-chi and killed them.

Then Shih Chi said, "We must kill the king as well."

They pursued the king, who fled to the Kao Mansion. One of Shih Chi's retainers, Chu Ku, carried the king on his back to the queen mother's palace. When the lord of Sheh heard that the lord of Pai had rebelled, he led his men to attack him. With the defeat of his followers, the lord of Pai fled into the mountains and killed himself. Shih Chi was captured and threatened with death in the cauldron if he refused to disclose where his master's corpse lay.

"Had we succeeded," replied Shih Chi, "I should have been a high minister. Now that we have failed, it is my duty to die in the cauldron." He refused to say where his lord had died and so he was boiled alive. Then they found King Hui and restored him to the throne.

The Grand Historian comments: How deeply resentment rankles in men's hearts! A ruler cannot afford to offend his subjects, much less one of his peers. Had Wu Tzu-hsu died with his father, he would have had no more significance than an ant. But setting aside minor scruples to wipe out a great wrong, he made a name that has come down to later ages. Alas for him! Whether hard pressed by the river or begging for food by the roadside, he never for a moment forgot the Chu capital. He endured disgrace to achieve great deeds and fame, and none but a true hero could have done this. If the lord of Pai had not aspired to the throne, his practical achievements and good advice would also have been remarkable.

KOU-CHIEN, KING OF YUEH

Kou-chien, king of Yueh, traced his ancestry back to Yu the Great through descendants of King Shao-kang of the Hsia Dynasty who were enfeoffed at Kuaïchi, where they kept up the sacrifices to Yu. They tattooed themselves, cut their hair short, and lived among brambles and weeds. After more than twenty generations there was Yun-chang, whose fight with King Ho-lu of Wu resulted in a feud. When Yun-chang died, his son Kou-chien succeeded him as king of Yueh.

In the first year of King Kou-chien,* King Ho-lu, hearing of Yun-chang's death, raised an army to attack Yueh. Kou-chien made his desperadoes challenge the enemy. In three parties they went to the Wu lines and with a great shout cut off their own heads. While the men of Wu were watching this Yueh launched a surprise attack at Tsuili, defeated Wu and wounded Ho-lu with an arrow. As he lay dying the king ordered his son Fu-cha, "Never forget Yueh!"

Three years later Kou-chien heard that King Fu-cha of Wu was training troops day and night to avenge himself. He thought of attacking before Wu's troops set out, but Fan Li advised against this, saying, "Think again. I have heard that arms are unlucky, war an evil force, and that disputes are minor affairs. If you plot with an evil force, by unlucky means, risking your life over a minor affair, you will be flouting Heaven's will and your campaign will not prosper."

"My mind is made up," said the king, and he raised an army.

When the king of Wu knew this, he sent picked troops against Yueh and won the battle of Fuchiao. Then with the

---

* 496 B.C.

five thousand men left to him, the king of Yueh withdrew to Kuaichi, where he was pursued and besieged by the king of Wu.

Kou-chien told Fan Li, "This comes of not following your advice. What shall I do now?"

Fan Li replied, "One who overcomes self-satisfaction gains the help of heaven, one who can turn a disastrous situation into a secure one gains the help of men, and one who practises frugality gains the help of the earth. Try to placate him with humble words and rich gifts. And if that fails, offer yourself as a hostage."

Kou-chien, approving, sent his minister Wen Chung to sue for peace. Approaching on his knees, Wen Chung kowtowed to the king of Wu, saying, "Your worthless subject Kou-chien sends his slave with the request that he may be your subject and his wife your serving-maid."

The king was about to agree when Wu Tzu-hsu said, "Heaven has delivered Yueh into our hands. Don't accept."

When Wen Chung reported this on his return, Kou-chien wanted to kill his wife and children, destroy his bronze vessels and jewels, and die fighting. But Wen Chung stopped him, suggesting, "Po Pi, the chancellor of Wu, is a grasping man who can be bribed. Let me go and talk to him secretly." So Kou-chien sent him with beautiful girls and jewels to the chancellor. Po Pi accepted these and got Wen Chung another audience with the king of Wu.

Wen Chung kowtowed and said, "I entreat Your Majesty to pardon Kou-chien and take all his bronze vessels! Unless you have mercy, he will kill his wife and children, destroy his jewels and fight to the last with his five thousand men, who can still do some damage."

Po Pi also advised the king, saying, "Kou-chien of Yueh has surrendered as your slave. If you pardon him, this will benefit our state."

Again the king of Wu was about to agree when Wu Tzu-hsu advanced to warn him, "If you do not destroy Yueh now, you will live to regret it. Kou-chien is an able ruler, while

Wen Chung and Fan Li are good ministers. If you let them return to Yueh they will make trouble for Wu." But the king, ignoring his advice, pardoned Yueh and withdrew his troops.

While besieged at Kuaichi, Kou-chien had sighed and asked, "Is this the end?"

Wen Chung told him, "King Tang of Shang was a captive in Hsiatai, King Wen of Chou was imprisoned in Yuli, Duke Wen of Tsin fled to Ti and Duke Huan of Chi to Chü; but they triumphed in the end. For all we know, this may lead to good fortune."

After being spared by Wu, Kou-chien returned to his state to lead a hard life and take anxious thought. He kept gall by his mat, looking at it while seated or lying down and tasting it while eating, to remind himself not to forget the disgrace of Kuaichi. He tilled the fields himself, made his wife spin cloth, went without meat and wore no coloured silks. He treated men of talent respectfully and his protégés handsomely, helping the poor, mourning the dead and sharing his people's toil.

Fan Li was asked to govern the state, but he said, "In military matters I am better than Wen Chung. But in governing a state and uniting the people, I am no match for him." So affairs of state were entrusted to Wen Chung while Fan Li and another minister, Cheh Chi, went to Wu to sue for peace and remained there as hostages. Two years later, Wu sent Fan Li back.

Seven years after his return from Kuaichi Kou-chien had succeeded in winning the support of his people, who were eager to take revenge on Wu. But his minister Feng Tung said, "Our state which was nearly destroyed is only just becoming self-supporting, prosperous and prepared for war. If we alarm Wu, we will inevitably bring disaster on ourselves. A hawk must keep out of sight before it swoops. The king of Wu is now attacking Chi and Tsin, while Chu and our state are his old enemies. So great is his prestige that he constitutes a threat to the House of Chou. His virtue is slight but his achievement great, and he is ambitious, exulting in his strength. Our best plan, therefore, is to ally with Chi, Chu and Tsin and keep on friendly terms with Wu. Since Wu aims at conquest, she will think nothing of fighting; but we shall have three other states as our allies against her, and by joining battle when Wu is exhausted we can defeat her."

"Very well," agreed Kou-chien.

Two years later the king of Wu decided to make war on Chi. Wu Tzu-hsu warned, "Don't do it yet. I have heard that Kou-chien eats only one dish at each meal and shares the joys and sorrows of his people. So long as this man lives, he is bound to be a threat to our state. Yueh is like a cancer in our belly, while Chi is nothing but a disease of the skin. I hope you will leave Chi alone and attack Yueh first."

The king paid no attention but attacked and defeated Chi at Ailing, capturing the ministers Kao and Kuo.

When blamed for giving the wrong advice, Wu Tzu-hsu said, "Don't laugh too soon, sir!" The king was angry and Wu Tzu-hsu determined to kill himself, but the king, hearing of this, stopped him.

Wen Chung, the minister of Yueh, said, "I fancy the king of Wu is over-confident. Let us test him by asking for a loan of grain."

The king of Wu agreed to a loan despite Wu Tzu-hsu's protests, to the secret delight of Yueh.

"The king will not listen to good advice," lamented Wu Tzu-hsu. "In three years Wu will be in ruins."

When Chancellor Po Pi heard this, he disputed with him. They had many arguments and Po Pi slandered him to the king, saying, "He may look loyal but in fact he is quite ruthless. If he cared nothing for his own father and brother, why should he care about his king? When you decided to attack Chi he argued against it. When you were successful he started grumbling again. Unless you take care, he will rebel."

He plotted with Feng Tung to abuse Wu Tzu-hsu to the king, who did not believe them at first and sent Wu Tzu-hsu as his envoy to Chi. He was enraged, however, to hear that

Wu Tzu-hsu had entrusted his son to the Pao family there. "So he really is deceiving me!" he exclaimed. "He means to rebel."

He sent a messenger to Wu Tzu-hsu with his sword *Shu-lou* and orders to kill himself.

Wu Tzu-hsu laughed. "I made your father a great conqueror and set you on your throne," he cried. "You offered me half your kingdom then, but I would not accept it. Yet now you are putting me to death because of slander. Ah, well! No man can stand alone." He told the messenger, "Pluck out my eyes and set them over the East Gate, so that I can watch the men of Yueh march into Wu."

After this all affairs of state were entrusted to Po Pi.

When three more years had passed, Kou-chien summoned Fan Li to ask, "The king of Wu has killed Wu Tzu-hsu and is surrounded by flatterers — is this our chance?"

The answer was, "Not yet."

The next spring King Fu-cha, escorted by his best troops, went north to Huangchih for a conference with all the heads of states, leaving only the old and infirm under the crown prince to guard Wu. And now when Kou-chien questioned Fan Li again, he agreed that the time had come. Yueh mobilized two thousand men sentenced to exile, forty thousand trained men, six thousand knights and a thousand officers. They attacked Wu, defeated the defenders and killed the crown prince.

When this disaster was announced to King Fu-cha at the conference, he kept it secret from the other states. After an agreement had been reached at Huangchih, he sent envoys with rich gifts to Yueh to sue for peace. And since Kou-chien felt unable to destroy Wu yet, he made peace.

Four years later Yueh attacked Wu again. Because the people of Wu were exhausted and their best troops had fallen in the wars with Chi and Tsin, Yueh routed their forces and besieged the capital for three years. Then the army of Wu was beaten and the king driven to Mount Kusu. He made

Kungsun Hsiung his envoy, to advance upon his knees with bared back and beg the king of Yueh for peace.

"Your subject Fu-cha presumes to lay bare his heart to you," said Kungsun Hsiung. "In days gone by he wronged you at Kuaichi, but complied with your request for peace. Now that you have advanced in majesty to mete out punishment, he must obey your commands. Will you pardon his offence, as he pardoned yours at Kuaichi?"

Kou-chien had not the heart to refuse, but Fan Li said, "At Kuaichi, Heaven delivered us into their hands, but they did not seize their chance. Now Heaven has delivered them into our hands: is Yueh to oppose the will of Heaven? Did you not hold court for long hours every day on account of Wu? Twenty-two years you have been planning this: how can you throw away your victory now? One who spurns what Heaven offers will suffer for it. As the saying goes, the woodcutter has not far to look for the example of an axe-handle. Have you forgotten what trouble you were in on Mount Kuaichi, sir?"

"I want to be guided by you," replied Kou-chien. "But I am sorry for the envoy."

Accordingly Fan Li sounded drums and ordered troops to advance. Then he announced, "His Majesty has left this in my hands. The envoy must leave or pay the penalty." Then the envoy of Wu left, weeping.

Kou-chien out of pity sent this message to the king of Wu, "I shall settle you east of Yung and make you lord over one hundred families."

But the king of Wu declined, saying, "I am too old to serve another King." He covered his face, crying, "How can I face Wu Tzu-hsu?" And with that he killed himself.

Kou-chien had the king of Wu buried and executed Chancellor Po Pi. After his conquest of Wu he advanced across the River Huai to meet the rulers of Chi and Tsin at Hsuchow. He presented tribute to the king of Chou, who sent an envoy to him with sacrificial meat and gave him the title of Lord Protector. Then Kou-chien returned south of the River Huai and gave the Huai Valley to Chu, returned the territory of Sung which Wu had annexed, and gave a hundred square *li* east of the River Szu to Lu. The army of Yueh was now supreme throughout the eastern Yangtse and Huai River valleys. All the states sent Kou-chien congratulations, and he called himself the Overlord.

Then Fan Li left, sending Wen Chung a letter from Chi in which he said, "When all the birds are killed the good bow is put away. When the cunning hares are dead the hounds are made into stew. The king of Yueh with his long neck and predatory mouth is a good companion in time of trouble but not in time of peace. You had better leave."

After receiving this letter, Wen Chung stayed away from court on the pretext of illness but slanderers accused him of plotting rebellion. Then Kou-chien sent him a sword with this message, "You told me of seven ways to conquer Wu and by using three of them I have overthrown it. That leaves you with four — why not try them with my kingly ancestors?" Thereupon Wen Chung committed suicide.

Kou-chien died and was succeeded by his son, Shih-yu. The throne passed from father to son, from Shih-yu to Pu-shou, Weng, Yi, Chih-hou and Wu-chiang. During the reign of Wu-chiang, Yueh attacked Chi in the north and Chu in the west, contending for power with the central states.

In the time of King Wei of Chu, Yueh struck north against Chi and King Wei of Chi sent an envoy to advise the king of Yueh, "Unless you attack Chu, you cannot be a king or a conqueror. I assume you have not yet done so because you lack the support of Hann and Wei, who will not attack Chu. If Hann defeated an army of Chu and killed its commander, the Hann cities of Sheh and Yangti would be endangered. If Wei destroyed an army of Chu and killed its commander, the Wei cities of Chen and Shangtsai would be endangered. These two states cannot help you unless they destroy the enemy's force. Why do you value their support so highly?"

The king of Yueh replied, "I am not asking these states to cross swords with Chu, let alone storm its cities. I simply want the Wei army to gather at Taliang, and the forces of Chi to muster at Nanyang and Chü and gather at Chang and Yen. Then the men of Chu would not dare march south of Fangcheng or east of the Huai and Szu Rivers. They would not have strength enough to defend themselves against Chin west of Shang, Yu, Hsi, Li and Sunghu, or against Yueh along the Yangtse and Szu Rivers. Chi, Chin, Hann and Wei would hold Chu at bay while the two states of Tsin, without resorting to arms, would get their share of Chu's territory, reaping a harvest without ploughing. Instead of this, however, they are contending by the Yellow River and Mount Hua for the territory of Chi and Chin. This is foolish behaviour; how can they become kings like that?"

The envoy of Chi replied, "Luck alone has saved Yueh from destruction. It is not wisdom to see fine hairs but not the eyebrow. In the same way, you see the folly of the states of Tsin but not the mistakes of Yueh. You do not expect Hann and Wei to fight for you or enter into a military alliance with you, but only want them to exhaust Chu's strength. But why place your hopes on them when Chu's forces are already scattered?"

The king of Yueh asked him to explain himself.

He said, "The three ministers of Chu are deploying their armies. They have laid siege to Chuwo and Wuchung in the north and their line extends 3,700 *li* to the Wuchia Pass. Ching Tsui's army is stationed in the north near Lu, Chi and Nanyang. Could they have covered a greater area? You are hoping that Hann and Wei will fight Chu, and unless they do your army will not advance. This is like a man who does not know that two fives add up to ten. Unless you attack Chu now, you will never become a conqueror or king. Chu gets its grain from Chou, Pang and Changsha, its timber from the mountains and marshes of Chingling. If you dispatch troops to the Wuchia Pass, those four districts will stop sending tribute to the capital of Chu. I have heard that a man who fails to become a king can at least become a conqueror. If you cannot be a great conqueror, it is because you have not followed the kingly way. I advise you, sir, to turn and attack Chu."

Then the king of Yueh called off his attack on Chi and turned against Chu, but King Wei of Chu raised an army and utterly routed the troops of Yueh, killing King Wuchiang and recapturing all the former territory of Wu up to the River Che. He also defeated the army of Chi at Hsuchow in the north.

Because of this, Yueh became disunited and many princes contended for power. Some took the title of prince, others of lord, and they ruled along the seacoast south of the Yangtse, acknowledging the suzerainty of Chu.

Seven generations later Lord Yao of Minyueh joined forces with other states to overthrow the Chin empire. The First Emperor of Han made him prince of Yueh to continue the Yueh dynastic sacrifices. The prince of Tungyueh and the lord of Minyueh were his descendants.

For more than twenty years Fan Li had toiled without sparing himself in the service of Kou-chien, advising the king till at last he overthrew Wu and avenged the disgrace of Kuaichi. When Kou-chien dispatched troops north of the River Huai to threaten Chi and Tsin, lorded it over all the central states and exhorted them to respect the House of Chou, he became Lord Protector with Fan Li as his supreme commander.

After his return Fan Li realized that he was too prominent now for his own safety, for Kou-chien was a good companion in danger but not in time of peace. He therefore sent a letter to the king, saying, "I have heard that if something preys on the ruler's mind, his minister should exert himself. If the ruler is disgraced, his minister should die. When you suffered disgrace at Kuaichi I did not die because I wished to take revenge, but now that we have wiped out our shame I beg to be punished."

"I want to share my kingdom with you," said Kou-chien. "If you refuse, I shall kill you."

However, Fan Li replied, "A sovereign gives commands, a subject does what he thinks right." So gathering together his jewels and precious possessions, he put out to sea with his followers and never returned to Yueh. Kou-chien designated Mount Kuaichi as his fief.

Fan Li went by sea to Chi, where he changed his name and called himself Master Wine-skin. He worked hard with his sons as a farmer on the coast, and amassed considerable property. Soon he had tens of thousands. The men of Chi, knowing his great ability, made him their prime minister.

Then Fan Li said with a sigh, "For a private citizen to make thousands of pieces of gold or for an official to become a minister are the highest attainments of ordinary men; but no good can come of a long period of fame and nobility." So he returned the minister's seal, gave all his money to his friends and neighbours and left quietly with his jewels to settle in Tao, a great commercial centre where a man could grow rich by trading. He now called himself Lord Chu of Tao. Here once more he and his sons tilled the soil, bred cattle, stored goods and sold them at the right season to make a ten per-cent profit. In a short time he had amassed tens of thousands again and his name was known throughout the land.

While in Tao, Lord Chu had a third son. When this boy grew up, the second son was arrested for murder in Chu.

"It is right that a murderer should die," said Lord Chu. "But I have heard that the son of a wealthy family need not die on the execution ground." He ordered his youngest boy to go and make inquiries, packing one thousand *yi** of gold** in sacks and loading these on an ox-cart. But as he was sending the young man off, his eldest son insisted on going instead.

When Lord Chu would not agree, his first-born said, "The eldest son of a family is the guardian of the house. Now my brother is charged with murder, yet you want to send my younger brother instead of me — I must be a bad son!" He threatened to kill himself.

---

* Ancient measure of weight corresponding to the modern catty.

** Some scholars hold that the word *chin* (gold), as it occurs in the books of the Chou and early Han Dynasties, really means brass. Owing to the lack of conclusive proofs it is translated in this book according to its usual connotation. — *Tr.*

His mother put in, "Sending the youngest may still not save the second, while the eldest dies first. What use is that?"

So Lord Chu was forced to send his eldest son. He wrote a letter to his old friend Master Chuang and told his son, "On your arrival, leave the thousand *yi* of gold with Master Chuang to dispose of as he thinks fit. Mind you don't argue with him!"

The eldest son set off, having added several hundred pieces of gold of his own. Upon reaching the Chu capital, he found that Master Chuang lived in the suburb in a very humble way, his gate choked with brambles. Still, he gave him the letter and gold as his father had told him.

"You may go straight back," said Chuang. "Don't stay here. And if your brother is released, don't ask the reason."

The eldest son withdrew but stayed on in the city, not calling upon Chuang but using the gold which he had brought separately to bribe a powerful noble of Chu.

Although Master Chuang lived in a poor neighbourhood, the whole state knew that he was incorruptible and he was respected by everyone from the king downwards. He had no intention of keeping Lord Chu's gold, but meant to return it as soon as he had succeeded. He told his wife, "This gold belongs to Lord Chu. It is like a disease which must not be left untended overnight. Later it must be returned. Don't touch it!"

Lord Chu's eldest son did not know this, however, but thought Chuang rather lacking in discrimination.

Chuang had an audience with the king of Chu and told him that a certain star in a certain quarter of the heavens boded harm to the state.

"What can be done?" asked the king, who trusted him implicitly.

"Only by doing good can you avert danger."

"Very well," said the king. "I shall take your advice." He sent a man to seal up the treasury.

Then the noble told Lord Chu's eldest son, "The king is going to declare an amnesty." Asked how he knew, he explained, "Before each amnesty the king always seals up the treasury. And yesterday evening he sent to seal it up."

The eldest son reflected that if there was to be an amnesty his brother would be released anyhow, and all the gold given Master Chuang would be wasted. So he went to see Chuang again.

"How is it you haven't left?" asked Chuang in surprise.

"I came hoping to save my brother," was the reply. "Now that an amnesty is to be proclaimed, he will be saved in any case. So I have come to bid you goodbye."

Knowing what he wanted, Chuang said, "Go in and take the gold."

The young man took the gold and left, very pleased with himself.

But Chuang, annoyed at being tricked by this youth, went back to the king and said, "Last time when I spoke of the stars, sir, you decided to avert bad luck by doing good. But now it is the talk of the town that the son of wealthy Lord Chu of Tao is in prison here for murder and his family has given your ministers substantial bribes. They say you are not declaring an amnesty out of the goodness of your heart but for the sake of Lord Chu's son."

The king retorted angrily, "I may not be a good man, but I would not do such a thing just for Lord Chu's son." He ordered the young man's execution, and a general amnesty was proclaimed the next day. So the eldest son had to take back his brother's corpse. When he reached home his mother and the rest of the household mourned. Only Lord Chu laughed.

"I knew he would kill his brother," he declared. "Not that he did not love him, he just could not help himself. He went through hard times with me when he was young, knows how difficult it is to make a living, and therefore hates parting with money. His younger brother has never seen me as otherwise than wealthy, riding in carriages or on fine horses to hunt the hare. Because he has no idea where money comes from, he is prodigal with it and never counts the cost. That is why I wanted to send him. But the eldest is incapable of that, and so he ended up by killing his brother. This is in the nature of things, not a cause for mourning. I have been waiting day and night for his corpse to be brought back."

Fan Li, who moved three times, won a great reputation throughout the land. And he never moved for nothing, but made a name for himself wherever he went. Since he grew old and finally died in Tao, he is known as Lord Chu of Tao.

The Grand Historian comments: Great were the achievements of Yu, who opened up the Nine Rivers and divided the Nine Regions so that the descendants of Hsia dwell in peace to this day. His descendant Kou-chien led a hard life and took anxious thought till at last he succeeded in overthrowing powerful Wu, manifesting the might of his arms to the central states, giving his support to the House of Chou and winning the title of an Overlord. Undoubtedly he was an able king and a worthy descendant of Yu. Fan Li moved three times but won fame wherever he went, and his name is remembered by later generations. Indeed, how could such a good minister fail to win glory?

LORD SHANG

Lord Shang was descended, through a concubine, from the royal house of Uei. His personal name was Yang, his clan name Kungsun, and his ancestors had been of the royal Chi clan. As a youth he was interested in the study of law and served as clan officer under Kungshu Tso, the prime minister of Wei, who recognized his ability but lacked opportunity to recommend him.

When Kungshu Tso fell ill, King Hui of Wei went in person to inquire after him and asked, "If anything should happen to you, what will become of my state?"

"My clan officer Kungsun Yang, although young, has remarkable gifts," replied Kungshu Tso. "I hope you will entrust affairs of state to him."

The king was silent and prepared to leave. The prime minister sent everyone else away and said, "If you do not mean to take my advice and employ him, then have Yang killed. Don't let him leave the country."

The king agreed to this, and left.

Then Kungshu Tso sent for Yang and told him regretfully, "Today the king asked me to suggest a successor. When I recommended you, I saw disapproval written on his face. So, putting my sovereign's interest first, I urged him to kill you if he would not use your services, and he agreed to do this. You must leave without delay, or you will be caught."

"If the king ignored your advice to employ me," said Yang, "why should he take your advice to have me killed?" And he did not leave.

After this interview King Hui told his followers, "I'm afraid the prime minister is in a bad way. He urged me to entrust affairs of state to Kungsun Yang — how absurd!"

After Kungshu's death, Yang heard that Duke Hsiao of Chin was trying to recruit men of talent to continue the achievements of Duke Mu and recover the territory Chin had lost in the east. He went west to Chin and obtained an audience with the duke through the offices of his favourite eunuch Ching. Yang held forth at great length but Duke Hsiao did not listen and kept dropping off to sleep. The duke afterwards complained to Ching, "Your friend is a fool. How could I use such a man?"

When Ching reproached Yang, the latter said, "I spoke to him about the emperors' way, but he lacks the necessary enlightenment." Five days later, at another audience, he did better, although it still was not what the duke wanted. Duke Hsiao complained once more to Ching, who reproached Yang again.

"I spoke about the kingly way," said Yang, "but he could not accept that either. I must beg for another audience."

This time the duke was pleased with Yang but did not take him into his service. After he had withdrawn, the duke told Ching, "Your protégé is all right. I can talk with him."

"I spoke of the conquerors' way," said Yang, "so now he is thinking of using me. I know how to talk with him next time I see him."

At their next meeting the duke unconsciously moved forward to sit closer to Yang. He spoke with him without wearying for several days.

"How did you make such a good impression?" asked Ching. "My master is delighted."

"I spoke to him first of the emperors' way and the kingly way, drawing comparisons with the Three Dynasties," Yang explained. "But the duke said, 'That would take too long, I cannot wait. A good ruler should make his mark in the world in his lifetime, not wait for a century to achieve the emperors' or the kingly way.' I then told him how to make his state powerful, and he was overjoyed. But he will hardly equal Shang and Chou."

Upon entering Duke Hsiao's employment, Yang asked to

61

introduce reforms, but the duke was afraid of popular discontent.

"Those who hesitate to act win no fame, those who falter in their course achieve nothing," reasoned Yang. "Those who outdo others are condemned by the world. Those who see further than others are mocked by the mob. Fools are blind to what already exists whereas the wise perceive what is yet to come. It is no use consulting the people at the start, but one can enjoy the fruits with them. Those whose virtue is highest do not compromise with the common herd, those whose achievements are greatest do not consult the mob. A wise ruler who knows how to strengthen his state will not abide by old traditions; one who knows how to profit the people will not cling to conventions."

The duke approved.

But Kan Lung* said, "Not so. A sage does not teach the people to change their ways, a wise sovereign does not rule by discarding tradition. He who educates the people in accordance with custom succeeds without any trouble; he who rules according to established laws will have competent officers and satisfied subjects."

Yang replied, "Kan Lung talks like one of the vulgar herd. The common run of men cling to conventions, while scholars are smothered by their own learning. They are all adequate at sticking to official routine, but not the sort of people with whom to discuss other matters. The Three Dynasties were each governed according to different traditions, and the Five Conquerors** each prevailed by different policies. The wise make laws; the foolish keep them. The able alter the conventions; the foolish are bound by them."

Tu Chih*** said, "Never change your way except for a hundredfold profit. Never alter a tool except for a tenfold ad-

---

* A minister of Chin.

** Duke Huan of Chi, Duke Wen of Tsin, Duke Hsiang of Sung, Duke Mu of Chin and King Chuang of Chu.

*** Another minister.

vantage. We cannot go wrong if we follow the ancient way. We cannot err by keeping to conventions."

"There are many ways of governing," retorted Yang. "To benefit the state we need not follow the ancients. Tang and Wu of old ruled as kings without following the ancients, and the Hsia and Shang Dynasties perished through keeping the conventions unchanged. We must not condemn those who oppose the ancients or praise those who abide by conventions."

"Well said!" approved Duke Hsiao. He appointed Yang adjutant general and laid down new laws.

The people were divided into groups of five and ten households, mutually responsible for each other. Those who failed to denounce a criminal would be cut in two; those who denounced him would be rewarded as if they had beheaded an enemy; those who harboured a criminal would be punished as if they had surrendered to the enemy. Families with two or more grown sons not living in separate households had to pay a double tax. Those who distinguished themselves in war would be rewarded with noble rank according to merit. Those who carried on private feuds would be punished according to their offence. The people had to work hard at the fundamental occupations of farming and weaving, and those who harvested most grain or produced most silk would be exempted from levies. Those who followed subsidiary occupations like trade, or who were idle and poor, would have their wives and sons enslaved. Nobles who failed to distinguish themselves in war would lose their noble status. The social hierarchy was clearly defined and each rank allotted its appropriate land property, retainers, women slaves and clothing. Those who achieved worthy deeds would be honoured; those who did not, even if they were wealthy, could not make a splendid display.

When these reforms were ready to be promulgated, the authorities, fearing that the people would disregard them, set up a wooden pillar thirty feet high at the south gate of the market and offered a reward of ten gold pieces to anyone who would move it to the north gate. The people were sceptical and no one dared move it. Then a reward of fifty gold pieces was offered. A man moved the pillar and received the reward, proving that the authorities meant what they said. After that, the new decrees were issued.

Within a year, the subjects of Chin were flocking to the capital in thousands to complain of the new measures. And then the crown prince broke the law.

"These reforms are not working because those at the top are breaking the law," said Yang. He wanted to penalize the crown prince, but, since the heir apparent could not be punished, his guardian Lord Chien was punished in his stead while his tutor Lord Chia had his face tattooed. From the next day on all the people of Chin obeyed the laws.

By the end of ten years the people were well content. Nothing lost on the road was picked up and pocketed, the hills were free of brigands, every household was comfortably off, men fought bravely in war but avoided private feuds, and villages and towns were well-governed. When some of the citizens who had first complained of the reforms now came to praise them, Yang said, "These are trouble-makers." These men were banished to frontier towns, after which no more discussion of the laws was heard.

Then Yang was promoted to the sixteenth rank, the highest rank in Chin being the twentieth. He led an army to besiege Anyi in Wei, and subjugated the city. Three years later, he built a palace with archways at Hsienyang, and the duke moved his capital there from Yung.

Then fathers, sons and brothers were forbidden to live in one house, small villages and towns were grouped together as counties, with magistrates and vice-magistrates over them. The state was divided into thirty-one of these counties; the old boundaries between the fields were abolished; regular taxation was introduced; and weights and measures were standardized. Four years later, the prince's guardian Lord Chien broke the law again and his nose was cut off. After five years Chin was so wealthy and powerful that the king of Chou sent sacrificial meat to the duke, and all the states offered congratulations.

The following year Chi defeated the army of Wei at Maling, capturing Crown Prince Shen and killing General Pang Chuan.

The next year Yang advised the duke, "Wei is like a cancer in our heart. Either Wei will annex us, or we must annex Wei. For they lie west of the mountains with their capital at Anyi, separated from us by the Yellow River but possessing all the advantages of the east. They can march west to invade us whenever they please, or hold their land in the east if they are weak. Thanks to Your Majesty's wisdom our state is prospering, whereas Wei was heavily defeated by Chi last year and all their allies have left them. This is the time to attack. When they withdraw, unable to resist us, we can seize the strongholds of the mountains and the Yellow River and control the other states in the east. This is the task for a king!"

The duke, approving, gave him an army to attack Wei, whose king dispatched troops under Lord Ang to resist. When both forces confronted each other, Yang sent Lord Ang this message, "We are old friends, yet now we are commanding hostile armies. I cannot bear the thought of fighting you. Let us meet to pledge our faith and feast together, then withdraw our troops so that our states may live at peace."

Lord Ang agreed to this. The two commanders made a pledge and, as they were drinking together, armed men whom Yang had set in ambush seized Lord Ang. Then the Chin troops fell upon the army of Wei and after routing it returned home. Since Wei had been defeated by both Chi and Chin, King Hui of Wei's resources were exhausted and his territory was dwindling away. In fear he sent an envoy to sue for peace, offering the land west of the Yellow River to the duke of Chin. Then King Hui moved his capital from Anyi to Taliang, saying, "I should have taken Kungshu Tso's advice!"

Upon Yang's return from defeating the Wei army, the duke gave him fifteen towns in Shang and Wu as his fief, and he became known as Lord Shang.

For ten years Lord Shang was prime minister of Chin, and many of the nobles hated him.

Chao Liang* asked for an interview with him, and Lord Shang told him, "I owe this introduction to Meng Lan-kao. May I ask you to be my friend too?"

"I must decline the honour," Chao Liang replied. "Confucius said, 'One who shows his love for the people by recommending good men succeeds. One who assembles inferior men to rule fails.' As an inferior individual, I dare not accept your friendship. I have heard that 'claiming a position not rightly yours is greed, claiming a name not rightly yours is ambition.' Were I to do as you ask, sir, I should be guilty of both greed and ambition. So I dare not accept."

"Do you disapprove of my way of governing Chin?"

"The wise man considers carefully what he is told, the enlightened man looks within, the strong man masters himself. Thus King Shun said, 'He who humbles himself makes himself great.' You should follow the sage king's way, sir, instead of consulting me."

Lord Shang rejoined, "The men of Chin used to be like the barbarian tribes of Jung and Ti, making no distinction between fathers and sons, and all living in the same room. Now I have changed those ways, segregating men and women. I have built palaces with archways like those of Lu and Uei. How would you say I compare with Paili Hsi** in governing the state?"

"A thousand sheepskins are not as good as one fox fur," replied Chao Liang. "A thousand sycophants are not as good as one outspoken man. King Wu prospered thanks to frank advisers, while King Chow, the last ruler of the Yin Dynasty, lost his state through silencing criticism. If you have no objection to King Wu's way, may I speak frankly without fear of punishment for the rest of my life?"

"As the old saying goes, 'Fair words are flowers, true words are fruit; reproof is medicine, flattery is disease.' By all means speak absolutely frankly. You will be adminis-

---

* A respected recluse of Chin.

** A minister of Duke Mu of Chin (659-621 B.C.).

tering medicine to me and I shall be guided by you, sir. Pray don't hesitate."

So Chao Liang said, "Paili Hsi, a borderer of Chu, wanted to come to Chin because he heard that Duke Mu was a good ruler. Since he had no money for the journey, he sold himself as a slave to a native of Chin. He wore rags and tended cattle for over a year till the duke, hearing about him, took him from the herd and raised him above common citizens to the highest position in the land. After he had been prime minister for six or seven years, Chin attacked Cheng in the east, appointed three different rulers of Tsin, and rescued Chu from ruin. He spread enlightenment throughout the state, and the men of Pa* sent tribute. His virtue spread through all the land and even barbarians submitted to his rule. When Yiu-yu** heard of him, he crossed the frontier to see him. While in office, he rode in a standing, not a sitting chariot, even if he was tired, and never used an awning in hot weather. He toured the country without any equipage or armed retainers. His noble deeds are recorded in the archives, his virtue has influenced later generations. At his death, every man and woman in Chin shed tears, the children stopped singing, the millers stopped chanting as they pounded rice — such was his goodness.

"As for you, sir, you obtained an audience with the king of Chin through his eunuch Ching, which was hardly proper. During your administration you have done nothing for the people, simply building a host of archways and palaces, which is hardly to your credit. You have punished and tattooed the crown prince's tutor and guardian and mutilated the people with harsh penalties, arousing resentment and making enemies. It is more effective for a ruler to influence men than to give them orders, and subjects are quicker to imitate their superiors than to obey their commands; yet you introduce wrong systems and mistaken measures, which is no way to educate

* In present-day Szechuan.

** A famous strategist of Tsin.

the people. You talk and act like a prince, and are pressing the nobles of Chin harder every day. The *Book of Songs* says, 'Even a rat knows what is proper, but some men do not. If a man does not know what is proper, the sooner he dies the better.' Judging by this, you are not likely to live long. For eight years Lord Chien has not ventured out of doors. You killed Chu Huan too and had Lord Chia tattooed. According to the *Book of Songs*, 'He who wins support will prosper, he who loses support will fall.' Your actions are not such as win support.

"You drive out followed by a dozen carriages of retainers and with others full of guards, flanked by strong men, with lancers and halberdiers beside you. You will not stir abroad without all these precautions. The *Book of Documents* says, 'Those who rely on virtue will prosper, those who rely on force will perish.' You are as vulnerable as the morning dew and your expectation of life can hardly be long.

"You would do better to return those fifteen towns, work on some vegetable farm outside the city and urge the duke to honour recluses who live in mountain caves, to care for the old and helpless, to show respect to elders, and to reward and honour men of achievements and virtue; for this would lessen your danger. If you cling to your rich estates, monopolize state power, and arouse the hatred of the common people, then the men of Chin will have ample reason to get rid of you once the duke dies. Your end will come as swift as a kick!"

But Lord Shang ignored his advice.

Five months later Duke Hsiao of Chin died, and the crown prince came to the throne. The followers of his guardian Lord Chien accused Lord Shang of plotting revolt, and officers were sent to arrest him. He fled and sought lodging for the night in a frontier inn but the inn-keeper, not knowing who he was, told him, "According to the laws of Lord Shang, I shall be punished if I take in a man without a permit."

Lord Shang sighed and said, "So I am suffering from my own laws!"

He went to Wei, but the men of Wei would not give him asylum, because his betrayal of Lord Ang and the defeat of their army still rankled. Before he could go elsewhere, they said, "Lord Shang is a traitor to Chin, and Chin is powerful. How can we let him escape through our territory?" So they turned him back.

Once in Chin again, Lord Shang fled to his fief and made his followers raise local troops to attack Cheng in the north. Chin sent an army against him and he was killed at Mienchih. King Hui of Chin had his corpse torn limb from limb by chariots as a warning to others, and decreed, "Let no man rebel like Lord Shang!" His family was wiped out.

The Grand Historian comments: Lord Shang had a cruel nature. His falseness was shown by the way in which he tried to impress the duke with the emperors' way and kingly way, just high-sounding talk in which he had no real interest. His inhumanity was revealed by the way he gained an audience through the duke's favourite, but after he was in power punished Lord Chien, tricked Lord Ang of Wei and turned a deaf ear to Chao Liang's advice. I have read his dissertations on law and government, agriculture and war, which correspond to his actions. The bad end he finally came to in Chin was no more than he deserved.

MENCIUS AND HSUN CHING

The Grand Historian comments: When I read *Mencius* and come to the words, "King Hui of Liang asked Mencius, 'How shall I profit my state?'" I lay the book aside and sigh. Alas! I say, how true it is that profit is the root of all evil. The master seldom spoke of profit, always trying to check it at the source. Thus Mencius said, "Going all out for profit often leads to dissatisfaction." The evil consequences of seeking profit are the same for a common citizen or an emperor.

Meng Ko,* a native of Tsou, was taught by a disciple of Tzu Szu. After he had mastered the Way he offered his services to King Hsuan of Chi, but King Hsuan could not use him. He went to Liang (Wei), but King Hui of Liang did not carry out his teachings, regarding Mencius as an impractical pedant.

This was the time when Chin was employing Lord Shang to enrich the state and strengthen the army, Chu and Wei were employing Wu Chi to defeat their weaker enemies, King Wei and King Hsuan of Chi were employing men like Sun Pin and Tien Chi, while all the other states turned east to pay homage to Chi. The whole realm was divided into alliances with or against Chin and fighting was held in high regard. Mencius, who spoke of the virtues of Yao and Shun and the Three Dynasties, could not get on with these rulers. So he retired with Wan Chang and some other disciples to expound the *Book of Songs* and *Book of Documents* and transmit the teachings of Confucius. His own writings filled seven books.

After him were the philosophers Tsou-tzu's. The state of Chi had three scholars surnamed Tsou. The first, Tsou Chi,

---

* Mencius.

so impressed King Wei by his performance on the lyre that he was set in charge of affairs of state, enfeoffed as Marquis Cheng and given the seal of prime minister. He lived before Mencius.

The second, Tsou Yen, came after Mencius. Tsou Yen saw that the rulers were becoming increasingly dissolute and extravagant, unable to first rectify themselves and then spread their virtue among the common people, as was taught in the ancient odes. Thereupon he delved deep into the interplay of the *yin* and *yang* and wrote more than a hundred thousand words about their strange transmutations, summarizing the ideas of the great sages. Using wild and magniloquent language, he went on from a study of some minor object to extend his deductions to infinity. Going back from modern times to the Yellow Emperor* and the common origin of all teachings, he covered the rise and fall of different ages, the good and bad omens, and the various institutions, tracing these to the remote past before Earth and Heaven were created, and to the mysterious and unknown origin of things. He began by tabulating the famous mountains, mighty rivers and valleys of China, its birds and beasts, products of water and land and precious objects, going on from these to things hidden from men's eyes beyond the Four Seas. He claimed that since the separation of Heaven and Earth all things must change according to the specific laws of the Five Elements and show definite manifestations. He maintained that what Confucians called the "Central States" were only one of eighty-one regions of the world. The Middle Kingdom, known as the Red Divine Land, comprised the nine "continents" of which Great Yu spoke, but these were not real continents. Outside the Middle Kingdom there were nine regions as large as the Red Divine Land, and these were the true Nine Continents. These were each surrounded by "small seas" separating the people and beasts on one from those on others and formed one region which made up one

---

* A legendary ruler to whom many Taoist teachings were ascribed.

continent. There were nine such continents, surrounded by a "great ocean" at the boundary of Earth and Heaven.

Tsou Yen's theories were all of this sort. Yet these were the premises for his conclusions about humanity, justice, frugality and the relationships between ruler and ruled, high and low, and kinsmen. Princes and nobles were impressed and influenced by their first acquaintance with his teachings, but they could never put them into practice.

Tsou Yen was highly regarded in Chi. When he went to Liang (Wei), King Hui welcomed him outside the city and treated him as an honoured guest. In Chao, Lord Pingyuan walked beside him and dusted the mat for him. In Yen, King Chao swept the path before him, asked to be allowed to sit with his students to study under him, and built Chiehshih Palace so that he himself might learn from him there. So Tsou Yen wrote *The Sovereign's Way*. Every state he visited received him with honour. How different from the case of Confucius, who underwent hunger in Chen and Tsai, or of Mencius who was hard put to it in Chi and Liang!

When, for the sake of humanity and justice, Wu attacked the king of Yin and became king himself, Po Yi refused to eat the grain of Chou. When Duke Ling of Uei asked about battle formations, Confucius refused to answer. When King Hui of Liang (Wei) planned to attack Chao, Mencius told him how King Wen had left the district of Pin. These men certainly never tried to follow the fashion or compromise with it. How can you fit a square peg into a round hole? Some point out, however, that Yi Yin served Tang as a cook before making him a king, and Paili Hsi grazed his oxen in front of Duke Mu's chariot before serving him and making him a conqueror; for they had to meet the ruler first before leading him to the right path. Although Tsou Yen's teachings were unorthodox, he may have had the same idea as these men.

After Tsou Yen came the scholars of the Chihsia Academy in Chi, men like Chunyu Kun, Shen Tao, Huan Yuan, Chieh Tzu, Tien Pien and Tsou Shih, who wrote about government to advise the princes of their time. They are too many to enumerate here.

Chunyu Kun, a native of Chi, had wide knowledge and a retentive memory and belonged to no particular school of thought. In offering advice he took Yen Ying as his model, but paid careful attention to the ruler's reactions. Once someone introduced him to King Hui of Liang (Wei), who twice dismissed everyone else to receive him in private, but not a word did Chunyu Kun say.

The astonished king told the man who had introduced him, "You recommended Master Chunyu as superior even to Kuan Chung and Yen Ying, but I have learned nothing from him. Am I unworthy of his advice? Or what is the reason?"

When this was repeated to Chunyu Kun, he said, "True. The first time I saw the king his thoughts were on charioteering. The second time his thoughts were on music. So I kept quiet."

As soon as the king was informed of this, he exclaimed in astonishment, "Ah, Master Chunyu must certainly be a sage! When he first came, I had just been given a fine horse and had no time to examine it. The second time, I had just been given some musicians but had no time to hear them. Although I dismissed everyone else, it is true that my thoughts were elsewhere."

Chunyu Kun subsequently saw the king again and they talked for three days and three nights without wearying. King Hui wished to make him a high minister, but he declined and withdrew. Then the king presented him with a fine carriage drawn by four horses, as well as rolls of silk, some jade and two thousand *yi* of gold. He accepted no official post all his life.

Shen Tao came from Chao, Tien Pien and Chieh Tzu from Chi, and Huan Yuan from Chu. These men studied the doctrines of the Yellow Emperor and Lao Tzu and propounded their own ideas according to these. Shen Tao was the author of twelve essays, Huan Yuan left two books of writing, and Tien Pien and Chieh Tzu both wrote essays too. Tsou Shih, another of the Tsou scholars of Chi, recorded the teachings of Tsou Yen in his writings. The king of Chi favoured these scholars. From Chunyu Kun down he gave them all the rank of ministers and honoured them by building large mansions, broad avenues and imposing gates for them. This was to show the protégés of other rulers that the king of Chi was a good patron.

Hsun Ching was a native of Chao who went to Chi when he was fifty to spread his teachings. Tsou Yen's arguments were diffuse and highflown, Tsou Shih had literary talent but his theories were difficult to put into practice, and if you spent long enough with Chunyu Kun you could occasionally catch words of wisdom. Hence the men of Chi commented, "Tsou Yen talks about heaven, Tsou Shih is a fine stylist, and Chunyu Kun is a fluent speaker."

Tien Pien and the scholars associated with him were dead by the time of King Hsiang of Chi, so that Hsun Ching was the doyen of the philosophers. Chi was filling vacancies in the ranks of its ministers, and Hsun Ching was three times appointed chief libationer. When some men of Chi slandered him he went to Chu, where Lord Chunshen made him magistrate of Lanling, a position he lost at the death of Lord Chunshen. Li Szu, later prime minister of Chin, was one of Hsun Chin's pupils.

Hsun Ching hated the corrupt governments of his day, the decadent states and evil princes who did not follow the Way but gave their attention to magic and prayers and believed in omens and luck. The Confucian scholars of his generation were petty and narrow-minded, while thinkers such as Chuang Chou were wild and destructive of public morality. So Hsun Ching expounded the advantages and disadvantages of practising the Confucian, Mohist and Taoist teachings. By the time of his death he had written tens of thousands of words. He was buried in Lanling.

Kungsun Lung was another man of Chao. He argued about similarities and differences and about solidity and whiteness. Chao also produced the philosophy of Chu Tzu. In Wei there was Li Kuei, who taught the proper use of natural resources. In Chu there were Shih Tzu, Chang Lu and Yu Tzu of Ah. Since the writings of these men from Mencius to Yu Tzu are well known, I shall not discuss them here.

Mo Ti was a minister of Sung who was skilled in military defence and advocated economy. Some say he was a contemporary of Confucius, and others that he lived later.

LORD MENGCHANG

Lord Mengchang's name was Tien Wen. His father Tien Ying, Lord Ching-kuo, was the youngest son of King Wei of Chi and a half brother of King Hsuan.

Tien Ying served in the government under King Wei and led troops with Tsou Chi the marquis of Cheng and Tien Chi in the campaign against Wei to rescue Hann. Then Tsou Chi and Tien Chi contended for power, the former slandered the latter, and Tien Chi in alarm tried to storm a border town of Chi but fled after defeat. Upon King Wei's death King Hsuan ascended the throne and, knowing that Tien Chi had been the victim of slander, he recalled him and made him a general.

In the second year of King Hsuan,* Tien Chi, Sun Pin and Tien Ying led troops against Wei and won the battle of Maling, capturing the crown prince Shen and killing General Pang Chuan.

In the seventh year of King Hsuan, Tien Ying went as an envoy to Hann and Wei to win them as allies for Chi. He escorted Marquis Chao of Hann and King Hui of Wei to a conference with King Hsuan south of Tungngo, where an agreement was reached.

The following year, the king of Chi conferred again with King Hui of Wei at Chien. Later that year King Hui died.

In the ninth year of King Hsuan, Tien Ying became prime minister of Chi. King Hsuan conferred with King Hsiang of Wei at Hsuchow, where both took the title of king. The news of this made King Wei of Chu angry with Tien Ying.

The following year Chu defeated Chi at Hsuchow and

_____
* 341 B.C.

dispatched men to drive away Tien Ying; but he sent Chang Chou to intercede with the king of Chu, who relented. Tien Ying remained prime minister of Chi for eleven years. Then King Hsuan died, King Min came to the throne, and three years later Tien Ying received Hsueh as his fief.

Tien Ying had more than forty sons. On the fifth day of the fifth month one of his low-born concubines gave birth to a son named Wen, and Tien Ying ordered her to abandon the child. She secretly kept him, however, and when he grew up induced his brothers to introduce him to his father.

Tien Ying was angry with the mother and said, "I told you to get rid of this child. How dare you bring him up?"

Wen bowed and asked, "What was your reason, sir, for abandoning a son born on that day?"

"When a child born on the fifth day of the fifth month grows as high as the door he will do his parents harm."

"Is man's fate controlled by Heaven or by the height of a door?" When his father could not answer, Wen continued, "If man's fate is controlled by Heaven, what's the good of worrying? If it is controlled by a door, why not make the door higher so that no one can equal its height?"

At that Tien Ying said, "Very well, you may go."

Some time later Wen asked his father, "What is the son of a son?"

"A grandson," was the reply.

"What is the grandson of a grandson?"

"A great-great-grandson."

"What is the grandson of a great-great-grandson?"

"I don't know."

"You have served as prime minister of Chi during three reigns," said Wen, "yet the territory of Chi has not increased. Your private estate is worth ten thousand pieces of gold, yet not one man of talent can be found among your followers. I have heard that a general's family should produce generals, a minister's family should produce ministers. Now your concubines are clothed in fine silk, while the gentlemen serving you wear ragged jackets; your slaves and concubines have grain and meat to spare, while your guests go hungry on husks. And you are amassing yet more wealth to leave to some unknown descendants, paying less and less attention to public affairs. To my mind, this is rather strange."

Tien Ying then treated him with more respect, putting him in charge of family affairs and of guests. Gradually more and more guests flocked to him so that his fame spread far and wide through the states. And when envoys from various states asked Tien Ying to make Wen his heir, he agreed to do so.

Tien Ying was given the posthumous title of Lord Ching-kuo. Tien Wen succeeded to his fief as Lord Mengchang of Hsueh.

Lord Mengchang invited gentlemen to Hsueh from various states as well as refugees and felons flying from justice, using his fortune to entertain them handsomely. So gentlemen came to him from all over the land. He entertained several thousand protégés, treating all like himself with no distinction of rank. When he sat talking with the guests he had invited, there was always a scribe behind the screen to record their conversations and ascertain their relatives' whereabouts; and after the visitors' departure he sent messengers with gifts for their families.

One night when he gave a banquet, one of his guests who was sitting in the shadow lost his temper, fancying that he was receiving inferior fare. He stopped eating and begged to take his leave. At once Lord Mengchang rose and took his own meal over to compare with this fellow's. Then the man killed himself for shame. For reasons like these many gentlemen flocked to Lord Mengchang, who treated all well without discrimination so that each felt he was the lord's special friend.

When news of this admirable behaviour reached King Chao of Chin, he sent Lord Chinyang as a hostage to Chi in order to invite Lord Mengchang to pay him a visit. The lord was eager to go, but all his protégés were against it. He turned a deaf ear, however, to their warnings.

Then Su Tai said, "This morning on my way here, I heard a wooden figure talking to one of clay. 'It is raining,' said the wooden figure. 'You will crumble and collapse.' The clay figure retorted, 'I am made of earth and if I crumble I shall simply return to the earth. But the rain will carry you off and there is no knowing where you will end.' Now Chin is like a tiger or wolf, yet you are eager to go there. If you fail to return, the clay figure will laugh at you." Then Lord Mengchang relinquished his plan.

In the twenty-fifth year of King Min of Chi, Lord Mengchang was none the less sent to Chin, and King Chao of Chin made him his prime minister.

Someone warned King Chao, "Lord Mengchang is an able man and related to the royal house of Chi. He is bound to put Chi's interests first, to the detriment of our state." Thereupon King Chao removed Lord Mengchang from office and put him under house arrest, meaning to kill him later. Lord Mengchang sent an appeal for help to the king's favourite concubine.

Her answer was, "I would like the lord's white fox fur."

Now Lord Mengchang, upon his arrival in Chin, had presented King Chao with a fox fur worth a thousand pieces of gold, which was without its equal in the world, and of course he had no other. In dismay, he consulted his protégés, but none of them could think of any solution. Among his humblest followers, however, was a thief who could pretend to be a dog, and this fellow said, "I can get that white fox fur for you." That night, passing himself off as a dog, he slipped into the palace storeroom and brought out the fur. When this was presented to the concubine, she interceded on Lord Mengchang's behalf and King Chao released him.

As soon as he was free he galloped off with forged documents in another name and reached the Hanku Pass by midnight. By then the king had regretted releasing him and summoned him, only to find that he had already left. Men were sent in hot pursuit.

Now the pass was closed and there was a rule that no one might go through before cock-crow. Lord Mengchang feared that he would be overtaken, but another of his humblest followers was able to imitate the crow of a cock, and because this set all the other cocks crowing too the fugitives were able to go through. In the time it takes to eat a meal the pursuers reached the pass, but finding Lord Mengchang gone went back again.

When Lord Mengchang first accepted these two men as protégés, the others had despised them, yet it was these two who saved him from danger in Chin. And after this no more was said against them.

When Lord Mengchang was passing through Chao, Lord Pingyuan entertained him. The people of Chao, who had heard of his fame, came out to see him but only jeered at him. "We expected the lord of Hsueh to be a powerful man," they said. "But now we see he is a puny fellow." When the lord heard this he was angry. His followers drew their swords and laid about them until they had killed several hundred men, nor did they stop till they had wiped out an entire county.

King Min of Chi regretted having sent Lord Mengchang away, and on his return made him prime minister in charge of the government.

Because he bore a grudge against the king of Chin, Lord Mengchang wanted to attack Chin instead of joining forces with Hann and Wei against Chu and he asked Western Chou for a loan of grain for the army.

Su Tai, on behalf of Western Chou, said to him, "For nine years you have attacked Chu to help Hann and Wei and strengthened them by taking land north of Wan and Sheh. Now if you attack Chin that will make Hann and Wei even stronger, and if they feel no threat from Chin in the west or Chu in the south, they will be a serious threat to you. They will fear Chin but despise Chi, and I think this is dangerous for you. It would be much better to let our state ally closely with Chin while you neither attack Chin nor borrow grain for the army. You can halt at the Hanku Pass while we convey your wishes to King Chao of Chin, saying, 'The lord of Hsueh will not defeat Chin to make Hann and Wei strong.

He has advanced in the hope that you will ask the king of Chu to give his eastern territory to Chi, while you send back King Huai of Chu to make peace.' If you let us do this favour to Chin, they will certainly consent, for they can avoid defeat by giving you Chu's eastern territory. And the king of Chou will also be grateful to Chi for his release. Chi will be strengthened by the acquisition of the eastern territory, and your fief of Hsueh will be secure for ever. Since Chin will thus still be powerful on the western frontiers of Hann and Wei, those states will have to treat Chi with respect."

The lord approved of this plan. He made Hann and Wei send gifts to Chin, called a halt to the joint expedition and refrained from borrowing grain from Western Chou.

At this time King Huai of Chu was detained in Chin and his state was anxious for his return, but in the event Chin did not let him go.

While Lord Mengchang was prime minister of Chi, his steward Wei Tzu, who collected revenue for him from his fief, went three times without once handing it over. When questioned, he replied that he had given the grain to a worthy man, and the lord angrily dismissed him.

A few years later, slanderers told King Min that Lord Mengchang was about to revolt. And subsequently the king suspected that Lord Mengchang was behind Tien Chia's attack upon him. So the lord ran away. When this news came to the ears of the worthy man to whom Wei Tzu had given grain, he wrote to the king declaring that Lord Mengchang would never rebel — he would stake his life on this. And he killed himself at the palace gate to prove the lord's innocence. The king was shocked into investigating the matter, found Lord Mengchang innocent, and recalled him. Lord Mengchang, on the pretext of illness, asked permission to go to his own fief and this was granted.

Later Lu Li, a general who had deserted from Chin, became prime minister of Chi. He wanted to injure Su Tai, who told Lord Mengchang:

"Chou Tsui has rendered great services to Chi, yet the

king dismissed him and on Chin Fu's advice has made Lu Li prime minister. This is because he wants to win over Chin. If Chi and Chin become allies, Chin Fu and Lu Li will hold power while you will count for nothing with Chi or Chin. Lose no time, then, in leading an army north towards Chao, making peace with Chin and Wei, and inviting Chou Tsui back to show your appreciation; for in this way you will regain the king's confidence and put a stop to all possible changes. Once Chi is independent of Chin, the other states will flock to us and Chin Fu will be forced to leave. Then the king will have to find someone else to manage affairs of state."

Lord Mengchang took his advice, but was hated by Lu Li for this. Fearing reprisals, the lord wrote to Wei Jan, the marquis of Jang and prime minister of Chin, "I hear that your king wants with Lu Li's help to win over Chi. But since Chi is a powerful state, you are bound to become less influential. Moreover when Chi and Chin combine against Hann and Wei, Lu Li will be prime minister in both our states. This is what will come of allying with Chi and exalting Lu Li. So long as Chi is not threatened by other states, it is bound to regard you as its worst enemy; so you had better persuade your king to attack it. If Chi is defeated, I can propose that the territory won from it should be given to you, and fear of the might of Hann, Wei and Chao will make the king of Chin rely on you to win them over. At the same time, since these states were threatened by Chi and fear Chin, they will rely on you to win Chin over. In this way you will gain credit by defeating Chi and gain power, thanks to Hann, Wei and Chao. Your fief will be enlarged and Chin and Hann, Wei and Chao will respect you more. On the other hand, if Chi is not defeated and Lu Li remains prime minister, you will find yourself in serious trouble."

Then the marquis of Jang advised King Chao of Chin to attack Chi, and Lu Li sought safety in flight.

The conquest of Sung later made King Min of Chi arrogant and he wanted to rid himself of Lord Mengchang, who took fright and went to Wei, where King Chao appointed him prime minister. Having allied with Chin and Chao in the west, Wei joined forces with Yen to attack Chi and King Min fled to Chü, where he died. When King Hsiang ascended the throne of Chi, Lord Mengchang became the ruler of an independent state. Since King Hsiang was newly come to the throne he feared the lord's power and made a pact with him, whereby they became reconciled.

At the lord's death he received the posthumous title of Lord Mengchang. His sons contended for the succession, but Chi and Wei together attacked and destroyed the state of Hsueh, so that no one succeeded to the title.

Before this, when Feng Huan heard that Lord Mengchang was good to his guests, he came to see him wearing straw sandals.

"You have come from far away, sir," said Lord Mengchang. "What instruction have you for me?"

"I hear that you are good to gentlemen," said Feng Huan, "and being poor I have come to seek your protection."

Lord Mengchang installed him in a hostel and ten days later asked the steward in charge, "What is our guest doing?"

The answer was, "Master Feng is very poor. He owns nothing but a sword with a plaited reed round its hilt. He beats his sword and sings, 'Let's go back, long sword! Here I have no fish to eat.'"

Then Lord Mengchang moved Feng Huan to a better hostel where he could have fish for his meals. Five days later he questioned the steward again and was told, "That guest is still beating his sword and singing, 'Let's go back, my long sword. Here I have no carriage to go out in.'" Then Lord Mengchang moved Feng Huan to a still better hostel, where he had the use of a carriage. Five days later he questioned the steward again and was told, "The gentleman is still beating his sword and singing, 'Let's go back, my long sword. Here I have no house of my own.'"

Lord Mengchang was annoyed. And Feng Huan stayed there for over a year without saying anything to him.

83

At that time Lord Mengchang was prime minister of Chi with a fief of ten thousand households at Hsueh, but since he was supporting three thousand protégés his income was not enough to meet his expenditure, so he used to lend money in Hsueh. Then there came a famine and he could not get his money back, for most of his debtors were unable to pay the interest. Worried because he could not meet his expenses, Lord Mengchang asked his men to recommend someone to go to Hsueh to collect debts for him.

His steward said, "Master Feng who stays in the best hostel seems a man of great eloquence and a fine-looking gentleman, but he has no other gifts. You might send him."

Lord Mengchang invited Feng Huan over and told him, "More than three thousand gentlemen, overestimating my talents, have honoured me with their presence. Since my income is insufficient to meet this outlay, I have put out money at interest in Hsueh. But the crops there have failed and the people have not paid the interest, so that I may be unable to defray my expenses. I would like to trouble you for your help."

Feng Huan accepted this mission and left. Upon his arrival in Hsueh, he summoned all Lord Mengchang's debtors who owed interest amounting to a hundred thousand coins. He prepared wine in abundance and fat oxen and invited them all to come whether they could discharge their debts or not, bringing with them records of their loans. On the appointed day, he had the oxen slaughtered and brought out the wine, and while they drank he checked their documents. He agreed to a date with those who were able to pay and burned the receipts of others who were too poor.

"Lord Mengchang lent you money to supply you with capital to make a start," he told them. "He asked for interest because he needs money to entertain his protégés. So now we are setting a time limit for those who are well off and burning the receipts of those too poor to discharge their debt. Eat and drink your fill, gentlemen, and do your best for a lord who treats you so well."

Then all the men rose from their seats and bowed their thanks.

When Lord Mengchang heard that Feng Huan had burned the receipts, he angrily recalled him.

"Because I have three thousand guests living on me, I lent money in Hsueh," he said. "Since my fief is small and my people do not always pay the interest, I was afraid I might not have enough for my guests and asked you to collect the money. But I hear that you used the funds to buy oxen and wine in abundance, after which you burned the documents. Why was this?"

"That is right," said Feng Huan. "If I hadn't prepared plenty of oxen and wine, not all of them would have come and I shouldn't have known which had money and which had not. I set a time limit for those in a position to pay. As for those who have no money, even if I were to wait around for ten years the interest would simply accumulate until in desperation they ran away. In that event, apart from receiving no payment, you would win the reputation of a miser with no regard for the people, while they would be guilty of absconding. This is no way to improve the people's morale and increase your reputation. Burning those useless deeds and not attempting to dun the destitute will endear you to the people of Hsueh and spread your fame. Why do you doubt this, sir?"

Then Lord Mengchang clapped his hands and apologized.

When slanderers from Chin and Chu convinced the king of Chi that Lord Mengchang's fame outdid his own and that he had usurped state power, the king dismissed him from office. And as soon as he ceased to be prime minister most of his protégés left.

"Lend me a chariot to go to Chin," said Feng Huan, "and I shall make the king of Chi think so highly of you that he will increase your fief. How would you like that?"

Lord Mengchang prepared a chariot and gifts and saw him off. Feng Huan travelled west to Chin and told the king, "All those travelling politicians who ride west in their chariots to Chin are eager to strengthen Chin and weaken Chi, while those who go east to Chi are eager to strengthen Chi and weaken Chin. These two states are rivals, they cannot both reign supreme. The one which proves superior will conquer the world."

The king of Chin sat up and asked, "How can I make Chin more powerful?"

"Have you heard, sir, that the king of Chi has dismissed Lord Mengchang?"

"Yes, I heard that."

"It was Lord Mengchang who gave Chi status in the eyes of the world. Now that the king has dismissed him because of slander, he must bear a grudge against Chi. If he comes here, he can give you a full and true account of that state and its people, enabling you to conquer Chi. Will that not make you more powerful? Make haste, sir; send a messenger with gifts and invite him over secretly. Don't let this opportunity slip! If the king of Chi awakes to his mistake and makes Lord Mengchang prime minister again, it is hard to say which state will prove supreme."

The king of Chin, well pleased with this advice, sent ten chariots bearing a hundred *yi* of gold with an invitation to Lord Mengchang. Feng Huan asked leave to go first and when he reached Chi he advised the king of Chi, saying:

"All those travelling politicians who ride east to Chi in their chariots are eager to strengthen Chi and weaken Chin, while those who go west to Chin are eager to strengthen Chin and weaken Chi. Since these two states are rivals, if Chin is strengthened Chi must be weakened. They cannot both reign supreme. Now I hear that the king of Chin has sent ten chariots bearing a hundred *yi* of gold to Lord Mengchang with an invitation. If the lord remains here, well and good; if he travels west to serve as prime minister of Chin, the world will follow Chin. It will be the superior state and yours the inferior, and your chief cities Lintzu and Chimo will be endangered. Why not restore the lord to his position and increase his fief to show your gratitude before the arrival of the envoy of Chin? He is bound to be pleased and accept, and however powerful Chin may be it can hardly invite another state's prime minister. In this way you can upset Chin's designs and thwart its scheme of conquest."

The king of Chi approved and sent a messenger to the frontier to look out for the envoy from Chin. As soon as the envoy's chariots had crossed the frontier the messenger galloped back to report to the king, who forthwith summoned Lord Mengchang and reinstated him as prime minister, restoring to him his former fief with an additional thousand households. When word of this reached the envoy from Chin, he turned his chariots round and drove home again.

When the king of Chi dismissed Lord Mengchang on account of slander, all the lord's protégés left him. Now that he was summoned to be reinstated, Feng Huan alone went to meet him.

While they were on the road Lord Mengchang sighed and said, "I used to enjoy collecting protégés and always treated them as well as I could. More than three thousand gentlemen lived upon me, as you know. But the day that they saw I was dismissed, they left without any regard for me at all. Thanks to your help I have been reinstated, but how can those men meet my eyes again? If they come to see me, I shall have to spit in their faces and insult them."

Feng Huan tied up his reins, got down from the chariot and bowed.

Lord Mengchang alighted to raise him up and asked, "Are you apologizing for those guests?"

"No, indeed," replied Feng Huan. "I disagree with you. Don't you know that all things must take their natural course and follow their own law?"

"I am too foolish to understand what you mean."

"All that lives must die: that is the nature of things. The rich and noble have many friends while the poor have few: that is the general law. Have you never noticed people going to the market? In the morning they crowd and shoulder their way through the gate, whereas after dusk they turn away without a look behind. This is not because they like the market in the morning and dislike it in the evening, but because the things they want are no longer there. The fact that all your guests left when you lost your position is no reason for you to complain. If you do, you will simply stop them from returning. I hope you will treat them exactly as before."

Lord Mengchang bowed and said, "With all respect I shall act upon your advice, sir."

The Grand Historian comments: I once visited the district of Hsueh and found many of the local people there were hot-tempered young men very different from those of Tsou and Lu. Upon asking the reason, I was told that Lord Mengchang had invited over sixty thousand families of gallant men and outlaws from far and wide to settle in Hsueh. Evidently there is truth in the report that Lord Mengchang loved entertaining protégés.

TIEN TAN

Tien Tan belonged to a distant branch of the royal house of Tien in the state of Chi. During the reign of King Min,* he was a minor official in Lintzu.

When Yueh Yi, a general of the state of Yen, defeated the army of Chi, King Min fled from his capital to the city of Chü, while the soldiers of Yen advanced unopposed to conquer Chi. Then Tien Tan fled to Anping and ordered his clansmen to saw off the projecting ends of their chariot-axles and fit iron guards round the stumps. When the troops of Yen took Anping by storm, the men of Chi fled and, in the mêlée on the road, the other chariots' axle ends broke and their occupants were captured. Tien Tan and his kinsmen were the only ones to escape, thanks to their reinforced axles, and they went east to defend Chimo. Alone of all the cities of Chi, Chü and Chimo were holding out against Yen.

As the men of Yen knew that King Min was in Chu, they attacked the city in strength. Nao Chih assassinated the king and defended Chu stubbornly, holding out against the besiegers for several years. Yen's troops then marched east to lay siege to Chimo. Its governor going out to give battle was defeated and killed.

The defenders at once chose Tien Tan to lead them, saying, "In the battle of Anping, Tien Tan's kinsmen escaped because of the iron guards fitted to their axles. He understands warfare." They made him their commander to defend Chimo.

Soon after this, King Chin of Yen died. His successor King Hui had an aversion to Yueh Yi, and when Tien Tan knew this he sowed further dissension between them by declaring,

---

* 323-284 B.C.

"Chi's king is dead and only two of its cities remain to be taken. But Yueh Yi dares not return for fear of punishment. Under the pretext of subjugating Chi, he is hoping to combine his forces with those of Chi and make himself king here. He is delaying his attack so that the men of Chi may come over to his side. The one thing we fear is that another general might be appointed, for then Chimo must be destroyed."

The king of Yen believed this and made Chi Chieh take over Yueh Yi's command, and Yueh Yi went back to Chao,* to the great indignation of the soldiers of Yen.

Then Tien Tan ordered the citizens of Chimo to sacrifice to their ancestors in the courtyard before each meal, so that birds flocked down to the city to find food, to the astonishment of the besiegers.

"I have been granted a divine revelation," announced Tien Tan. Then he told the citizens, "A man with supernatural powers will be our teacher."

"Can I be that teacher?" cried a soldier, and was running off when Tien Tan stood up and led him to a seat facing east, treating him as a teacher.

"I was fooling, sir," said the soldier. "I have no special powers."

"Hush!" whispered Tien Tan. He treated the man as a teacher with divine powers, and attributed all the orders he gave to his divine teacher. He also declared, "My one fear is lest the soldiers of Yen cut off their captives' noses and place these men in the front ranks against us. For then Chimo is doomed."

The men of Yen, hearing this, acted upon it. And when the defenders saw this mutilation of all who had surrendered, they were so angry that they resisted manfully, determined not to be captured.

To add fuel to the fire Tien Tan also said, "Heaven help us if the invaders dig up the graves outside the city and defile our ancestors!"

---

* His native state.

90

When the men of Yen dug up the graves and burned all the corpses, the defenders watching from the city wall wept with redoubled rage, longing to go out and fight.

Now that he knew that his men were ready for battle, Tien Tan himself set to work with them to repair the defences, enrolling his wife and concubine in the ranks and sharing all his food and wine with the soldiers. He ordered the men in armour to keep out of sight while the old, the weak and the women mounted the city walls and an envoy was sent out to treat for surrender. At this a great cheer went up in the enemy ranks.

Tien Tan collected a thousand *yi* of gold from the people and made some wealthy citizens present this sum to the enemy general, saying, "The city is about to surrender. We entreat you to spare our wives, concubines and kinsmen, and let us live in peace!" The Yen general very gladly agreed to this. And the invaders further relaxed their vigilance.

Then Tien Tan assembled more than one thousand bulls, swathed them in red silk, painted them different colours so that they looked like dragons, tied daggers to their horns and tied straw soaked in oil to their tails. At night the straw was set alight and the bulls were let out through dozens of breaches in the city wall. They were followed by five thousand stout fellows. Goaded into fury by their burning tails, the bulls charged the army of Yen, taking the invaders completely by surprise. The flaming torches on their tails cast a lurid light, and to the men of Yen the bulls seemed like so many dragons sowing death and destruction. After them rushed the five thousand, their mouths gagged, followed by the inhabitants, shouting and drumming. The old and infirm beat so loudly on copper vessels that the tumult shook heaven and earth. Yen's forces fell back in terror. And when their general Chi Chieh was killed, the enemy fled in confusion, pursued by the host of Chi. Every town and city they passed threw off Yen's yoke and flocked to Tien Tan's support.

Tien Tan's ranks swelled after each fresh victory, as Yen's grew daily weaker. When at last the enemy was thrown back to the river,* all Chi's cities — seventy and more — had been recovered. Then Tien Tan invited King Hsiang back from the city of Chü to govern in Lintzu, and the king enfeoffed him Lord of Anping.

The Grand Historian comments: In war, regular tactics are used to fight a battle and surprise tactics to win it. Skilled commanders show endless resourcefulness in devising an infinite variety of tactics, moving endlessly between regular and surprise ones. First passive as a young girl in face of the enemy, then swift as an escaped hare that cannot be overtaken — these were Tien Tan's surprise tactics.

Previously, when Nao Chih assassinated King Min, the citizens of Chü sought out the king's son Fa-chang, whom they found working as a gardener for Taishih Chiao. The daughter of the family had taken pity on him and treated him well. He told her who he was, and they became lovers. After the citizens made him king of Chi to hold Chu against Yen, the girl became his queen with the title of Chief Lady.

When the forces of Yen first entered Chi, they heard that Wang Chu of Houyi was a virtuous man. An order was issued forbidding troops to go within thirty *li* of where he lived, and messengers were sent to him, saying, "The men of Chi speak so highly of your virtue that we will make you a general with a fief of ten thousand households." When Wang Chu declined this offer, the envoys said, "If you do not agree, we shall bring troops to wipe out this district."

"A loyal subject cannot serve two masters, a chaste woman cannot change her husband," replied Wang Chu. "Since the king of Chi ignored my advice I retired to till the fields. Now that our land is conquered I have nothing to live for, and today you are trying to force me to be your general. If I consented, I should be aiding a tyrant. I would rather die in the cauldron than live without virtue."

---

* The north boundary of Chi.

He tied a halter to a tree and with one leap hanged himself.

When the ministers of Chi heard this they said, "Wang Chu was an ordinary citizen, yet he would not submit to Yen. What an example for those of us who have official positions and government emoluments!" So they went to Chü to find the prince and set him up as King Hsiang.

FAN SUI AND TSAI TSE

Fan Sui was a native of Wei whose courtesy name was Shu. After roaming through different states as an orator he wanted to serve King Chao of Wei, but being too poor to buy himself a post he first worked for the palace adviser Hsu Chia and accompanied him when he went as Wei's envoy to Chi. They remained there for several months without concluding any agreement.

Then King Hsiang of Chi, having heard that Fan Sui was an orator, sent him ten catties of gold, some beef and some wine, which Fan Sui dared not accept. When Hsu Chia learned this he was very angry, imagining that Fan Sui had divulged state secrets. He told him to accept the beef and wine but refuse the gold.

On their return to Wei, Hsu Chia, still highly incensed, reported the matter to Wei Chi, the prime minister and a member of the royal house, who in his rage made his stewards beat Fan Sui till his ribs were broken and his teeth knocked out. Then Fan Sui, pretending to be dead, was wrapped in a mat and thrown into the privy. And the guests who were tipsy took turns to urinate on him, meaning by this shameful treatment to make him a warning to others to avoid careless talk.

From inside the mat Fan Sui begged the guard, "Get me out and I will repay you handsomely!" The guard asked permission to throw out the corpse in the mat, and Wei Chi who was drunk consented. So Fan Sui escaped. On second thoughts, Wei Chi sent to arrest him again. Cheng An-ping of Wei, hearing this, carried the fugitive off and Fan Sui went into hiding, changing his name to Chang Lu.

Just at this time King Chao of Chin sent Wang Chi, his

master of ceremony, to Wei. Cheng An-ping, disguised as a soldier, waited on him.

"Are there any men of talent in Wei who would come west with me?" inquired Wang Chi.

"In my lane lives a Master Chang Lu who would like to meet you to discuss world affairs," replied Cheng. "Because he has an enemy, he dare not call on you by day."

"Bring him tonight," said Wang Chi.

So that night Cheng An-ping took Fan Sui to see Wang Chi. They did not converse at great length, but Wang Chi gauging Fan Sui's worth arranged to meet him south of Santing, and on this understanding they parted. When Wang Chi left Wei, he took Fan Sui with him in his carriage to Chin. At Hukuan, they saw chariots and horsemen approaching from the west.

Fan Sui asked, "Who is that coming?"

"Marquis Jang, the prime minister of Chin," said Wang Chi. "He is travelling east on a tour of inspection."

"I have heard that Marquis Jang has absolute power in Chin and dislikes all visitors from outside," said Fan Sui. "I do not want to be insulted, so I had better hide in the carriage."

A little later the marquis did in fact come up and stop to greet Wang Chi.

"What news is there from east of the Passes?" he asked.

"No news," said Wang Chi.

"Have you brought anyone back from the eastern states? Those men are no good: they only stir up trouble."

"I wouldn't even think of it," replied Wang Chi.

Then the marquis went on his way.

Fan Sui said, "I have heard that the marquis is shrewd but slow in the uptake. He suspected that there was someone in your carriage, but it didn't occur to him to make a search." With that he alighted, explaining, "He is bound to think better of it."

And sure enough, after driving ten *li* or more, the marquis sent horsemen back to search the carriage. When they could not find anyone that was the end of the matter. Wang Chi and Fan Sui proceeded to Hsienyang.

The report on his mission made, Wang Chi told the king, "Master Chang Lu of Wei is a great orator. He says that your kingdom is in greater peril than eggs placed one on top of the other. He has a plan to make it safe, but since he would not put this down in writing I have brought him back with me."

The king did not believe this, however. He had Fan Sui fed a very poor diet and lodged in one of the humblest hostels, where he stayed for a year and more.

By now,* King Chao of Chin had reigned for thirty-six years. He had won Yen and Ying from Chu in the south, holding King Huai of Chu prisoner in Chin till he died. He had moreover defeated Chi in the east, so that King Min of Chi renounced the title of emperor which he had taken. Chin had also repeatedly worsted Hann, Chao and Wei. But the king disliked orators and had no faith in them.

Marquis Jang and Lord Huayang were younger brothers of King Chao's mother, Queen Dowager Hsuan. Lord Chingyang and Lord Kaoling were his own younger brothers. While the marquis was prime minister, the three lords served in turn as commander and received fiefs. Thanks to the favour of the queen dowager, they had larger fortunes than the king himself. And Marquis Jang, now commander-in-chief, was planning to cross Hann and Wei to attack Kangshou in Chi, in order to enlarge his fief at Tao.

Then Fan Sui wrote this memorial to the king: "I have heard that under an enlightened ruler men of merit must be rewarded and men of ability appointed to office; the heavier the responsibility the larger the emolument, and the greater the merit the nobler the rank; thus one capable of governing the masses should hold the highest office. For then those of no ability will not dare to aspire to position, while the able will not go unnoticed. If you approve my words, sir, I hope you will put them into practice to the greatest possible ad-

---

* 271 B.C.

vantage. If you disagree with them, then no purpose is served by keeping me here.

"There is a saying, 'A foolish monarch rewards those he loves and punishes those he hates; but a wise monarch rewards only the deserving and punishes only those who do wrong.' Since I have no wish to lay myself on the chopping-block or to be cut in two, how dare I court punishment by questionable statements? You may despise my humble condition, but you should respect the man who recommended me and trust his loyalty. I have heard that Chou, Sung, Wei and Chu have four famous pieces of jade: the *ti-yi, chieh-lu, hsuan-li* and *ho-pu*. These, when quarried, were ignored by skilled jade-carvers, but now these treasures are known far and wide. In the same way, a man rejected by a wise sovereign may still be able to render great service to the state.

"I have heard that those skilled in enriching their families do so at the expense of the state, whereas those skilled in enriching the state do so at the expense of other states. When there is a wise sovereign the feudal lords will not arrogate power to themselves, for that would be encroaching on his sovereignty. A good physician can tell whether a patient will live or die; a sagacious sovereign knows whether enterprises will succeed or fail. He undertakes those that are advantageous, abandons those that are harmful, and tries out on a small scale those whose outcomes are doubtful. Even the great Yu and Shun, were they alive today, could do no more. I dare not commit my inmost thoughts to writing and my more trivial proposals are hardly worth your hearing. Perhaps your idea is that one as stupid as myself can have nothing to interest you. It cannot be that the man who recommended me is too low to deserve your trust. If he is not too low, I crave the favour of an audience when you are at leisure. If my words prove worthless, I beg to be cut in two!"

King Chao was very pleased with this letter. He expressed his approval to Wang Chi and sent a carriage to summon Fan Sui to his presence.

Fan Sui, granted an audience in the country palace, pretended to have lost his way and blundered in as if by mistake. At the king's approach, the angry eunuchs tried to drive Fan Sui away, crying, "Here comes the king!"

"King? What king has Chin?" retorted Fan Sui hotly, deliberately trying to provoke the king. "Chin has only the queen dowager and Marquis Jang."

King Chao heard this altercation with the eunuchs as he was close by and invited Fan Sui over to apologize to him. "I ought to have received your instructions long ago," he said. "But the situation in Yichu was so grave that I was consulting the queen dowager day and night. Now that this trouble is settled I would like to entertain you as my guest, although I am conscious of my lack of wisdom."

Fan Sui made a courteous reply, while the ministers looked on with expressions of awe.

The king dismissed his attendants and, when they were alone, straightened up* to ask, "What instructions have you for me?"

"I am at your service, sir," Fan Sui replied.

Presently the king straightened up to ask again, "What instructions have you for me?"

Once more Fan Sui replied, "I am at your service."

When this had happened three times, the king straightened up to inquire, "Are you unwilling to instruct me, then?"

"How dare I refuse?" replied Fan Sui. "But I have heard that Lu Shang, when he first met King Wen, was a fisherman by the River Wei. Despite the great difference in standing between them, Lu's conversation so pleased the king that he made him the grand preceptor and took him back in the royal carriage. This was because he spoke out frankly. Thanks to Lu Shang, King Wen succeeded in ruling the world. If the king had made Lu Shang keep his distance and not spoken frankly with him, the House of Chou would never have conquered the world, nor would Wen and Wu have succeeded in their kingly task.

_____

* There were no chairs in ancient China. People knelt down and sat on their heels, straightening up whenever there was need for ceremony.

"I am a native of another state and far below Your Majesty; moreover, what I have to say concerns your government and your own flesh and blood. I wish to show my humble loyalty but do not know your will, sir. That is why I dared not reply to your three questions. It is not fear of any man that keeps me silent. I know that for what I say today I may lose my head tomorrow, but this does not deter me. If you, great king, listen to my advice and adopt it, neither death nor banishment can dismay me, nor should I count it a disgrace to lacquer my body and bring it out in sores or go about with dishevelled hair like a madman.

"All men must die, even sages like the Five Sovereigns, paragons of virtue like the Three Kings, able princes like the Five Conquerors, powerful men like Wu Huo and Jen Pi, and brave fellows like Cheng Ching, Meng Pen, Prince Ching-chi and Hsia Yu. No man, then, can escape death. I ask nothing more than to submit to my fate, if by so doing I can be of some slight service to Chin. So I have no qualms.

"Wu Tzu-hsu escaped in a sack through the Chao Pass and travelled by night, hiding himself by day, till he reached the River Ling. Having nothing to eat, he crawled along with bare shoulders, kowtowing and drumming on his belly or playing on a flute to beg for food in the market. Yet finally he made Wu a great power and King Ho-lu a great conqueror. If like Wu Tzu-hsu I could see my plans adopted, although I were imprisoned in a dark dungeon never to look upon your face again, I should have no regret. Chi Tzu and Chieh Yu lacquered their bodies to bring them out in sores and went about with tousled hair like madmen, yet they could not assist their sovereign. If by imitating Chi Tzu I could be of service to a worthy sovereign, I should count this no shame at all but a great honour. My one fear is that if I am killed for my loyalty, my death will make men keep their mouths shut, halt their steps and turn away from Chin.

"Above, you fear to offend the queen mother, below, you are influenced by evil ministers. Spending all your time in the palace surrounded by guards, you are kept in ignorance and cannot see what is wrong. If things go badly, your line will be ended; at the very least, your own life is in danger. This is what I fear, not poverty, disgrace, death or banishment. If my death profits Chin, I would rather die than live."

The king fell on his knees protesting, "How can you suggest such a thing, sir! Chin is an outlying state and I am a worthless fool, but the fact that you have honoured us with your presence means that Heaven has sent you to me, unworthy as I am, to save my line. I am privileged to hear your instructions because Heaven looks kindly on my ancestors and will not abandon their descendant. Why, then, speak as you did? I beg you to instruct me on all matters, great and small, whether concerning the queen dowager or my ministers. Have no scruples, I entreat you!"

Then Fan Sui bowed and the king returned his bow.

"Your country has strong barriers on all sides, great king," said Fan Sui. "In the north are the Kanchuan and Kukou Mountains, in the south the Ching and Wei Rivers, in the west the Lung and Shu Mountains, in the east the Hanku Pass and Mount Yao. You have a million fighting men, a thousand war chariots. You can go out to attack when you see your chance and fall back on these to defend yourself if defeated; this is the land for a conqueror. Since your people do not engage in personal feuds but fight bravely for the state, they are the people for a conqueror. So you have the right land and the right people. With your brave soldiers and your host of chariots and horses, you can deal with other states as easily as a swift hound catches a limping hare. It is within your power to become a conqueror; but your ministers are not good enough. You have remained within the Pass fifteen years without showing your strength east of the mountains; this is because Marquis Jang has not served Chin loyally and your plans miss the point."

The king, straightening up, said, "Please tell me what is wrong with them."

Since many of the king's followers were eavesdropping, Fan Sui was afraid to speak of home affairs and spoke first of foreign policy, to sound the king out. So he moved closer to the king and said:

"Marquis Jang's plan to cross Hann and Wei to attack Kangshou in Chi is not a good one. For a small force will be unable to inflict any damage on Chi, while sending out a large one would weaken Chin. I assume you plan to send a small force and make use of the armies of Hann and Wei, but this is not fair to them. Crossing their territory to launch an attack is no good way to treat your allies. This policy is not well considered.

"When King Min of Chi attacked Chu in the south, defeating Chu's army, killing its general and conquering a thousand *li* of land, he did not keep one foot of ground. This was not because he did not want the territory, but because the circumstances did not permit it; the other states, seeing Chi exhausted and its king and minister at loggerheads, raised armies and smashed it. In the humiliation of defeat, the men of Chi asked their king, 'Who is to blame?' and he replied, 'Tien Wen.' At that the ministers stirred up such trouble that Tien Wen had to flee. Chi suffered this great reverse because in attacking Chu it benefited Hann and Wei. This is what is known as 'supplying weapons and food to brigands.'

"You would be better advised to ally with distant states and attack your neighbours, for then you can keep every inch of land you win. It is certainly a mistake to attack distant states instead. Chungshan with five hundred *li* of territory was swallowed up by Chao alone, bringing Chao such fame and such advantages that no other states could harm it. Now Hann and Wei are central states holding a key position. If you want to become a conqueror, you should maintain close relations with these central states in order to impress Chu and Chao with your might. Then if Chu is strong you can ally with Chao, if Chao is strong you can ally with Chu. When both these states are your allies, Chi will take fright and cultivate your friendship with humble words and rich gifts. And once Chi is on your side, you can seize Hann and Wei."

"I have long wanted close relations with Wei," said the

king. "But it has been impossible because they keep changing their policy. Please tell me how to set about it."

"First woo them with humble words and rich gifts," said Fan Sui. "If that fails, offer territory. If that too fails, attack with your army."

"I shall carry out your instructions," said the king.

He made Fan Sui an honorary minister and consulted him on military affairs. On his advice he sent Wan, a noble of the fifth rank, to attack Wei and capture Huai. Two years later Hsingchiu was taken.

Once more Fan Sui advised the king, saying, "The boundaries of Chin and Hann interlace like threads in embroidery. To Chin, Hann is like dry rot in wood or a cancer in the heart. If the world is at peace, well and good. But if trouble starts, none can damage Chin more than Hann. You had better subdue Hann, sir."

"I am only too eager to do so," replied the king. "But Hann will not submit. What can I do?"

"Hann will have to submit! Send an army to attack Yingyang and block the roads to Kung and Chengkao. Then cut the road to Taihang in the north and bottle up their forces in Shangtang. In this way you will divide Hann into three and, when they see that they are doomed, they will submit. Once that happens, you can plan to conquer the world."

"Very good," said the king and sent an envoy to Hann.

Fan Sui daily rose in favour. After he had advised the king for several years, he took an opportunity to say, "When I lived back in the east, I heard of Tien Wen but never of the king of Chi. Similarly, I heard of the queen dowager, Marquis Jang, Lord Huayang, Lord Kaoling and Lord Chingyang, but never of the king of Chin. Now a king should rule the state, meting out rewards and punishments and holding the power of life and death; but the queen dowager does exactly as she pleases, Marquis Jang undertakes missions without reporting on them to you, Lord Huayang and Lord Chingyang pass arbitrary judgements, and Lord Kaoling comes and goes without asking permission. No country with four such nobles could escape disaster. With four such nobles in control, there might as well be no king! His sovereignty is inevitably undermined and the orders do not come from him.

"I have heard that a good ruler should strengthen his authority at home and increase his power abroad. Marquis Jang has usurped the royal prerogative: he acts as an arbitrator between other states; he sends his envoys throughout the world, and undertakes military expeditions against other states. When these campaigns are successful, his fief of Tao reaps the benefit and the other states suffer. When these campaigns are unsuccessful there is popular discontent and our state suffers the consequences. The old song runs:

> Boughs laden with fruit will break,
> Boughs broken damage the tree;
> Too great a capital weakens the state,
> Too high a subject brings his sovereign low.

"When Tsui Shu and Nao Chih were in control of Chi, they shot the king in the thigh with an arrow, slashed his tendons and hung him from a temple beam, so that he died the next day. When Li Tui had control of Chao, he imprisoned the king at Shachiu for a hundred days and finally starved him to death. Now I hear that the power in Chin is held by the queen dowager and Marquis Jang, assisted by Lord Kaoling, Lord Huayang and Lord Chingyang, while the king has no place. This is like the case of Nao Chih and Li Tui.

"The Three Dynasties perished because their last rulers delegated all authority to their ministers while they caroused and hunted, ignoring affairs of state. But those entrusted with power envied men of talent, lorded it over the people, acted in their own selfish interests and hid the truth from their king. They did not have their sovereigns' interests at heart, but because the kings did not know this they lost their realms. Now all officers from the lowest to the highest, as well as all court attendants, are followers of the prime minister. You are completely isolated at court, which makes me fear that after your passing some other than your descendant will reign over Chin."

King Chao in great dismay replied, "You are right."

He degraded the queen dowager and sent Marquis Jang, Lord Kaoling, Lord Huayang and Lord Chingyang beyond the Pass. Having made Fan Sui prime minister, he took back Marquis Jang's seal of office and ordered him to return to Tao. The government had to use more than a thousand carts to move his property. And his treasures, examined at the Pass, outnumbered those of the king. Fan Sui was given the district of Ying and enfeoffed as Marquis Ying. This was in the forty-first year of King Chao of Chin.*

Now Fan Sui had become Chin's prime minister under the name of Chang Lu, but the men of Wei did not know this, imagining that Fan Sui was long since dead. When word reached the king of Wei that Chin meant to strike east against Hann and his own state, he dispatched Hsu Chia as his envoy to Chin. Fan Sui, learning of this, went incognito in shabby clothes and on foot to Hsu Chia's hostel.

At sight of him, Hsu Chia exclaimed in surprise, "So you are all right, Fan Sui!"

"Yes, as you see."

Hsu Chia smiled, "Are you advising the king of Chin?"

"No, I came here as a fugitive after offending the prime minister of Wei. How could I offer advice to the king?"

"What are you doing, then?"

"Working as a hired hand."

Pitying the man, Hsu Chia asked him to a meal. "Imagine your coming to such a sorry pass!" he said, and gave Fan Sui one of his own silk gowns. "Do you know this Chang Lu, prime minister of Chin?" he asked. "I hear he stands well with the king and decides all affairs of state. Whether I can stay or not depends on him. Do you know anyone close to him, my boy?"

* 266 B.C.

"Yes, my master knows him well. I could arrange an interview for you with Master Chang."

"My horses are worn out and my carriage wheels are damaged. I must go there in a large carriage drawn by four horses."

"I will borrow my master's carriage and horses for you."

Fan Sui went back to fetch a carriage and horses and, acting as Hsu Chia's groom, drove up to the prime minister's residence. When the men there saw him, all who recognized him kept out of the way, to Hsu Chia's astonishment. When they reached the gate of the prime minister's living quarters, Fan Sui said to Hsu Chia, "Wait here while I announce you."

Hsu Chia waited at the gate in the carriage for some time, then asked the attendants, "Why hasn't Fan Sui come back?"

"There is no one here called Fan Sui," was the reply.

"I mean the man who brought me in this carriage."

"That was our prime minister, Chang Lu."

Hsu Chia, dumbfounded by the trick played on him, bared his shoulder and fell on his knees, begging the attendants to apologize to the prime minister for him. Fan Sui then received him among splendid hangings and troops of attendants. Hsu Chia kowtowed and pleaded for mercy.

"I little knew you would ascend to such heights, sir," he said. "From now on I shall not presume to read any more books or meddle with worldly affairs. I deserve to be thrown into a boiling cauldron. I beg to be exiled among the barbarians. My life is in your hands!"

"How many crimes are you guilty of?" asked Fan Sui.

"More crimes than the number of hairs on my head, were I to enumerate them one by one."

"Your crimes are three," retorted Fan Sui. "In the time of King Chao of Chu, Shen Pao-hsu repulsed the army of Wu for him, and the king offered him a fief of five thousand households in Ching; but Shen declined because his ancestral graves were in Ching. My ancestral graves are in Wei, yet you suspected me of working for Chi and accused me to Wei Chi. That was your first crime. When Wei Chi insulted me

105

by throwing me into the privy, you did not stop him. That was your second crime. You even sank low enough to urinate on me when you were drunk. That was your third crime. I shall spare your life, however, because your gift of a silk gown showed that you still had some feeling for an old friend." With that he dismissed him. And he advised King Chao to send him away.

When Hsu Chia came to take his leave, Fan Sui prepared a great banquet to which he invited envoys from all the states. As they sat feasting in the hall, Hsu Chia was placed below the steps and two tattooed criminals were ordered to seize him and force him to eat straw and beans like a horse.

"Tell the king of Wei to send Wei Chi's head here at once," ordered Fan Sui. "Otherwise all Taliang will be put to the sword."

When Hsu Chia went back and reported this, Wei Chi fled in terror to Chao to take refuge with Lord Pingyuan.

After Fan Sui became prime minister Wang Chi told him, "There are three contingencies about which we can do nothing. First, the king's death. Secondly, your sudden death. Thirdly, my own death. If the king dies, however much we regret it, we can do nothing about it. If you die, however much I regret it, I can do nothing. If I die, however much you regret it, you can do nothing."

Fan Sui was distressed and went in to the king to say, "If not for Wang Chi's friendship, I could never have entered the Hanku Pass. If not for Your Majesty's sagacity, I could never have become a noble. Now I am prime minister with the rank of a marquis, while Wang Chi is still a palace steward. He expected better things."

Then King Chao sent for Wang Chi and appointed him governor of Hotung, exempting his district from taxation for three years. He also enlisted Cheng An-ping's services and made him a general.

Fan Sui rewarded from his own pocket all who had helped him in distress. He would repay even the kindness of a single meal, take vengeance on even an unfriendly glance.

In the forty-second year of King Chao, the second year in which Fan Sui was prime minister, Chin's army attacked Hann and took Shaochu and Kaoping. King Chao knew that Wei Chi was staying with Lord Pingyuan and, because he wanted to avenge Fan Sui, he sent the lord this friendly invitation, "Having heard of your noble character, I would like to be on friendly terms with you, just like two ordinary citizens. Won't you come and drink with me for ten days?"

Lord Pingyuan, who stood in awe of Chin, accepted the invitation. When King Chao had drunk with him for a few days he said, "In ancient times King Wen of Chou had Lu Shang, whom he made the Patriarch. Duke Huan of Chi had Kuan Chung, whom he honoured with the title of uncle. Now I regard Fan Sui as my own uncle, and his enemy is in your house. I hope you will send a man back to fetch me his head. If not, I shall keep you here."

"Even the rich and noble cleave to old friends who are obscure and poor," retorted Lord Pingyuan. "Wei Chi is my friend. Even if he were in my house — which he is not — I could not surrender him."

Then King Chao of Chin sent this message to the king of Chao, "Your younger brother is here, and Fan Sui's enemy Wei Chi is in his house. Unless you promptly send me Wei Chi's head, I shall dispatch an army against your state and hold your brother prisoner."

King Hsiao-cheng of Chao sent troops to surround Lord Pingyuan's house. Wei Chi in desperation fled at night to Yu Ching the prime minister. And Yu Ching, fairly sure that the king would prove adamant, relinquished his seal of office and left with Wei Chi. Travelling in secret, they could not escape quickly to another state but went to Taliang, hoping that Lord Hsinling would help them to find refuge in Chu. But fear of reprisals from Chin made Lord Hsinling hesitate to admit them.

"What sort of man is this Yu Ching?" he asked.

Hou Ying who was beside him replied, "Men are not easy to understand, and to understand men is not easy. This Yu

Ching appeared before the king of Chao in straw sandals with an umbrella over his shoulder. After the first interview he was given two white jade discs and two thousand *yi* of gold; after the second he was made a high-ranking minister, after the third he received the prime minister's seal and was made a noble with a fief of ten thousand households, so that all the world courted his acquaintance. When Wei Chi turned to him in desperation, Yu Ching, without a thought for his high position, relinquished his seal of office and his fief to help a gentleman in trouble escape. But now that they come to you, you ask, 'What sort of man is he?' Truly, men are not easy to understand, and to understand men is not easy!"

Then Lord Hsinling, much ashamed, went by carriage to the country to welcome them. Wei Chi, however, had heard of his initial reluctance and in his anger killed himself with his own sword. When the king of Chao learned this he had the head sent to the king of Chin, who allowed his hostage Lord Pingyuan to return to Chao.

In the forty-third year of King Chao, Chin attacked the district of Fenhsing in Hann and took it, then built a stronghold at Kuangwu by the Yellow River. Five years later the king of Chin, on the advice of Fan Sui, tricked Chao by spreading a rumour which induced the king of Chao to appoint Chao Kuo, son of Chao Sheh entitled Lord of Mafu, in Lien Po's place as commander. Then Chin routed the army of Chao at Changping, and laid siege to their capital, Hantan.

Fan Sui, who disliked Pai Chi, Lord Wu-an, spoke against him and had him killed. Cheng An-ping was made commander of the forces attacking Chao, but he was surrounded by the enemy and forced to surrender with twenty thousand men. Then Fan Sui, sitting on a straw mat, asked for punishment. For according to the law of Chin, when an officer proved worthless the man who recommended him should receive the same punishment, and therefore the whole family of Fan Sui should have been arrested. But because King Chao did not want to harm Fan Sui, he forbade any mention of the Cheng An-ping affair throughout the country, on pain of receiving the same punishment. And to reassure Fan Sui, he increased his daily gifts of food to him. Two years later Wang Chi, then governor of Hotung, was executed for his illicit dealings with other states, and this made Fan Sui even more alarmed.

While holding court one day King Chao sighed. Fan Sui stepped forward to say, "It is said that when the ruler is anxious his minister should feel ashamed. When the ruler is disgraced his minister should die. Now you, great king, are showing anxiety at court, I beg to be penalized."

"I have heard that Chu's iron swords are sharp but its singers and jesters are clumsy," said King Chao. "This means that its soldiers are brave and that their ambitions are high. I fear that Chu, with its high ambition and brave men, may try to conquer us. When no preparations have been made there is no way of dealing with an emergency. I am anxious now because since Lord Wu-an's death and Cheng An-ping's revolt we have had no good commanders and are surrounded by enemies." The king's implied reprimand so alarmed Fan Sui that he did not know what to do. When word of this reached Tsai Tse, he went to Chin.

Tsai Tse was a native of Yen who as an itinerant scholar had tried his luck in many states without success. One day he consulted the physiognomist Tang Chu. "Is it true," he asked, "that you predicted to Li Tui that within a hundred days he would hold state power?"

"It is true," replied Tang Chu.

"Can you tell my future?"

After a careful look at him Tang Chu answered with a smile, "You have a snub, upturned nose, massive shoulders, a prominent forehead and bow legs. The saying 'A sage is ill-favoured' may apply to you."

Aware that Tang Chu was mocking him, Tsai Tse said, "Wealth and rank I can get for myself. What I want to ask you is how long I shall live?"

"Another forty-three years, sir," was the answer.

Tsai Tse thanked him with a smile and left. He told his

driver, "Forty-three years is long enough to enjoy good food, ride swift horses and, with a golden seal in my hands and a purple tassel round my waist, bow before my sovereign and savour the joys of rank and riches."

He went to Chao but was driven away, and was robbed of his cooking vessels while travelling on the road to Hann and Wei. When he heard that both Cheng An-ping and Wang Chi were in trouble and that Fan Sui, who had recommended them, was troubled by a guilty conscience, he made his way to Chin.

Before being received by King Chao, he sent someone to provoke Fan Sui and tell him, "This Tsai Tse from Yen is a great man known everywhere for his wisdom and eloquence. Once the king of Chin sees him, he will think less of you and dismiss you from your post."

Fan Sui replied, "I am well versed in the hundred schools of thought, as well as all the historical events of the Three Dynasties and the reigns of the Five Emperors. I can refute any orator however eloquent. How could he embarrass me or seize my position?" And so he sent for Tsai Tse.

Tsai Tse, coming in, merely bowed. And seeing his insolent manner Fan Sui, who was already displeased, demanded, "Is it true that you intend to take my place as prime minister of Chin?"

"That is correct," replied Tsai Tse.

"May I ask how?"

"Why, how can you be so slow-witted? Just as the four seasons change, what has reached completion gives place to something new. What man does not want to be healthy and active, clear-sighted and sharp of hearing, with the wisdom of a sage?"

"Nobody," agreed Fan Sui.

Is it not the aim of a wise and eloquent man to be kind and just, do what is right, and achieve his ambition in such a way that the whole world loves, respects and honours him, and is eager to be ruled by him?"

Again Fan Sui agreed.

Tsai Tse went on, "When a man has rank, riches, fame and honour, when he makes all things follow the proper course and lives out his full span of life, the world can carry forward and maintain his tradition. Such a man lives up to his name, his salutary influence spreads a thousand *li*, and later generations never cease to praise him, for he is as immortal as Heaven and Earth. Is this not the result of virtue, what the sages called beneficent goodness?"

Once more Fan Sui agreed.

"Is it good enough, in your view, to aspire to equal Lord Shang of Chin, Wu Chi of Chu, or Wen Chung the minister of Yueh?"

Aware that Tsai Tse hoped to worst him in argument, Fan Sui deliberately countered, "Why not? When Lord Shang served Duke Hsiao, he devoted himself completely to the state with no thought of private interest. He set up swords and saws to discourage evil-doers, made rewards and punishments certain in their application to bring about good government, took all blame upon himself and even deceived his old friend Lord Ang to make Chin secure and benefit its people, capturing the enemy general, defeating his army, and extending Chin's territory for hundreds of *li*.

"Wu Chi, when he served King Tao of Chu, never let his private interest interfere with the public interest, never let slanderers injure loyal subjects, never compromised in word or deed or modified his conduct in face of danger. He risked his own safety to do what was right, and braved calamity to make the state strong and his king a conqueror. Wen Chung served the king of Yueh with untiring loyalty through disgrace and trouble, straining every nerve and not leaving him when his king's position was helpless; he was neither puffed up by success nor did he relax his efforts when he grew rich and noble. Those three were paragons of virtue and justice. So a superior man who dies for justice looks on death as a homecoming and prefers death with honour to a life of disgrace. Indeed, some men have killed themselves to win fame, for

111

an upright man can die without regret. Why should I not aspire to equal these three men?"

"A sage ruler and worthy ministers bring happiness to the world," replied Tsai Tse. "An intelligent ruler and honest ministers bring happiness to the state. A kind father and filial sons, a faithful husband and a chaste wife, bring happiness to the family.

"Pi Kan, for all his loyalty, could not save the Shang Dynasty; Wu Tzu-hsu, for all his astuteness, could not preserve Wu; and Shen Sheng, for all his piety, could not prevent confusion in Tsin. How was it that such loyal ministers and such a filial son could not save these states? It was because they had no intelligent sovereigns or worthy father to listen to them; and that is why the world condemns those others and sympathizes with Pi Kan, Wu Tzu-hsu and Shen Sheng.

"Lord Shang, Wu Chi and Wen Chung were good ministers, whose rulers were misguided. Thus men say they did great deeds which went unrewarded, but no one can admire their unfortunate deaths. If men could prove their loyalty and make a name by death only, Wei Tzu would not be known for his humanity, Confucius acclaimed as a sage, or Kuan Chung admired for his greatness. A man who distinguishes himself is bound to hope to make a good end. The best thing is to live and win fame. The next best is to win fame and die. But worst of all is living on in shame."

Again Fan Sui approved.

Tsai Tse took occasion to add, "Of course, we may emulate Lord Shang, Wu Chi or Wen Chung, who were loyal ministers and achieved so much; but Hung Yao who served King Wen and the duke of Chou who assisted King Cheng were loyal and wise ministers too. How do the other three compare with them?"

"The other three do not measure up to them."

"How does your king compare with Duke Hsiao of Chin, King Tao of Chu and the king of Yueh in benevolence? In his trust in loyal ministers, concern for old friends, respect for the able, close ties with the good, and fair treatment of deserving subjects?"

"That is hard to say."

"Your king is no better than Duke Hsiao, King Tao of Chu or the king of Yueh in his relation to loyal ministers. You, thanks to your wisdom, have saved the state from peril, reformed the government, settled disorders, strengthened the army, overcome calamities, removed dangers, extended the territory and increased the grain supply. You have enriched the country and people, making the sovereign mighty, the state exalted and the royal house glorious, so that no one in the world dares offend your king, whose might is felt far and wide, whose reputation has spread for thousands of *li* and whose fame will endure for ever. How do you compare with Lord Shang, Wu Chi or Wen Chung?"

"I cannot compare with them."

"So your king falls short of Duke Hsiao, King Tao and King Kou-chien in his treatment of loyal ministers and old friends, while your achievements and the trust and favour shown you fall short of those of Lord Shang, Wu Chi and Wen Chung, although in rank and riches you surpass them. Obviously, unless you resign, you will meet an even worse end than these three men. My heart bleeds for you.

"The proverb says, 'When the sun reaches its zenith it must decline, when the moon is full it must wane, and what is ripe must decay.' This is a universal law. The sage's way is to advance or retreat, expand or retrench, according to the times. Thus Confucius said, 'When the True Way prevailed in his land, he served the state; but when the True Way ceased to prevail, he became a hermit.' The sage said, 'When a dragon flies through the sky, it will be beneficial to meet a great man.' 'Wealth and rank without justice are no more to me than floating clouds.' Now that you have avenged the wrongs against you and repaid your debts of gratitude, you have fulfilled your ambitions yet are not considering any change. To my mind, this is hardly worthy of you, sir!

"The kingfisher, swan, rhinoceros and elephant are eager

113

to avoid death, yet perish at last because they are tempted by bait. Su Chin and Lord Chih were astute enough to keep themselves from disgrace and death, yet they met their end owing to inordinate greed. A wise ruler establishes rites, curbs his desires, and is moderate in his levies on the people, whom he uses with restraint and in the proper seasons. His ambition has its bounds and his behaviour is moderate. Since he treads the right path and never diverges from it, his reign continues without interruption. Duke Huan of Chi united all the states and set the world in order, but because of his arrogance at the Kueichiu conference nine states turned away from him. The troops of King Fu-cha of Wu were invincible, but he despised the other states because of his might and threatened Chi and Tsin; finally he was killed and his state overthrown. The war-cries of Hsia Yu and Taishih Chiao could strike dread into a whole army, yet both died at the hands of ordinary men. For all these in their triumph went to extremes and strayed from the ' proper path, not acting humbly or practising frugality and moderation.

"When Lord Shang served Duke Hsiao of Chin, he clarified the laws, stemmed evil at its source, never failed to reward the worthy or to punish the guilty, unified weights and measures and abolished old boundaries. He gave the people a settled livelihood, did away with different local customs, encouraged men to farm and make full use of the land, forbidding any other occupations but toil in the fields to amass grain and military training. So when its troops marched out, Chin extended its territory; and when they were at rest, the country prospered. Thus Chin became invincible, striking awe into other states, and achieved its mission. But the man responsible for this was torn asunder by chariots!

"Chu had thousands of *li* of territory and a million halberdiers, yet Pai Chi with a few tens of thousands of men attacked it. In his first campaign he captured Yen and Ying and burned the royal tombs. In the second, having annexed Hanchung and Shu in the south, he crossed the territory of Hann and Wei to attack mighty Chao, defeated the lord of

Mafu in the north and massacred more than four hundred thousand of his troops at Changping. Blood flowed in torrents as, amid the thunder of battle, he advanced to besiege Hantan and carve out an empire for Chin. Chu and Chao had been powerful states and Chin's chief opponents, but these campaigns left them too cowed to fight back again. All this was thanks to Pai Chi, who conquered more than seventy cities. Yet in the end, in spite of these achievements, he was ordered to kill himself at Tuyu.

"Wu Chi established laws for King Tao of Chu, curtailed the power of the ministers, dismissed incompetent and useless officials, abolished sinecures, ended nepotism, unified the customs throughout the land and checked travelling politicians. He trained peasants and soldiers, conquered the Yangyueh tribesmen in the south and annexed Chen and Tsai in the north. He destroyed hostile alliances, closed the mouths of wandering orators, prohibited rival factions among the people, reformed the government and with the might of Chu's arms struck awe into other states. But although he accomplished all this, he was finally dismembered.

"Wen Chung made far-sighted plans for the king of Yueh, rescued the state in its hour of peril at Kuaichi, saved it from destruction and turned disgrace into glory. He brought barren land under cultivation, repopulated whole districts, opened up new territory and started plantations, gathering men from all sides and uniting high and low. He assisted his good king Kou-chien to take revenge on King Fu-cha and finally conquer powerful Wu, making Yueh a mighty state. Yet conspicuous as were his services, his ungrateful monarch killed him.

"Calamity befell these four men because they did not step aside once their work was done. They knew how to advance but not how to retreat, how to expand but not how to retrench. Fan Li, who knew better, withdrew from the court to live on as Lord Chu of Tao. You must have observed how some gamblers stake all on one throw, whereas others divide their stakes. You know this well, sir. Now, as prime minister

115

of Chin, you draw up plans from your seat and control the other states without leaving the court. You have opened up Sanchuan and strengthened Yiyang, cut the hazardous Yangchang route, blocked the Taihang road and obstructed the highways in Hann, Chao and Wei to prevent the six other states from forming an alliance against Chin. You have also made a plank-road a thousand *li* long through the mountains to Shu and Hanchung, so that all the world trembles before the might of Chin. Chin has achieved its end and you can accomplish no more, for this is the time for Chin to divide its stakes. Now, unless you withdraw, you will meet with the same fate as Lord Shang, Pai Chi, Wu Chi and Wen Chung.

"There is a proverb, 'Man's face is reflected by water, his fate is reflected by other people.' And it is written, 'Good fortune is short-lived.' Why should you court the disaster that befell these four men? Far better relinquish the prime minister's seal now to some worthy successor while you retire to live among hills and streams like a second Po Yi. Then the title of Marquis Ying will be handed down for generations, you will be like Hsu Yu and the prince of Yenling, who gave up thrones, and will live as long as Prince Chiao and the Master of the Red Pine. Surely this is better than disgrace and death? The choice is up to you. If you cannot bear to resign, cannot make up your mind, you will share the fearful fate of those four men. The *Book of Change* says, 'The dragon repents its height.' This refers to those who climb high and cannot come down, who are self-willed and cannot bend to circumstances, who go forward but cannot go back. I hope you will give this careful consideration."

"Well said!" approved Fan Sui. "I have heard that a man who cannot curb his desires will lose what he desires. One dissatisfied with what he has will lose what he has. I shall act on the good advice you have given me, sir." He entertained Tsai Tse as an honoured guest.

A few days later, at court, Fan Sui told King Chao, "A certain Tsai Tse, who has just come from the east, is a brilliant orator with such a thorough understanding of the Three Kings and Five Conquerors and the changes in human affairs that he can be entrusted with governing our state. Of all the men I have seen he is the ablest, and I beg to report that I am no match for him."

King Chao summoned Tsai Tse and was so much impressed by his conversation that he made him an honorary minister. Fan Sui asked leave to resign on the pretext of illness and, when the king urged him to carry on, insisted that his health was unequal to it. After Fan Sui's retirement the king, approving Tsai Tse's plans, made him prime minister, and he annexed Chou in the east.

When Tsai Tse had held office for several months, he found that he had enemies and to avoid trouble retired on the grounds of illness, receiving the title of Lord Kangcheng. He remained for ten years and more in Chin, serving under the kings Chao, Hsiao-wen and Chuang-hsiang, and finally under the First Emperor. For three years he served as Chin's envoy to Yen and that state sent Crown Prince Tan as a hostage to Chin.

The Grand Historian comments: Well did Han Fei Tzu say, "Long sleeves are good for dancing and much money is good for trade." Fan Sui and Tsai Tse were great orators, who tried to impress different lords with their eloquence, yet had no luck until their hair turned white. This was not for any lack of eloquence, but because their prospective patrons were too weak. When they later went as strangers to Chin, each in turn became a minister and prime minister and accomplished great deeds known to all the world, due to the difference in Chin's relative strength. None the less, much depends on chance. For the number of men as able as these two whose ambitions were frustrated is past counting. It was desperation, moreover, that goaded them on.

LORD HSINLING

Wu-chi, younger son of King Chao of Wei and step-brother of King An Hsi, was made Lord Hsinling when King Chao died and King An Hsi succeeded to the throne. At that time Fan Sui had fled from Wei to become the prime minister of Chin; and because he hated Wei Chi, the Chin armies besieged the Wei capital Taliang and routed the forces of Wei at Huayang, putting General Mang Mao to flight. The king of Wei and Lord Hsinling were sorely troubled.

Lord Hsinling was a kindly, unassuming man, who showed courtesy to all he met whether they had talent or not and did not stand on his dignity because of his wealth and position. So followers flocked to him from hundreds of *li* around until he had about three thousand protégés; and when the other feudal lords saw his ability and the number of his supporters, they dared not attack Wei. Thus more than ten years passed without further alarms.

One day Lord Hsinling was playing draughts with the king of Wei when word was brought that beacon fires had been lit on the northern border and the king of Chao was about to invade their territory. The king rose from the table to summon a council of ministers at once, but Lord Hsinling stopped him.

"The king of Chao is only out hunting," he assured him. "This is no invasion."

Lord Hsinling played calmly on, while the king was too worried to concentrate on the game. Presently another messenger arrived from the north to report that the king of Chao had come out to hunt, not to launch any attack.

"How did you know this, sir?" the astonished king asked Lord Hsinling.

"Among my protégés are men who know all the secrets of the king of Chao. They tell me at once what he is doing. That is how I knew."

Then the king began to fear his step-brother's abilities and no longer dared entrust affairs of state to him.

There was an old man of seventy in Wei, named Hou Ying, who lived in poverty and served as the warden of Yi Gate in Taliang. When Lord Hsinling knew this he called on him with gifts, but Hou Ying declined them.

"I have lived simply for many years to cultivate virtue," he said. "Poor as I am, I cannot accept your gifts, sir."

Some time later Lord Hsinling prepared a great banquet to which he invited many guests. When they had taken their seats he drove with a retinue to Yi Gate to fetch Hou Ying in person, leaving the left seat in his chariot empty for the old man. Dusting off his tattered clothes and cap, Hou Ying promptly took the seat of honour without one polite word of protest, watching Lord Hsinling to see how he would take this. But Lord Hsinling, reins in hand, appeared more respectful than ever.

"I have a friend who is a butcher in the market-place," said Hou Ying. "Would you mind passing that way?"

So Lord Hsinling drove his chariot into the market, where Hou Ying alighted to speak to his friend, Chu Hai. He deliberately stood for a long time chatting to the butcher, stealing sidelong glances at Lord Hsinling, who showed no sign of impatience. Meanwhile the generals, ministers, nobles and protégés of Wei who thronged Lord Hsinling's hall were waiting for his return to start the feast. The whole market was staring to see him act as charioteer, while all his outriders were cursing Hou Ying under their breath. When the old warden saw how imperturbably Lord Hsinling was waiting, he took leave of his friend and mounted the chariot again.

Upon reaching his mansion, Lord Hsinling made Hou Ying take the seat of honour and introduced him to his guests, to the amazement of all. And during the feast he went across to toast him.

119

"I put you to a hard test today, my lord," said Hou Ying. "I am only a warden at Yi Gate, yet you drove your chariot through the crowds to bring me here, calling for me in person and unnecessarily going out of your way. And when I further tried your famed courtesy by making you wait so long in the market-place with your chariot and outriders while I called on a friend, I observed that you looked more courteous than ever. The whole market despised me then, but admired you for your noble humility."

After this feast Hou Ying became one of Lord Hsinling's most honoured guests. One day he told him, "Chu Hai, the butcher I called on, is an able man. But because no one has recognized his talents he is living in obscurity as a butcher."

Lord Hsinling called on Chu Hai several times, but to his surprise the butcher showed no sign of appreciation.

In the twentieth year of King An Hsi,* King Chao of Chin routed the army of Chao at Changping and advanced to besiege Hantan. Lord Hsinling's elder sister had married Lord Pingyuan, younger brother of King Hui-wen of Chao, and now she sent repeatedly to her brothers, the king of Wei and Lord Hsinling, to beg for aid. But when the king of Wei dispatched General Tsin Pi with a hundred thousand men to Chao's assistance, the king of Chin sent an envoy to him with this warning:

"Chao is about to fall. If any other state dare go to its aid, I shall lead my troops against it as soon as I have conquered Chao."

The panic-stricken king of Wei immediately ordered Tsin Pi to advance no further but simply to garrison Yen,** ostensibly aiding Chao while actually sitting on the fence. Then carriage after carriage of envoys came from Lord Pingyuan to Wei.

"I was eager to ally with you by marriage," Lord Pingyuan reproached Lord Hsinling, "because you were famed for your

---

* 257 B.C.

** A city on the border between Wei and Chao.

high-minded generosity and for helping those in distress. Now our capital may fall to Chin at any moment, but we have had no assistance from Wei. Is this your way of helping friends in need? Of course, you may think so poorly of me that you do not care if I fall captive to Chin; but have you no feeling for your sister?"

Time and again, in great distress, Lord Hsinling pleaded with the king and sent protégés and orators to reason with him; but for fear of Chin the king ignored their advice. Realizing that the king was not to be persuaded, and unwilling to live to see the downfall of Chao, Lord Hsinling preferring to perish with Chao mustered from among his retainers a force of more than a hundred chariots and riders to attack the army of Chin. Passing Yi Gate he explained his mission to Hou Ying and took his leave of him.

"Farewell then, my lord," said Hou Ying. "I am too old to follow you."

Lord Hsinling rode for several *li* with a growing sense of grievance. "The whole world knows how much I have done for Hou Ying," he thought. "Yet now that I am going to die, he has not a word to say to me. Can I have offended him in any way?"

He drove back to question the old man.

"I knew you would be back," said Hou Ying with a smile. "You are famed far and wide for your generosity to able men; yet now that trouble has arisen you can think of nothing better than to pit yourself against the army of Chin. This is like tossing meat to a hungry tiger — what good can come of it? What has been the use of making so many friends? You have treated me so well that, when I did not see you off, I knew you would resent it and come back."

Lord Hsinling bowed and begged for his advice, whereupon Hou Ying sent everyone else away.

"I have heard that Tsin Pi's army tally is kept in the king's bed-chamber," he whispered. "Lady Ju, the king's favourite, is in and out of his chamber all the time and could easily steal the tally. I have heard, too, that after Lady Ju's father was

121

murdered she thirsted three years for revenge and appealed in vain to everyone from the king down to his ministers to avenge her. When she pleaded with you, however, you sent a man to cut off her enemy's head and presented it to her. This lady would risk any danger, even death itself, to repay you, but she has not yet had the chance. She will certainly consent to get you the tally. And once you have it you can take over Tsin Pi's troops, march north to Chao's aid and beat back the forces of Chin, a campaign worthy of the five conquerors of old!"

Lord Hsinling, acting on Hou Ying's advice, prevailed on Lady Ju to steal the tally. As he was about to leave, Hou Ying cautioned him, "A general at the front is not bound to obey his sovereign's orders if they endanger the state. So even though you have the right half of the tally, Tsin Pi may refuse to hand over his command until he receives confirmation from the king, in which case there will be trouble. You had better take my friend the butcher with you, for he is a powerful man. If Tsin Pi agrees, well and good; if not, Chu Hai can kill him."

Lord Hsinling was moved to tears.

"Why are you weeping?" asked Hou Ying. "Are you afraid of death?"

"Tsin Pi is a veteran commander and completely fearless," Lord Hsinling replied. "He is not likely to obey me and I may have to kill him. That is why I shed tears, not because I am afraid of death."

When he asked Chu Hai to accompany him the butcher laughed and said, "I am a butcher who chops up meat in the market, yet you have called on me time and again. I did not show my gratitude before because such small courtesies are meaningless; but now that you have need of me, my life is at your disposal."

So he accompanied Lord Hsinling, who left the city by the Yi Gate in order to thank Hou Ying.

"I would go with you were I not so old," said Hou Ying. "As it is, I shall estimate the time it will take you to reach

Tsin Pi, and that day I will face north and kill myself to prove my loyalty."

Lord Hsinling, reaching Yeh, claimed that he had orders from the king to take over Tsin Pi's command. But although the two halves of the tally fitted each other Tsin Pi had certain misgivings and, raising a protesting hand, he looked hard at Lord Hsinling.

"As commander of a hundred thousand men at the frontier, I have a great responsibility to the state," he said. "How is it you have arrived in a single chariot to replace me?"

He was about to refuse when Chu Hai killed him with a forty-pound iron pestle which he had hidden under his coat. Then Lord Hsinling took over the command and announced to his troops, "If father and son are both serving here, the father may go home. If there are brothers, the elder may go home. And if any soldier is an only son, he may go home to support his family."

Then with eighty thousand picked troops he advanced to the attack. The army of Chin withdrew, the siege of Hantan was raised and Chao was saved. The king of Chao and Lord Pingyuan went to the boundary to meet him in person, and Lord Pingyuan carried his quiver and went before as his guide. "History knows no greater man than you, sir!" said the king of Chao with a bow. And Lord Pingyuan felt unworthy to be compared with him.

After Lord Hsinling left Hou Ying and reached the army, the old man faced north as he had promised and killed himself.

Aware that he had incurred the king of Wei's anger by stealing the tally and killing Tsin Pi, once Chin had withdrawn and Chao was safe Lord Hsinling ordered a general to lead the troops back to Wei while he and his protégés remained in Chao. King Hsiao-cheng of Chao was so grateful for his help that after discussing the matter with Lord Pingyuan he decided to present Lord Hsinling with five cities. And when the latter knew of this, he began to plume himself on his achievement.

"There are things a man should remember and things he should forget," a protégé warned him. "If someone does you

123

a good turn, by all means remember it; but if you do someone else a good turn, forget it. Taking over Tsin Pi's command on feigned orders from the king of Wei to rescue Chao, you did Chao a good service but were disloyal to Wei. This is not an achievement of which to be too proud."

Lord Hsinling at once admitted his mistake, ready to sink into the ground for shame. The king of Chao swept the path himself to welcome him into the palace by the west steps,* but Lord Hsinling declined and went up by the east steps instead, saying that he was guilty of injuring his own country while doing little for Chao. The king of Chao entertained him with wine till the evening, but in view of his humility did not mention the gift of five cities. Lord Hsinling stayed on, however, in Chao, where he was given the district of Huo. The king of Wei also kept Hsinling for him.

During Lord Hsinling's stay in Chao he heard tell of a retired gentleman named Mao who lived in obscurity among gamblers, and another named Hsueh who lived among porridge-venders. When he tried to meet them they concealed themselves, but eventually he discovered where they lodged, called on them and started enjoying their company.

This came to the ears of Lord Pingyuan, who told his wife, "I had heard that your brother was a man of unmatched qualities, but now they tell me he is wasting his time with gamblers and porridge-venders. He must be a fool after all!"

When his sister told this to Lord Hsinling, he said he must leave them, explaining, "Under the impression that Lord Pingyuan was a great man, I wronged the king of Wei to rescue Chao for his sake. But apparently he is gathering followers merely to impress the world, not to find talented men. While still in Taliang I heard of the excellence of these two good men, and my one fear after coming here was that I might not meet them — I was afraid they would think me beneath them. If Lord Pingyuan considers that disgraceful, his company can hardly be worth having."

---

* The west steps were for guests of honour.

He was packing up to leave when his sister repeated this to Lord Pingyuan, who took off his hat and apologized, begging his brother-in-law to remain. When word of this reached Lord Pingyuan's protégés, half of them left him and joined Lord Hsinling. Other gentlemen from near and far also sought his patronage, and eventually he won the allegiance of virtually all Lord Pingyuan's followers.

Lord Hsinling remained for ten years in Chao, during which time Chin took advantage of his absence to send many expeditions eastward to attack Wei. At last the king of Wei, in desperation, dispatched envoys to beg his half-brother to return. But Lord Hsinling, afraid that the king still bore him a grudge, warned his followers that any man who dared to deliver a message from Wei would be killed. All his protégés then left Wei and came to Chao, and no one ventured to speak to him of returning. One day, however, his two friends Mao and Hsueh called to see him.

"You are highly regarded in Chao and your fame is known to all the feudal lords solely because of Wei's existence," they told him. "Now Chin is attacking Wei, yet you appear quite unmoved by your country's danger. Suppose Chin takes Taliang by storm and razes your ancestral temples, how will you be able to face the world again?"

Lord Hsinling turned pale before they had finished speaking. Calling for his carriage, he raced back to the aid of his country. At his meeting with the king of Wei they both wept, and he was appointed as high marshal.

In the thirtieth year of King An Hsi, Lord Hsinling sent envoys to all the states, and when they knew that he was Wei's commander-in-chief they dispatched troops to his aid. Then at the head of the troops from five states he routed Chin's army south of the Yellow River, put General Meng Ao to flight and drove the enemy into the Hanku Pass, striking such fear into the men of Chin that they dared not sally forth again. His military prowess shook the world, and wise men from various states sent him stratagems which he compiled in one volume under his name. This collection is generally known as *Lord Hsinling on the Art of War*.

In great alarm, the king of Chin bribed a former follower of Tsin Pi with ten thousand catties of gold to slander Lord Hsinling.

"Lord Hsinling has been away for ten years," this man told the king of Wei. "Yet now he commands not only our troops but the forces of other states, whose rulers have heard of Lord Hsinling but not of the king of Wei. If he aspires to seize the throne, the other states which fear his might will support him."

Envoys were also sent from Chin to alienate Lord Hsinling from the king of Wei by offering him congratulations and inquiring whether he had yet ascended the throne. At last the king, who could not but believe the slander he heard daily, sent another general to take over the command. Then Lord Hsinling, aware of why he had been removed, absented himself from court on the pretext of illness and spent all his time drinking strong wine with his friends or enjoying himself with women. After four years of continuous carousing, he drank himself to death. King An Hsi died the same year.

When word of Lord Hsinling's death reached Chin, Meng Ao attacked Wei again and took twenty towns, which became Chin's Eastern Province. Chin went on nibbling at Wei's territory, and eighteen years later captured the king of Wei and massacred the inhabitants of Taliang.

During his youth our first emperor heard so much of the exploits of Lord Hsinling that, after becoming emperor, he sacrificed at Lord Hsinling's shrine whenever he passed through Taliang. In the twelfth year of his reign, returning from a punitive expedition against Ching Pu, he appointed five families to act as guardians of Lord Hsinling's tomb. Since then seasonal sacrifice has been offered to Lord Hsinling four times a year.

The Grand Historian comments: When I visited the ruins of Taliang, I asked the whereabouts of Yi Gate and learned that it was the east gate. Other noble lords enjoyed having protégés too, but Lord Hsinling even sought out recluses in mountain caves and no one, however humble, was beneath his notice. Little wonder, then, that his fame spread among the states and that our first emperor, when passing his shrine, decreed that sacrifices should be offered to him for ever.

LORD PINGYUAN AND YU CHING

Chao Sheng, Lord Pingyuan, was a member of the royal house of Chao, the ablest of all the young lords. He was a great patron whose protégés numbered thousands. Prime minister under King Hui-wen and King Hsiao-cheng, he resigned three times and three times was reappointed. His fief was Tungwucheng.

Lord Pingyuan's storeyed mansion stood next to a commoner's house from which a lame man once limped out to draw water, only to be heartily laughed at by one of the lord's concubines. Next day the lame man came to the lord's gate and said, "I hear you are such a great patron that worthy men come to you from a thousand *li* away, because you value them more than your concubines. It is my misfortune to be lame, but one of your concubines has laughed at me. I want that lady's head."

Lord Pingyuan consented with a smile. Once the lame man had gone, however, he said with a laugh, "What a fool, wanting me to kill my beauty because of one laugh! Ridiculous!" And he did not kill her.

Within a year or so, more than half of his protégés and retainers had left one after the other.

"I have never treated you gentlemen impolitely. Why are you all leaving like this?" he asked in surprise.

One of them stepped forward to answer, "By not killing the lady who laughed at the lame man you showed that you love feminine beauty but despise worthy men. That is why so many are leaving."

Then the lord cut off the head of the offending concubine and himself presented it with apologies to the lame man. After that his protégés gradually returned.

At this time, Lord Mengchang in Chi, Lord Hsinling in Wei and Lord Chunshen in Chu were trying to outdo each other in their treatment of worthy men.

When the army of Chin besieged Hantan, Chao ordered Lord Pingyuan to seek aid by entering into an alliance with Chu. He decided to take with him twenty strong, fearless protégés skilled in the arts of peace as well as of war. "If we can succeed by peaceful means, well and good," he said. "If not, let us take an oath on blood in the hall to bring back an agreement. I shall not seek men elsewhere, only in my own household."

He selected nineteen men, but could not decide on the twentieth. Then one of his retainers, Mao Sui, came forward and recommended himself, saying, "I hear you want to join Chu in an alliance against Chin, my lord, and that you mean to choose twenty men from your own household but are still one short. Will you take me to make up the number?"

"How many years have you been here?" asked Lord Pingyuan.

Mao Sui answered, "Three."

"An able man in this world, like an awl kept in a bag, quickly shows himself. If you have been here for three years, praised by none and unknown to me, you can hardly have any talent. No, no, you had better stay here."

"I am asking now to be put in the bag," said Mao Sui. "Had I been put there earlier, the awl would have thrust right through instead of simply showing its tip outside." So finally the lord agreed to take him. The other nineteen exchanged amused glances in silence.

By the time they reached Chu, Mao Sui had convinced the other nineteen of his ability in argument.

At sunrise Lord Pingyuan and the king of Chu began to discuss the advantages and disadvantages of an alliance, but no agreement had been reached by noon.

Then the nineteen others urged Mao Sui, "Go up, sir!"

Mao Sui, his hand on his sword, mounted the steps and said to Lord Pingyuan, "Whether this alliance is advantageous or not can be settled in two words. How is it that negotiations started at sunrise yet no agreement has been reached by noon?"

The king of Chu demanded, "Who is this man?"

Lord Pingyuan answered, "One of my retainers."

"What impudence!" shouted the king of Chu. "I am discussing matters with your master. What business have you here?"

His hand on his sword, Mao Sui advanced and said, "Your Majesty dares to shout at me because Chu has powerful forces; but within these ten paces they are no help to you. Your life is in my hands. How dare you shout at me in my master's presence? I have heard that King Tang ruled the world although he only started with seventy *li* of land, and King Wen with his kingdom of a hundred *li* ruled over all other states. These kings had no great armies, yet they could control events and exercise their might. Now with Chu's five thousand *li* of territory and million halberdiers, you have the resources to become a great conqueror. The whole world should be powerless to withstand you. Yet that young cur Pai Chi with a few tens of thousands of men in one battle took the cities Yen and Ying, in another burned the royal tombs at Yiling, and in a third brought shame upon your ancestors. We blush for you over this undying disgrace, yet you are not ashamed. We are proposing this alliance for your sake, not for our own. How dare you shout at me in my master's presence?"

"Yes, yes," said the king of Chu. "Just as you say. My state shall ally with yours."

"Is that settled, then?" asked Mao Sui.

The king said, "It is."

Then Mao Sui ordered the king's followers to fetch the blood of a cock, dog and horse. On his knees he presented the bronze dish of blood to the king of Chu, saying, "You must make a blood pact, sir. Then my master will pledge himself, then I." So the alliance was concluded in the court.

Then holding the dish of blood in his left hand, Mao Sui beckoned to the other nineteen with his right. "You shall swear with blood too," he said. "You yes-men can only reap what others have sown."

Having made the alliance and returned to Chao, Lord Pingyuan said, "I shall never set myself up as a judge of men again. I have judged perhaps a thousand men, or several hundreds at least, and thought I could not miss any man of talent; but I was mistaken in my judgement of Mao Sui. His going to Chu has made our prestige higher than that of the nine tripods of Hsia or the great bell of Chou. His three inches of tongue have proved mightier than an army a million strong! I shall never set myself up as a judge of men again." Thereafter he treated Mao Sui as his most honoured guest.

After Lord Pingyuan's return to Chao the king of Chu sent Lord Chunshen with an army to Chao's rescue, while Lord Hsinling of Wei took over General Tsin Pi's army by trickery to aid Chao. Before the arrival of these forces, however, the troops of Chin were pressing Hantan so hard that the city was on the verge of surrender, and Lord Pingyuan was desperately worried.

Li Tung, the son of a steward in a hostel, asked, "Don't you care if the state of Chao is overthrown?"

"If Chao falls I shall be captured," replied Lord Pingyuan. "Of course I care."

The citizens of Hantan are in such sore straits they are using bones for fuel and exchanging their sons to eat," rejoined Li Tung. "Yet in your inner palace are hundreds of slave girls and concubines who wear silk and embroidery and have grain and meat and to spare, while the people lack sackcloth to cover their nakedness and would welcome husks to eat. Exhausted, with no weapons left, they are sharpening sticks to serve as spears and arrows; yet your bronze vessels, bells and chimes remain intact. All these will be lost if Chin conquers Chao. But if Chao is saved, you will have no lack of such things. You should make your ladies take part in the work of the troops and distribute all you have to supply our men. In their desperate state, it is easy to win their gratitude."

Lord Pingyuan took his advice and assembled three thousand

131

men ready to risk their lives. With Li Tung they charged the soldiers of Chin and made them fall back thirty *li*. Just at that juncture Chu and Wei came to their assistance. Then the men of Chin raised the siege and Hantan was saved. Li Tung fell in battle, but his father was enfeoffed as marquis of Li.

Because Lord Hsinling had saved Hantan, Yu Ching decided to ask for a larger fief for Lord Pingyuan. When Kungsun Lung heard this he drove by night to see Lord Pingyuan and said, "I hear that Yu Ching means to ask for a larger fief for you because Lord Hsinling saved Hantan. Is this true?" Told that it was, he said, "That would be very wrong. It was not because you are the wisest man in Chao that the king made you his chief minister, nor was it because you had achieved much and all others nothing that he gave you Tungwucheng as your fief. He did so because you are his kinsman. And you accepted the chief minister's seal and fief without declining on the grounds of unworthiness, also because you are his kinsman. Now if you accept a fief because Lord Hsinling saved the capital, this would mean that you had accepted cities in the past as a member of the royal family and were now asking for a reward like a common citizen. That would be most improper. Yu Ching stands to gain either way. If he succeeds you will be indebted to him; if he fails you will have to be grateful to him for trying. You must not listen to him, sir!"

So Lord Pingyuan declined Yu Ching's offer.

Lord Pingyuan died in the fifteenth year of Hsiao-cheng.* His descendants held the title after him until the fall of Chao. Lord Pingyuan gave very generous treatment to Kungsun Lung, a skilled logician, until he was ousted from favour by Tsou Yen, who came to Chao to expound the origin of things.

Yu Ching was an itinerant politician. Shod in straw sandals and carrying an umbrella, he spoke with King Hsiao-cheng of Chao. After one interview he was given a hundred *yi* of gold

* 251 B.C.

and a pair of white jade discs, while after a second interview he was made chief minister. Thus he was known as Yu Ching or Minister Yu.

In the battle against Chin at Changping, the men of Chao were worsted and lost their commander. The king consulted Lou Chang and Yu Ching, saying, "Our army has been defeated and our commander killed. What if I attack with all our men at arms?"

"That would be useless," said Lou Chang. "Better send some high-ranking envoy to treat for peace."

But Yu Ching said, "Lou Chang proposes peace for fear our army will be beaten, but making peace depends on Chin. In your view, does Chin want to destroy our army or not?"

"Chin is going all out to destroy us," replied the king.

Yu Ching said, "If you take my advice, you will send envoys with rich gifts to Chu and Wei. Wanting our gifts, these states will admit our envoys. Once our envoys enter Chu and Wei, Chin will take fright, suspecting that all the other states have allied against it. That is the only way to achieve peace."

The king did not accept this advice, however, but told Lord Pingyuan to negotiate and sent Cheng Chu to Chin. When Chin accepted his envoy, the king of Chao summoned Yu Ching and said, "I have asked Lord Pingyuan to negotiate for us, and Chin has accepted our envoy Cheng Chu. What do you say to that?"

Yu Ching answered, "You will fail to make peace, the army will be destroyed, and all the world will go to congratulate Chin on its victory. Cheng Chu is a nobleman, and the king of Chin and the marquis of Ying (Fan Sui) are bound to make a great show of respect for him. When Chu and Wei see you are treating for peace with Chin they will not come to your rescue, and when Chin sees that it will not agree to make peace."

Sure enough, the marquis of Ying paraded Cheng Chu before all the envoys from different states who came to congratulate Chin on its victory, and Chin refused to make peace. Then

133

the great defeat at Changping was followed by the siege of Hantan, so that Chao became the laughing-stock of the world.

After Chin raised the siege of Hantan, the king of Chao held court and told Chao Shih to sue for peace and offer Chin six counties.

Yu Ching asked, "Has Chin withdrawn because it is exhausted? Or do you think it is still strong enough to advance but has called off the attack for your sake?"

The king answered, "Chin went all out in its attack. This withdrawal must be owing to exhaustion."

"So Chin attacked as hard as it could, yet was unable to take the city and has withdrawn, exhausted. If you give it what it was unable to take, you are helping Chin to attack us. Next year it will attack again, and you will be doomed."

The king repeated this to Chao Shih, who said, "Can Yu Ching really know the strength of Chin? Suppose, knowing that Chin can do no more, we keep back these small patches of land, if it attacks again next year you will have to give up your palace to obtain peace."

"If I take your advice and give Chin these counties, can you guarantee no further attack next year?"

"I can't promise that," said Chao Shih. "In the past the three states of Tsin were on good terms with Chin, whereas now Chin is friendly with Han and Wei but has attacked us. This shows that we have not served Chin as well as Han and Wei have done. Now I can enter the Pass, present gifts, and serve Chin as well as Han and Wei have done. If there is an attack on us alone next year, that will mean you are still not serving Chin as well as Han and Wei — I cannot be responsible for that."

The king repeated this to Yu Ching, who countered, "Chao Shih says that if we do not make peace, next year when Chin attacks again we shall have to give your palace to obtain peace; but if we make peace with Chin, he cannot guarantee no further attack. What is the use, then, of giving up six cities? If Chin attacks again next year and to make peace we give up more land which it cannot take, we shall be cutting our own throats!

134

Better not make peace. Although Chin launches strong attacks, it cannot take our six cities. Although we have given ground, we have not lost these six cities. Now Chin has withdrawn, exhausted, its troops tired out. If we use these cities to induce other states to attack Chin, exhausted as it is, we shall receive compensation for our cities from Chin. Our country is still strong. Why should we tamely surrender territory, weakening ourselves and making Chin even more powerful?

"Chao Shih says Chin is friendly with Han and Wei but has attacked Chao, implying that Han and Wei will not help us, that we are standing alone, and that this shows we have not served Chin as well as Han and Wei. He wants you to give up six cities to Chin each year, which will soon amount to taking the surrender of all our cities lying down. Next year when Chin asks for cities, will you give it them or not? If you refuse, all past efforts will have been wasted and you will be asking for trouble. If you agree, you will soon have no more to give.

"The proverb says, 'When the powerful launch strong attacks, the weak must give ground.' If you let Chin have its way, it will add to its territory without fighting, and that will strengthen Chin while weakening Chao. Chin as it grows stronger will never cease seizing land from us as we grow weaker. There is a limit to your territory, but none to their ambition. If things go on like this, Chao will disappear."

Unable to make up his mind, the king consulted Lou Huan, just back from Chin. "Which is better, to give Chin land or not?"

"That is not for me to say," replied Lou Huan.

"Still, what is your private opinion?"

"Does Your Majesty know the story of Kungfu Wen-po's mother? Kungfu served in the state of Lu, and when he fell ill and died two women killed themselves in their chambers. His mother, receiving word of this, did not mourn for him. Asked the reason by his nurse she said, 'The sage Confucius was driven away from Lu, but he did not follow Confucius. Now two of his wives have killed themselves because of his death, which shows how little he thought of elders, how much of women.' These words spoken by his mother prove that she was a good mother, whereas if spoken by his wife they would simply have shown jealousy. Thus the same words may have a different meaning, depending upon the speaker. Now I have just come from Chin. If I urge you not to cede these cities, it would be bad advice. If I urge you to cede them, you may suspect me of speaking on behalf of Chin. So I dare say nothing. If I were you, I would give up these cities." The king agreed with him.

When Yu Ching knew this he went to the king and said, "He is hiding his real motives. You must not agree!"

Lou Huan, learning of this, went back to see the king, who told him what Yu Ching had said. Lou Huan replied, "No, Yu Ching sees one side only, not the other. Now all other states are gloating over this trouble between Chin and Chao. Why? They hope to side with the stronger to take advantage of the weaker. They have sent congratulations to Chin on defeating our army. We had better give up some land at once to make peace, to sow doubts in the others and placate Chin. Otherwise they will take advantage of Chin's might and of our weakness to carve up our state as if it were a melon. That would mean the end of Chao and all these speculations about Chin. This is why I say Yu Ching sees one side only, not the other. I hope Your Majesty will make up your mind and not hesitate any longer."

Word of this reached Yu Ching, who went back to the king and said, "What a dangerous proposal! Lou Huan is working for Chin. This would make the other states suspect you more without placating Chin. Why didn't he say that this would show the world your weakness? Besides, when I advised you not to cede those cities, I had something else in mind. Chin has asked you for six cities. Well then, offer six to Chi, Chin's sworn enemy. For then, if asked to join in an attack on Chin in the west, Chi will agree before you finish your speech. In this way you will cede something to Chi but gain compensation from Chin, while both you and Chi can take your revenge and display your power to the world. If you make known your intention then Chin will send rich gifts and sue for peace before your armies set out. When you accept and Han and Wei hear of it, they will think highly of you and send rich gifts too. So at one stroke you will make friends with three states, while your position and Chin's will be reversed."

The king approved and sent Yu Ching eastwards to the king of Chi to discuss an alliance against Chin. Before Yu Ching's return, an envoy from Chin had reached Chao. When Lou Huan knew this, he fled. The king enfeoffed Yu Ching with a city.

Later Wei offered to ally with Chao and the king summoned Yu Ching to consult him. Yu Ching first saw Lord Pingyuan, who said, "I hope you will speak in favour of the alliance." Then he went in to the king. When told of the proposal Yu Ching said, "Wei is making a mistake."

"That is why I have not agreed," rejoined the king.

"Then Your Majesty is making a mistake."

"You say Wei is mistaken in seeking an alliance, and I am mistaken in refusing. Are we then not to consider an alliance at all?"

Yu Ching replied, "I have heard that when a small state allies with a large one, it is the large state that benefits if all goes well, while if there is trouble the small state suffers. Now Wei as a small state is asking for trouble, while you with your large state are missing a golden opportunity. That is why I say that both Wei and Your Majesty are mistaken. I think the alliance would be to our advantage."

The king approved and entered into an alliance with Wei.

For the sake of Wei Chi, Yu Ching gave up his fief of ten thousand families and the seal of a chief minister. He fled with Wei Chi from Chao and found himself in difficulties at Taliang. After Wei Chi's death he was not so highly regarded, and therefore he started to write a book based on material from the past as well as his observation of recent events. There were eight chapters in all, including the chapters "On Character", "On Titles", "On Speculation" and "On Policy".

137

This book, passing judgement on good government and bad, has been handed down as the *Annals of Yu Ching*.

The Grand Historian comments: Lord Pingyuan was a fine nobleman in troubled times, but he failed to keep in sight what was most important. As the proverb says, "Profit makes fools of the wise." Lord Pingyuan, led astray by Feng Ting's bad advice, was responsible for making Chao lose more than four hundred thousand men in the Battle of Changping and nearly losing Hantan.

Yu Ching was a man of shrewd judgement and great insight, and his plans for Chao were certainly well devised. Yet he let pity for Wei Chi involve him in trouble at Taliang. Even an ordinary man should not be such a fool, let alone a man of his talent! However, if not for his troubles and misfortunes, he would have been unable to write his book which has been handed down to posterity.

LIEN PO AND LIN HSIANG-JU

Lien Po was an able general of Chao. In the sixteenth year of King Hui-wen,* he commanded the Chao army against Chi and defeated its troops, taking the city of Yangtsin. Then he was made a chief minister and was known for his prowess to all the states.

Lin Hsiang-ju, a man of Chao, was the steward of Mu Hsien the chief eunuch.

King Hui-wen had come into possession of the jade of Pien Ho, a man of Chu. When King Chao of Chin knew this, he sent an envoy with a letter to the king of Chao, offering fifteen cities in exchange for the jade. The king took counsel with General Lien Po and his chief ministers, who feared that if the jade were sent to Chin they might be cheated and get no cities in return, yet if they refused the soldiers of Chin might attack. They could neither hit on a plan nor find an envoy to take their answer to Chin.

Then Mu Hsien the chief eunuch said, "My steward Lin Hsiang-ju would make a good envoy."

"How do you know?" asked the king.

He replied, "Once I did something wrong and secretly planned to escape to Yen, but my steward stopped me, asking, 'How can you be sure of the king of Yen?' I answered, 'I met him at the frontier with our king, and he privately grasped my hand and offered me his friendship. That is how I know, and why I mean to go there.' Lin said, 'Chao is strong and Yen is weak, and because you stood well with our lord the king of Yen desired your friendship. But if you now fly from Chao to Yen, for fear of Chao he will not dare to keep you

* 283 B.C.

and will have you sent back in chains. Your only possible way out is to bare your shoulder and prostrate yourself before the axe and block for punishment.' I took his advice and Your Majesty pardoned me. To my mind he is a brave, resourceful man, well fitted to be our envoy."

The king thereupon summoned Lin Hsiang-ju and asked him, "Should I accept the king of Chin's offer of fifteen cities in exchange for my jade?"

"Chin is strong, we are weak," replied Lin Hsiang-ju. "We cannot refuse."

"What if he takes my jade but will not give me the cities?"

"If we refuse Chin's offer of cities in exchange for the jade, that puts us in the wrong; but if we give up the jade and get no cities, that puts Chin in the wrong. Of these two courses, the better one is to agree and put Chin in the wrong."

"Who can be our envoy?"

"If Your Majesty has no one else, I will gladly take the jade and go on this mission. If the cities are given to Chao, the jade will remain in Chin. If no cities are given, I shall bring the jade back unscathed."

So the king of Chao sent Lin Hsiang-ju with the jade west to Chin.

The king of Chin sat in his pleasure pavilion to receive Lin Hsiang-ju, who presented the jade to him. The king, very pleased, had it shown to his ladies and attendants, and all his attendants cheered.

Seeing that the king had no intention of giving any cities to Chao, Lin Hsiang-ju stepped forward and said, "There is a blemish on the jade. Let me show it to you, sir."

As soon as the king gave him the jade, Lin Hsiang-ju retreated to stand with his back to a pillar. His hair bristling with fury, he said, "To get this jade, great king, you sent a letter to the king of Chao. When our sovereign summoned his ministers to discuss the matter, they said, 'Chin is greedy and, relying on its strength, hopes to get our jade in return for empty promises. We are not likely to receive the cities.' They were against giving you the jade. It seemed to me, however, that if even fellows in homespun can trust each other, how much more can powerful states. Besides, how wrong it would be to offend mighty Chin for the sake of a piece of jade! So the king of Chao, after fasting for five days, sent me with a letter and the jade to your court. Why? To show the respect and awe in which we hold your great country. Yet on my arrival you received me in a pleasure pavilion and treated me with contempt. You took the jade and passed it among your ladies to make a fool of me. I can see you have no intention of giving Chao those cities in return, so I have taken back the jade. If you use force against me, I will smash my head and the jade against this pillar."

With that, glancing at the pillar, he raised the jade and threatened to smash it.

To save the jade, the king of Chin apologized and begged him to stop, then ordered the officer in charge to look up the map and point out the boundaries of the fifteen cities to be given to Chao.

Lin Hsiang-ju, thinking this was a subterfuge and that Chao would never really get the cities, declared, "The jade of Pien Ho is a treasure known throughout the world, but for fear of Chin the king of Chao dared not withhold it. Before parting with it he fasted for five days. So it is only right, great king, that you too should fast for five days and then prepare a grand court reception. Only then dare I hand it over."

Since he could not seize the jade by force, the king agreed to fast for five days, during which time Lin Hsiang-ju should be lodged in the Kuangcheng Hostel.

Lin Hsiang-ju suspected that despite his fast the king would not keep his promise to give the cities. So, dressing one of his followers in rags and concealing the jade on his person, he made him hurry back to Chao by paths and byways.

When the king of Chin had fasted for five days, he prepared a grand reception for Chao's envoy.

Lin Hsiang-ju, arriving, announced to the king, "Since the time of Duke Mu of Chin, not one of the twenty-odd princes of your state has kept faith. Fearful of being deceived by

Your Majesty and letting my country down, I sent a man back with the jade. He should be in Chao by now. Chin is strong and Chao is weak. When you, great king, sent a single messenger to Chao, we immediately brought the jade here. If your mighty state had first given us fifteen cities, we should not have dared offend you by keeping the jade. I know I deserve death for deceiving you and beg to be boiled in the cauldron. Consider this well with your ministers, great king!"

The king and all his ministers gaped at each other. Some attendants prepared to drag Lin Hsiang-ju away, but the king said, "Killing him now will not get us the jade but would spoil our relations with Chao. Better treat him handsomely and send him back. The king of Chao dare not risk offending Chin for the sake of a piece of jade."

Thereupon he entertained Lin Hsiang-ju in his court, dismissing him when the ceremony was over.

The king of Chao was so pleased with the skill with which Lin Hsiang-ju had saved the state from disgrace that he made him a high councillor on his return. Neither did Chin give the cities to Chao, nor Chao give the jade to Chin.

After this, Chin attacked Chao and took Shihcheng.

The following year twenty thousand men of Chao were killed in another attack. Then the king of Chin sent an envoy to the king of Chao, proposing a friendly meeting at Minchih south of Hsiho. The king of Chao was loath to go, for fear of Chin. But Lien Po and Lin Hsiang-ju reasoned with him saying, "Not to go, sir, would make our country appear weak and cowardly."

So the king went, accompanied by Lin Hsiang-ju.

Lien Po saw them to the frontier, where he bade the king farewell saying, "I reckon that Your Majesty's journey there, the meeting and the journey back should not take more than thirty days. If you fail to return in that time, I suggest that we set up the crown prince as king, to thwart the designs of Chin."

The king, having agreed, went to meet the king of Chin at Minchih.

The king of Chin, merry after drinking, said, "I have heard that the king of Chao is a good musician. Will you play the cithern for me?"

The king of Chao did as he asked. Then the Chin chronicler stepped forward and recorded, "On such-and-such a day the king of Chin drank with the king of Chao and ordered the king of Chao to play the cithern."

Lin Hsiang-ju then advanced and said, "The king of Chao has heard that the king of Chin is a good hand at Chin music. Will you entertain us with a tune on the pitcher?"

The king of Chin angrily refused. But Lin Hsiang-ju went forward to present a pitcher and, kneeling down, requested him to play. Still the king refused.

"I am only five steps from you," cried Lin Hsiang-ju. "I can bespatter you, great king, with the blood from your throat!"

The attendants wanted to kill him, but he glared and shouted so fiercely that they shrank back. Then the king of Chin sullenly beat once on the pitcher, whereupon Lin Hsiang-ju turned to bid the Chao chronicler record, "On such-and-such a date, the king of Chin played the pitcher for the king of Chao."

Then the ministers of Chin said, "We hope Chao will present fifteen cities to the king of Chin."

Lin Hsiang-ju retorted, "We hope Chin will present Hsienyang* to the king of Chao!"

At this feast, then, the king of Chin was unable to get the better of Chao. Nor dared he make any move because of the strong guard brought by the king of Chao.

Upon their return to Chao after this meeting, Lin Hsiang-ju was appointed a chief minister for his outstanding service, taking precedence over Lien Po.

Lien Po protested, "As a general of Chao I have served the state well in the field and stormed many cities. All Lin Hsiang-ju can do is wag his tongue, yet now he is above me.

* The capital of Chin.

143

I'd think shame to work under such a base-born fellow." He swore, "When I meet Lin Hsiang-ju I shall humiliate him!"

When Lin Hsiang-ju got word of this, he kept out of Lien Po's way and absented himself from court on grounds of illness, not wanting to compete for precedence. Once when he caught sight of Lien Po in the distance on the road he drove his carriage another way.

His stewards reproached him saying, "We left our kinsmen to serve you because we admired your lofty character, sir. Now you have the same rank as Lien Po, but when he insults you in public you try to avoid him and look abjectly afraid. This would disgrace even a common citizen, let alone generals and ministers! We are afraid we must beg to resign."

Lin Hsiang-ju stopped them, asking, "Is General Lien Po as powerful in your eyes as the king of Chin?"

"Of course not," they replied.

"If, useless as I am, I lashed out at the mighty king of Chin in his court and insulted his ministers, why should I be afraid of General Lien Po? To my mind, however, were it not for the two of us, powerful Chin would not hesitate to invade Chao. When two tigers fight, one must perish. I behave as I do because I put our country's fate before private feuds."

When word of this reached Lien Po, he bared his shoulders, fastened a switch of thorns to his back and had a protégé conduct him to Lin Hsiang-ju's gate. He apologized, "Contemptible boor that I am, I could not understand your magnanimity, sir!"

They became close friends, ready to die for each other.

That year Lien Po attacked Chi in the east and defeated one of its armies. Two years later he took another city of Chi. Three years later he stormed Fangling and Anyang in Wei. Four years later Lin Hsiang-ju led an army against Chi, but withdrew after reaching Pingyi. The following year Lien Po defeated the army of Chin at Oyu.

Chao Sheh was a tax-collector in Chao. When Lord Pingyuan's family refused to pay the land tax, he punished them in accordance with the law, executing nine of their stewards. In his rage, Lord Pingyuan wanted to kill him.

Chao Sheh reasoned with him, "You are a noble of Chao yet you flout the law, allowing your family to evade taxation. When the law is flouted, the state will grow weak and other states will invade and destroy us; and when Chao is no more, what will become of your wealth? If you, a noble, pay taxes according to the law, society will be at peace, the state of Chao will be strong and secure and you, sir, as a member of the royal house, will not be despised by the world."

Impressed by Chao Sheh's worth, Lord Pingyuan recommended him to the king, who put him in charge of the state revenues, and he managed these so well that the people prospered and the treasury was full.

Then Chin invaded Han and stationed an army at Oyu. The king of Chao summoned Lien Po and asked, "Can we go to their aid?"

Lien Po replied, "The road is long and over very mountainous country. It would be hard."

The king consulted Yueh Sheng, who made the same answer. He then consulted Chao Sheh, who replied, "The way is far and lies through ravines. The combatants would be like two rats fighting in a hole — the braver would win."

Then the king ordered Chao Sheh to lead troops to rescue Han.

When the army was only thirty *li* from Hantan, Chao Sheh issued this order: "Criticism of the plan of campaign will be punished with death."

The men of Chin were stationed west of Wu-an. The roll of their drums when they drilled set the tiles on the roofs of Wu-an vibrating. A scout of the Chao army who urged that they should make haste to rescue the town was executed by Chao Sheh on the spot. Having fortified his camp, he stayed there without advancing for twenty-eight days, simply building more and more ramparts. When a Chin spy came to the camp, Chao Sheh gave him a good meal and sent him away. The spy reported this to his commander, who gloated, "Their army is only thirty *li* from their capital, yet already they have stopped to strengthen their defences. They will never recapture Oyu."

After Chao Sheh had dismissed the spy, he commanded his troops to advance in light marching order at full speed. In two days and one night he reached Oyu and stationed his best archers fifty *li* from the city. No sooner had they dug in than the men of Chin, hearing of their approach, came in full force.

An officer named Hsu Li asked permission to make a suggestion. When Chao Sheh had him brought to his tent, Hsu Li said, "The men of Chin never thought we would get so far. They are in a confident mood. You must mass your troops to resist their attack, or we shall be defeated."

Chao Sheh replied, "I shall take your advice."

"I beg to die by the axe," said Hsu Li.

"Wait until we get to Hantan," was the answer.

Hsu Li gave him some more advice, saying, "The first to take the North Hill will win. The late-comers will be defeated."

Again Chao Sheh agreed and sent ten thousand men to storm the hill. The troops of Chin, coming later, could not retake it. Then Chao Sheh launched an attack and inflicted a heavy defeat on the Chin army, which scattered and fled. Thereupon he raised the siege of Oyu and returned. King Hui-wen of Chao made him the lord of Mafu and promoted Hsu Li to be marshal. So now Chao Sheh ranked equal with Lien Po and Lin Hsiang-ju.

Four years later, King Hui-wen died and King Hsiao-cheng ascended the throne. In the seventh year of his reign, Chin fought Chao at Changping. As Chao Sheh was now dead and Lin Hsiang-ju mortally ill, Lien Po led the troops against Chin. After several defeats he strengthened his defences and refused to give battle. Though repeatedly challenged by Chin, he would not fight.

Then a spy from Chin told the king of Chao, "All Chin fears is that Chao Kuo, son of Chao Sheh, lord of Mafu, may be appointed commander." Because the king believed this, he made Chao Kuo take over Lien Po's command.

Lin Hsiang-ju protested, "If you are sending him because of his father's fame, that is like playing the cithern with fixed frets. All Chao Kuo can do is read his father's treatises: he has no idea how to apply or modify them." But the king did not listen to him and made Chao Kuo commander.

Chao Kuo had studied military science and discussed strategy since boyhood. He was confident that no one in the world was a match for him. Once he even worsted his father Chao Sheh in a discussion on strategy, yet he could not win Chao Sheh's approval. When Chao Kuo's mother asked him why, Chao Sheh said, "War is a matter of life and death, but he makes light of it. I can only hope he never becomes our state's commander. If he does, he will destroy our army."

So when Chao Kuo was about to set out with his troops, his mother wrote to beg the king not to send him. Asked for her reasons, she replied, "When I was first married to his father, who was then a commander, he offered food and wine to dozens of men at his meals and treated hundreds as his friends, distributing his gifts from Your Majesty and others of the royal house among his officers and friends. From the day he took the command he gave no further thought to family affairs. But as soon as Chao Kuo became a commander he put on such airs that none of his officers or men dare look him in the eye. When you give him gold and silk he takes it home, and he looks every day for cheap property to buy. How does he compare with his father, would you say? Since father and son are so different, I hope you will not send him."

"Leave it to me," said the king. "I have made the decision."

Then she asked, "If you must send him, will you spare me from punishment if he does badly?" The king agreed to this.

After Chao Kuo took over from Lien Po, he rescinded all previous orders and appointments. When General Pai Chi of Chin knew this, he made a surprise attack, feigned a retreat, cut Chao's supply route and split the army into two so

147

that both officers and men lost heart. When his army was starving some forty days later, Chao Kuo led picked troops out to fight and the men of Chin shot and killed him. Chao was defeated and hundreds of thousands of its men surrendered, only to be buried alive by Chin. In all, Chao lost four hundred and fifty thousand men.

The following year the Chin army besieged Hantan. For more than a year the capital was under siege and would have fallen if not for help sent from Chu and Wei, who managed to raise the siege. Because Chao Kuo's mother had warned him, the king of Chao did not have her executed.

Five years after the relief of Hantan, Yen attacked Chao on the advice of its minister Li Fu, who said, "All the able-bodied men of Chao were wiped out at Changping, and their orphans are not yet fully grown." But Lien Po as Chao's commander utterly routed the men of Yen at Hao, killed Li Fu and laid siege to the capital of Yen. To make peace, Yen offered five cities which were accepted. Then Chao gave Lien Po the district of Weiwen as his fief, making him Lord Hsinping and acting chief minister.

When, deprived of his command, Lien Po had returned home from Changping, all his protégés had left him because he was out of power. Upon his reappointment they came back, but he ordered them away.

"Ah, how lacking you are in understanding," they told him. "All friendship in this world follows the rules of the market. When you have power we follow you, when you lose power we leave you. This is only natural. Why should you complain?"

Six years later, Chao sent Lien Po against Fanyang in Wei and he captured it. After the death of King Hsiao-cheng of Chao, his son King Tao-hsiang came to the throne and made Yueh Sheng take over the army command. Lien Po in his anger attacked Yueh Sheng, who fled. Then Lien Po went to Taliang, the capital of Wei. The following year Chao appointed Li Mu commander against Yen, and he took Wusui and Fangcheng.

Lien Po remained many years in Wei but was never trusted

there or given a post. Because Chao was so hard pressed by Chin, the king wanted to have him back. Lien Po too was eager to serve his own country again. The king of Chao sent an envoy to see whether Lien Po could still command an army, but an enemy of his named Kuo Kai gave the envoy a large bribe to slander him. When the envoy came to see him, Lien Po ate a whole peck of rice and ten catties of meat, then buckled on his armour and mounted his horse to show that he was still fit for active service.

On his return, however, the messenger told the king, "Though old, General Lien Po still enjoys his food. But in the short time I was with him, he went out three times to relieve himself." Then the king decided he was too old to recall.

When the men of Chu heard that Lien Po was in Wei, they secretly invited him to their state. But as a general of Chu he had no success and sighed, "If only I had some men of Chao under me!" He finally died in Shouchun.

Li Mu was an able general on Chao's northern frontier, who remained in Yenmen in the land of Tai to guard against the Huns. He appointed officers as he saw fit and had all the market taxes sent to his headquarters to meet army expenses. He slaughtered several oxen daily for his troops, trained his men in mounted archery, kept the beacons in readiness, made full use of spies and treated his soldiers handsomely. He enjoined on his men, "When the Huns make a raid, withdraw quickly to the ramparts. Whoever dares engage the enemy will lose his head."

So whenever they were raided by the Huns, they lit the beacon fires and withdrew without fighting. This went on for several years, with no losses incurred. The Huns, of course, considered Li Mu a coward, while even his frontier troops thought him faint-hearted. But when the king of Chao reprimanded him, he carried on as before. Then the king angrily recalled Li Mu, sending someone else to take over the command.

For over a year the Chao troops gave battle every time the Huns raided, and were always defeated with heavy losses. The men of Chao could no longer farm or breed cattle on the frontier. But when asked to go back, Li Mu shut himself behind closed doors, pleading illness, till the king ordered him to get up and take command.

"Very well, if Your Majesty insists," he said. "But only if I can carry on as before."

The king agreed to this. And Li Mu on his return used his old tactics. For several years the Huns could get no advantage, yet still they thought him a coward. And the frontier troops, daily rewarded yet kept out of action, were spoiling for a fight. Then Li Mu chose thirteen hundred chariots, thirteen thousand horsemen, fifty thousand brave fighters, and a hundred thousand archers. Having trained them well, he let cattle and men wander all over the plain. When the Huns made a small raid, he pretended to be defeated and abandoned several thousand men to the enemy. The khan of the Huns, hearing this, attacked in full force. Then Li Mu, resorting to unconventional stratagems, deployed both wings of his army in attacks from right and left and routed and killed more than a hundred thousand of the Hun horsemen. He wiped out the tribes of Tanlan, defeated those of Tunghu, and subjugated those of Linhu. The khan fled and for ten years and more dared not approach the frontier again.

In the first year of King Tao-hsiang of Chao,* as Lien Po had fled to Wei, Li Mu was sent to attack Yen and he captured Wusui and Fangcheng. Two years later Pang Hsuan defeated the army of Yen, killing Chu Hsin. Seven years later Chin defeated Chao, killed its commander Hu Che at Wusui and wiped out a hundred thousand men. Then Li Mu was made commander-in-chief to attack the Chin army at Yi-an, where he routed the men of Chin and forced General Huan Yi to flee. For this he was enfeoffed as lord of Wu-an. Three years later Chin attacked Panwu, but Li Mu defeated its army and resisted Hann and Wei in the south.

In the seventh year of King Chien of Chao, Chin sent Wang

_____

* 244 B.C.

Chien to attack Chao, and Li Mu and Szuma Shang were ordered to resist him. Chin bribed the king's favourite, Kuo Kai, to act as its agent and slander both these generals by accusing them of plotting treason. Then the king of Chao sent Chao Tsung and Yen Chu, a general from Chi, to take over Li Mu's command. When Li Mu refused to give it up, the king sent men to take him by surprise and kill him, while Szuma Shang was also dismissed. Three months later Wang Chien routed the men of Chao with a surprise attack, killing Chao Tsung and capturing King Chien and General Yen Chu. The state of Chao was thus extinguished.

The Grand Historian comments: A man who knows he must die acts courageously, for it is not hard to die, only hard to face death. When Lin Hsiang-ju prepared to smash the jade on the pillar and lashed out at the attendants of the king of Chin, the worst that could befall him was death. Other men, of course, might have been paralysed with fear, but he summoned up courage to strike awe into the enemy. When later he gave way to Lien Po, he won a name for himself as great as Mount Tai. Truly he was a paragon of resourcefulness and courage combined!

LU PU-WEI

Lu Pu-wei was a great merchant of Yangti. He travelled about buying cheap and selling dear till he had amassed thousands of catties of gold.

In the fortieth year of King Chao of Chin* the crown prince died. In his forty-second year, the king's second son Lord Ankuo was made crown prince.

Lord Ankuo had more than twenty sons. But his favourite concubine Lady Huayang, whom he made his chief wife, was childless.

Tzu-chu, Lord Ankuo's son by a secondary wife Lady Hsia, who was not a favourite, was sent as a hostage to Chao. Because Chin had attacked Chao many times, Tzu-chu was treated there with scant ceremony. As the son of a concubine sent as a hostage to another state, he was not well off for equipage and funds but had a poor time of it under hard conditions.

Lu Pu-wei, in Hantan on business, saw the prince and pitied him. "This rare merchandise would be a sound investment," he said.

He called on Tzu-chu and told him, "I can put you up in the world."

With a laugh Tzu-chu retorted, "Put yourself up first, sir!"

"You do not understand," replied Lu Pu-wei. "I depend on you for that."

Then Tzu-chu caught his meaning, made him take a seat and had a frank talk with him.

"The king of Chin is old and Lord Ankuo is crown prince," said Lu Pu-wei. "I hear that Lord Ankuo loves Lady

---

* 267 B.C.

Huayang, who is childless, and that she alone can appoint a successor to him. You have more than twenty brothers, are neither the senior nor the most favoured among them, and have long been a hostage in another state. When the king dies and Lord Ankuo ascends the throne, what chance have you of becoming crown prince compared with your eldest brother and the others who are before him day and night?"

"True. But what can I do?" asked Tzu-chu.

"You are poor and a stranger here," replied Lu Pu-wei, "without the means to present gifts to your relatives or to win protégés. Although I am poor myself, let me travel west for you with a thousand pieces of gold to persuade Lord Ankuo and Lady Huayang to make you their heir."

Tzu-chu bowed at that and said, "If your plan succeeds, sir, you must let me divide Chin and share the state with you."

Then Lu Pu-wei gave Tzu-chu five hundred pieces of gold as spending money to win protégés, and laid out another five hundred on rare objects and trinkets for gifts. He travelled west to Chin, obtained an interview with Lady Huayang's elder sister and presented all his gifts to Lady Huayang. He spoke of Tzu-chu's worth and wisdom, the friends he had in all the different states, and how often he said, "I look on Lady Huayang as Providence. Day and night I shed tears thinking of the crown prince and her ladyship." The lady was highly delighted.

And so Lu Pu-wei induced Lady Huayang's sister to advise her, "I have heard that favour won by beauty will cease once beauty fades. Now you serve the crown prince, who loves you dearly although you are childless. If you attach yourself in good time to one of his sons who is able and filial, making him the heir and adopting him as your son, as long as your husband lives you will be respected, and after his death when your adopted son becomes king you will not lose your power. This is what is known as 'lasting gain resulting from one single word.' While you are still blooming you must provide for the future, for once your beauty has faded and his love has died it will be too late to speak. Now Tzu-chu is a worthy youth, but he knows that as a concubine's son he has no claim to the succession; and since his mother is not a favourite he has attached himself to you. If you really have him appointed as successor now, you will be favoured in Chin so long as you live."

Lady Huayang approved and, when the crown prince was at leisure, told him blandly that Tzu-chu, now a hostage in Chao, was a most worthy youth praised by all who had travelled that way. Then with tears she said, "I am lucky to be one of your concubines, but unlucky to have no son. Will you make Tzu-chu your heir, so that I may have someone to rely on?"

Lord Ankuo agreed and gave her an engraved jade tally as a pledge that Tzu-chu should succeed him. Then Lord Ankuo and Lady Huayang sent rich presents to Tzu-chu and asked Lu Pu-wei to be his tutor. After this, Tzu-chu's fame spread through the different states.

Lu Pu-wei had taken as his mistress the best dancer and prettiest courtesan in Hantan, and now she was with child. Tzu-chu saw her one day when he was with Lu Pu-wei, and took a fancy to her. Rising to offer a toast, he asked if he might have her. Lu Pu-wei was very angry, but reflecting that he had nearly beggared his family for Tzu-chu in the hope of fabulous returns, he gave him the girl, who concealed the fact that she was pregnant. When her time came she gave birth to a son, Cheng. Then Tzu-chu made her his wife.

In the fiftieth year of King Chao of Chin, Wang Yi was sent to lay fierce siege to Hantan and the men of Chao wanted to kill Tzu-chu. But he consulted Lu Pu-wei and contrived to escape by bribing his guard with six hundred pieces of gold. He fled to the Chin army, then returned home. The men of Chao wanted to kill his wife, but since she came of a wealthy Chao family she succeeded in hiding herself. In this way both mother and child escaped with their lives.

In the fifty-sixth year of his reign, King Chao of Chin died.

Lord Ankuo became king with Lady Huayang as his queen and Tzu-chu as crown prince. Chao sent Tzu-chu's wife and son Cheng back to Chin.

After a reign of one year the king of Chin died and was posthumously entitled King Hsiao-wen. The crown prince, Tzu-chu, succeeded him as King Chuang-hsiang. His foster-mother, Queen Huayang, became Queen-Dowager Huayang, while his own mother Lady Hsia was honoured with the title Queen-Dowager Hsia.

In the first year of his reign, King Chuang-hsiang appointed Lu Pu-wei his assistant chancellor. He was enfeoffed as marquis of Wenhsin and given the revenues of a hundred thousand households in Honan and Loyang.

After a reign of three years King Chuang-hsiang died and the crown prince, Cheng, became king. He honoured Lu Pu-wei by appointing him chancellor with the title of 'Second Father'. The king was still young and the queen-dowager maintained illicit relations with Lu Pu-wei.

Lu Pu-wei had as many as ten thousand household slaves. At this time Lord Hsinling in Wei, Lord Chunshen in Chu, Lord Pingyuan in Chao and Lord Mengchang in Chi were all great patrons who vied in keeping protégés. Thinking it would be shameful not to equal them when Chin was so powerful, Lu Pu-wei also invited guests and treated them handsomely, until he had three thousand protégés.

In the different states at this time there were many orators. Men like Hsun Kuang wrote books which spread through the world. Lu Pu-wei also made his guests record all their knowledge, compiling more than two hundred thousand words divided into Eight Observations, Six Discussions and Twelve Records. Believing that this work dealt with everything in heaven and earth, comprising all ancient and all modern knowledge, he entitled it *The Annals of Master Lu*. It was displayed at the gate of Hsienyang market, with a thousand pieces of gold hung above it. Itinerant scholars and protégés from other states were invited to read it, and the gold was offered to anyone who could add or subtract a single word.

As the First Emperor grew older, the queen-dowager remained as wanton as ever. Lu Pu-wei, fearing disaster if they were discovered, secretly found a man named Lao Ai with a large penis and made him his retainer. Some times for amusement he made Lao Ai walk round with a *tung*-wood wheel on his penis, seeing to it that the queen-dowager heard of this, in order to inflame her. And sure enough, when word of this reached her ears, she secretly sought for Lao Ai. Lu Pu-wei presented him to her and had someone accuse him of a crime deserving castration.

Then Lu Pu-wei told the queen-dowager in private, "If we make a pretence of having him castrated, you can get him to serve in the palace."

So she surreptitiously bribed the officer in charge of castration to make a false report and pluck Lao Ai's beard and eyebrows to make him look like a eunuch. Then he entered the service of the queen-dowager, who had secret intercourse with him and doted on him. Later she became pregnant and, fearing discovery, gave out that an oracle had told her to retire for a season. She moved from the palace to Yung, where Lao Ai was in constant attendance upon her. She showered him with rich gifts and he it was who decided her affairs. Lao Ai had several thousand household slaves, while more than a thousand would-be officials became his retainers.

In the seventh year of the First Emperor,* King Chuang-hsiang's mother, Queen-Dowager Hsia, died. The consort of King Hsiao-wen, who was also known as Queen-Dowager Huayang, had been buried with him at Shouling. Since King Chuang-hsiang the son of Queen-Dowager Hsia was buried at Chihyang, she chose to be interred separately east of Tuyuan. "I shall see my son on my east, my husband on my west," she said. "One hundred years from now there will be a city of ten thousand households beside me."

In the ninth year of the First Emperor, the king was informed that Lao Ai was not a real eunuch, that he had illicit relations

_____

* 240 B.C.

with the queen-dowager, that she had two sons by him both of whom had been concealed, and that he had plotted with her saying, "Once the king dies, our sons will succeed him."

The king of Chin ordered an investigation, and when the truth came out the chancellor Lu Pu-wei was implicated. In the ninth month Lao Ai was executed and all his kinsmen wiped out. The queen-dowager's two sons were also executed and she was removed to Yung. All Lao Ai's followers had their property confiscated and were exiled to Shu.

The king wanted to put Lu Pu-wei to death, but spared him on account of his services to the last king and because his many orators and protégés, who travelled about as sophists, spoke up for him.

In the tenth month of the tenth year, the king of Chin dismissed Lu Pu-wei from his post as chancellor. Mao Chiao of Chi persuaded the king to welcome the queen-dowager back to Hsienyang from Yung, and Lu Pu-wei was sent to his fief south of the Yellow River.

A year and more later the highways were so thronged with envoys and visitors from various states on their way to see the marquis of Wenhsin, that the emperor feared a revolt. He wrote to him, "What have you done for Chin, sir, to deserve a fief of a hundred thousand households south of the river? What relation are you to Chin that you should be entitled 'Second Father'? Go with your family and followers to Shu!"

Realizing that disobedience would mean execution, Lu Pu-wei drank poison and died. Once Lu Pu-wei and Lao Ai who had incurred the king of Chin's wrath were dead, Lao Ai's former followers were recalled from Shu.

In the nineteenth year of the First Emperor, the queen-dowager died. She was posthumously entitled the empress-dowager and buried with King Chuang-hsiang at Chihyang.

The Grand Historian comments: Lu Pu-wei and Lao Ai were ennobled and the former enfeoffed as marquis of Wenhsin. Lao Ai heard of his impeachment while the king was still investigating witnesses and had not yet taken action. When the king went to the suburb of Yung, Lao Ai, fearing disaster, plotted with his men to forge the queen-dowager's seal and send troops to take Chinien Palace. Officers were dispatched to attack him and he fled in defeat. He was overtaken and beheaded at Haochih, after which his clan was wiped out. From this followed Lu Pu-wei's downfall. Lu Pu-wei was surely the sort of man whom Confucius described as one whose good reputation was belied by his conduct.

THE FIRST EMPEROR OF CHIN

Shih Huang Ti was the son of King Chuang-hsiang of Chin, who while a hostage in Chao fancied one of Lu Pu-wei's concubines and took her. She gave birth to the First Emperor in Hantan in the first month of the forty-eighth year of King Chao of Chin.* At his birth he received the name Cheng, with Chao as his surname.

When he was thirteen his father died and he succeeded to the throne of Chin. By now Chin had annexed Pa, Shu and Hanchung, pushed beyond Wanchiu, taken Yingtu and set up the province of Nanchun. In the north it included the territory east of Shangchun, with the provinces of Hotung, Taiyuan and Shangtang. Eastward it had reached Yingyang, conquered Eastern and Western Chou and set up the province of Sanchuan.

Lu Pu-wei, the prime minister, had a fief of a hundred thousand families and the title marquis of Wenhsin. He mustered protégés and wandering scholars in the hope of conquering the whole of the land. Li Szu was the imperial steward. Meng Ao, Wang Yi and Lord Piao commanded the army. As the king was still young and newly come to the throne, the rule devolved upon the chief ministers.

In the first year of his reign, General Meng Ao quelled the revolt in Tsinyang.

In the second year, Lord Piao led troops against Chuan and killed thirty thousand men.

In the third year, Meng Ao attacked Hann and captured thirteen cities. General Wang Yi died. In the tenth month

---

* 259 B.C.

General Meng Ao attacked Chang and Yukuei in Wei. This was a year of great famine.

In the third month of the fourth year, after the conquest of Chang and Yukuei, the army was recalled. The prince of Chin held as a hostage in Chao came back, and the crown prince of Chao returned to his own country. In the tenth month, a swarm of locusts from the east darkened the sky and plague stalked the land. For a thousand piculs of grain, commoners could purchase a noble rank.

In the fifth year, General Meng Ao stormed twenty cities of Wei, among them Suantsao, Yen, Hsu, Changping, Yungchiu and Shanyang. The province of Tungchun was established. There was thunder that winter.

In the sixth year, Hann, Wei, Chao, Uei and Chu launched a joint attack against Chin and took Shouling; but when Chin sent out troops the five states withdrew their armies. With Uei conquered, the forces of Chin advanced on Tungchun. Chiao, prince of Uei, led his followers to Yehwang to hold the mountains and keep the territory north of the Yellow River.

In the seventh year a comet appeared, first in the east, then in the north. In the fifth month it appeared again in the west. General Meng Ao died. The forces of Chin attacked Lung, Ku and Chingtu, then turned against Ji. The comet reappeared in the west for sixteen days. The queen-dowager Hsia died.

In the eighth year the king's younger brother, Cheng-chiao, lord of Changan, led troops against Chao. He rebelled but died at Tunliu. All his officers were executed and his people were transferred to Lintao. The commander committed suicide. The corpses of all the soldiers who had mutinied were mutilated. There was a great flood, and to get food men rode east on horseback or in fast carriages.

Lao Ai, enfeoffed marquis of Changhsin, was ordered to live in the region of Shanyang. Lao Ai had his own palace, equipage, livery, forest and hunting ground. All affairs of state, great and small, were in his hands. The province of Taiyuan west of the Yellow River was also his fief.

In the ninth year a comet was seen to cross the whole sky. Chin attacked Weiyuan and Puyang. In the fourth month the king took up residence at Yung. He came of age, was capped and girded on a sword.

The plot of Lao Ai, marquis of Changhsin, was discovered. He used the royal seal and queen-dowager's seal to call out the royal troops, guards, government cavalry, foreign chiefs and his retainers, meaning to start a revolt by attacking Chinien Palace. The king, learning of this, ordered the state councillor, the lord of Changping, and the lord of Changwen to raise troops to subdue Lao Ai. At the Battle of Hsienyang several hundred rebels were killed. All the king's men were promoted, the eunuchs who had taken part in the action being promoted one rank. Lao Ai and his defeated forces fled. A reward of a million cash was offered throughout the land for his capture alive, half a million for his dead body. Lao Ai and his men were all caught. Some twenty of his followers, including Chieh the captain of the palace guard, Szu the metropolitan prefect, Chieh the assistant archery officer, and Chi the chief palace steward, were dismembered and their heads hung high as a warning to others. Punishment was meted out even to his retainers, minor offenders being punished with conscript labour or deprivation of rank. More than four thousand families were removed to Fanling in Shu.

The fourth month was bitterly cold and men froze to death. Yang Tuan-ho attacked Yenshih. A comet appeared in the west, then in the north, remaining for eighty days south of the Dipper.

In the tenth year, the chancellor Lu Pu-wei was dismissed on account of Lao Ai. Huan Yi was made a general. Envoys sent by Chi and Chao were feasted.

Mao Chiao of Chi advised the king: "Now Chin is out for world conquest, yet you are reported to have sent away the queen-dowager, your mother. I fear that when other states know this, they will oppose you." Then the king went to Yung to invite the queen-dowager back, escorting her to Hsienyang to take up her quarters again in Kanchuan Palace.

A great search was made for wandering politicians and an order issued for their expulsion, but on Li Szu's advice this order was rescinded.

Li Szu urged the king to conquer Hann in order to intimidate the other states, and he was sent to demand Hann's surrender. The prince of Hann in his anxiety consulted Han Fei on means to weaken Chin.

Wei Liao of Taliang came to advise the king saying, "Now Chin is so strong that the other states are like your subject provinces and counties. But what if they ally together and launch a sudden attack? This is how Lord Chih, King Fu-cha and King Min of Chi perished. I hope you will upset their scheme by begrudging no expenditure to bribe their powerful ministers. For then three hundred thousand pieces of gold will enable you to conquer all the states."

The king followed this plan. And thereafter he treated Wei Liao as an equal, sharing clothes, food and drink with him. But Wei Liao said, "The king of Chin has a waspish nose, eyes like slits, a chicken breast and a voice like a jackal. He is merciless, with the heart of a tiger or wolf. When in difficulties he willingly humbles himself, when successful he swallows men up without a scruple. I am a plain citizen in homespun clothes, yet he treats me as if I were his superior. Should he succeed in conquering the empire, we shall all become his captives. There is no staying long with such a man." He prepared to leave but the king forced him to stay, made him commander of the Chin army and adopted his plans. Then Li Szu came to power.

In the eleventh year Wang Chien, Huan Yi and Yang Tuanho attacked Yeh and took nine cities. Wang Chien also attacked Oyu and Laoyang. Then these forces were combined into one army which Wang Chien commanded for eighteen days. Upon the army's return, only two out of every ten sergeants were allowed to remain. Yeh and Anyang were conquered and Huan Yi was made commander.

In the twelfth year Lu Pu-wei, marquis of Wenhsin, died and was buried in secret. Those of his followers from Tsin who attended his funeral were expelled, those of Chin above the six hundred piculs rank were degraded and moved elsewhere. Those who did not attend the funeral and were below the five hundred piculs rank were moved to another district but not deprived of their rank. It was decreed that in future high ministers who committed crimes comparable to those of Lao Ai and Lu Pu-wei should have their families enslaved and their property confiscated. That autumn the followers of Lao Ai who had been banished to Shu were recalled. For six months there was a great drought. Rain fell only in the eighth month.

In the thirteenth year Huan Yi attacked Pingyang in Chao, killing General Hu Che and slaughtering a hundred thousand men. The king went to the land south of the river. In the first month a comet appeared in the east. In the tenth month Huan Yi attacked Chao.

In the fourteenth year Huan Yi fought the men of Chao at Pingyang and took Yi-an by storm, killing its commander. Then he conquered Pingyang and Wucheng. Han Fei went as an envoy to Chin and the king, on Li Szu's advice, kept him. He died later in Yuyang. The king of Hann asked to become a vassal of Chin.

In the fifteenth year a great force was mobilized. One army advanced to Yeh, another to Taiyuan, taking Langmeng. There was an earthquake.

In the ninth month of the sixteenth year, troops were sent to take over Nanyang from Hann, and Teng was appointed provisional governor. A general census was taken. Wei presented Chin with some territory which became the district of Liyi.

In the seventeenth year the city prefect Teng attacked Hann and captured King An, annexing all his territory which was made into the province of Yingchuan. There was an earthquake. The queen-dowager Huayang died. There was a great famine.

In the eighteenth year a great army was mobilized against Chao. Wang Chien led the troops in Shangti to take Chinghsing, Yang Tuan-ho led the troops north of the Yellow River, and Chiang Hui also launched an attack on Chao. Yang Tuan-ho laid siege to Hantan.

In the nineteenth year Wang Chien and Chiang Hui defeated Chao, taking the district of Tungyang and capturing the king of Chao. Next, in preparation for an attack on Yen, they stationed their troops at Chungshan. The king of Chin went to Hantan and buried alive all the enemies of his mother's family at the time of his birth, after which he returned by way of Taiyuan and Shangchun. The king's own mother, the queen-dowager, died. A noble of Chao named Chia took several hundred men of his clan to Tai and made himself king there, then joined forces with Yen in the east and encamped at Shangku. There was a great famine.

In the twentieth year Crown Prince Tan of Yen, fearing an invasion from Chin, sent Ching Ko to assassinate the king of Chin. When this was discovered, the king dismembered Ching Ko as a warning to others, then sent Wang Chien and Hsin Shen to attack Yen. Yen and Tai dispatched their armies to engage Chin, but were defeated west of the River Yi.

In the twenty-first year Wang Pen attacked Chi and Wang Chien's army was reinforced. Then they defeated the troops of Crown Prince Tan, captured the city of Chi and obtained Tan's head. The king of Yen annexed Liaotung in the east and ruled over it. Wang Chien asked leave to retire on the grounds of ill health. A revolt broke out in Hsincheng. The lord of Changping moved his capital to Ying. There was a great snowfall, twenty-five inches deep.

In the twenty-second year, Wang Pen attacked Wei and diverted the river to flood the city of Taliang. The city wall crumbled, the king of Wei surrendered, and all his land was annexed.

In the twenty-third year, the king of Chin recalled Wang Chien and forced him to take command, sending him against Chu. All the land south of Chen was conquered as far as Pingyu and the king of Chu was captured. The king of Chin

164

visited Ying and Chen. Hsiang Yen, a general of Chu, set up the lord of Changping as king of Chu and revolted against Chin south of the River Huai.

In the twenty-fourth year, Wang Chien and Meng Wu attacked Chu and defeated its army. The lord of Changping was killed and Hsiang Yen took his own life.

In the twenty-fifth year a great force was mobilized. Wang Pen, ordered to take command, attacked King Hsi of Yen at Liaotung and captured him, then turned to attack Tai and captured its king, Chia. Wang Chien conquered the territory of Chu south of the Yangtse, forced the prince of Yueh to surrender and set up the province of Kuaichi. In the fifth month there were celebrations and feasting throughout the land.

In the twenty-sixth year, King Chien of Chi and his prime minister Hou Sheng dispatched troops to defend the western frontier and cut communications with Chin. The king of Chin sent General Wang Pen south from Yen to attack Chi and captured Chien, king of Chi. So now Chin was in control of the whole land.

The king told his prime minister and chief counsellor, "Formerly the king of Hann offered us his territory and royal seal, begging to become our subject; but when he broke faith to ally with Chao and Wei against us, we raised a punitive force and captured him. I consider this well done, for it led to the cessation of hostilities.

"When the king of Chao sent his minister Li Mu to pledge friendship with us, we returned the prince of theirs we held hostage; but after they broke faith and revolted at Taiyuan we raised a punitive force and captured the king. When Chia, a noble of Chao, made himself king of Tai, we raised troops to destroy him. The king of Wei promised to surrender, but when he plotted with Hann and Chao to launch a surprise attack, our officers and men punished him and defeated him. The king of Chu, after presenting us with the land west of Chingyang, broke faith and attacked Nanchun; so we sent troops against him and captured him, conquering his land. The king of Yen was a muddle-headed fool and let the crown prince Tan send Ching Ko out to assassinate us; so our officers and men punished them and destroyed their state. The king of Chi took Hou Sheng's advice and severed relations with Chin; so our army punished and captured him, conquering his land.

"Insignificant as I am, I have raised troops to punish the rebellious princes; and thanks to the sacred power of our ancestors all six kings have been chastised as they deserved, so that at last the empire is pacified. Now unless we create a new title, how can we record our achievements for posterity? Pray discuss the question of an imperial title."

The prime minister Wang Kuan, the chief counsellor Feng Chieh and the chief justice Li Szu returned this reply: "In the past the Five Emperors ruled over a thousand square *li* of territory, beyond which were the barons and barbarians. The barons were free to pay homage or not as they pleased, for the emperor had no control over them. Now Your Majesty has raised an army of justice to punish tyrants, subjugating the whole empire so that all lands within the seas have become our provinces and counties and all the law-codes have been unified. This is something never before achieved, which not even the Five Emperors could match. We have consulted learned men and, as in ancient times there were the Heavenly Sovereign, Earthly Sovereign and Supreme Sovereign, of whom the last named was paramount, we presume to suggest the exalted title *Tai-huang* or Supreme Sovereign. Your Majesty's commands should be known as 'edicts', your orders as 'decrees', and you should refer to yourself as 'our royal self'."

The king replied, " 'Supreme' may be omitted and 'Sovereign' adopted with the title of 'Emperor' used since ancient times. Let my appellation be *Huang-ti*, Sovereign Emperor. I approve your other proposals." An edict was issued and King Chuang-hsiang was retitled the Exalted Sovereign.

The edict read: "We have heard that in remote antiquity kings had titles but no posthumous appellations. The kings of later days not only had titles but after their death were given appellations based on their conduct. In other words, sons passed judgement on their fathers, subjects on their sovereigns. This is improper and we will not countenance it. Posthumous titles are herewith abolished. We are Shih-huang-ti, First Sovereign Emperor, and our successors shall be known as the Second Emperor, Third Emperor and so on for generations without end."

According to the theory of the Cycle of Five Powers, the emperor decided that as successor to the Chou Dynasty, which was under the Power of Fire, Chin must have the Power to vanquish Fire. So began the era of the Power of Water. The start of the year was changed to the first day of the tenth month, when the court celebration was held. Black became the paramount colour for garments, flags and pennants, and six the paramount number. Tallies and official hats were six inches long, carriages six feet wide, one 'pace' was six feet, and the imperial carriage had six horses. The Yellow River was renamed the River of Power. It was held that to inaugurate the Power of Water there must be firm repression with everything determined by law. Only ruthless, implacable severity could make the Five Powers accord. So the law was harsh and for long there were no amnesties.

The prime minister Wang Wan and some others said, "The states are newly conquered and unless we set up princes in such remote regions as Yen, Chi and Chu, how are we to control them? We beg your permission to make your sons princes there."

The First Emperor laid this proposal before his ministers. All approved except the chief justice Li Szu, who said, "King Wen and King Wu of Chou gave fiefs to their sons, younger brothers and many other members of their clan, but later their descendants fell out and finally set on each other. And when the states fought together, the king of Chou was powerless to stop them. Now thanks to Your Majesty's divine might, all lands within the Four Seas have become your provinces and counties. If you give the princes and men who have served you well public revenues and rich rewards, they will be easy to control and there will be no dissension throughout the land. This is the way to secure peace, not by setting up princes."

The emperor said, "The world has had no respite from warfare because of the states. Now thanks to the divine might of our ancestors, we have pacified all under heaven. Setting up new states would mean establishing armies, and peace and quiet would be hard to secure. The chief justice is right."

So the empire was divided into thirty-six provinces, each with a governor, an army commander and an inspector. The common people were renamed the Black-Headed People. There were great celebrations. All the weapons were collected and brought to the capital Hsienyang, where they were melted down to make bronze bells and twelve bronze statues of giants, each weighing two hundred and forty thousand catties, and these were placed in the courts and palaces. All weights and measures were standardized, all carriages had gauges of the same size. The script was also standardized.

The empire extended in the east to the ocean and the land of Chaohsien, in the west to Lintao and Chiangchung, in the south to Peihsianghu, in the north to the fortresses by the Yellow River and along Mount Yinshan to Liaotung. One hundred and twenty thousand wealthy families were brought from all over the empire to Hsienyang. The imperial ancestral temples, Changtai Palace and the Shanglin Gardens were constructed on the south bank of the River Wei. Each time Chin had conquered a state, a replica of its palace was rebuilt on the hills north of the capital overlooking the River Wei in the south; while eastward from Yungmen to the Ching and Wei Rivers, in a series of courts, walled-in avenues and pavilions, were kept the beautiful women and musical instruments captured from different states.

In the twenty-seventh year the emperor inspected Lunghsi and Peiti, crossed Mount Chitou and passed Huichung. The Hsin Palace was built on the south bank of the River Wei and the emperor decreed that it be the Paramount Temple, representing the apex of heaven. From the Paramount Temple a path led to Mount Li where a front hall of the Kanchuan

Palace was built, and the temple was connected with Hsienyang by a walled road. This year officers were promoted one rank. Post-roads were constructed.

In the twenty-eighth year the First Emperor travelled east through his provinces and counties, ascended Mount Tsouyi and erected a stone monument. After some discussion with the scholars of Lu, he had a stone inscription made to celebrate the virtue of the Chin Empire. They also discussed the imperial sacrifice to Heaven and Earth and the sacrifices to mountains and rivers. Then the emperor ascended Mount Tai, erected a stone monument and offered sacrifice to Heaven. On his way down he was caught in a storm and sheltered under a tree, which was given the title of Minister of the Fifth Rank. The sacrifice to the Earth was offered at Mount Liangfu. And a stone monument was erected with this inscription:

The Sovereign Emperor came to the throne, made decrees and laws which all his subjects heeded;
In his twenty-sixth year the land was unified, all obeyed his rule;
He inspected the black-headed people in distant parts, ascended Mount Tai and viewed the eastern extremity;
His obedient subjects remember his achievements, trace them from the start and celebrate his virtue.
Beneath his wide sway all things find their place, all is decreed by law;
Great and manifest, his virtue is handed down to ages yet to come, to be followed without change.
The sage emperor who has pacified all under heaven is tireless in his rule;
He rises early, goes to sleep late, makes lasting benefits and offers wise instructions;
Wide spread his teachings, all far and near is well ordered according to his will;
High and low are set apart, men and women observe the proprieties, fulfil their different tasks;

> Public and private affairs are clearly distinguished; peace
> reigns and will endure till a future age;
> His influence knows no end, his will is obeyed and his
> orders will remain through eternity.

The emperor proceeded east from Pohai past Huang and Chui to the tip of Mount Cheng, then climbed Mount Chihfu to erect a stone monument extolling the virtue of Chin. From there he went south to ascend Mount Langya and was so struck by the place that he stayed there for three months. He moved thirty thousand families of the black-headed people to the foot of this mountain, exempting them from taxation and conscription for twelve years. The emperor had a tower built on Mount Langya and a stone inscription set up to praise the power of Chin and make clear his will. The inscription read:

> In the twenty-eighth year of his reign
> A new age is inaugurated by the Emperor;
> Rules and measures are rectified,
> The myriad things set in order,
> Human affairs are made clear
> And there is harmony between fathers and sons.
> The Emperor in his sagacity, benevolence and justice
> Has made all laws and principles manifest.
> He set forth to pacify the east,
> To inspect officers and men;
> This great task accomplished
> He visited the coast.
> Great are the Emperor's achievements,
> Men attend diligently to basic tasks,
> Farming is encouraged, secondary pursuits discouraged,
> All the common people prosper;
> All men under the sky
> Toil with a single purpose;
> Tools and measures are made uniform,
> The written script is standardized;
> Wherever the sun and moon shine.
> Wherever one can go by boat or by carriage,

Men carry out their orders
And satisfy their desires;
For our Emperor in accordance with the time
Has regulated local customs,
Made waterways and divided up the land.
Caring for the common people,
He works day and night without rest;
He defines the laws, leaving nothing in doubt,
Making known what is forbidden.
The local officials have their duties,
Administration is smoothly carried out,
All is done correctly, all according to plan.
The Emperor in his wisdom
Inspects all four quarters of his realm;
High and low, noble and humble,
None dare overshoot the mark;
No evil or impropriety is allowed,
All strive to be good men and true,
And exert themselves in tasks great and small;
None dares to idle or ignore his duties,
But in far-off, remote places
Serious and decorous administrators
Work steadily, just and loyal.
Great is the virtue of our Emperor
Who pacifies all four corners of the earth,
Who punishes traitors, roots out evil men,
And with profitable measures brings prosperity.
Tasks are done at the proper season,
All things flourish and grow;
The common people know peace
And have laid aside weapons and armour;
Kinsmen care for each other,
There are no robbers or thieves;
Men delight in his rule,
All understanding the law and discipline.
The universe entire
Is our Emperor's realm,

Extending west to the Desert,
South to where the houses face north,
East to the East Ocean,
North to beyond Tahsia;
Wherever human life is found,
All acknowledge his suzerainty,
His achievements surpass those of the Five Emperors,
His kindness reaches even the beasts of the field;
All creatures benefit from his virtue,
All live in peace at home.

Since conquering all under heaven, the king of Chin has assumed the title of Sovereign Emperor and made a tour of inspection of his eastern territory, coming to Langya. In his escort are the enfeoffed nobles Wang Li marquis of Wucheng and Wang Pen marquis of Tungwu, the nobles without fief Chao Hai marquis of Chiencheng, Cheng marquis of Changwu and Feng Wu-chai marquis of Wuhsin, as well as the prime ministers Wei Lin and Wang Wan, the ministers Li Szu and Wang Mu, the ministers of the fifth rank Chao Ying and Yang Chiu. These took counsel together at the coast and said, "The territory of the ancient overlords never exceeded a thousand square *li* and the local rulers had their own states; some paid homage to the central power, but not so others. They never ceased from violence and war among themselves, yet had their deeds recorded on stone and bronze. The Five Emperors and Three Kings of old pursued different policies and had no clear legal system. They posed as divine to deceive subjects far away, but their deeds did not measure up to their fame and so their rule could not endure. Even before their death their barons rebelled and their orders were not obeyed.

"Now our Sovereign Emperor has united all the land within the Four Seas as his provinces and counties. All under heaven is at peace, to the glory of the imperial ancestral temple. The emperor carries out the True Way and practises virtue, living up to his exalted title. So we, his subjects, praise his virtuous deeds and have inscribed them on bronze and stone as examples and models for all."

After this inscription was made, Hsu Fu of Chi and others presented a memorial saying, "In the ocean are three fairy islands called Penglai, Fangchang and Yingchou, where immortals live. We beg to be sent in search of these with some young boys and girls after fasting and purification." Accordingly the emperor sent Hsu Fu with several thousand boys and girls out to sea to find the immortals.

The emperor broke his return journey at Pengcheng where he fasted, purified himself and sacrificed at the shrine, in the hope of recovering the bronze tripod of Chou from the River Szu. A thousand divers searched for it, but in vain. The emperor continued southwest, crossed the River Huai and proceeded to the Heng Mountains and the province of Nanchun. He then sailed down the Yangtse to the Temple of Mount Hsiang, but a great gale sprang up and the ship had difficulty in crossing the river.

The emperor asked his learned men, "Who is the goddess called the Princess of the River Hsiang?"

"They say she was Emperor Yao's daughter and the wife of Emperor Shun," they replied. "She is buried here."

Then the emperor in his rage made three thousand convicts cut down all the trees on Mount Hsiang, leaving the mountain bare, after which he returned from Nanchun to the capital by way of the Wu Pass.

In the twenty-ninth year the emperor, travelling east to Polangsha in the county of Yangwu, was threatened by an assassin. A search was made for the man but he could not be found. Thereupon a ten days' search was ordered throughout the empire. The emperor ascended Mount Chihfu and had the following inscription carved on stone:

In the twenty-ninth year in mid-spring, the start of the sunny season,

The Emperor made a tour of inspection in the east, ascended Mount Chihfu and reached the ocean;

His subjects, following in his train, think of his illustrious virtue and recall the beginning;

Under the Great Sage's rule, laws were set down, principles made manifest;

He taught other states, shed the light of his kindness abroad to illumine the right;

The six states, insatiable and perverse, would not make an end of slaughter,

Till, pitying the people, the Emperor sent troops to punish the wicked and to display his might.

His penalties were just, his actions true, his power spread far, all submitted to his rule;

He wiped out tyrants, rescued the black-headed people, brought peace to the four corners of the earth;

His enlightened laws spread far and wide as examples to all under heaven till the end of time.

Great is he, indeed! The whole universe obeys his sagacious will;

His subjects praise his achievements and have asked to inscribe them on stone for posterity.

The inscription on the eastern monument was as follows:

In the spring of the twenty-ninth year, the Emperor inspected distant parts;

As far as the coast he went, and ascended Chihfu to face the bright morning sun;

Gazing at that splendid view, his retinue recalled his illustrious ways:

At the beginning of his sagacious rule, he cleansed the state, punished tyrants beyond the border;

His growing might made earth's four corners shake, destroyed the six princes;

Then he unified all under heaven, uprooted evil, put an end to war.

Great is the Emperor's virtue! He rules the earth, tireless
in his exertions,
Sets a standard of proper bearings and signs for all
things;
His subjects follow their respective callings, knowing their
duties, acting without hesitation;
The black-headed people are reformed; he surpasses the
ancients and is free from errors;
All tasks are assigned, and later generations will follow
his sagacious rule;
His subjects, delighting in his virtue and noble deeds, have
asked that they be inscribed at Chihfu.

Then the emperor returned to Langya, thence back to his
capital by way of Shangtang.

In the thirtieth year nothing of moment occurred.

In the twelfth month of the thirty-first year, gifts were
bestowed on the common people, each village receiving six
piculs of rice and two sheep. The emperor left the capital incognito accompanied by four armed guards. Going out at
night he met with brigands at Lanchih and his life was endangered, but his guards killed the brigands. Then for twenty
days a great search was made for brigands within the Pass.
The price of rice was no higher than sixteen hundred cash a
picul.

In the thirty-second year the emperor went to Chiehshih
and sent a scholar of Yen named Lu to find the immortals
Hsien Men and Kao Shih. The walls of Chiehshih were pulled
down, its moats and fortifications abolished. An inscription
was carved on the city gate which read:

Troops raised to punish the lawless have wiped out rebels,
The wicked are put down by force, the innocent are peace-
fully rewarded and the people obey from their hearts;
Merit is rewarded with gifts of cattle and fertile lands;
The Emperor in his might overcame other states by virtue
and was the first to unify the empire.

City walls are demolished, moats and defences dug up,
    all barriers levelled;
The land is subdued, an end made to conscript labour, the
    world is at peace.
Men take pleasure in farming and women care for the
    home; there is order in all things;
His kindness extends to all, the land is shared out, all
    live content with their lot.
His ministers, admiring his virtue, ask to have this in-
    scribed on stone as a model for all time.

The emperor ordered Han Chung, Hou and a scholar named
Shih to go in search of the elixirs of the immortals. Then he
inspected the northern frontier, returning by way of Shangchun. A scholar named Lu of Yen came back from the sea
with accounts of spirits and deities who had predicted Chin's
overthrow by "Hu". Then the emperor ordered General Meng
Tien to lead three hundred thousand troops against the Huns
in the north, and conquered the land south of the Yellow
River.

In the thirty-third year those who had evaded conscription,
men living with their wives' families, and tradesmen were
conscripted to conquer Luliang; then the provinces of Kueilin,
Hsiangchun and Nanhai were created and convicts sent to
garrison them. The Huns in the northwest were driven back.
The region from Yuchung to east of the Yellow River was
incorporated with Yinshan, making thirty-four counties. Ramparts were built along the river as frontier defences. Then
Meng Tien was sent across the Yellow River to conquer Kao-
chueh, Taoshan and Peichia. Outposts and defences were set
up to resist the tribesmen and convicts were sent to populate
the new counties. The sacrifice to the Morning Star was
forbidden. A comet was seen in the west.

In the thirty-fourth year, officers of justice who had done
wrong were sent to build the Great Wall or to Southern Yueh.
The emperor gave a feast in Hsienyang Palace, and seventy
learned men came and offered toasts.

The archery officer Chou Ching-chen recited this eulogy: "Formerly Chin covered no more than a thousand square *li*. Now thanks to your divine sagacity all the land within the Four Seas has been conquered and the barbarian tribes driven far away. All men under the sun and the moon acknowledge your sovereignty, the various states have been made provinces and counties; the people enjoy peace with no fear of war, and so it will be for ten thousand generations. From ancient times there has been no match for Your Majesty's might and virtue." The emperor was pleased.

Then up stepped Chunyu Yueh, a scholar of Chi, who said, "I have heard that the Shang and Chou Dynasties lasted more than a thousand years because fiefs were given to younger members of the royal house or meritorious ministers, who set up tributary states. Now Your Majesty holds all the land within the Four Seas, yet your relations are still commoners. Should you have such disloyal subjects as Tien Chang of Chi or the six lords of Tsin, how could the dynasty be saved without the assistance of barons? I have yet to hear of anything able to endure that was not based on ancient precedents. Chou Ching-chen's flattery will lead you into error. He is not a loyal subject."

The emperor ordered his ministers to debate this question.

The prime minister Li Szu said, "The Five Emperors did not emulate each other nor did the Three Dynasties adopt each other's ways, yet all had good government. This is not paradox, because times had changed. Now Your Majesty has built up this great empire to endure for generations without end. Naturally this passes the comprehension of a foolish pedant. Chunyu Yueh spoke about the Three Dynasties, but they are hardly worth taking as examples. In times gone by different barons fought among themselves and gathered wandering scholars. Today, however, the empire is at peace, all laws and order come from one single source, the common people support themselves by farming and handicrafts, while students study the laws and prohibitions.

"Now these scholars learn only from the old, not from

177

the new, and use their learning to oppose our rule and confuse the black-headed people. As prime minister I must speak out on pain of death. In former times when the world, torn by chaos and disorder, could not be united, different states arose and argued from the past to condemn the present, using empty rhetoric to cover up and confuse the real issues, and employing their learning to oppose what was established by authority. Now Your Majesty has conquered the whole world, distinguished between black and white, set unified standards. Yet these opinionated scholars get together to slander the laws and judge each new decree according to their own school of thought, opposing it secretly in their hearts while discussing it openly in the streets. They brag to the sovereign to win fame, put forward strange arguments to gain distinction, and incite the mob to spread rumours. If this is not prohibited, the sovereign's prestige will suffer and factions will be formed among his subjects. Far better put a stop to it!

"I humbly propose that all historical records but those of Chin be burned. If anyone who is not a court scholar dares to keep the ancient songs, historical records or writings of the hundred schools, these should be confiscated and burned by the provincial governor and army commander. Those who in conversation dare to quote the old songs and records should be publicly executed; those who use old precedents to oppose the new order should have their families wiped out; and officers who know of such cases but fail to report them should be punished in the same way.

"If thirty days after the issuing of this order the owners of these books have still not had them destroyed, they should have their faces tattooed and be condemned to hard labour at the Great Wall. The only books which need not be destroyed are those dealing with medicine, divination and agriculture. Those who want to study the law can learn it from the officers." The emperor sanctioned this proposal.

In the thirty-fifth year a highway was built through Chiuyuan to Yunyang. To make it straight, hills were razed and valleys filled.

The emperor said, "Hsienyang is overcrowded and the palaces of the former kings are too small. I have heard that King Wen of Chou had his capital at Feng, King Wu at Hao. The region between Feng and Hao is fit to be an imperial capital."

He had palaces constructed in the Shanglin Gardens south of the River Wei. The front palace, Apang, built first, was five hundred paces from east to west, and five hundred feet from south to north. The terraces above could seat ten thousand, and below there was room for banners fifty feet in height. One causeway round the palace led to the South Hill at the top of which a gateway was erected; another led across the River Wei to Hsienyang, just as the Heavenly Corridor in the sky leads from the Apex of Heaven across the Milky Way to the Royal Chamber. Before the completion of this palace, the emperor wished to choose a good name for it. But because of its proximity to the old palace, it was commonly called Apang, which means beside the palace. A labour force of more than seven hundred thousand — men punished by castration or sentenced to penal servitude — was drafted to build Apang Palace and the emperor's tomb on Mount Li. Stone was quarried from the northern hills, timber shipped from Shu and Chu. Three hundred palaces were built within the Pass, and east of it more than four hundred.

A stone monument was set up on Mount Chu near the eastern coast as the East Gate of the Chin Empire. Thirty thousand families were settled in Liyi and fifty thousand in Yunyang, with ten years' exemption from taxation and conscription.

The scholar Lu reported to the emperor, "Our search for magic fungus, rare herbs and immortals has come to nothing. It seems some sinister influence was against us. It is my sincere opinion that you would be well advised to change your quarters secretly from time to time, in order to avoid evil spirits; for in their absence some pure being will come. For subjects to know their sovereign's whereabouts detracts from his divinity. A pure being is one who cannot be wet by water or burned by fire, who rides on the clouds and air and endures as long as heaven and earth. Since he who governs the empire cannot lead a pure, simple life, we hope Your Majesty will not let it be known in which palace you are staying, for then we should be able to obtain the herb of immortality."

"I wish to be a pure being," replied the emperor. "I shall refer to myself in this way and stop using the royal 'we'." He gave orders for the two hundred and seventy palaces and pavilions within two hundred *li* of Hsienyang to be connected by causeways and covered walks and furnished with hangings, bells, drums and beautiful ladies, each in the appointed place. Disclosure of his whereabouts became punishable with death.

When the emperor went to his palace at Liangshan he was displeased to see from the mountain what a great retinue the prime minister had. One of the palace eunuchs informed the prime minister, who thereupon reduced his retinue. The emperor was angry and said, "Someone here has been telling tales." When none of the eunuchs whom he cross-examined would admit it, he had all those with him at the time seized and killed. After this his movements were kept secret, but it was always in Hsienyang Palace that he heard his ministers' reports and made decisions.

The scholars Hou and Lu took counsel together, saying, "The emperor is stubborn and self-willed. Starting as the prince of one state, he conquered the whole empire, and now that all his ambitions are realized he thinks no one since time immemorial can compare with him. He relies solely on the law officers, whom he trusts. Although there are seventy court scholars, their posts are just sinecures for he never listens to them. The prime minister and other high officials only deal with routine matters on which the decisions have already been made, leaving all to the emperor. He loves to intimidate men with punishments and death, so that to avoid being charged with crimes those who draw stipends dare not speak out loyally. The emperor, never hearing his faults condemned, is growing prouder and prouder while those below cringe in fear and try to please him with flattery and lies. According to the law of the realm, no man may practise two arts and anyone who fails in his task may be executed. No fewer than three hundred astrologers are watching the stars, but these good men, for fear of giving offence, merely flatter the emperor and dare not speak of his faults. It is he who decides all affairs of state, great or small. He even has the documents weighed every morning and night, and will not rest until a certain weight has passed through his hands. How can we find herbs of immortality for such a tyrant?" And so they ran away.

When the emperor learned of their flight he flew into a passion. "I collected all the writings of the empire and got rid of those which were no use," he fumed. "I assembled a host of scholars and alchemists to start a reign of peace, hoping the alchemists would find marvellous herbs. But I am told no more has been heard of Han Chung and those who went with him, while Hsu Fu's crowd has wasted millions without obtaining any elixir — all I hear of them is charges of corruption! Handsomely as I treated Lu and the other scholars, they are libelling me, making out that I lack virtue. I have had inquiries made about the scholars in the capital and I find that some of them are spreading vicious rumours to confuse the black-headed people."

He ordered the chief counsellor to try the scholars, who incriminated each other to save their own necks. Over four hundred and sixty, found guilty of breaking the law, were buried alive in Hsienyang as a warning to the whole empire. Even more were banished to the frontier regions.

Fu-su, the emperor's eldest son, protested, "The empire is newly established and the black-headed people in distant parts have not yet settled down. All those scholars uphold the teachings of Confucius, and now that you have punished them so severely I fear there may be panic throughout the land. Will you not reconsider the matter?" Angered by this, the emperor sent Fu-su north to Shangchun to supervise Meng Tien's army.

In the thirty-sixth year Mars approached the Scorpion's Heart. A shooting star changed into a stone when it fell to earth at Tungchun, and someone inscribed on the stone, "After the First Emperor's death the land will be divided." When word of this reached the emperor, he sent the chief counsellor to investigate. Since no one admitted to the deed, all those in the vicinity were executed and the stone was destroyed by fire.

The emperor, unable to find happiness, ordered the court scholars to write poems about immortals and pure beings, and wherever he went he made musicians set these to music and sing them. That autumn an envoy from east of the Pass, travelling down the Pingshu Road by night, was stopped at Huaiyin by a man with a jade disc who said, "Please give this for me to the Lord of Haochih." He added, "This year the Primal Dragon will die." When the envoy asked what he meant the stranger vanished, leaving the disc behind.

The envoy presented the disc to the emperor and told him what had happened. After a long silence the emperor remarked, "These mountain spirits can only see a year ahead." Leaving the court, he said, "The Primal Dragon means the first among men." When he ordered the Imperial Treasury to examine the jade, they discovered that this was the disc thrown into the water when he crossed the Yangtse in the twenty-eighth year. Then the emperor consulted an oracle, which said that the time was auspicious for travel and removal. Thirty thousand families were moved to Peiho and Yuchung. Officers were promoted one rank.

In the tenth month of the thirty-seventh year, the emperor set out on a tour of inspection accompanied by the junior prime minister Li Szu, while the deputy prime minister Feng Chu-chi remained in the capital. Young Hu-hai, the emperor's favourite son, asked permission to join the tour and this was granted.

In the eleventh month they reached Yunmeng and sacrificed to Emperor Shun at Mount Chiuyi. Then they sailed down the Yangtse to inspect Chiko, crossed Haichu, passed Tanyang and reached Chientang, coming to the River Che. Since the waves were high, they proceeded west for another hundred and twenty *li* to cross where the river was narrower. They then ascended Mount Kuaichi and sacrificed to Yu the Great. Reaching the southern coast, they set up a tablet in praise of the dynasty's power. The inscription on it read:

> Illustrious the Sovereign Emperor who has united and pacified the land, whose kindness remains for ever.
>
> In the thirty-seventh year he toured his realm, inspecting all the distant regions;
>
> He ascended Mount Kuaichi, examined local customs; all the black-headed people bowed in respect.
>
> His ministers praise the Emperor's achievements and review his deeds to extol his lofty splendour.
>
> When this sage King of Chin came to the throne, laws were amended, old ways made manifest;
>
> He was the first to standardize regulations, distinguish different posts and establish a lasting order;
>
> But the six princes were rebellious, rapacious, despotic, glorying in their hosts;
>
> They committed evil, boasted of their strength, moved armies into battle;
>
> They exchanged envoys secretly to conspire against us, did what was wrong;
>
> With guile in their hearts they invaded our land, and so they came to grief.
>
> The Emperor quelled them with his justice and might; the tyrants were wiped out, the rebels perished.
>
> Wide-spread, all-embracing his sagacious power, bestowing kindness for ever throughout the world.
>
> Since the Emperor conquered all below the sky, he governs all things, there is quiet far and near;
>
> He regulates all things, verifies facts, gives each its proper name;
>
> High and low, good and bad are visible to him from whose eyes nothing is hidden;

He makes reforms, teaches virtue: If a widow with a son
    remarries, she is faithless, unchaste;
The sexes are strictly separated, licence is ended, men and
    women are pure and honest;
If a man commits adultery, it is no crime to kill him,
    thus men must observe the proper rules of conduct;
If a woman elopes with a lover her son may disown her;
    thus women become chaste and good.
His great rule purifies society, all come under his in-
    fluence, know his beneficence;
All men keep to the path, live in peace and harmony and
    obey his orders;
The black-headed people are cleansed, delight in the same
    rules and enjoy lasting peace;
Later ages will respect his law, his rule will endure for
    all time, like carriages and boats that hold their course.
The ministers in his train extol his greatness and inscribe
    this stone as a monument to his glory.

Starting back, the emperor crossed the river at Chiang-cheng
and proceeded north along the coast to Langya. Hsu Fu and
the other alchemists who had gone to sea to find magic herbs
but failed after many years and much expense, told a lie to
escape being punished. "The herbs are to be had on Penglai,"
they said. "But we were so harassed by monstrous whales
that we could not reach the fairy isles. We would like to
take some good archers with us so that when next we see
the whales they can shoot them with repeating crossbows."

The emperor dreamed that he had a fight with a sea god
which had assumed human form. He consulted his scholars
about this dream and they said, "The gods of the sea are
invisible but they may take the form of giant fish, sea-serpents
or dragons. Though you have taken such care to offer prayers
and sacrifice, this evil spirit has appeared. It must be driven
away so that good spirits will come in its place."

Then the emperor ordered sailors to prepare implements to
catch a great fish, and he waited with a repeating crossbow

for the monster to appear so that he might shoot it himself. He went north from Langya to Mount Jungcheng but found nothing. Upon reaching Chihfu, however, he saw some great fish and shot and killed one of them. Then he went westward, inland. At Pingyuanchin he fell ill.

Since the emperor could not bear to talk of death, his ministers dared not mention the subject either. When his illness grew worse, he wrote a letter under the imperial seal to Prince Fu-su saying, "On my death, come to Hsienyang for the funeral." This sealed letter was entrusted to Chao Kao, keeper of the chariots, who kept it in the place where tallies were issued but did not give it to a messenger.

In the seventh month, the First Emperor died at Pingtai in Shachiu. Since he died away from the capital, the prime minister Li Szu hushed the matter up for fear that the princes and others in the land start trouble, and no preparations were made for the funeral. The coffin was borne in a litter escorted by the emperor's favourite eunuchs, who presented food and official reports as usual and issued the imperial orders from the covered litter. The only ones who knew that the emperor was dead were his son Hu-hai, Chao Kao and five or six other trusted eunuchs.

Chao Kao had taught Hu-hai writing and the legal codes, and the prince was attached to him. So now Chao Kao conspired with Hu-hai and Li Szu to destroy the emperor's sealed letter to Prince Fu-su and forge a decree supposed to have been given Li Szu at Shachiu, making Hu-hai the crown prince. Another letter, sent to Prince Fu-su and General Meng Tien, charged them with crimes and ordered them to die. (This is told in detail in the life of Li Szu.) So the cortège proceeded from Chinhsing to Chiuyuan. It was summer and the litter began to reek. To disguise the stench the escort was told to load a cart with a picul of salted fish.

They took the direct road back to Hsienyang, then announced the funeral. The crown prince Hu-hai succeeded to the throne as the Second Sovereign Emperor. In the ninth month the First Emperor was buried at Mount Li.

As soon as the First Emperor became king of Chin, excavations and building had been started at Mount Li, while after he won the empire more than seven hundred thousand conscripts from all parts of the country worked there. They dug through three subterranean streams and poured molten copper for the outer coffin, and the tomb was filled with models of palaces, pavilions and offices, as well as fine vessels, precious stones and rarities. Artisans were ordered to fix up crossbows so that any thief breaking in would be shot. All the country's streams, the Yellow River and the Yangtse were reproduced in quicksilver and by some mechanical means made to flow into a miniature ocean. The heavenly constellations were shown above and the regions of the earth below. The candles were made of whale oil to ensure their burning for the longest possible time.

The Second Emperor decreed, "It is not right to send away those of my father's ladies who had no sons." Accordingly all these were ordered to follow the First Emperor to the grave. After the interment someone pointed out that the artisans who had made the mechanical contrivances might disclose all the treasure that was in the tomb; therefore after the burial and sealing up of the treasures, the middle gate was shut and the outer gate closed to imprison all the artisans and labourers, so that not one came out. Trees and grass were planted over the mausoleum to make it seem like a hill.

The Second Emperor was twenty-one when he ascended the throne. Chao Kao became his chamberlain, in charge of affairs of state. The Second Emperor decreed that more sacrifices should be made at the First Emperor's temple and to the hills and rivers.

His ministers, ordered to find ways to honour the First Emperor's temple, bowed to the ground and replied, "In ancient times the Son of Heaven had seven temples, the feudal princes five and ministers three, a practice unchanged for countless generations. Now the First Emperor's temple is supreme. All regions within the Four Seas have sent their tribute and the number of sacrifices has been increased; the ceremonies are complete and no more can be added. However, since the temples of the former kings are in Hsiyung or Hsienyang, only the temple of the First Emperor should have the imperial sacrifice. All imperial sacrifices to the former rulers from Duke Hsiang downwards may be abolished, leaving only seven temples where ministers may sacrifice as ceremony demands, exalting the First Emperor's temple to be the Primal Temple of Emperors. And our sovereign should refer to himself as 'we'."

The Second Emperor took counsel with Chao Kao, saying, "I am young and newly come to the throne and the black-headed people have not yet rallied to me. My father toured the provinces and counties to show his might and pacify the realm. If I remain passive and make no tour of inspection, I shall seem weak, unfit to govern the empire."

So in the spring the Second Emperor, accompanied by Li Szu, made a tour of the eastern provinces and counties. He went to Chiehshih, then south along the coast to Kuaichi. He had an inscription carved on the sides of the monuments set up by his father, listing all the chief ministers that had accompanied their sovereign, to show the First Emperor's achievements and abundant virtue. The inscription read:

> The emperor said, "These inscriptions on bronze and stone were the work of the First Emperor. He had the title of First Sovereign Emperor, but since this was not used in these inscriptions they may come to be attributed to later rulers, belying his achievements and abundant virtue." So his subjects the prime ministers Li Szu and Feng Chu-chi and the secretary of state Teh made bold to suggest, "We beg to have your imperial decree inscribed on stone, to make all clear. This we propose even at the risk of our lives." And the Emperor sanctioned this.

They went on to Liaotung, then returned to the capital.

The Second Emperor, on the advice of Chao Kao, reaffirmed the laws and ordinances and secretly consulted his chamberlain saying, "The chief ministers question my rule, the officials still have great power, and the princes are bound to contest my authority. What should I do?"

"I have been wanting to raise this but did not dare," said Chao Kao. "The chief ministers of the last emperor came from noble families famed throughout the land for generations, whose feats have long been handed down. I am humble and obscure, yet Your Majesty graciously raised me up to hold high office and order affairs in the palace. This has offended the chief ministers, who only make a show of obeying me but are resentful at heart. If you seize this chance to make an example of those provincial governors and military tribunes whose crimes you discovered during your tour of inspection, you will awe the land and do away with those against us. This is no time for politeness — might is right. I beg you to take prompt action before these officials have time to lay their plots, so that as a wise sovereign you win over the rest of your subjects, ennobling the humble, enriching the poor and making the distant close. Then high and low will rally round you and the empire will be secure."

The Second Emperor approved. He sentenced the chief ministers and princes to death and had accusations brought against those close to his person, dismissing three captains of the Imperial Guards and killing six princes at Tu. Prince Chiang-lu and his two brothers, imprisoned in the palace, were the last to be condemned. But the Second Emperor sent Chiang-lu the message, "You are a disloyal subject and deserve to die. The officers will execute the law."

The prince protested, "In court ritual I never dared disobey the master of ceremonies; in my government post I never overstepped my authority; when accepting orders and making my replies I never said anything wrong. In what way have I been disloyal? Let me know my crime before I die."

The messenger replied, "My duty is to carry out orders, not ask for reasons."

Prince Chiang-lu raised his eyes to the sky and three times he cried, "Heaven! I have done no wrong!" Then all three brothers, shedding tears, drew their swords and killed themselves.

Thus all members of the imperial house were intimidated while ministers who protested were accused of slander. So high officials drew their stipends but did nothing, and the common people were afraid.

In the fourth month the Second Emperor, back in Hsienyang, said, "My father, finding the Hsienyang court too small, had Apang Palace built as a residence but died before its completion. Then work stopped while the builders carried earth to Mount Li. Now Mount Li is nearly finished. If we leave Apang Palace uncompleted, it will imply that the last emperor was wrong. The work on it must be resumed and the barbarians at the frontier subdued, according to the plan of the First Emperor."

He summoned fifty thousand picked men to garrison the capital and ordered them to teach archery, hunting and hawking. As there were many mouths to feed in the capital and not enough provisions, grain and fodder were levied from the provinces, transport workers were ordered to supply their own rations, and all grain within three hundred *li* of Hsienyang was commandeered. The laws were enforced even more rigorously.

In the seventh month Chen Sheh and other conscripts revolted in the former land of Chu to restore that state. Chen Sheh made himself king of Chu with Chen as his capital, and sent out generals to conquer other districts. The young men in the eastern provinces, suffering under the Chin officials, killed the local governors, tribunes, magistrates and assistant magistrates and rose in revolt, working in league with Chen Sheh to make themselves marquises and princes. They joined forces and marched westward to attack Chin, and their number was past counting.

When an envoy from the eastern territory reported these revolts, the Second Emperor in a rage committed him to trial. So the next messenger to be questioned by the emperor answered, "They were bands of brigands and have all been captured now by forces sent by the local governors and magistrates. There is no cause for alarm." Then the emperor was pleased.

Wu Chen made himself prince of Chao, Wei Chiu became prince of Wei, and Tien Tan prince of Chi. Liu Pang revolted in the district of Pei and Hsiang Liang rose in arms in the province of Kuaichi.

In the winter of the second year, Chen Sheh's general Chou Chang and others advanced west to Hsi with several hundred thousand men. The Second Emperor in great dismay took counsel with his ministers.

The revenue officer Chang Han said, "The rebel army is approaching, and it is a powerful host. It is too late now to summon troops from neighbouring counties, but there are many conscripts on Mount Li. Why not pardon these slaves and arm them to resist?"

Thereupon the Second Emperor proclaimed a general amnesty and made Chang Han his commander. Chang Han routed the army of Chou Chang, who fled away and met his death at Tsaoyang. Then the Second Emperor dispatched the prime ministers' secretaries Szuma Hsin and Tung Yi to help Chang Han suppress the rebels. They killed Chen Sheh at Chengfu, routed Hsiang Liang at Tingtao and destroyed Wei Chiu at Linchi. Once the well-known rebel generals of Chu were killed, Chang Han crossed the Yellow River to attack Hsieh, prince of Chao, and others at Chulu in the north.

Then Chao Kao advised the Second Emperor, saying, "The last emperor governed the realm for many years, till his ministers dared not do any wrong or put forward incorrect proposals. Now you are in your prime, newly come to the throne. You had better not take decisions at court in front of the ministers, for then any mistake would reflect badly on you. The sovereign refers to himself as 'we' because his own voice is not heard." So after that the Second Emperor kept to the inner palace, deciding matters with Chao Kao alone while other ministers seldom had access to him.

Uprisings increased and troops had to be sent again and

again from within the Pass to attack the rebels in the east. The junior prime minister Feng Chu-chi, the senior prime minister Li Szu and General Feng Chieh asked for an audience and told the emperor, "Brigands are rife east of the Pass and, although our government troops have suppressed and killed a great many of them, they are not yet wiped out. The reason for all this brigandage is the bitter burden of garrison duty, building and transport service, and heavy taxation. We propose calling a halt to the work on Apang Palace, reducing transport duties and garrison service."

The Second Emperor replied, "According to Han Fei Tzu, 'Yao and Shun neither polished their oak rafters nor trimmed their thatched hut, and they ate and drank from earthen bowls, so that no gatekeeper could have lived more frugally. When Yu cut a channel through Lungmen to Tahsia to let the Yellow River flow into the ocean, he carried pestle and pick himself, and worked till he rubbed all the hair off his legs. No slave could have toiled harder.'

"But what is splendid about possessing an empire is being able to do as you please and satisfy your desires. By stressing and clarifying the laws, a ruler can stop his subjects from doing evil and so control the land within the seas. If rulers like Shun and Yu, exalted as the Son of Heaven, have to lead poor, arduous lives to set an example to the people, what use are laws? In name we are the lord of ten thousand chariots, but not in fact. So I want a retinue of a thousand, no, ten thousand, chariots to live up to my title.

"My father began as the lord of a single state but conquered the realm so that all under heaven was at peace. He drove back the barbarians from every side to pacify the frontiers and built palaces to show his success. You, my lords, saw the orderly sequence of his achievements. Now during the two years of my reign brigands have been rising on every side, yet instead of suppressing them you urge me to give up my father's tasks. You are neither carrying out the First Emperor's wishes nor working loyally for me. You are not fit for your posts!"

191

He had the three men brought to trial on various different charges. Feng Chu-chi and Feng Chieh said, "Generals and ministers will not accept disgrace," and they killed themselves. Li Szu went to prison and suffered the Five Tortures.

In the third year Chang Han and others laid siege to Chulu. Hsiang Yu, the high marshal of Chu, led troops to raise the siege.

That winter Chao Kao became prime minister. He condemned Li Szu and had him put to death.

Because Chang Han and the others had suffered many reverses that summer, the Second Emperor dispatched a messenger to reprimand him. Chang Han in dismay sent his secretary Szuma Hsin to ask instructions from Chao Kao. But Chao Kao would not see him or believe his account. In great alarm Szuma Hsin fled, and the men Chao Kao sent in pursuit failed to overtake him.

Then Szuma Hsin told Chang Han, "Chao Kao is now in charge at court. Whether you win or lose, you will be condemned." So when Hsiang Yu launched a sudden attack against Chin and captured Wang Li, Chang Han went over with his men to the rebels.

In the eighth month Chao Kao, eager to usurp power, made a test to see if the officials would obey him or not. He presented a stag to the emperor, describing it as a horse.

The emperor said with a laugh, "Haven't you made a mistake, prime minister? This is a stag, not a horse." But when he appealed to the officials present, some remained silent, others said it was a horse to please Chao Kao, and yet others said it was a stag. Then Chao Kao secretly impeached and punished those who had said it was a stag, after which all the officials were afraid of him.

Chao Kao had maintained more than once that the rebels east of the Pass could do little damage. But after Hsiang Yu captured Wang Li and other generals of Chin before Chulu and started advancing, Chang Han and his fellow commanders suffered several defeats and sent repeated requests for reinforcements. Now Yen, Chao, Chi, Chu, Hann and Wei all set up princes of their own, while in most regions east of the Pass men rose against the Chin officials to join the rebel leaders advancing west. The lord of Pei at the head of several tens of thousands captured the Wu Pass, massacred its defenders and sent a messenger in secret to Chao Kao. Afraid to incur the emperor's wrath and punishment, Chao Kao stayed away from the palace on the pretext of illness.

The Second Emperor was disturbed and puzzled by a dream that a white tiger had bitten and killed the left horse of his carriage. He consulted a diviner who told him, "An evil influence from the River Chin is at work." So the emperor purified himself in Wangyi Palace and prepared to sacrifice to the river god by drowning four white horses in the stream. He also sent a messenger to reprimand Chao Kao for not suppressing the rebels. Chao Kao in his alarm plotted with his son-in-law Yen Lo, the magistrate of the capital, and his younger brother Chao Cheng.

"The emperor never takes good advice," he said. "In this crisis he means to hold us responsible. I would like to set up Prince Tzu-ying in his place, for Tzu-ying is a kindly, frugal prince who has made a favourable impression on the people."

They enlisted the help of the chamberlain of the palace, who announced that rebels had broken into the palace and ordered Yen Lo to bring officers and troops to seize them. Holding Yen Lo's mother in his house as a hostage, Chao Kao sent him with more than a thousand men to the gate of Wangyi Palace. There they bound the captain of the guards and the archery officer, demanding, "Why didn't you stop the rebels from entering?"

The captain retorted, "What rebels? How could anyone break through our cordon of guards?"

Yen Lo beheaded the captain and led his men straight in, discharging arrows. The guards and eunuchs were thrown into confusion. Some fled, others resisted. The few dozen who offered resistance were cut down and killed. Then the chamberlain and Yen Lo went inside and shot at the hangings of the throne. The emperor shouted angrily for his followers, but they were far too panic-stricken to fight. One eunuch alone did not abandon his master, who going into his inner apartment asked him, "Why didn't you speak out earlier, before it came to this?"

"My life was spared because I did not dare to speak," said the eunuch. "Had I spoken before, I would be a dead man now and not have lived to see this day."

Then Yen Lo came up to the emperor and denounced him. "Tyrant! Heartless executioner!" he cried. "The whole empire is against you. Choose how you will die."

The emperor asked, "May I see the prime minister?"

Yen Lo answered, "No, you may not."

"I will consent to be the prince of a province."

But this was refused.

"A marquis, then, with a fief of ten thousand households."

Another refusal.

"Let me live with my wife and children as a common citizen like the other princes."

Yen Lo replied, "I am charged by the prime minister to put you to death on behalf of the whole empire. However much you plead, I am adamant." With that he called in his troops. Then the Second Emperor killed himself.

Yen Lo returned to report to Chao Kao, who thereupon summoned all the high ministers and princes and told them that the emperor had been punished with death.

"Chin was formerly a princely state," he said. "Not till he became ruler of the whole realm did the First Emperor assume the imperial title. Now that the six states have become independent again and our territory has diminished, it would be wrong to retain the empty title of emperor. Let us rather have a king as before." So Tzu-ying, son of the Second Emperor's elder brother, was made king of Chin. The Second Emperor was buried like a common citizen in the Yichun Gardens south of Tu.

Chao Kao asked Tzu-ying to observe a fast before going to the ancestral temple to receive the royal jade seal. After fasting for five days Tzu-ying told his two sons, "The prime minister Chao Kao had the Second Emperor murdered in Wangyi Palace. Fearing the condemnation of other officials he pretended to enthrone me because that was right. I have heard that Chao Kao has agreed with the forces of Chu to wipe out the House of Chin and set himself up as a prince within the Pass. This ceremony he has arranged at the temple must mean he will kill me there. I shall excuse myself on the score of illness so that he has to come here. Then I shall kill him."

Chao Kao sent several summons to Tzu-ying, who ignored them all. Then the prime minister went in person to say, "This ceremony is of the utmost importance. Why don't you come?"

Tzu-ying had him assassinated in his palace and all the Chao clan wiped out as a warning to the citizens of Hsienyang.

Tzu-ying had been king of Chin for forty-six days when Liu Pang, the lord of Pei, commanding the forces of Chu, routed the men of Chin, marched through the Wu Pass to Pashang and sent an envoy to demand Tzu-ying's surrender. A rope round his neck, the imperial seal and tally in his hands, Tzu-ying drove out in a plain carriage with white horses to surrender at Chihtao Station. Then the Lord of Pei entered Hsienyang, sealed up the palaces and treasuries and once more stationed his troops at Pashang. More than a month later came the forces of the allied princes, headed by Hsiang Yu. Then Tzu-ying was killed with other princes and members of the House of Chin. There was a massacre in Hsienyang, palaces were burned, boys and girls carried off as slaves, jewels and treasures looted and the spoils divided among the different princes.

After the destruction of Chin, its territory was divided into three regions under the princes of Yung, Sai and Ti, and these became known as the three states of Chin. Hsiang Yu, the overlord of Western Chu, was responsible for sharing out the land between the princes and barons. Thus Chin was overthrown. Five years later the Han Empire was founded.*

---

* The end of this record, consisting of Chia Yi's essay condemning the Chin Dynasty and a chronological summary of the reigns of earlier kings, is omitted.

CHEN SHEH

Chen Sheng, whose other name was Sheh, was a native of Yangcheng. Wu Kuang, or Wu Shu, was a native of Yanghsia. Chen Sheh was a farm hand when young. One day when resting from his labours he climbed up a mound and brooded morosely for some time.

"If I become rich and noble, I will not forget the rest of you," he said.

The other farm hands laughed.

"How can a farm labourer become rich and noble?" they asked.

"Ah!" said Chen Sheh with a deep sigh. "Can a sparrow know a wild swan's ambition?"

In the seventh month of the first year of the Second Emperor of Chin,* nine hundred men from the poor end of their village were conscripted for garrison service at Yuyang. On the way they stopped at Tatsehsiang. Chen Sheh and Wu Kuang, who were among the conscripts, were camp leaders. There was heavy rain, the roads were impassable, and they saw that they could not arrive on time. The penalty for delay was decapitation. Chen Sheh and Wu Kuang took stock of the situation.

"Desertion means death and so does revolt," they argued. "Since the risk is the same, why not die for our country?"

"The people have groaned long enough under Chin," said Chen Sheh. "I have heard that the Second Emperor is a younger son and not the rightful heir. Prince Fu-su was the rightful heir, but because he often disagreed with his father he was given a frontier command. Now they say the Second Emperor has killed him, although he had done no wrong. Many

---

* 209 B.C.

197

of the common folk have heard well of him, but do not know of his death. Then there is General Hsiang Yen of Chu, who is popular there for his many deeds of daring and the good care he takes of his men. Some say he is dead and some that he may have gone into hiding. If we pretended to be Prince Fu-su and Hsiang Yen and called on the people to rise, many would respond."

Wu Kuang agreed with him and they consulted a diviner, who, knowing what they had in mind, declared, "You will succeed in all you undertake and achieve great deeds. But why not ask aid from the spirits?"

Chen Sheh and Wu Kuang, pleased with this suggestion, said, "He means us to awe men first."

So they wrote "Chen Sheh will be king!" in vermilion on silk and placed it in the belly of a fish someone had caught. When the conscripts bought the fish and cooked it, they were amazed to find this writing in its belly.

Chen Sheh secretly sent Wu Kuang at night with a lantern to the forest shrine near their camp, to cry like a fox, "Great Chu will rise again! Chen Sheh will be king!"

The conscripts were terrified at hearing this cry at night. The next day they kept talking among themselves with many a side-long glance at Chen Sheh.

Wu Kuang was good to his men, all of whom obeyed him. One day when the commanding officers were drunk, he persuaded the conscripts to run away and goaded the officers to punish him and thus enrage the men. Sure enough, the officers had Wu Kuang flogged. But when one of them drew his sword, Wu Kuang snatched it away and killed him. Chen Sheh came to his aid and killed the other officer too.

Then they called their men together and said, "This rain has already made all of us late, and the penalty for this is decapitation. Even if we do not lose our heads, seven out of ten will die at the frontier. If a stout fellow must die, let it be for some great cause. How can our birth prevent us from becoming princes and barons, generals and ministers?"

"We will do whatever you say," responded the men.

To win popular support they gave out that their leaders were Prince Fu-su and General Hsiang Yen. Baring their right arms, they called themselves the army of Great Chu. They built an altar and made an oath, using the officers' heads as sacrifice. Chen Sheh made himself general with Wu Kuang as his chief commander. After storming Tatsehsiang they took the county of Chi and sent Ko Ying of Fuli with troops to take the districts east of Chi. Chih, Tso, Ku, Cheh and Chiao all fell to them. As they advanced, their ranks swelled. By the time they reached Chen they had about seven hundred chariots, more than a thousand cavalrymen and several tens of thousands of infantry. When they attacked the county seat of Chen the magistrate was away and the deputy magistrate held the city gate against them. But they defeated the defenders, killed the deputy magistrate and occupied the city. A few days later they summoned the elders and chief citizens to a conference.

"My lord," said these men, "you have come wearing armour and carrying sharp weapons to attack an unjust government, to punish the Chin tyranny and re-establish the kingdom of Chu. Your achievements fit you to be our king."

So Chen Sheh made himself king, calling himself the Magnifier of Chu. Thereupon all in the provinces and counties who hated the rule of Chin rose against their governors and magistrates and killed them in order to follow Chen Sheh's lead. Wu Kuang, made vice-regent over the other generals, advanced west against Yingyang. Chen Sheh also ordered Wu Chen, Chang Erh and Chen Yu, all natives of Chen, to conquer Chao, and Teng Tsung of Juyin to take the province of Chiuchiang. By this time Chu had countless bands of troops, each several thousand strong.

When Ko Ying reached Tungcheng he set up Hsiang Chiang as king of Chu. Later, hearing that Chen Sheh had proclaimed himself king, he killed Hsiang Chiang and went back to report. But when he reached Chen, Chen Sheh had him executed. Then Chen Sheh sent Chou Shih, a native of Wei, to conquer Wei in the north. Wu Kuang laid siege to Yingyang but the city was defended by Li Yiu, governor of Sanchuan, and he could not take it.

Chen Sheh summoned all the chief citizens of his kingdom to a conference and appointed Tsai Tzu, lord of Fang and a native of Shangtsai, as his chief minister.

Chou Wen, a talented citizen of Chen, had been the astrologer in General Hsiang Yen's army and had also served under the lord of Chunshen. As he claimed that he was well-versed in strategy, Chen Sheh gave him the seal of a general and ordered him to strike west at Chin. He gathered troops on his way to the Hanku Pass till he had a thousand chariots and several tens of thousands of men, and he stationed this army by the River Hsi.

Chin ordered its privy treasurer, Chang Han, to free the conscript labourers and slaves at Mount Li and send them to counter-attack. The Chu army was routed and Chou Wen fled back through the Pass to station his men at Tsaoyang. After two or three months Chang Han came after him and defeated him again. Then Chou Wen stationed his troops at Minchih; but after ten days or so Chang Han attacked once more and utterly routed them. Chou Wen fell on his sword and his troops were put out of action.

When Wu Chen reached Hantan, he made himself king of Chao with Chen Yu as his grand marshal and Chang Erh and Shao Sao as his senior and junior chancellors. Chen Sheh in anger arrested their relations, meaning to have them killed, but his chief minister Tsai Tzu protested, "Chin is not yet overthrown. If you execute the families of the king of Chao and his ministers, you are only making another enemy. You had better recognize him as king."

So Chen Sheh sent an envoy to congratulate Wu Chen, moved his relatives and those of his ministers into his palace, enfeoffed Chang Erh's son Chang Ao as lord of Chengtu, and urged the troops of Chao to advance at once against Chin.

Wu Chen took counsel with his generals and ministers, who said, "It was not Chen Sheh's plan that you should be king of Chao. After he has overthrown Chin he will attack us.

Instead of advancing west, we had better conquer Yen in the north in order to enlarge our territory. When we have the Yellow River in the south and Yen and Tai in the north, even if Chen Sheh defeats Chin he will not dare to lord it over us. And should he fail to defeat Chin, he will have to respect us. Then we can take advantage of the fall of Chin to do whatever we please."

Wu Chen agreed with them. Instead of advancing west, he sent Han Kuang, former army secretary of Shangku, to conquer Yen in the north.

Then the nobles and chief citizens of Yen advised Han Kuang saying, "Now Chu has set up a king and so has Chao. Though Yen is small, it was also once a kingdom of ten thousand chariots. We hope you will set yourself up as king of Yen."

"I cannot," said Han Kuang. "My mother is still in Chao."

"Chao fears Chin in the west and Chu in the south," they replied. "It is in no position to interfere with us. Besides even Chu, for all its strength, dared not harm the family of the king of Chao. How could the king of Chao dare harm yours?"

Han Kuang took their advice and made himself king of Yen. A few months later Chao sent Han Kuang's mother and the rest of his family to him.

During this period many generals made conquests. Chou Shih marched north and conquered the land up to the district of Ti. A man of Ti named Tien Tan, who had killed the magistrate of Ti and made himself king of Chi, attacked and routed Chou Shih with the forces of Chi. Chou Shih returned to Wei and wanted to enthrone Chiu, former lord of Ningling and a descendant of the House of Wei. But Chiu was then in Chen Sheh's territory and could not come to Wei. After Wei was conquered, therefore, the people tried to make Chou Shih their king, but he refused. Five times they sent envoys to Chen Sheh, until finally he agreed to make the lord of Ningling the king of Wei and sent him back to his kingdom. Chou Shih in the end became his chancellor.

Tien Tsang and some other generals plotted together saying, "Now that Chou Wen's army has been routed, the troops of

Chin may be here any time. We are besieging Yingyang but cannot take it. If the Chin army comes, we shall certainly be beaten. We had better leave a few troops to defend our position here, and advance with all our best men against Chin. This vice-regent is proud and knows nothing about fighting. We must not discuss this with him. Unless we kill him, we are hardly likely to succeed."

Pretending to be acting on Chen Sheh's orders, they killed Wu Kuang and presented his head to Chen Sheh. Then Chen Sheh sent an envoy to give Tien Tsang the seal of the chancellor of Chu and appointed him as a high marshal. Tien Tsang ordered Li Kuei and the other generals to defend Yingyang, while he led picked troops west to attack the Chin army at Aotsang, but in the battle that ensued Tien Tsang was killed and his army defeated. Then Chang Han advanced to attack Li Kuei and the others before the city of Yingyang, defeating and killing them too.

Teng Yueh of Yangcheng, in command of troops at Chia, was defeated by an auxiliary force sent by Chang Han. His army scattered and he fled to the city of Chen. Wu Hsu of Chih, in command of forces at Hsu, was also defeated by Chang Han and fled to Chen. But Chen Sheh had him executed.

When Chen Sheh first declared himself king, Chin Chia of Ling, Tung Hsieh of Chih, Chu Chi-shih of Fuli, Cheng Pu of Chulu and Ting Chi of Hsu all raised troops and besieged Ching, governor of Tunghai, at Tan. When Chen Sheh knew this, he appointed Pan, lord of Wuping, as general in charge of all the forces at Tan. Chin Chia would not accept this, however, but made himself the commander-in-chief, refusing to take orders from the lord of Wuping.

"The lord of Wuping is too young," he told his officers. "He has no military experience. We must not listen to him." Pretending to act on orders from Chen Sheh, he had the lord of Wuping executed.

After defeating Wu Hsu, Chang Han attacked the city of Chen and killed Tsai Tzu, Chen Sheh's field marshal. He then advanced to attack Chang Ho's army west of the city. Chen

Sheh himself came out to direct the battle, but his army was defeated and Chang Ho killed.

In the twelfth month Chen Sheh went to Juyin, then turned back to Hsiachengfu, where his charioteer Chuang Chia killed him and surrendered to Chin. Chen Sheh was buried at Tang with the posthumous title of King Yin.

Chen Sheh's former palace attendant, General Lu Chen, rallied troops to form a black-turbaned army at Yingyang. He took Chen, killed Chuang Chia and made Chen into the state of Chu again.

When Chen Sheh first reached Chen, he sent Sung Liu of Chih with troops to conquer Nanyang and advance through the Wu Pass. Sung Liu had taken Nanyang, but after Chen Sheh's death it fell under Chin's control again and he could not enter the Wu Pass. Instead he went east to Hsintsai, where he encountered the Chin army and surrendered with all his men. He was sent to Hsienyang and torn limb from limb by chariots to serve as a warning to others.

After Chin Chia and his men heard of Chen Sheh's defeat and flight, they made Ching Chu king of Chu and advanced with troops to Fangyu to attack the Chin army at Tingtao. They sent Kungsun Ching to Tien Tan, king of Chi, asking him to join forces with them.

"We do not know whether Chen Sheh is alive after his defeat," said Tien Tan. "How could you appoint another king of Chu without consulting us?"

"You set yourself up as king in Chi without asking us," retorted Kungsun Ching. "Why should we consult you? Besides, as Chu started the revolt, she should be the leader of all the other states."

At this Tien Tan had Kungsun Ching killed.

The left and right armies of Chin attacked and retook the city of Chen. General Lu Chen fled but rallied his troops and was joined by Ching Pu, lord of Tangyang, who was one of the brigands of Po. Having defeated the Chin army at Chingpo, they once again made Chen into the state of Chu. Then Hsiang

Liang appointed as king of Chu Hsin, the grandson of King Huai of Chu.

Chen Sheh was king for six months in all, with his capital at Chen. When one of the men who had been an agricultural labourer with him heard this, he went to Chen and knocked on the palace gate.

"I've come to see Sheh!" he said.

The chief palace gate-keeper wanted to arrest him. After lengthy explanations he let him go, but still refused to announce him. So when Chen Sheh went out, this fellow blocked his way and shouted his name. The king, hearing his voice, called him over and took him back in his own chariot to the palace, where at sight of the great halls and hangings the man exclaimed, "Whew, Chen Sheh! You're wallowing in wealth, now you're a king!" (The people of Chu say "Whew!" when they feel overwhelmed. This is how the expression, "Whew! Even Chen Sheh can be king!" spread over the whole country.)

This old friend took to wandering in and out of the palace quite freely and telling stories about Chen Sheh's past. Someone warned the king, "This ignorant fool with his careless talk is damaging your prestige." Chen Sheh then had him beheaded, and after that all his old friends went away and nobody else got on close terms with him again.

Chen Sheh had appointed Chu Fang his supervisor and Hu Wu his censor to keep watch over his ministers and officers. When victorious generals came back, these two men could arrest and punish them if they had not obeyed orders. Indeed, they regarded fault-finding as such a proof of loyalty that instead of sending men to the proper authorities they tried them themselves. As Chen Sheh placed so much trust in these two he lost the support of his generals. This was why he failed.

Although Chen Sheh himself was killed, it was he who started the revolt and the nobles, kings, generals and officials whom he appointed and sent out succeeded in overthrowing Chin. In the time of Emperor Kao-tsu of Han, thirty families were put in charge of his grave at Tang, where sacrifices to him continue to this day.

HSIANG YU

Hsiang Chi, whose other name was Yu, was a man of Hsiahsiang. He was twenty-four when he first rose in arms. His uncle Hsiang Liang was the son of Hsiang Yen, a general of Chu who was killed by the Chin general Wang Chien. For many generations the heads of the clan had been enfeoffed in Hsiang as generals of Chu; hence Hsiang became their family name.

As a lad Hsiang Yu studied to be a scribe. Failing in this, he took up swordsmanship. When he failed in this too, Hsiang Liang was angry with him, but he said:

"All scribes do is make lists of names, and swordsmen can only fight a single foe: that is not worth learning. I want to learn how to fight ten thousand foes."

Then, to his great joy, Hsiang Liang taught him military strategy. But once he had a general grasp of the subject, Hsiang Yu again refused to study to the end.

Hsiang Liang was arrested at Yoyang, but procured a letter from Tsao Chiu, gaoler of Chi, and presented this to Szuma Hsin, the gaoler of Yoyang, who thereupon let him go. Later Hsiang Liang killed a man and fled from vengeance with Hsiang Yu to Wu. As all the local figures lacked his ability, Hsiang Liang generally took charge of large labour conscriptions or important funerals. And in secret he trained his followers and young men in the arts of war, to test their abilities.

When the First Emperor of Chin crossed the River Che on a visit to Kuaichi, Hsiang Liang and Hsiang Yu looked on.

"Why not take over from him?" exclaimed Hsiang Yu.

"Don't talk so wildly!" said Hsiang Liang, stopping his nephew's mouth. "Do you want our clan wiped out?" But this sent Hsiang Yu up in his estimation.

Hsiang Yu was over six feet tall and so strong that he could carry a bronze cauldron. He was more brilliant and ambitious than others, so that all the young men in the district stood in awe of him.

In the seventh month of the first year of the Second Emperor,* Chen Sheh and his men rose in Tachai. In the ninth month Yin Tung, governor of Kuaichi, summoned Hsiang Liang and said:

"All the lower reaches of the Yangtse have revolted. Heaven is about to destroy the House of Chin. Whoever strikes first, they say, becomes a leader, while those who delay are led. I want to raise troops with you and Huan Chu as my generals." Huan Chu was then an outlaw in the marshes.

"Huan Chu is an outlaw," replied Hsiang Liang, "and no one but Hsiang Yu knows where he is." He withdrew and told Hsiang Yu to wait outside with his sword. Then he went back, sat down again by the governor and said, "Please summon Hsiang Yu to take your orders to Huan Chu."

When the governor agreed, Hsiang Liang called Hsiang Yu in. After a moment he glanced at him and said, "The time has come!" Then Hsiang Yu drew his sword and cut off the governor's head. Hsiang Liang picked up the head and hung Yin Tung's seal and insignia on his own belt. The governor's men panicked and were thrown into confusion. Hsiang Yu killed several scores of them. The whole office cowered in terror and no one dared stand against him. Then Hsiang Liang summoned the chief citizens and some officers whom he knew, gave them his reasons for raising a revolt, and took command of the army of Wu. He sent officers to conscript men from the various districts and gathered a picked force of eight thousand men, appointing the best local men as his lieutenants, scouts and sergeants. One man complained that he had received no post, but Hsiang Liang retorted:

"When I asked you to see to something at so-and-so's funeral, you let me down. That is why you are being passed over."

All agreed that this was just. Hsiang Liang became the

* 209 B.C.

governor of Kuaichi with Hsiang Yu as his adjutant, and they took over all the districts in that province.

Chao Ping, a native of Kuangling, attacked that city for Chen Sheh but failed to take it. When he heard of Chen Sheh's defeat and flight and of the Chin army's approach, he crossed the Yangtse and, pretending that he was acting on Chen Sheh's orders, conferred on Hsiang Liang the title of chief minister of Chu.

"You have conquered the land to the east," he said. "Lose no time now but lead your army west against Chin."

Hsiang Liang at the head of his eight thousand men crossed the river and marched west. When he learned that Chen Ying had taken Tungyang, he sent an envoy to propose that they join forces and advance west together. Chen Ying had been secretary to the magistrate of Tungyang and was respected throughout the county for his integrity. After the young men there killed their magistrate, several thousands of men banded together and looked for a leader. Finding no one suitable, they approached Chen Ying. He declined with the excuse that he lacked ability, but they finally prevailed on him to take charge and some twenty thousand men of the county followed him. Then the young men wanted to set him up as their king and form a black-turbaned rebel force of their own.

Chen Ying's mother told him, "Since I married into your family, I have never heard that any of your ancestors ever attained noble rank. It is not safe to win fame overnight: you would do better to serve as a subordinate. Then if all goes well, you will be made a marquis; if things go badly, you can easily escape because you are not known to all."

So Chen Ying did not venture to become king. "The Hsiang family has produced generals for several generations," he told his officers. "They are well known in Chu. If we want to revolt, we must have them on our side. With the help of such a distinguished family, Chin can certainly be destroyed."

They took his advice and put their troops under Hsiang Liang's command. After Hsiang Liang crossed the River Huai,

Ying Pu* and General Pu also came over to him with their men. The army, now nearly seventy thousand strong, encamped at Hsiapei.

Meanwhile Chin Chia had made Ching Chu king of Chu and stationed his troops east of Pengcheng to block Hsiang Liang's way.

"Chen Sheh was the first to rise," said Hsiang Liang to his officers. "But since his defeat we do not know what has become of him. Now Chin Chia has turned against him and made Ching Chu king. This is vile treachery!"

He led his men against Chin Chia and put him to flight. Hsiang Liang pursued him to Huling, where Chin Chia turned to give battle. At the end of the day Chin Chia was dead and his men had surrendered. Ching Chu fled and perished in the land of Liang.

Hsiang Liang took over Chin Chia's army and camped at Huling before marching west.

By now the Chin army led by Chang Han had reached Li. Hsiang Liang sent his generals Chu Chi-shih and the lord of Yufan against him; but the lord of Yufan was killed and Chu Chi-shih's army, routed, retreated to Huling. Hsiang Liang led his men to Hsueh and killed Chu Chi-shih. He had sent Hsiang Yu to storm Hsiangcheng, but the city resisted stubbornly. After taking it by storm, Hsiang Yu put all the defenders to the sword before going back to report to Hsiang Liang.

When Hsiang Liang heard for certain that Chen Sheh was dead, he summoned his generals to Hsueh for a council. By this time Liu Pang, who had risen in Pei, had joined him.

Fan Tseng of Chutsao, a man of seventy who held no public office, was a good strategist. Now he went to offer advice to Hsiang Liang saying, "Chen Sheh deserved to fall. Of the six kingdoms conquered by Chin, Chu was the most blameless. Ever since King Huai went to Chin and failed to return, the people of Chu have never ceased to mourn him. That is why Nan-kung of Chu said, 'So long as three households are left in

---

* Also known as Ching Pu.

Chu, she will be the land to overthrow Chin.' But when Chen Sheh rebelled, he set himself up as king instead of one of the House of Chu; thus his power was short-lived. Once you took up arms in the east, men of power in Chu raced to put themselves under your command, because you come of a line of generals of Chu and have it in your power to restore the royal house."

These words convinced Hsiang Liang, who had a search made for the late King Huai's grandson Hsin, who turned out to be herding sheep among the common people, and set him up as King Huai of Chu to satisfy popular feeling. Chen Ying was appointed his chief minister and given five counties as his fief. King Huai's capital was Hsuyi. Hsiang Liang himself took the title lord of Wuhsin.

Some months later he led his army against Kangfu, then joined forces with Tien Jung of Chi and Marshal Szuma Lung-tzu to relieve Tunga, routing the forces of Chin there. Then Tien Jung led his troops back to Chi and drove away King Chia, who fled to Chu. His chief minister Tien Chueh fled to Chao. Tien Chueh's younger brother Tien Chien, a former general of Chi, remained in Chao, not daring to return. Then Tien Jung made Fu, son of Tien Tan, king of Chi. After defeating the forces of Chin at Tunga, Hsiang Liang set out in pursuit of them and sent several envoys to urge the generals of Chi to advance west with him.

Tien Jung's answer was, "We will send troops only if you kill Tien Chia and the king of Chao kills Tien Chueh and Tien Chien."

"Tien Chia is the king of a friendly state who turned to us in time of need," objected Hsiang Liang. "It would not be right to kill him." Neither would the king of Chao kill the other two men to please Chi. So Chi sent no troops to aid Chu.

Hsiang Liang dispatched Liu Pang and Hsiang Yu to attack Chengyang. They slaughtered all the defenders and advanced west to defeat the Chin army east of Puyang. When the Chin forces withdrew into Puyang, Liu Pang and Hsiang Yu attacked Tingtao but failed to take it. They marched west and occupied all the districts up to Yungchiu, where they inflicted another crushing defeat on the forces of Chin and beheaded Li Yu. They turned back to attack Waihuang, but could not take it.

Meanwhile Hsiang Liang had set out from Tunga and marched northwest to Tingtao, where once again he defeated the forces of Chin; and now that Hsiang Yu and the others had beheaded Li Yu, he began to underestimate Chin and to grow arrogant.

Sung Yi warned him, "A general who is arrogant and soldiers who slack off after a victory are sure to be defeated. Now your troops are taking it easy while the Chin army grows stronger every day. I am worried to think what will become of you."

Hsiang Liang paid no attention, but sent Sung Yi as his envoy to Chi. On the way Sung Yi met Chi's envoy, Lord Hsien of Kaoling.

"Are you going to see the lord of Wuhsin (Hsiang Liang)?" he asked him.

The other replied, "I am."

"I can tell you," said Sung Yi, "that the lord of Wuhsin is sure to be defeated. If you travel slowly, you may escape with your life. If you hurry, you will run into trouble."

All Chin's men were mobilized to reinforce Chang Han, who attacked and routed the Chu army at Tingtao and killed Hsiang Liang.

Liu Pang and Hsiang Yu had left Waihuang to attack Chenliu, but the city was stubbornly defended and could not be taken. So they took counsel together. "Now that Hsiang Liang's army has been routed, our men are scared," they said. They decided to go east with Lu Chen's troops. Lu Chen encamped east of Pengcheng, Hsiang Yu west of Pengcheng and Liu Pang at Tang.

After defeating Hsiang Liang, Chang Han thought he had nothing to fear from the other Chu forces. He crossed the Yellow River to attack Chao and routed its army completely. Chao Hsieh, the king of Chao, fled with his general Chen Yu and his chief minister Chang Erh to the city of Chulu. Chang Han ordered Wang Li and Sheh Chien to besiege the city, while he stationed his own army to the south and constructed a fortified road to supply them with grain. The Chao commander Chen Yu camped with several tens of thousands of men north of the city. This force was known as the Army North of the River.

After the defeat of the Chu army at Tingtao, King Huai of Chu took fright and moved from Hsuyi to Pengcheng, where he combined the forces of Hsiang Yu and Lu Chen under his own command. He appointed Lu Chen his chief commissary and his father Lu Ching prime minister. Liu Pang he made governor of Tang and marquis of Wu-an, in command of the troops of Tang.

Lord Hsien of Kaoling, Chi's envoy whom Sung Yi had once met and who was in the Chu army, informed King Huai, "Sung Yi predicted the lord of Wuhsin's defeat, and a few days later his army was indeed routed. Here is a man who understands warfare, who foresees defeat before a battle is fought."

King Huai summoned Sung Yi for a talk and was so impressed that he appointed him commander-in-chief to rescue Chao, and made Hsiang Yu the duke of Lu and his second in command with Fan Tseng as third in command. All the other generals took orders from Sung Yi, whose title was Lord Chief Marshal. They marched to Anyang and camped there for forty-six days without advancing.

"I hear that Chin is besieging the king of Chao at Chulu," said Hsiang Yu. "If we cross the river quickly and attack from outside while the men of Chao strike from within, we are bound to defeat the Chin army."

"No," objected Sung Yi. "A gadfly which can sting a bull may not be able to kill a flea. Now Chin is attacking Chao. If her men win they will be exhausted and we can take advantage of their weakness. If they lose we can march west with sounding drums and will certainly defeat them. Better let Chin and Chao fight it out first. In feats of arms I am no match for you, but in strategy you are no match for me."

Then he issued this order to the troops: "Any man who is fierce as a tiger, stubborn as a sheep, greedy as a wolf, or disobedient to orders, will lose his head."

He appointed his son Sung Hsiang chief minister to the king of Chi and saw him to Wuyen, where he gave a banquet. The day was raw, a heavy rain was falling, and the men were hungry and cold.

Hsiang Yu reflected, "Instead of hitting out hard at Chin, he has made us stay here all this time without moving. The harvest has failed, the people are destitute, and for lack of grain our men are eating taros and beans; yet he holds a great banquet! Instead of leading our troops across the river to get food from Chao and join forces with Chao to attack the enemy, he claims he is waiting for Chin to be exhausted. In fact, Chin is so powerful that if she attacks the newly formed state of Chao, she is bound to defeat it. Once Chao falls, Chin will grow even stronger. There will be no exhaustion for us to profit by. Besides, our men have recently been defeated, our king sits uneasy on his throne and has put all the resources of the kingdom at the command of Sung Yi. Our whole country's future is at stake. Yet instead of caring for his troops, Sung Yi attends to private affairs. He is betraying our country."

So one morning when he went to pay his respects to the marshal he entered Sung Yi's tent and cut off his head. Coming out he announced to the army, "Sung Yi was plotting with Chi against our state. King Huai sent me secret orders to execute him."

At this all the generals were awed into submission. "Your family first established our state," they said. "Now you have killed a traitor." They made Hsiang Yu their acting commander-in-chief and sent men to Chi to capture and kill Sung Yi's son. General Huan Chu was sent to report this to King Huai, who appointed Hsiang Yu as commander-in-chief with the lord of Tangyang and General Pu under him.

By killing the Lord Chief Marshal Sung Yi, Hsiang Yu struck terror into the whole of Chu and his fame spread to other states. He sent the lord of Tangyang and General Pu across the river with twenty thousand men to raise the siege of Chulu. As they met with little success, Chen Yu asked for reinforcements. Thereupon Hsiang Yu led his entire force across the river.

They sank all their boats, smashed their cooking vessels, burned their huts, and carried only three days' rations with them, to show their determination to fight to the death and never to turn back. They besieged Wang Li's troops, fought nine battles with the Chin army, cut its supply route and defeated it utterly. The Chin general Su Chueh was killed, Wang Li captured, and Sheh Chien who refused to surrender perished in the fire.

By now the army of Chu outmatched all others. Ten or more armies from different states had entrenched themselves outside Chulu to rescue the city, but none had dared take the field. When Chu attacked Chin, the others watched from their ramparts. Each soldier of Chu was a match for ten of the enemy. Their war-cries rent the sky, striking terror into the hearts of all who heard them. Thus when they defeated Chin and Hsiang Yu summoned the other generals to his camp, they entered on their knees and none dared look up. Then Hsiang Yu became commander-in-chief of the forces of these different states and their leaders took orders from him.

Chang Han's army at Chiyuan and Hsiang Yu's army south of the River Chang confronted each other for some time without fighting. Because the Chin army had several times retreated, the Second Emperor sent an envoy to censure Chang Han. Then the latter dispatched his secretary Szuma Hsin in alarm to Hsienyang to ask for instructions. Three days Szuma Hsin waited outside the palace gate, but Chao Kao would not see him as he did not trust him. At that Szuma Hsin was afraid and returned to the army by a different route. The pursuers Chao Kao sent after him failed to overtake him.

Back with the army, Szuma Hsin reported, "With Chao Kao in control there is nothing we can do. If we fight and win, he will envy our success. If we lose, he will have us killed. I hope you will think this over carefully."

Chen Yu sent Chang Han a letter, saying:

"When Pai Chi was a general of Chin, he conquered Yen and Ying in the south and wiped out the army of the lord of Mafu in the north. He captured cities and territories past counting, yet at last he was ordered to die. Meng Tien, another general

213

of Chin, drove away the Huns in the north and extended the territory of his state by several thousand square *li*; yet in the end his head was cut off at Yangchou. Why was this? Because their achievements were too great for Chin to reward with fiefs large enough; hence some legal pretext was found for their execution.

"Now you have been a general of Chin for three years and lost hundreds of thousands of men, while rebellions in the different states are becoming more frequent. Chao Kao has deceived and flattered the emperor so long that now the position is desperate he wants to make you a scapegoat to avoid being executed himself. He will take away your command to save his own skin.

"You have long been absent from the capital and have many enemies at court. You will be executed whether you win battles or not. Besides, Chin is destined to fall — wise and foolish alike can see that. Now you have no voice in the government, and if you remain at the front you will soon have no country of your own. Alone and unfriended you are, alas, doomed! Why not turn your army back and ally with the other states to attack Chin and divide the empire between you? Then you can be a king and reign supreme. This is surely better than dying by the axe and bringing destruction upon your own wife and children."

Chang Han began to waver and secretly sent his officer Shih Cheng as an envoy to seek for some agreement with Hsiang Yu. Before an agreement was reached, Hsiang Yu dispatched General Pu with troops to cross Sanhu ford by night to the south bank of the River Chang, where Pu attacked and defeated the army of Chin. Then Hsiang Yu led his entire force against the Chin troops on the bank of the River Yu and completely routed them. When Chang Han sent another envoy to seek for an agreement, Hsiang Yu summoned his officers to discuss the matter.

"Our food supply is low," he said. "We had better accept his offer."

When his officers approved, Hsiang Yu appointed a time

214

to meet Chang Han on the ruins of the old capital of Yin south of the River Huan, and there they reached an agreement. Chang Han told Hsiang Yu with tears what Chao Kao had done, and Hsiang Yu made him king of Yung and kept him in the Chu army. His secretary Szuma Hsin was appointed marshal of the Chin troops to lead them ahead of the main army to Hsinan.

Before this, the frontier garrisons conscripted from the eastern states had often received rough treatment at the hands of the soldiers of Chin when they passed through their territory. Now that the Chin forces had surrendered, the triumphant soldiers of the other states took their revenge by treating them as slaves and captives, humiliating and abusing them.

The men of Chin whispered among themselves, "Our commander Chang Han tricked us into surrendering. If we enter the Pass and conquer Chin, well and good. But if we fail, they will send us east as captives and Chin will kill our parents, wives and children."

Hsiang Yu's generals heard this talk and reported it, whereupon he summoned the lord of Tangyang and General Pu. "Chin's officers and men are still a large force," he said, "and in their hearts they have not submitted to us. Once inside the Pass, any disobedience would be dangerous. Before we enter Chin we had better kill them all but Chang Han, Szuma Hsin his secretary, and Tung Yi his lieutenant."

So the Chu army attacked by night and massacred more than two hundred thousand Chin troops south of Hsinan.

They advanced conquering the land of Chin till they found their way barred by a force defending the Hanku Pass, which they were unable to storm. When word came that Liu Pang, lord of Pei, had already taken Hsienyang, Hsiang Yu flew into a passion. He made the lord of Tangyang and others storm the Pass and followed them to a place west of the River Hsi.

Liu Pang's army was now at Pashang. Before he could meet with Hsiang Yu, his left marshal Tsao Wu-shang sent Hsiang Yu this message: "The lord of Pei intends to be king inside the Pass, with Tzu-ying* as his prime minister. He will keep all the jewels and treasures for himself."

In a rage Hsiang Yu swore, "Tomorrow I shall feast my men, and then we will attack and smash Liu Pang's army!"

Hsiang Yu then had four hundred thousand men encamped at Hungmen near Hsinfeng, and Liu Pang had one hundred thousand at Pashang.

Fan Tseng also told Hsiang Yu, "When the lord of Pei was living east of the mountains, he was greedy for wealth and fond of beautiful women; but since entering the Pass he has taken neither loot nor women. This shows that he aims high. I sent men to watch the heavenly signs above his camp. They are of all colours and shaped like dragons and tigers — the signs of a Son of Heaven. You must lose no time in attacking him!"

Hsiang Yu's uncle Hsiang Po, the vice-chancellor of Chu, was a friend of Chang Liang, marquis of Liu, then in the service of Liu Pang. Hsiang Po galloped in secret to Liu Pang's camp that night to visit Chang Liang and tell him what had happened. He urged Chang Liang to go away with him.

"Otherwise you will perish!" he warned him.

But Chang Liang replied, "The king of Hann** sent me here with the lord of Pei. It would not be right to desert him in the hour of danger. I must report this to him."

He went in and related everything to Liu Pang.

"What shall I do?" asked Liu Pang in great alarm.

"Who advised you to take this course?" inquired Chang Liang.

"A fool of a scholar advised me to hold the Pass and not let the others in, for then I should be able to rule all Chin. I followed his plan."

"Do you think, my lord, that your troops can stand up to Hsiang Yu?"

"Of course not," answered Liu Pang after a pause. "But what shall I do?"

---

* The last ruler of Chin, who had surrendered.

** Previously one of the Seven Warring States, now a nominal kingdom. It was Chang Liang's native land.

"Let me tell Hsiang Po that the lord of Pei dares not oppose Hsiang Yu."

"How do you happen to know Hsiang Po?"

"We became acquainted in the time of Chin, and I saved Hsiang Po's life once when he killed a man. Now that we are in danger, he was good enough to come and warn me."

"Which of you is the elder?"

"He is."

"Please ask him in. I shall treat him as I would an elder brother."

Chang Liang brought Hsiang Po in to see Liu Pang, who offered him a goblet of wine, drank a toast to him, and pledged to link their families by marriage.

"Since I came through the Pass, I have not touched so much as a hair," he declared. "I have made a register of officials and citizens and sealed up the treasuries until the commander's arrival. I have sent officers to guard the Pass to prevent bandits going through it and to be ready for any emergency. Night and day I have been awaiting the commander. How dare I rebel against him? Please make it clear to him that I could not be so ungrateful."

Hsiang Po agreed to do so, adding, "You must come early tomorrow morning to apologize in person to Lord Hsiang Yu."

This Liu Pang promised to do.

Then Hsiang Po went back by night to Hsiang Yu's camp and told him all Liu Pang had said.

"If the lord of Pei had not conquered Chin, you would not have been able to enter," he pointed out. "It is wrong to attack a man who has done you so great a service. You had better treat him handsomely."

Hsiang Yu agreed.

The next day Liu Pang, followed by some hundred horsemen, came to Hsiang Yu's camp at Hungmen and made his apologies.

"I, your humble servant, joined with you to attack Chin," he said. "You fought north of the Yellow River while I fought south. I had not expected to be the first to enter the Pass and conquer Chin, so that we meet again here. Now some evil-minded man has been sowing doubt in your mind."

"It was your own officer Tsao Wu-shang," replied Hsiang Yu. "Otherwise such a thing would never have occurred to me."

Hsiang Yu invited Liu Pang to stay for a banquet. He and Hsiang Po sat facing east, the patriarch Fan Tseng faced south; Liu Pang faced north and Chang Liang, who was in attendance upon him, faced west. Several times Fan Tseng shot Hsiang Yu meaningful glances and three times, as a hint, raised his jade *chueh*.* But Hsiang Yu did not respond. Finally Fan Tseng rose and went out. Summoning Hsiang Chuang, he said:

"Our lord is too kind-hearted. Go in, drink a toast and offer to perform a sword dance. Then strike the lord of Pei down where he sits. If you don't do this, we will all end up his captives."

Hsiang Chuang went in to offer a toast, after which he said, "Our prince is drinking with the lord of Pei, but we have no entertainers in the army. May I perform a sword dance?"

"Very well," said Hsiang Yu.

Hsiang Chuang drew his sword and began the dance, and Hsiang Po followed suit, shielding Liu Pang with his body so that Hsiang Chuang could not strike him.

Chang Liang went out to the gate of the camp to see Fan Kuai, who asked, "How are things in there?"

"Touch and go," replied Chang Liang. "Hsiang Chuang has drawn his sword to dance. He means to kill the lord of Pei."

"This is serious!" said Fan Kuai. "Let me go in and have it out with him."

Sword and shield in hand he entered the gate. Guards with crossed halberds tried to bar the way, but he charged and knocked them down with his tilted shield. Bursting into the tent, he lifted the curtain and stood facing west, glaring at Hsiang

---

* An ornament in the form of a broken ring. He was hinting that Hsiang Yu should break with Liu Pang.

Yu. His hair bristled, his eyes nearly started from his head. Hsiang Yu raised himself on one knee and reached for his sword.

"Who is this stranger?" he asked.

"This is the lord of Pei's bodyguard, Fan Kuai," answered Chang Liang.

"Stout fellow!" said Hsiang Yu. "Give him a stoup of wine."

Wine was poured and presented to Fan Kuai, who bowed his thanks and straightened up to drink it standing.

"Give him a leg of pork," directed Hsiang Yu.

A raw leg of pork was given to Fan Kuai, who set his shield upside down on the ground, placed the pork on it, carved it with his sword and began to eat.

"Stout fellow!" cried Hsiang Yu. "Can you drink any more?"

"I am not afraid of death; why should I refuse a drink?" retorted Fan Kuai. "The king of Chin had the heart of a tiger or a wolf. He killed more men than one could count and tortured others cruelly. So the whole world revolted against him. King Huai promised his generals that the first to conquer the land of Chin and enter its capital should be its king. Now the lord of Pei has conquered Chin and taken Hsienyang. But he has not touched anything. He sealed up the palaces, withdrew his troops to Pashang to wait for you, and sent men to guard the Pass against bandits and other emergencies. Yet though he has laboured so hard and achieved so much, you do not reward him with noble rank but listen to worthless talk and decide to kill this hero. This is to go on in the way that led to the downfall of Chin. Please do not act like this, Your Majesty."

Hsiang Yu could not answer.

"Sit down," he said.

Fan Kuai took a seat next to Chang Liang. Presently Liu Pang got up and went out to the privy, beckoning Fan Kuai to go with him. Hsiang Yu ordered his lieutenant Chen Ping to call him back.

"I've come out without taking leave," said Liu Pang. "What shall I do?"

"Where big issues are at stake you cannot trouble about trifles," said Fan Kuai. "In matters of consequence you cannot observe the minor courtesies. They are the chopper and board, we the fish and meat. Why should we take our leave?"

So Liu Pang started off, telling Chang Liang to stay behind to make his excuses.

"What gifts did you bring with you, my lord?" asked Chang Liang.

"A pair of white jade discs for Lord Hsiang Yu, and a pair of jade wine cups for the patriarch Fan Tseng. Seeing how angry they were, I dared not present them. Will you please do so for me?"

"Very good, my lord," said Chang Liang.

Now Hsiang Yu's camp was at Hungmen and Liu Pang's at Pashang, some forty *li* away. Leaving his chariot and retinue, Liu Pang rode off alone, followed on foot by Fan Kuai, Hsia-hou Ying, Chin Chiang and Chi Hsin, who carried swords and shields. Skirting Mount Li, they took a short cut to Chihyang.

"By this route it is only twenty *li* to my camp," Liu Pang had told Chang Liang. "Wait until you think I have got there before you go back in."

When enough time had passed for him to reach his troops, Chang Liang went in to apologize for him.

"The lord of Pei had too much to drink and was unable to take his leave," he said. "He asked your humble servant to present this pair of white jade discs to Your Lordship and this pair of jade wine cups to the Patriarch."

"Where is he now?" asked Hsiang Yu.

"Knowing that your Lordship meant to censure him, he left alone. He must be in his camp by now."

Hsiang Yu accepted the discs and placed them on his mat. But Fan Tseng put the jade cups on the ground, drew his sword and smashed them to pieces.

"Bah!" he cried. "Advice is wasted on a fool. The lord of Pei will wrest your empire from you and take us all captive."

As soon as Liu Pang reached his camp, he had Tsao Wu-shang executed.

A few days later Hsiang Yu led his troops west, massacred the citizens of Hsienyang, killed Tzu-ying, the last king of Chin who had surrendered, and set fire to the Chin palaces. The conflagration raged for three whole months. Having looted the city and seized the women there, he started east.

Someone advised him, "The region inside the Pass is surrounded by mountains and rivers which form natural barriers, and the soil is fertile. You could make this your capital and rule supreme."

But now the Chin palaces were destroyed by fire and Hsiang Yu longed to go back to his home in the east.

"What use are wealth and rank if you do not go home?" he retorted. "That is like wearing embroidered clothes at night when nobody can see you."

"They say the men of Chu are apes with hats on," observed a wit later. "It's really true."

When Hsiang Yu heard this, he had the man thrown into a boiling cauldron.

Hsiang Yu sent a messenger to report to King Huai.

"Let it be as we agreed," replied the king.

Then King Huai received the title of Righteous Emperor. Hsiang Yu, who wished to be a king, first made the other generals and ministers kings.

"When the revolt broke out, we set up the descendants of different royal houses as a temporary measure to attack Chin," he said. "We are the ones, however, who took up arms, started the revolt and risked our lives on the battlefield for three years until Chin was overthrown and the empire pacified. The Righteous Emperor has done nothing. Let us divide up his land and make ourselves kings."

The generals agreed to this and they divided the empire, making themselves lords and kings.

Hsiang Yu and Fan Tseng suspected that Liu Pang meant to seize the whole realm. But having settled their dispute with him, they hesitated to break their word for fear the other leaders might not support them. So they plotted together saying, "The lands of Pa and Shu are mountainous and impassable. That is where all the exiles used to be sent by Chin." Then, announcing that Pa and Shu were also inside the Pass, they made Liu Pang king of Han to rule over Pa, Shu and Hanchung, with his capital at Nancheng. And Chin was divided into three kingdoms under the Chin generals who had surrendered, as buffer states against Han.

Hsiang Yu made Chang Han king of Yung to rule over the territory west of Hsienyang with his capital at Feichiu. His secretary Szuma Hsin, the former gaoler of Yoyang who had helped Hsiang Liang, was also made a king. So was the army commander Tung Yi, who had advised Chang Han to surrender to Hsiang Yu.

Szuma Hsin became king of Sai, ruling over the territory east of Hsienyang as far as the Yellow River, with his capital at Yoyang. Tung Yi was made king of Ti to rule Shangchun Province with his capital at Kaonu. King Pao of Wei was sent west to be king of West Wei, ruling over Hotung with his capital at Pingyang. Shen Yang of Hsiachiu, Chang Erh's favourite who had conquered the province of Honan and surrendered to the Chu army by the river, was made king of Honan with his capital at Loyang. King Cheng of Hann remained where he was, with Yangchai as his capital. Szuma Ang, a general of Chao who had conquered Honei and won several victories, was made king of Yin over Honei with his capital at Chaoko. King Hsieh of Chao was transferred to be king of Tai. Chang Erh, the able chief minister of Chao who had accompanied the Chu army through the Pass, was made king of Changshan ruling over Chao with his capital at Hsiangkuo.

Ying Pu, lord of Tangyang, who had proved the bravest general of the Chu army, was made king of Chiuchiang with his capital at Liu. Wu Jui, lord of Po, who had led the Pai Yueh tribesmen as reinforcements to the feudal princes and followed Hsiang Yu through the Pass, was made king of Hengshan with his capital at Dju. Kung Ao, the Righteous

Emperor's minister who had led troops against Nanchun and won many victories, was made king of Linchiang with his capital at Chiangling.

Han Kuang, king of Yen, was transferred to be king of Liaotung. The Yen general Tsang Tu, who had joined the Chu forces to rescue Chao and accompanied Hsiang Yu through the Pass, was made king of Yen with his capital at Chi. Tien Fu, king of Chi, was transferred to be king of Chiaotung. The Chi general Tien Tu, who had joined the Chu forces to rescue Chao and accompanied Hsiang Yu through the Pass, was made king of Chi with his capital at Lintzu.

Then there was Tien An, grandson of the former king of Chi, who was conquered by Chin. When Hsiang Yu crossed the river to rescue Chao, Tien An took several cities north of the River Chi and came over to Hsiang Yu with his forces. He was therefore made king of Chipei, with his capital at Poyang.

Tien Jung, who had often disobeyed Hsiang Liang's orders and refused to aid Chu against Chin, was given no title. Though Chen Yu, lord of Chengan, had abandoned his commander's seal and refused to follow Hsiang Yu into the Pass, he was known to be a talented man who had served Chao well. When it was learned that he was at Nanpi, he was given three adjacent counties. Mei Chuan, a general under the lord of Po who had many bold deeds to his credit, received a fief of one hundred thousand households. As for Hsiang Yu, he set himself up as Overlord of West Chu, with nine provinces as his kingdom and Pengcheng as his capital.

In the fourth month of the first year of Han,* the various kings withdrew their troops and returned to their own countries. When Hsiang Yu reached his kingdom, he gave orders for the removal of the Righteous Emperor, saying, "In ancient times an emperor who had one thousand square *li* of territory always lived on the upper reaches of a river." His envoy told the emperor to move to the district of Shen in Changsha, and

---

* 206 B.C.

kept urging him to go till one by one the emperor's ministers left him. Then Hsiang Yu secretly ordered the kings of Hengshan and Linchiang to attack and kill the emperor on the river.

As King Cheng of Han had won no victories, Hsiang Yu prevented his return to his kingdom by taking him to Pengcheng. There, having degraded him to the rank of a marquis, he killed him. When Tsang Tu went to his state of Yen, he tried to drive away the former king, Han Kuang, to Liaotung. As Han Kuang refused to go, Tsang Tu attacked and killed him at Wuchung and annexed his territory.

When Tien Jung heard that Hsiang Yu had removed the king of Chi to Chiaotung, setting up the Chi general Tien Tu in his stead, he was very angry and refused to let Tien Tu take up his new position in Chi but rose in arms and attacked him. Tien Tu fled to the land of Chu. Since King Tien Shih was afraid of Hsiang Yu, he fled to Chiaotung, his new realm. Tien Jung pursued him in anger and killed him at Chimo. Then Tien Jung made himself king of Chi and marched west to attack and kill Tien An, king of Chipei. He now ruled over Chi, Chiaotung and Chipei. Tien Jung gave Peng Yueh a commander's seal and ordered him to revolt in the land of Wei. Chen Yu also sent Chang Tung and Hsia Yueh in secret to advise him.

"Hsiang Yu has not divided the country fairly," they said. "He has made all the former kings rulers of poor lands, but made his generals and ministers kings of rich districts. He drove the former king of Chao north to the land of Tai. We do not think this is right. Now we hear Your Highness has taken up arms, unable to endure this injustice. We hope you will lend us troops to attack Changshan and restore the king of Chao. We will gladly serve as your bulwark."

Tien Jung agreed and sent troops to the land of Chao. Chen Yu mobilized the men of his three counties and together they attacked Changshan and routed Chang Erh, who fled to Han. Then Chen Yu welcomed back the former king of Chao from Tai, and the king made Chen Yu king of Tai.

At this time, the Han army turned back and conquered the

224

three kingdoms of Yung, Sai and Ti. When Hsiang Yu heard that the king of Han had gained control of all the land within the Pass and was about to march east, and that Chi and Chao had rebelled, he was very angry. He made Cheng Chang, former governor of Wu, king of Hann to repel the king of Han's advance, and ordered Chiao the lord of Hsiao and others to attack Peng Yueh. But Peng Yueh defeated them.

The king of Han dispatched Chang Liang to conquer Hann, and he wrote to Hsiang Yu saying, "The king of Han has not received the territory promised him within the Pass. As soon as the agreement is carried out, he will halt and not advance any further east." He also sent Hsiang Yu letters showing that Tien Jung and Peng Yueh meant to revolt, that Chi would ally with Chao to overthrow Chu.

Then instead of advancing west, Hsiang Yu proceeded north to attack Chi. He ordered Ying Pu, the king of Chiuchiang, to bring up reinforcements; but Ying Pu did not join him on the pretext of illness, merely sending a general with several thousand men. Hsiang Yu hated him for this.

In the winter of the second year of Han, Hsiang Yu went north to Chengyang, where Tien Jung joined battle with him. Tien Jung was defeated and fled to Pingyuan, to be killed by the people there. Hsiang Yu advanced further north, and burned or razed to the ground all the suburbs of Chi, massacred Tien Jung's men who had surrendered, and took captive the old and infirm as well as the women. He conquered the land up to Peihai, spreading havoc and destruction. Then the men of Chi gathered together and rebelled. Tien Jung's younger brother, Tien Heng, rallied what was left of the army, numbering tens of thousands of men, and raised a revolt at Chengyang. Hsiang Yu was forced to stop and launch several assaults against the city, but he failed to take it.

The following spring, the king of Han advanced east at the head of the allied troops of five states, five hundred and sixty thousand strong, to attack Chu. When Hsiang Yu received word of this, he sent his generals to subdue Chi in the north, while he himself led thirty thousand picked troops south through Lu to Huling.

In the fourth month, the Han soldiers entered Pengcheng, sacked the city, seized the women, and gave all their time to carousing. Hsiang Yu struck at dawn from Hsiao in the west and fell upon the Han army at Pengcheng in the east. By noon the Han forces were completely routed. They fled in disorder to the Ku and Szu Rivers, where more than one hundred thousand of them were drowned. The rest retreated south to the hills, but the army of Chu pursued them to the banks of the River Sui, east of Lingpi. The Han troops fell back, hard pressed by the men of Chu. Some hundred thousand soldiers of Han were cut down and their bodies, thrown into the Sui, blocked the flow of the river. The pursuers threw three cordons round the king of Han. But just then a great wind sprang up from the northwest. It blew down trees and houses and raised swirling clouds of sand so that all grew dark and day turned into night. This storm beat against the army of Chu and threw it into confusion. Their ranks broke, enabling the king of Han to escape with several dozen horsemen.

The king of Han set out for Pei, meaning to take his family west with him. But as Hsiang Yu also sent pursuers to Pei, the king's family fled and missed him. On the road he met his son, later Emperor Hui, and his daughter, later Queen Yuan of Lu, and made them ride in his carriage. When the Chu cavalry came hot on their heels, the king in desperation pushed his children out; but Hsia-hou Ying, lord of Teng, got down and helped them in again. This happened three times.

"No matter how hard pressed we are, we cannot drive any faster," protested Hsia-hou Ying. "How can you abandon them?"

When they had made good their escape, the king of Han looked in vain for his father and his wife, later Empress Lu. They, escorted by Shen Yi-chi, were searching for him when they ran into some Chu troops instead. The men of Chu reported their capture to Hsiang Yu, who kept them in his army.

At this time Empress Lu's brother, Lu Chai, was in command

of the Han troops at Hsiayi. There the king of Han went, rallying stragglers on the way. By the time he reached Yingyang all his defeated soldiers had reassembled. Hsiao Ho also mobilized all the old and weak within the Pass who had not been conscripted, and sent them to Yingyang. Thus their army became a force to reckon with again.

The Chu troops, advancing from Pengcheng, followed up their victory and fought the Han army south of Yingyang between Ching and Soting. But the men of Han defeated them there, checking their advance further west.

While Hsiang Yu was relieving Pengcheng and pursuing the king of Han to Yingyang, Tien Heng was able to reconquer Chi and set up Tien Jung's son, Tien Kuang, as king there. After Han's defeat at Pengcheng, all the other kings went over to Hsiang Yu. The king of Han camped at Yingyang and constructed a walled road to the Yellow River to convey grain from Aotsang.

In the third year of Han, Hsiang Yu repeatedly cut this supply route so that the Han army ran short of food. The king of Han in alarm sued for peace, claiming only the territory west of Yingyang. Hsiang Yu would have agreed, but Fan Tseng marquis of Liyang said, "The Han army is easy to crush. If you let them go, you will be sorry later." So Hsiang Yu and Fan Tseng hammered at Yingyang.

In this desperate situation the king of Han adopted a plan devised by Chen Ping to sow dissension between Hsiang Yu and Fan Tseng. When an envoy from Hsiang Yu arrived, the king made ready a feast; but as it was being served he pretended to show great surprise on seeing who the envoy was.

"I thought you were Fan Tseng's envoy," he explained. "I see you come from Hsiang Yu."

He had the feast removed and more common fare brought in.

When the envoy went back and reported this, Hsiang Yu suspected Fan Tseng of being in league with Han, and little by little deprived him of his authority. Fan Tseng was very angry.

"The empire is nearly won," he said. "Your Highness can manage alone. Allow me to retire to the ranks."

Hsiang Yu gave his consent. But before Fan Tseng reached Pengcheng he had an abscess on his back and died.

Then Chi Hsin, a general of Han, said to the king, "We are in desperate straits, sir. Let me impersonate you to deceive the Chu army so that you may escape."

One night the king sent the women of Yingyang together with two thousand soldiers out through the east gate, and the Chu troops attacked them from all sides. Chi Hsin, in the carriage with the yellow canopy and the feather pennant on the left, came out to declare, "There is no food left in the city. The king of Han surrenders."

While all the Chu soldiers were cheering, the king of Han slipped out through the west gate with a few dozen horsemen and fled to Chengkao. When Hsiang Yu saw Chi Hsin, he demanded:

"Where is your king?"

"His Majesty had already left," was the answer.

Hsiang Yu had Chi Hsin burned alive.

The king of Han had entrusted the defence of Yingyang to his chief counsellor Chou Ko, Lord Tsung and Pao, once king of Wei. Chou Ko and Lord Tsung took counsel together and said, "A rebel king can hardly be trusted to defend the city." Thereupon they killed Pao.

Then the Chu army stormed the city and captured Chou Ko alive.

"If you will serve as my general, I will make you a chief marshal with a fief of thirty thousand families," said Hsiang Yu.

But Chou Ko swore at him, "Unless you surrender soon, the king of Han will capture you. You are no match for him."

In a rage, Hsiang Yu had him thrown into the cauldron and killed Lord Tsung as well.

After escaping from Yingyang, the king of Han fled south to Wan and Sheh. He won over Ying Pu, king of Chiuchiang, and raised troops to defend Chengkao.

In the fourth year of Han, Hsiang Yu laid siege to Chengkao. The king fled alone with Lord Teng through the north gate, crossed the river and went to Hsiuwu to join the army of Chang Erh and Han Hsin. One by one his generals escaped from Chengkao and joined him. When the Chu army took Chengkao and started westwards, the king of Han sent troops to hold Kung and check their advance.

At this point Peng Yueh crossed the river and attacked Tunga in Chu, killing the Chu general Lord Hsueh. So Hsiang Yu turned east to fight Peng Yueh. Now that the king of Han had Han Hsin's army, he wanted to cross the Yellow River and head south, but on Cheng Chung's advice he stayed in his positions north of the river, sending Liu Chia with troops to aid Peng Yueh and burn the Chu supplies. In the east Hsiang Yu defeated Peng Yueh and put him to flight.

The king struck across the river and recaptured Chengkao, stationed his army on Mount Kuangwu and drew supplies from Aotsang. Having conquered the land in the east, Hsiang Yu marched west again. He, too, stationed his army opposite Mount Kuangwu, confronting the forces of Han. This stalemate lasted for some months.

Meanwhile Peng Yueh continued to rebel in Liang and to intercept the Chu army's grain supply, which seriously worried Hsiang Yu. He had a high scaffold built on which he set the king of Han's father.

"Surrender at once, or I shall boil your father alive!" he threatened.

"Together we received King Huai's orders and swore to be brothers," replied the king of Han. "That makes my father yours as well. If you insist on boiling your own father, do send me a bowl of the soup!"

In a great rage Hsiang Yu prepared to kill the old man, but Hsiang Po reasoned with him saying, "It is not yet settled who will win the empire, and a man who aspires to be emperor will not trouble about his family. Killing him could serve no purpose but only make for trouble."

Hsiang Yu listened to his advice.

For a long time Chu and Han had battled yet neither had won a decisive victory. The able-bodied men were weary of fighting while the old and weak were exhausted by grain transportation. Hsiang Yu made a proposal to the king of Han.

"Because of us, the empire has been in a tumult for years. Let us settle the issue now by hand-to-hand combat instead of involving all these other men."

The king declined with a smile.

"I prefer to fight with my wits," he said, "not with brute force."

Then Hsiang Yu ordered his best fighters to challenge the men of Han to single combat. In the Han army there was a skilled mounted archer named Lou Fan, who with his arrows killed each Chu warrior after a few rounds of fighting. Hsiang Yu in a fury buckled on armour himself and rode out with his halberd to do battle. As Lou Fan raised his bow, Hsiang Yu glared and bellowed so fiercely that the bowman dared not meet his eyes or shoot but fled back to the rampart, too terrified to take the field again. When the king of Han sent to ask the reason and found that this warrior was Hsiang Yu himself, he was terrified. Hsiang Yu called to the king across the lines on Mount Kuangwu. The king enumerated Hsiang Yu's faults, while Hsiang Yu angrily challenged him to a fight, but his challenge was not accepted. Then Hsiang Yu shot him with a crossbow he had concealed, and the king fled, wounded, to Chengkao.

When Hsiang Yu learned that Han Hsin had conquered the land north of the Yellow River, defeated the armies of Chi and Chao and was about to invade Chu, he sent General Lung Chu to attack him. Han Hsin and Kuan Ying, the cavalry commander, struck back and utterly routed the Chu army, killing Lung Chu. Han Hsin then set himself up as king of Chi.

Alarmed to hear of General Lung Chu's defeat, Hsiang Yu sent Wu Sheh, a native of Suyi, to win Han Hsin over, but with no success.

Meanwhile Peng Yueh had reconquered Liang and cut the Chu army's supply route. Hsiang Yu told his high marshal Tsao

Chiu, marquis of Haichun, and the other generals, "See you defend Chengkao well. If the Han army challenges you, do not give battle. Simply stop them advancing eastwards. In fifteen days, when I have killed Peng Yueh and retaken Liang, I shall join you again."

He marched east and attacked Chenliu and Waihuang on the way, but Waihuang held out against him for several days before it finally surrendered. In his rage he ordered all the men above fifteen to be taken to the east of the city, where he meant to have them massacred.

The thirteen-year-old son of the magistrate's steward went to him and said, "Peng Yueh forced Waihuang to rebel, and because the city was afraid it submitted to him, waiting for Your Highness to come to the rescue. But now that you are here you want to butcher our men. How can you win the hearts of the people like this? East of here there are more than a dozen cities of Liang, and now they will all be afraid to surrender to you."

Hsiang Yu saw the truth in what this lad said, and pardoned those who were to have been massacred. When this became known, all the cities east to Suiyang promptly surrendered.

The Han army challenged the Chu troops in Chengkao several times, but they would not be drawn. Then men were sent to insult them, until after five or six days the high marshal Tsao Chiu lost his temper and started leading his men across the River Szu. When half the army was across, the men of Han attacked and routed them, capturing all the treasure of the kingdom of Chu. The high marshal Tsao Chiu, the secretary Tung Yi and Szuma Hsin, king of Sai, killed themselves by the river. Tsao Chiu, former gaoler of Chi, and Szuma Hsin, former gaoler of Yoyang, had been trusted by Hsiang Yu because of the help they had once given Hsiang Liang.

At this time Hsiang Yu was at Suiyang. When he learned of his army's defeat he led his troops back. The soldiers of Han were besieging Chungli Mo east of Yingyang. At Hsiang Yu's approach, they withdrew in fear to the heights.

Now the Han army was strong and had ample supplies, while Hsiang Yu's troops were exhausted and had no food. The king of Han dispatched Lu Chia to ask Hsiang Yu to send his father back, but Hsiang Yu refused. Then the king sent Lord Hou to persuade him. This time Hsiang Yu agreed to divide the empire into two. The land west of Hungkou should go to Han, that east of Hungkou to Chu. This agreement reached, Hsiang Yu handed over the king's father and wife, while all the soldiers cheered. The king of Han called Lord Hou the Leveller of States, but would not let him appear again.

"This man is the world's greatest orator," he explained. "Wherever he goes, he causes kingdoms to fall. That is why I call him the leveller of states."

After making this agreement, Hsiang Yu led his army east. The king of Han prepared to go west, but Chang Liang and Chen Ping advised against this saying, "You now have the greater half of the empire and the support of all the states, while the army of Chu is exhausted and has no food. Heaven has decreed Hsiang Yu's downfall. You should seize this opportunity to crush him. To let Hsiang Yu go now would be like bringing up a tiger — simply asking for trouble in future."

The king took their advice.

In the fifth year of Han, the king pursued Hsiang Yu to south of Yangchia and stationed his troops there, appointing a date to attack with Han Hsin, marquis of Huaiyin, and Peng Yueh, marquis of Chiencheng. But when he reached Kuling their armies failed to appear. Hsiang Yu attacked and defeated the men of Han, who retreated to their ramparts and strengthened their defences.

"The marquises have failed me. What shall I do?" the king of Han asked Chang Liang.

"Chu is about to be crushed, but Han Hsin and Peng Yueh have not been given fiefs," replied Chang Liang. "No wonder they stayed away. If you will divide the empire with them, they will come immediately. If not, the issue is by no means certain. Give Han Hsin the land from Chen east to the coast, give Peng Yueh the land from Suiyang north to Kucheng, so that they will be fighting for themselves. Then Chu can easily be defeated."

"Very good," said the king of Han.

He sent envoys to inform Han Hsin and Peng Yueh, "If you join us to attack Chu, I will give all the land between Chen and the sea to Han Hsin, king of Chi, all that between Suiyang and Kucheng to Chancellor Peng Yueh when Hsiang Yu is defeated."

After the envoys reached them, Han Hsin and Peng Yueh agreed to send troops at once. Han Hsin advanced from Chi while Liu Chia led his army from Shouchun, took Chengfu and wiped out its defenders. Then both forces reached Kaihsia. Marshal Chou Yin also rebelled against Hsiang Yu and marched from Shu to take Liu and massacre its defenders. In addition, the army of Ying Pu, king of Chiuchiang, followed the armies of Liu Chia and Peng Yueh. These forces converged upon Hsiang Yu at Kaihsia.

Hsiang Yu's army at Kaihsia, with only a handful of troops and right out of supplies, was hemmed in by the men of Han and the other states. At night he heard the besiegers all about him singing Chu songs.

"Has Han already conquered Chu?" he asked in dismay. "They have so many men of Chu with them!"

He rose that night to drink in his tent. With him was the lovely Lady Yu, who followed wherever he went, and Chui, the swift steed which he always rode. Now Hsiang Yu chanted a tragic air, setting words to it himself:

> My strength uprooted mountains,
> My spirit overtopped the world;
> But the times are against me,
> And Chui can gallop no more.
> When Chui can gallop no more
> What can I do?
> And what is to become
> Of Lady Yu?

He sang this song several times and Lady Yu joined in.

Tears coursed down his cheeks, while all his followers wept and bowed their heads in sorrow. Then he mounted his horse and rode into the night with little more than eight hundred staunch followers. Breaking through the enemy lines to the south, they galloped away.

By dawn the Han army knew that he had escaped, and the cavalry officer Kuan Ying was sent with five thousand horsemen in pursuit. By the time Hsiang Yu crossed the River Huai, there were little more than a hundred horsemen with him. At Yinling he lost his way and asked an old man in the fields to direct him. "Bear left!" The old man deliberately deceived him, and going left he was bogged down in the marshes so that the Han cavalry came up with him.

So Hsiang Yu turned back east to Tungcheng. By now only twenty-eight horsemen remained with him, while his pursuers numbered several thousand. He knew that he could not escape and told his men:

"It is eight years since I rose in arms. In that time I have fought more than seventy battles. I swept all obstacles from my path, conquered every foe I attacked, and was never defeated. That is how I won the empire. But now suddenly I am hemmed in here. This is because Heaven is against me and not because my generalship is at fault. Today I shall perish here, but for your sake I shall fight gallantly and overcome the enemy three times. For you I shall break through their lines, kill their commander and cut down their flag, so that you may know it is Heaven that has destroyed me, not my generalship that is at fault."

He divided his horsemen into four groups, facing in four directions. The Han forces had surrounded them on all sides.

"Watch me kill one of their commanders for you!" he cried.

He ordered his men to gallop down in four directions and reassemble in three groups east of the hill. Then with a mighty battle-cry he charged. The Han troops scattered before him and he struck down one of their commanders. A cavalry commander named Yang Hsi, the marquis of Chihchuan, pursued him. But Hsiang Yu glared and bellowed at him so fiercely that Yang Hsi's horse bolted and fled, terrified, for several *li*.

Hsiang Yu rejoined his men, who by now had reassembled in three groups. The Han forces, not knowing which group he was in, divided into three to surround them again. Once more Hsiang Yu charged through their lines and killed a military tribune as well as several dozen men. When he rallied his followers again, he had lost only two of them.

"How was that?" he asked.

His men bowed and replied, "You were as good as your word, Your Majesty."

Hsiang Yu now considered crossing the River Wuchiang and going to the east of the Yangtse. The station master there had a boat moored and waiting. "There is not much land east of the Yangtse," he said to Hsiang Yu. "But a thousand square *li* and several hundred thousand men are enough for a kingdom. You must cross quickly, Your Highness! Mine is the only boat here. When the Han army comes, they will not be able to cross."

"Heaven is against me," replied Hsiang Yu with a laugh. "What use is it to cross the river? Besides, I once crossed the Yangtse and went west with eight thousand young men from the east, but now I have come back alone. Even if the elders made me king out of pity, how could I face them again? Though they said nothing, how could I hold up my head?" He turned to the station master. "I can see you are a worthy man. For five years I have ridden this horse, sweeping all before me, often galloping a thousand *li* in one day. I cannot bear to kill him. I give him to you."

He ordered his men to dismount for hand-to-hand combat. Hsiang Yu alone killed several hundred men of Han and was wounded some dozen times. Then, turning to see the cavalry officer Lu Ma-tung, he exclaimed:

"Isn't that my old friend Lu?"

Lu Ma-tung, facing him, pointed him out to Wang Yi.

"There is Hsiang Yu!"

Hsiang Yu said, "I hear the king of Han has offered a reward of a thousand gold pieces and a fief of ten thousand families for my head. Let me do you a good turn!" With that he cut his own throat.

Wang Yi seized his head, while the other horsemen trampled and jostled each other for his body — several dozen of them fought and killed each other. Finally a cavalryman of the guard, Yang Hsi, the cavalry marshal Lu Ma-tung, and the knights Lu Sheng and Yang Wu secured one limb each. When the five of them fitted the limbs together, it was seen that they were indeed those of Hsiang Yu, and the fief was divided among them. Lu Ma-tung was made marquis of Chungshui, Wang Yi marquis of Tuyen, Yang Hsi marquis of Chihchuan, Yang Wu marquis of Wufang, and Lu Sheng marquis of Niehyang.

After Hsiang Yu's death all the districts in Chu surrendered except Lu. The king of Han prepared to muster the troops of the whole country to massacre the inhabitants. But because they had proved loyal and ready to die for their master, Hsiang Yu's head was displayed to them. And thereupon the elders of Lu surrendered.

As King Huai of Chu had made Hsiang Yu lord of Lu and this district was the last to surrender after his death, Hsiang Yu was buried at Kucheng with the rites befitting the lord of Lu. The king of Han, before leaving, conducted the funeral in person and shed tears.

Instead of punishing Hsiang Yu's kinsmen, the king made Hsiang Po marquis of Yiyang. The marquises of Tao, Pingkao and Hsuanwu, all of whom belonged to the Hsiang clan, were given the royal surname Liu.

The Grand Historian comments: I heard from the scholar Chou that Emperor Shun had double pupils in his eyes, and they say Hsiang Yu was the same. Does this mean that he was a descendant of Shun? His rise was remarkably sudden. When the Chin government abused its power and Chen Sheh started a rebellion, the brave men who flocked to him were too many to count. Hsiang Yu had no inch of territory at the start, yet, taking this chance to rise in the countryside, within three years he commanded five states and overthrew the House of Chin. He carved up the empire and enfeoffed kings and barons. He was supreme, styling himself the Overlord, and though his rule did not endure his achievement was surely unique in recent times.

But when he gave up the land within the Pass to return to Chu, banished the Righteous Emperor and set himself up in his stead, he could hardly complain when the kings and barons turned against him. He boasted of his conquests, trusted only his personal judgement and did not follow ancient precedents. Considering himself the overlord, he tried to win the empire by military conquest, so that within five years he lost his kingdom and met his death at Tungcheng. Yet he never realized his mistake or blamed himself for his folly. What a fool he was to say that Heaven was against him and that it was not his generalship that was at fault!

CHANG LIANG, MARQUIS OF LIU

The ancestors of Chang Liang, marquis of Liu, came from the state of Hann. His grandfather Kai-ti served as prime minister to Marquis Chao, King Hsuan-hui and King Hsiang-ai of Hann. His father Ping was prime minister to King Hsi and King Tao-hui. Chang Ping died in the twenty-third year of King Tao-hui,* and twenty years later Hann was conquered by Chin. Chang Liang, still young, held no official position in Hann. At the time of the fall of Hann he still had three hundred slaves, yet when his younger brother died he did not bury him but used his patrimony to find an assassin who would kill the king of Chin to avenge his state, because his grandfather and father had been ministers of Hann during five reigns.

Chang Liang went east to study ceremony at Huaiyang, where he met Lord Tsang-hai and found a strong man whom he armed with an iron hammer one hundred and twenty catties in weight. When the First Emperor of Chin made a tour of the east, Chang Liang and the assassin attacked him at Polangsha, but by mistake struck at his attendant's carriage. In fact, Chang Liang was the cause of the urgent, countrywide search for brigands ordered by the emperor in his rage. But Chang Liang escaped to Hsiapi and went into hiding under an assumed name.

One day he was strolling idly across the bridge at Hsiapi when an old man in rough homespun approached, dropped a shoe under the bridge and, turning to Chang Liang, said, "Boy! Go down, and fetch my slipper!" Chang Liang was astounded and wanted to hit the fellow. But controlling himself on account of the other's age, he went down to fetch the shoe.

---

* 250 B.C.

"Put it on for me," ordered the old man. And since Chang Liang had already fetched the shoe, he knelt down to put it on. The old man stretched out his foot for it, then left with a smile while Chang Liang watched in amazement. After going some distance the old man came back. "You can be taught, boy," he said. "Meet me here five days from now at dawn."

Chang Liang, his curiosity aroused, knelt down to answer, "I will."

At dawn five days later he went back to the place. The old man, there before him, said angrily, "What do you mean by keeping an old man waiting? Come earlier five days from now." With that he left.

Five days later Chang Liang went earlier, only to find the old man already there. He was told to come back after another five days.

This time Chang Liang went before midnight. Presently the old man arrived. "That's right!" he said approvingly and handed him a book with the injunction, "Read this and you will become the teacher of kings. Ten years from now you will prosper. Thirteen years from now you will once more encounter me, as the yellow rock at the foot of Mount Kucheng north of the River Chi." Without another word he left and did not appear again.

When day broke Chang Liang examined the book and found it was *The Patriarch Lu Shang's Art of War*. Prizing this work, he pored over it again and again. He remained in Hsiapi as a champion of justice and helped to conceal Hsiang Po after he killed a man.

Ten years later Chen Sheh and the others revolted, and Chang Liang gathered a band of more than a hundred young men. When Ching Chu made himself the acting king of Chu in Liu, Chang Liang decided to join him; but on the way he met Liu Pang, then in command of several thousand men who were conquering the region west of Hsiapi, and he threw in his lot with him. Liu Pang made him a cavalry officer. Chang Liang expounded *The Patriarch's Art of War* to him on several occasions and he approved of the book and made use of its strategies, although Chang Liang found others could not understand them. Struck by Liu Pang's natural genius, he followed him instead of joining Ching Chu.

When Liu Pang went to Hsueh to see Hsiang Liang, who had set up King Huai of Chu, Chang Liang advised Hsiang Liang saying, "You have enthroned a descendant of the royal house of Chu. Lord Cheng of Hengyang of the House of Hann is also a worthy man. If you make him a king you will win another ally."

So Hsiang Liang sent him to find Lord Cheng and make him king of Hann with Chang Liang as his minister. Chang Liang went with the king of Hann and over a thousand men to conquer the territory of Hann in the west, but each time they took a city the army of Chin recaptured it. So they carried on mobile warfare in Yingchuan.

When Liu Pang marched south from Loyang through Huanyuan, Chang Liang led his men to join him and together they captured more than ten cities of Hann and routed Yang Hsiung's army. Then Liu Pang ordered King Cheng of Hann to defend Yangti while he went south with Chang Liang and stormed Wan before advancing west through the Wu Pass. He planned to lead twenty thousand men against the forces of Chin at the Yao Pass, but Chang Liang said, "Don't underestimate the men of Chin — they are still a powerful force. I hear their general is a butcher's son, and tradesmen are easily tempted by gain. Why not entrench yourself here, send a force ahead with provisions for fifty thousand and set up banners on all the hills around to dismay the enemy, while Li Yi-chi goes with rich gifts to bribe him?"

The Chin general did in fact surrender and offered to advance west with Liu Pang against Hsienyang. Liu Pang would have agreed, but Chang Liang warned, "The general is willing to surrender but I doubt if his troops will follow suit. That would put us in a dangerous position. Better strike while they are off their guard." So Liu Pang attacked and defeated the army of Chin, then marched north to Lantien where he routed the Chin forces again. When he reached Hsienyang, Tzu-ying, king of Chin, surrendered.

Liu Pang, entering the Chin palaces, found there hangings, curtains, hounds, horses, treasures and women by the thousand. Tempted to stay there, he ignored the advice of Fan Kuai, who urged him to camp outside.

Chang Liang said, "You are here because Chin did not rule well. And now that you have rid the world of a tyrant, you should trade on frugality. If the moment you enter Chin you indulge in its pleasures, you will just be out-doing the despot. 'Home truths grate on the ears yet are good guides to action; strong medicine tastes bitter yet helps to cure disease.' I hope you will take Fan Kuai's advice." Then Liu Pang withdrew his troops and stationed them at Pashang.

When Hsiang Yu, arriving in Hungmen, decided to attack Liu Pang, Hsiang Po hastened by night to their camp and secretly urged Chang Liang to leave with him.

But Chang Liang said, "I came on behalf of my prince to help Liu Pang. It would not be right to desert him in his hour of danger."

He reported the whole matter to Liu Pang, who asked in consternation, "What shall I do?"

"Do you really intend to oppose Hsiang Yu?" asked Chang Liang.

"A worthless fellow advised me to hold the Pass against the other princes so that I could rule over the whole of Chin. I acted on his advice."

"Do you believe you can defeat Hsiang Yu?"

After quite a long silence he answered, "No, of course not. What shall I do?"

Then Chang Liang urged Hsiang Po to come in and see Liu Pang, who drank a toast to him, promised to link their families by marriage, and asked him to explain to Hsiang Yu that he would never think of betraying him and had simply held the Pass against brigands. So Hsiang Po went back and cleared up this matter, as has been recorded in the account of Hsiang Yu.

In the first month of the first year of Han,* Liu Pang became king of Han ruling over Pa and Shu. He gave Chang Liang a hundred *yi* of gold and two pecks of pearls, all of which Chang Liang presented to Hsiang Po. Liu Pang also sent rich gifts to Hsiang Po through Chang Liang with a request for Hanchung, and since Hsiang Yu agreed Liu Pang obtained this district.

When Liu Pang set off to his kingdom, Chang Liang accompanied him as far as Paochung before he was told to return. He advised Liu Pang saying, "Why not burn the plank road through the mountains? This would show the world you have no intention of marching east again and reassure Hsiang Yu." Liu Pang, having sent him off, went on, destroying the plank road on his way.

Upon his return to Hann, Chang Liang found that King Cheng had not been allowed to go there but had been taken east by Hsiang Yu, because Chang Liang was on the side of Liu Pang. He told Hsiang Yu, "Liu Pang has destroyed the plank road and has no intention of coming east again." He also informed him of the revolt of King Tien Jung of Chi. Then Hsiang Yu set his mind at rest about Liu Pang in the west, and led an army north against Chi. He would not let King Cheng go, however, but made him a marquis and then had him killed at Pengcheng.

Chang Liang fled to join Liu Pang, who by then had marched back and conquered the three states of Chin. Chang Liang, made marquis of Chenghsin, went east with the army of Han to attack Chu.

At Pengcheng the Han army was defeated and Liu Pang retreated to Hsiayi. Unsaddling his horse to squat on the saddle, he said, "I mean to give up all the land east of the Pass to someone who will make common cause with me. Can you suggest anyone?"

Chang Liang stepped forward and said, "Ying Pu, king of Chiuchiang, is an able Chu general who hates Hsiang Yu. Or

---

* 206 B.C.

there is Peng Yueh, who has rebelled with King Tien Jung of Chi in Liang. Both men would serve in this emergency. Of your own generals, Han Hsin alone is capable of great things and can play an independent part. If you mean to give up this territory, give it to these three men. Then Hsiang Yu can be defeated."

Liu Pang sent Sui Ho to win over Ying Pu and another envoy to make an alliance with Peng Yueh. And when King Pao of Wei rebelled, he dispatched Han Hsin against him with an army. So he conquered Yen, Tai, Chi and Chao. And the final overthrow of Chu was thanks to these three men. Chang Liang's health was poor and he never commanded an army, but in his capacity as an adviser he was constantly with the king.

In the third year of Han, Hsiang Yu beset Liu Pang so hard at Yingyang that in alarm he asked Li Yi-chi how to weaken the power of Chu.

"When Tang conquered King Chieh of the Hsia Dynasty," said Li Yi-chi, "he gave the land of Chi to his descendants. When King Wu conquered King Chow of the Shang Dynasty, he gave Sung to his descendants. But Chin, abandoning virtue and justice, has abolished the ancestral sacrifices of the six princes and disinherited their descendants, leaving them not a single inch of land. If you restore the descendants of the six royal houses and present them with seals, then they, their ministers and their people will acknowledge your virtue and turn towards you in admiration, willing to be your subjects. When you have done such deeds of virtue and justice, you can rule as the overlord and Hsiang Yu will have to submit to your sovereignty."

"Good!" said Liu Pang. "Have the seals cut at once and you can set out with them."

Chang Liang happened to come in before Li Yi-chi left on this mission. Liu Pang who was at his meal called, "Come over here! Someone has proposed a plan to weaken Chu's power." Having told Chang Liang all Li Yi-chi had said, he asked, "What do you think?"

243

"Who made this plan?" asked Chang Liang. "This will be your ruin!"

"In what way?" asked Liu Pang.

"Give me your chopsticks and let me explain. When Tang conquered the Hsias, he gave Chi to his descendants because he had power of life and death over them. Have you power of life and death over Hsiang Yu?"

"No, I have not."

"Fallacy number one. When King Wu conquered the Shangs, he gave Sung to his descendants because he knew he could cut off the head of the Shang king. Can you cut off Hsiang Yu's head?"

"No, I cannot."

"Fallacy number two. When King Wu took the Shang capital, he honoured Shang Jung's lane, released Chi Tzu from prison and enlarged Pi Kan's grave. Are you in a position to enlarge a sage's grave, honour a good man's lane or a wise man's gate?"

"No, I am not."

"Fallacy number three. King Wu was able to distribute the grain stored at Chuchiao and the money stored at Lutai among the poor. Are you able to distribute grain and money to the poor?"

"No, I am not."

"Fallacy number four. After his conquest of Shang, King Wu converted war chariots into carriages, while shields and spears were laid down and covered with tiger skins to show the world that there would be no more war. Are you in a position to lay down arms, practise the arts of peace and end all wars?"

"No, I am not."

"Fallacy number five. King Wu grazed his horses south of Mount Hua to show that there would be no more unrest. Are you in a position to turn your horses loose?"

"No, I am not."

"Fallacy number six. King Wu pastured his cattle north of Taolin to show that there would be no more transport duty. Are you in a position to do that?"

"No, I am not."

"Fallacy number seven. Itinerant scholars from all over the world have left their homes, ancestral graves and friends to follow you just in the hope of getting a little land. If you restore the six states and enthrone the descendants of the royal houses of Hann, Wei, Yen, Chao, Chi and Chu, all these gentlemen will go back to serve their old masters, returning to their homes, friends and ancestral graves. Then who will help you to win your empire? This is fallacy number eight. Your main task now is to stop Chu from growing stronger. If the six states are restored and follow Hsiang Yu, how can you subjugate Chu? If you really adopt this plan, it will be your ruin."

Liu Pang stopped eating and spat the food out of his mouth. "That fool of a pedant nearly did for me!" he swore. He gave orders at once to have the seals cancelled.

In the fourth year of Han, Han Hsin conquered Chi and wanted to make himself king there. Liu Pang was angry, but Chang Liang persuaded him to give Han Hsin the seal of a king, as is recorded in the account of Han Hsin.

That autumn Liu Pang pursued Hsiang Yu to south of Yangchia; then, being worsted in battle, he entrenched himself in Kuling, but the other commanders failed to come to his aid. Only when he acted on Chang Liang's advice did the reinforcements come, as is recorded in the account of Hsiang Yu.

In the first month of the sixth year of Han, fiefs were given for outstanding services. Chang Liang had never distinguished himself in battle, but the emperor said, "The strategies you planned in your tent won battles for us a thousand *li* away — that is your achievement. Take your choice of any thirty thousand households in Chi."

Chang Liang answered, "After I rebelled at Hsiapi I met you at Liu. Heaven sent me to you, and I am glad that some of the plans I proposed proved useful. I shall be satisfied with the district of Liu as my fief. I cannot accept thirty thousand households." So Chang Liang was made marquis of Liu at the same time as Hsiao Ho and the others were enfeoffed.

That same year, after the emperor had enfeoffed more than twenty men with great achievements to their credit, the others disputed day and night and could not reach agreement, so that the work of enfeoffment was held up. One day in his Southern Palace in Loyang, the emperor looked down from a terrace and saw some generals sitting by the river and talking together.

"What are they discussing?" he asked.

"Don't you know, sir?" replied Chang Liang. "They are plotting rebellion."

"Peace has just been restored. Why should they revolt?"

"You started out as a common citizen but with their help won the empire. Since becoming the emperor you have ennobled close friends like Hsiao Ho and Tsao Shen and punished all your former enemies. Now these officers, comparing their achievements, think you have not land enough to give fiefs to all. They fear you may not ennoble them, or may even punish them for past shortcomings. That is why they are gathering together to plot revolt."

The emperor was disturbed and asked, "What shall I do?"

"Is there any man they all know you abominate?"

"Yung Chih is one of my old confederates, but he keeps plaguing and insulting me. If not for all he's done, I'd kill him."

"Then lose no time in giving Yung Chih a fief. When the others see him enfeoffed, they will rest assured."

So the emperor gave a feast at which he made Yung Chih marquis of Shihfang and ordered the prime minister and chief counsellor to decide on the other fiefs. After this feast the officers were pleased and said, "If even Yung Chih is made a marquis, we need have no worry."

Liu Ching advised the emperor to make his capital within the Pass. The emperor was in two minds about this. As most of his attendants and high ministers came from east of the mountains, they urged him to make Loyang the capital. "East of Loyang there is Chengkao, west Mount Yao and the River Min," they said. "With the Yellow River behind and the Yi and Lo Rivers before, it is surely impregnable!"

But Chang Liang objected, "Though Loyang has these advantages, it covers no more than a few hundred *li*, the land is not fertile and the city is open to attack on four sides. It is not strategically situated. Within the Pass, however, we have Mount Yao and the Hanku Pass to the east, the Lung and Shu ranges to the west, and a thousand *li* of fertile fields; while to the south is the wealth of Pa and Shu, to the north the advantage of the Hunnish pastures. With natural barriers on three sides, we need only cope with the barons in the east. So long as they are quiet, ships can sail along the Yellow River and the Wei to all parts of the empire to bring back grain to the capital in the west. And if the barons make trouble, we can sail downstream with supplies and reinforcements. This is truly a mighty stronghold of solid gold, a thousand-*li* wall of bronze, a natural treasure-house! Liu Ching is right."

That same day the emperor drove west in his carriage to make his capital within the Pass, and Chang Liang accompanied him. As his health was poor, Chang Liang practised breath control and ate no grain, not venturing out of his house for a year and more.

The emperor wished to depose the crown prince in favour of Prince Ju-yi of Chao, his son by Lady Chi; but because many of his chief ministers objected, he had not reached a final decision. Empress Lu was alarmed and did not know what to do till someone suggested, "The marquis of Liu is a shrewd schemer and the emperor trusts him."

Accordingly Empress Lu sent Lu Tse, marquis of Chiencheng, to enlist Chang Liang's help saying, "You have always advised the emperor. Now that he wants to disinherit the crown prince, how can you lie easy on your pillow?"

"When the emperor was in difficulties he used several of my plans," replied Chang Liang. "Now the empire is at peace and, if he wants to substitute his favourite son for the crown prince, this is between his own flesh and blood. A hundred or more ministers like myself can do nothing."

But Lu Tse insisted, "Think of some plan for us!"

"Hard to talk him out of this," was Chang Liang's answer.

"But there are four men the emperor has failed to win over. These four men are old and, because they think his manner insulting, they have hidden themselves in the hills and refuse to serve the House of Han. The emperor has a high regard for these men. Now if you spare no expense on gold and rich gifts, get the crown prince to write a letter couched in humble terms, send comfortable carriages for them and an eloquent speaker to press the invitation, it is possible they may come. If they do, you can entertain them as guests, taking them from time to time with you to the palace, where the emperor will notice them, wonder who they are and make inquiries. When he learns that they are these four worthies, that should help your case."

Then Empress Lu made Lu Tse send a messenger with the crown prince's letter, inviting these four men with humble words and rich gifts. Upon their arrival, Lu Tse made them his guests.

In the eleventh year of Han, Ying Pu rebelled. The emperor, who was ill, wanted the crown prince to command the army sent against him. The four worthies said to each other, "We came here to preserve the crown prince. If he commands the army he will be endangered." So they told Lu Tse, "If the crown prince commands the army and is successful that will not improve his position, while if he returns unsuccessful that will be disastrous. Besides, all the generals under him will be redoubtable veterans who helped his father to win the empire. The crown prince at their head will be like a lamb commanding a pack of wolves. As they will not fight well for him, his failure is certain.

"We have heard that whoever loves the mother will fondle her child. Now Lady Chi waits on the emperor day and night so that Prince Ju-yi is always dandled before him, and the emperor has declared that no unworthy son shall ever rule over a son whom he loves. It is obvious that he is going to replace the crown prince. Lose no time, then, in urging Empress Lu to find some chance to plead to the emperor with tears. She can say that Ying Pu is a formidable fighter, a brilliant commander known throughout the world. Since our generals are all the emperor's old comrades-in-arms, setting the crown prince at their head would be like setting a lamb at the head of wolves — they would never obey him. And once Ying Pu knew this, he would march west towards the capital to the roll of drums. Although the emperor is unwell, he should make the effort to lead this campaign and direct his troops from a carriage, for then his generals will not dare to shirk. Hard as it is, the emperor should do this for the sake of his wife and child."

Lu Tse went that same night to see the empress, who did as the four worthies suggested, seizing an opportunity to plead to the emperor with tears in her eyes.

"I suppose the boy is not up to it," said the emperor. "Your old man will have to go!" So he led his army eastwards. The ministers left in charge saw him off at Pashang. Although Chang Liang was ill, he forced himself to get up and see the emperor at Chuyiu.

"I should have accompanied you," he said, "but I am too ill. The men of Chu are swift. Don't risk a head-on clash." He persuaded the emperor to give the crown prince the command of the troops within the Pass.

"Although you are ill," said the emperor, "do your best to help the crown prince from your couch." At this time Shusun Tung was the prince's senior guardian, so Chang Liang acted as the junior guardian.

In the twelfth year of Han the emperor returned after defeating Ying Pu. His illness had grown worse and he was more determined than ever to depose the crown prince. When Chang Liang's advice against this was disregarded, he retired on the pretext of illness. The senior guardian Shusun Tung, quoting precedents ancient and modern, put up such a hard fight for the crown prince that the emperor pretended to agree, though he still meant to change his heir.

One day there was a feast and wine was served. The crown prince came to wait on his father, attended by four old men each over eighty. Their beards and eyebrows were white, their hats and gowns most imposing.

The emperor asked in surprise, "Who are these men?"

Then the four advanced and gave their names as Master Tung-yuan, Scholar Luli, Chili Chi and Master Hsia-huang.

The emperor exclaimed in astonishment, "I tried for several years to get hold of you, yet you always kept away. What are you doing with my son?"

The four men replied, "You insult gentlemen, sir, and are addicted to swearing. Unwilling to put up with humiliation, we ran away in fear. Then we heard that the crown prince was kind, pious and courteous to all, and that the people of the empire are ready to die for him, and so we came."

The emperor said, "Take good care of the crown prince!"

After the four had paid their respects they rose to leave, and the emperor watched them go. He called Lady Chi and pointed them out to her, saying, "I meant to depose the crown prince, but these four men have come to his aid. His feathers are grown, it would be hard to dislodge him. Empress Lu is going to be your mistress now."

Lady Chi shed tears, at which the emperor said, "Dance one of the dances of Chu for me, and I shall sing a song of Chu for you." With that he sang:

> High flies the wild .swan,
> Soaring a thousand *li*;
> His feathers grown,
> He sweeps freely across the four seas;
> Sweeps freely across the four seas,
> And what can we do?
> Even our stringed shafts
> Are powerless against him.

He sang this several times while Lady Chi wept and sobbed. Then he rose and left the feast. So thanks to these four men invited at the suggestion of Chang Liang, the crown prince retained his position.

Chang Liang accompanied the emperor on his expedition

against Chen Hsi in Tai, he devised the stratagem at Mayi, and it was he who urged that Hsiao Ho be made prime minister. In his leisure he advised the emperor on various matters, but since these were not vital affairs of state they need not be recorded.

Then Chang Liang announced, "My forefathers were ministers of the state of Hann and after the state was overthrown I gave up a fortune to avenge Hann against mighty Chin, causing a great stir in the world. With my ready tongue I became the adviser of an emperor, was given a fief of ten thousand households and made a marquis. This is all a common citizen could desire, and I am satisfied. Now I mean to turn my back on worldly affairs and follow the Master of the Red Pine." He abstained from grain and studied breath control so that he might fly through the air.

When the emperor died, Empress Lu was so grateful to Chang Liang that she insisted on his taking nourishment and said, "A man's life passes as swiftly as a white charger seen through a crack in the door. Why should you mortify yourself in this way?" So Chang Liang had to take food.

Eight years later he died and was given the posthumous title of Marquis of Wen-cheng. His son Pu-yi succeeded to his title.

As for the old man who met him on the bridge at Hsiapi and gave him *The Patriarch Lu Shang's Art of War,* when Chang Liang went north of the Chi River with the emperor thirteen years after their meeting, he found a yellow stone at the foot of Mount Kucheng which he took away and worshipped. After his death this stone was buried with him, and during the summer and winter sacrifices men sacrificed to the stone too. In the fifth year of Emperor Wen, Chang Liang's son Pu-yi was charged with impiety and deprived of his fief.

The Grand Historian comments: Most scholars deny the existence of ghosts and spirits, but admit that marvels take place. The story of Chang Liang's meeting with the old man who gave him the book is certainly a strange one. It was surely the will of Heaven that Chang Liang was so often able to save the first emperor of Han when he was in trouble. The emperor said, "When it comes to scheming in the commander's tent to win a battle a thousand *li* away, I am no match for Chang Liang." So I had always visualized him as a tall, imposing figure, yet when I saw his portrait he looked like a woman or a pretty girl. Confucius said, "Judging by appearances I have been mistaken in the case of Tzu-yu." The same might be said of Chang Liang.

PRIME MINISTER CHEN PING

Prime Minister Chen Ping was a citizen of Huyu in Yangwu county. In his boyhood his family was poor but he loved reading. He lived with his elder brother, who tilled their thirty *mou* of land, letting him leave home to study.

Chen Ping was tall and handsome. Once someone asked, "What do you eat to grow so plump, poor as you are?"

His sister-in-law, who disliked him because he did nothing to help on the farm, replied, "He eats both the grain and the husks. Such a brother is worse than none!"

When her husband heard this he drove her away and divorced her.

When Chen Ping was old enough to take a wife, no rich family would give him a daughter and he scorned to marry a poor girl. There was a wealthy old woman in Huyu, Dame Chang, whose grand-daughter had been betrothed five times but all of her betrotheds had died, so that no one dared marry her. Chen Ping, however, wanted her as his wife. Whenever there was a funeral in the town, Chen Ping, being poor, would hire out his services, going early and leaving late in the hope of getting better payment. At one funeral Dame Chang was struck by him and, late as it was when he left, she followed him to his home. She found he lived in a poor lane at the foot of the city wall with only some worn-out matting as a door, yet with many wheel marks outside made by the carriages of prominent men.

Upon her return home, Dame Chang told her son Chung, "I mean to marry my grand-daughter to Chen Ping."

"That pauper who does nothing for a living!" protested her son. "He is the laughing-stock of the whole county. Why give him my daughter?"

But Dame Chang said, "A fine-looking man like Chen Ping will not always be poor." She married her grand-daughter to him, and since Chen Ping was poor she lent him money for the betrothal gifts as well as providing wine and meat at the wedding. Moreover she warned her grand-daughter, "Don't be disrespectful to him because he is poor. You must wait on his elder brother as if he were your father and on his sister-in-law as if she were your mother."

After marrying this daughter of the Chang family, Chen Ping became better off and acquired more connections. He officiated at the local sacrifices and made a fair division of the sacrificial meat.

All the elders said, "How well young Chen takes charge!"

"Ah!" replied Chen Ping. "Put me in charge of the government and I should do equally well."

When Chen Sheh rose in revolt and became king of Chen, he sent Chou Shih to conquer Wei, set up Wei Chiu as king there, and fought the Chin troops at Linchi. Chen Ping, who had already left his brother, went with some other young men to join the king of Wei at Linchi. He was appointed master of the carriages, but his advice to the king was not accepted; so when someone slandered him he went away.

Later, when Hsiang Yu advanced to the Yellow River, Chen Ping joined him and accompanied him to Chin, where he was made a minister. Hsiang Yu went east to make Pengcheng his capital, while Liu Pang turned back to conquer the land of Chin and advanced east, and the king of Yin revolted against Chu. Then Hsiang Yu made Chen Ping the lord of Hsinwu and sent him with the king of Wei's troops in Chu to attack the king of Yin, who surrendered.

Upon Chen Ping's return, Hsiang Yu sent Hsiang Han to appoint him a chief commander and present him with twenty *yi* of gold. Almost at once, however, Liu Pang conquered Yin, and Hsiang Yu in his rage decided to punish the officers in charge there. Chen Ping, afraid he would be executed, returned his gold and seal through a messenger to Hsiang Yu and armed only with a sword fled alone by secret ways.

When he was crossing the river, the boatman suspected that this fine-looking man travelling alone must be some run-away officer carrying gold, jade or other treasures. There was murder in the ferryman's eyes. Chen Ping stripped off his clothes in alarm and helped to punt the boat. The boatman saw that he had nothing, and gave up his plan.

Chen Ping went to Hsiuwu and surrendered to Liu Pang, gaining an audience through the good offices of Wei Wu-chih. Liu Pang's chamberlain at this time was Shih Feng, known as the Lord of Ten Thousand Piculs, who interviewed Chen Ping and introduced him.

After Chen Ping and six others had been received and given food, Liu Pang dismissed them saying, "All right, go back now to your hostel."

"I have come on business," objected Chen Ping. "What I have to say cannot wait until tomorrow."

Liu Pang talked with him and was favourably impressed. "What post did you have in Chu?" he asked.

Chen Ping answered, "I was an army officer."

That same day Liu Pang appointed him an army officer and his attendant in the royal carriage, making him the officer in charge of army discipline. The other officers were dumb-founded and complained, "The king has just got hold of this deserter from Chu and, with no idea of his ability, he is letting him share the royal carriage and control us."

When Liu Pang heard this, he showed even greater favour to Chen Ping. The men of Han marched east to attack Hsiang Yu but suffered a reverse at Pengcheng and withdrew, regrouping their scattered forces at Yingyang. Chen Ping, made lieutenant general under King Hsin of Hann, encamped his troops at Kuangwu.

Then Chou Po, Kuan Ying and others spoke slightingly of him. "Chen Ping is a fine-looking fellow," they said, "but jade ornaments on a cap do not mean there is anything inside the head. We hear that at home he had an affair with his sister-in-law; not doing well in Wei he fled to Hsiang Yu; but failing to please him, he fled to us. Now Your Majesty

255

has honoured and trusted him, making him the officer in charge of army discipline, yet we hear that he accepts bribes from the officers. Those who give the most get good jobs, those who give little get inferior posts. He is obviously a dangerous turncoat. We hope you will look into this, sir."

Liu Pang, his suspicions aroused, summoned Wei Wu-chih and reproached him for recommending Chen Ping.

"I recommended him for his ability," replied Wei Wu-chih. "But Your Majesty is questioning his private conduct. If you had men with the virtue of Wei Sheng and Hsiao Chi who could not help to win the war, what use would they be to you, sir? Now that Chu and Han are fighting it out, all I consider when I recommend a brilliant strategist is whether his plans will benefit our state or not. What does it matter if he had an affair with his sister-in-law or accepted bribes?"

Then Liu Pang sent for Chen Ping and reproached him saying, "You failed to do well in the service of Wei, then left the service of Chu, and now you have come to me. Is it right to chop and change so often?"

"The king of Wei would not take my advice: that is why I left him to serve Hsiang Yu," said Chen Ping. "But Hsiang Yu is incapable of trusting others and employs or favours only his own clan or his wives' relatives, and is unable to make use of men of talent. That is why I left him. I came here because Your Majesty had the reputation of knowing how to use men. I arrived empty-handed and should have had nothing to live on had I not accepted some money. If my plans are any good, you can adopt them. If not, I still have the money and shall give it to the treasury, and then beg leave to go home."

Liu Pang apologized and loaded him with gifts, appointing him provost marshal to supervise the actions of all his generals, who after that dared say no more.

Later the Chu army launched a sudden attack, cut off Han's grain supply and besieged Liu Pang at Yingyang till in his alarm he sued for peace, offering Hsiang Yu all the land west of Yingyang. But Hsiang Yu refused his terms.

The king said to Chen Ping, "The land is in utter confusion — shall we never have peace?"

"King Hsiang Yu is courteous and considerate," answered Chen Ping. "That is why men of honour who value ceremony flock to him. But when it comes to rewarding distinguished service with ranks and fiefs, he is tight-fisted, and for this reason no one stays with him long. You, sir, are so insulting and rude that men of honour do not come to you, while your generosity with fiefs make shameless fools who are out for profit flock to you. Could you get rid of both faults and adopt both virtues, you might pacify the empire as easily as raising a finger. But your overbearing ways will never win over men of honour. Of course, Chu is vulnerable too. Hsiang Yu has only a few officers as staunch as Fan Tseng, Chungli Mo, Lung Chu and Chou Yin. If you, sir, would spend a few tens of thousands of pieces of gold to spread rumours and sow dissension between him and these men, he will doubt their loyalty. What with Hsiang Yu's suspicious nature and his proneness to listen to slander, they are bound to be set at odds. Then if you raise an army to attack them, you will undoubtedly triumph."

Liu Pang, approving this plan, gave him forty thousand pieces of gold to use at his discretion, not asking for any account.

Chen Ping used most of this gold to sow dissension in the Chu army. Word was spread that generals like Chungli Mo, who had served Hsiang Yu well yet never been granted fiefs or made princes, meant to join Han to destroy Hsiang Yu and divide up his land. Then, sure enough, Hsiang Yu began to distrust these men.

Hsiang Yu, his misgivings already aroused, sent an envoy to Liu Pang, who prepared a great feast for him. But when the man entered, Liu Pang made a show of surprise. "I thought you were from the Patriarch Fan Tseng," he said. "But I see you come from Hsiang Yu." The feast was removed and poorer dishes brought in.

When the envoy went back and reported this, Hsiang Yu

257

grew very suspicious of Fan Tseng and, not trusting him, would not allow him to attack the city of Yingyang.

As soon as he knew that Hsiang Yu doubted him, Fan Tseng told him angrily, "Now that the fate of the empire is virtually settled you can manage for yourself, sir. Please allow me to go home." So he left, but an abscess broke out on his back and he died before reaching Pengcheng.

Then Chen Ping sent two thousand women out by night through the east gate of Yingyang, and while the Chu army attacked them he and Liu Pang slipped out by the west gate. Re-entering the Pass, they collected their scattered troops and marched east again.

The following year Han Hsin conquered Chi, made himself the king there and sent an envoy to announce this to Liu Pang. Liu Pang flew into a passion and started swearing, till Chen Ping trod on his foot and he took the hint. Having treated the envoy handsomely, he sent Chang Liang to confirm Han Hsin's new title. He gave Chen Ping the fief of Huyu, and by using his strategies finally defeated Chu. Chen Ping later accompanied the emperor as provost marshal to crush the revolt of Tsang Tu, king of Yen.

In the sixth year of Han, someone submitted a letter reporting that Han Hsin was plotting revolt. The emperor consulted his generals, all of whom advised, "Send out a force at once to destroy the upstart."

The emperor was silent for a time, then summoned Chen Ping to ask for his opinion. Declining to give it, Chen Ping inquired, "What do your generals say?" When told he asked, "Does anyone know that this letter has been sent?"

"No," said the emperor.

"Does Han Hsin know?"

"Not yet."

"How do your troops compare with his?"

"They are no better."

"Have you any commanders who can out-general him?"

"No, they are no match for him."

"So neither your troops nor your generals are as good as his.

If you lead an army against him you will be forcing his hand. That strikes me as risky."

"Then what shall I do?"

"The emperors of old used to make imperial tours of inspection and summon all the nobles to meet them. You can give out that you are going south to Yunmeng Marsh to meet the nobles of different states at Chen on the western boundary of Chu. When Han Hsin hears that you are on a goodwill trip, he will feel secure and come out to pay homage. Then you can have him seized. All you need for that is a strong man."

The emperor, approving, sent envoys to summon different nobles to Chen on his way south to Yunmeng. He set out with a retinue and was met by Han Hsin on the road to Chen. The emperor had guards ready. They arrested Han Hsin and bound him to a rear carriage.

"Now the empire is won," cried Han Hsin, "I suppose I deserve to be thrown into the cauldron!"

"Hold your tongue!" shouted the emperor, looking back. "Your treason is known."

Then the guards trussed Han Hsin up and took him away, while the emperor went on to meet other nobles at Chen and pacified the land of Chu. Returning to Loyang, he pardoned Han Hsin and made him marquis of Huaiyin. This was when the emperor gave tallies of office and fiefs to his followers according to their merit.

A tally was given to Chen Ping with the promise that his title, marquis of Huyu, should be retained by his descendants.

Chen Ping declined, saying, "I have done nothing to merit this."

"It was through using your plans that I defeated my enemy," retorted the emperor. "Isn't that your merit?"

"But if not for Wei Wu-chih's recommendation, I could never have entered your service," said Chen Ping.

"I am glad you don't forget the man to whom you owe your advancement," replied the emperor and rewarded Wei Wu-chih too.

The following year Chen Ping accompanied the emperor as

provost marshal to Tai to suppress the revolt of King Hsin of Hann. Suddenly surrounded by the Huns at Pingcheng, they were cut off from supplies for seven days. Chen Ping suggested a ruse to the emperor, who sent a message to the wife of the Hunnish khan so that the siege was raised and they escaped. What this ruse was is still a mystery.

The emperor, travelling south, ascended the city wall of Chiuyu and was impressed by the number of large buildings there. "What a magnificent town!" he exclaimed. "In all my journeys through the empire I have seen no place but Loyang to compare with this." He turned to his secretary and asked, "What is the population of Chiuyu?"

"Under Chin there were more than thirty thousand households," was the answer. "Since then, many citizens have fled or gone into hiding because of all the fighting. There are now only five thousand households."

The emperor ordered his secretary to appoint Chen Ping marquis of Chiuyu with the whole district as his fief instead of Huyu. In his capacity as provost marshal Chen Ping later accompanied the emperor on his expeditions against Chen Hsi and Ying Pu. In all he suggested six ingenious ruses and his fief was six times enlarged. But these ruses were closely guarded secrets, not known to the world.

The emperor, wounded while fighting against Ying Pu, travelled back by easy stages to Changan. Then King Lu Wan of Yen rebelled and the emperor sent the state chancellor Fan Kuai with an army to attack him. After Fan Kuai's departure, some men spoke ill of him to the emperor, who exclaimed in anger, "Fan Kuai knows I am ill and is hoping I will die!" On Chen Ping's advice he summoned Chou Po, marquis of Chiang, to his bedside and gave these orders: "Chen Ping will escort you at once by post carriage to take over Fan Kuai's command. When you reach the army Chen Ping will cut off Fan Kuai's head."

Having received these orders, the two men set off with all speed. But on the road they talked things over and said, "Fan Kuai is an old friend of the emperor and has many achievements to his credit. Besides, he is the husband of Lu Hsu, younger sister to Empress Lu. He is close to the throne and high in rank. In his rage the emperor has ordered his death, but he may regret it later. We had better arrest Fan Kuai and take him to court for the emperor to mete out the punishment himself." So before reaching the army they erected a dais and summoned Fan Kuai with the imperial credentials. Having announced the imperial command, they arrested Fan Kuai, put him in a cage on a cart and sent him to Changan while Chou Po took over the army and led it to subdue the insurgent districts of Yen.

On his way back Chen Ping received news of the emperor's death and, afraid that the empress and her sister might slander him in their anger, he travelled post-haste. On the road he met a messenger and received orders to station himself with Kuan Ying at Yingyang. But instead he went straight to the palace where, having lamented bitterly before the coffin, he reported to Empress Lu all that had passed.

"You have done your best," she said, taking pity on him. "Now go and rest." But Chen Ping, fearing defamation, begged to be allowed to stay in the palace.

The empress appointed him chief of the palace guard and told him, "You must help to educate the young emperor." After that Lu Hsu could no longer speak evil of him. Fan Kuai upon arriving was pardoned and his fiefs were restored to him.

In the sixth year of Emperor Hui, the chancellor Tsao Shen died and Wang Ling, marquis of Ankuo, was made senior prime minister, with Chen Ping as junior prime minister.

Wang Ling was a native of Pei and a prominent figure in that district. Before the First Emperor of Han rose to power he treated Wang Ling as his elder brother. Wang Ling was unconventional, impulsive, and frank in his speech. When the emperor raised an army at Pei to march against Hsienyang, Wang Ling had a troop several thousand strong at Nanyang but he did not follow the emperor. Not till the emperor turned east to attack Hsiang Yu did Wang Ling and his men come over to Han. Hsiang Yu detained Wang Ling's mother in his army, and when Wang Ling's messenger arrived he placed her in a seat of honour, hoping to win her son over to his side. Wang Ling's mother secretly saw the messenger off and, weeping, said, "Tell my son to serve his prince well. The king of Han is a good man and Ling must not break faith with him because of me. Let my death speed you on your way!" With that she drew a sword and killed herself. Hsiang Yu in his fury threw her corpse into the cauldron.

So Wang Ling helped Liu Pang win the empire. But because he was friendly with Yung Chih, whom the emperor hated, and had not at first intended to follow the emperor, he was not enfeoffed as marquis of Ankuo till late. After he had served as senior prime minister for two years, Emperor Hui died and Empress Lu consulted Wang Ling as to whether she might make the members of her family princes. His answer was "No". But when she consulted Chen Ping, he approved. Then the empress in her displeasure transferred Wang Ling to the post of senior tutor, which was in fact a sinecure. Angrily resigning on grounds of illness, he stayed at home, absenting himself from the court, dying seven years later.

After Wang Ling's dismissal, Empress Lu made Chen Ping the senior prime minister and Shen Yi-chi, marquis of Piyang, the junior prime minister. Shen Yi-chi did not work in the ministry but in the palace. He, too, was a native of Pei. When Liu Pang was defeated west of Pengcheng and the Chu army seized his father and wife as hostages, Shen Yi-chi served as steward to the empress. He later joined the army which defeated Hsiang Yu and was made a marquis. The empress favoured him. So when he became prime minister and worked in the palace, all officials had to go to him to get anything done.

Lu Hsu still bore a grudge against Chen Ping for advising the First Emperor to arrest Fan Kuai. She spread rumours about him saying, "Chen Ping does none of the work of a minister but spends his days drinking and playing about with women."

Chen Ping, knowing this, only indulged himself more each

262

day. And when the empress heard this she was secretly pleased. One day in Lu Hsu's presence she told him, "The proverb says, 'Ignore the tattle of children and women.' I judge you by the way you behave to me. Never mind my sister's slander."

Chen Ping had pretended to agree when the empress made members of her family princes, but after her death it was he who drew up the plan whereby he and Grand Marshal Chou Po had all the Lu family killed and set Emperor Wen on the throne. Then Shen Yi-chi was dismissed from office.

After Emperor Wen came to the throne he considered that Grand Marshal Chou Po had rendered him the greatest service by commanding the troops which killed the princes of the Lu clan. Chen Ping, to defer to Chou Po, resigned on the pretext of illness. The emperor, who was newly enthroned, questioned him about this in surprise.

"In the time of the First Emperor," said Chen Ping, "Chou Po did less than I. But in overthrowing the Lu family he did more. I would like to resign my position as senior prime minister in favour of him."

Then Emperor Wen gave Chou Po the highest post of senior prime minister while Chen Ping ranked second as junior prime minister. Chen Ping also received a thousand catties of gold and had his fief increased by three thousand households.

Some time later, when the emperor was more acquainted with affairs of state, he asked his senior prime minister at court, "How many law-suits are settled in the empire every year?"

Chou Po answered ruefully, "I do not know."

"What is the empire's annual revenue and expenditure in terms of money and grain?"

Again Chou Po had to admit, "I do not know." He was sweating with embarrassment at being unable to answer.

When the emperor put the same question to the junior prime minister, Chen Ping replied, "There are officers in charge of such matters."

"What officers?" asked the emperor.

"If you want to know about law-suits, sir, ask the chief

263

justice," said Chen Ping. "If you want to know about money and grain, ask the minister of revenue."

"If there are officers in charge of these matters, what is your function?" asked the emperor.

"Pardon my presumption," answered Chen Ping humbly. "Your Majesty, overestimating my mean capacity, has honoured me with the post of prime minister. The prime minister's duty is to help his sovereign to regulate the principles of *yin* and *yang*, to carry out projects according to the four seasons, to nurture all things, to control foreign tribes and the nobles, to rule the people with kindness and see that the ministers and officers perform their duties well."

The emperor approved of this answer. Chou Po, however, was thoroughly mortified and once they were outside he reproached Chen Ping, saying, "You never taught me how to answer such questions."

Chen Ping retorted with a laugh, "You should know what your post entails. If His Majesty asked you the number of thieves and robbers in the capital, would you try to answer that too?"

Then Chou Po realized how much inferior he was to Chen Ping. Later he asked to resign on the grounds of illness and Chen Ping became the sole prime minister.

In the second year of Emperor Wen, Chen Ping died and was given the posthumous title of Marquis Hsien. He was succeeded by his son Mai, Marquis Kung, who died two years later. Mai was succeeded by his son Hui, Marquis Chien, who died twenty-three years later. Hui was succeeded by his son Ho; but twenty-three years later Ho was executed on the charge of abducting another man's wife, and the fief was abolished.

Chen Ping once said, "All my crafty devices run counter to the Taoist Way. Once my descendants decline, they will never rise again, because of all the evil I have done." His great-grandson Chen Chang, it is true, became related by marriage to the noble house of Wei and asked to have the old fief restored, but this was never done.

The Grand Historian comments: Prime Minister Chen Ping in his youth was attracted to the teachings of the Yellow Emperor and Lao Tzu. While carving up the sacrificial meat he already had high ambitions. He vacillated between Chu and Wei before finally joining the First Emperor of Han, and he devised many ingenious plans to overcome difficulties and to save the state from danger. In the time of Empress Lu, although troubles beset him, he not only succeeded in extricating himself but restored the dynasty so that he died a dignitary and was known to posterity as an able minister. Truly, "a good beginning makes a good ending." None but a wise man could have accomplished this.

HAN HSIN, MARQUIS OF HUAIYIN

Han Hsin, Marquis of Huaiyin, was a man of Huaiyin. Starting life as a poor and undistinguished commoner, he was neither recommended for any official post nor able to make a living by trade. He kept sponging on others and was generally disliked. After he had imposed for several months on the hospitality of the constable of Nanchang in the local township, the constable's wife lost patience. One morning she cooked early and ate in bed so that Han Hsin, arriving for breakfast, found no food prepared. Taking the hint, he went off in a rage.

Another time he went fishing by a river where some old women were bleaching silk, and one of them, noticing how famished he looked, fed him for twenty or thirty days until the work was finished.

Han Hsin was very grateful. "I promise to repay you well some day," he said.

The old woman retorted angrily, "You're a grown man yet you can't keep yourself. I fed you out of pity, sir, not in the hope of repayment."

A young butcher in Huaiyin sneered at Han Hsin, saying, "You may be hefty and like to wear a sword, but at heart you are a coward." Then he taunted him publicly and swore, "If you want to die, stab me. If not, crawl between my legs."

Han Hsin surveyed him carefully, then squatted down and crawled between the man's legs, while the whole market jeered at his cowardice.

When Hsiang Liang crossed the River Huai, Han Hsin girded on his sword and joined him, but failed to make a name under his command. After Hsiang Liang's defeat he joined Hsiang Yu, who made him one of his bodyguards. He advised Hsiang

Yu on strategy several times, but his advice was never taken.

When Liu Pang went to Shu, Han Hsin left Hsiang Yu to join Han but still did not win fame, merely serving as an officer in charge of guests. He was condemned to death for some offence. Thirteen others were beheaded before him, but when it came to Han Hsin's turn he looked up and saw Lord Teng.

"Does our prince not want to conquer the empire?" he cried. "Why behead a brave man?"

Impressed by his words and struck by his appearance, Lord Teng pardoned him, spoke with him, and liked all he said. He recommended him to Liu Pang, who made him the commissary general but still did not appreciate his ability.

Han Hsin had several talks with Hsiao Ho, who was much impressed by him. On the way to Nancheng several dozen officers deserted and Han Hsin, reflecting that Hsiao Ho and others had recommended him several times to no purpose, deserted too. As soon as Hsiao Ho knew this, he set off in pursuit without stopping to ask permission. Others reported, "The prime minister has gone too!" and Liu Pang was as furious as if he had lost an arm. A couple of days later, however, Hsiao Ho returned to Liu Pang who, torn between joy and anger, swore at him.

"Why did you desert?" he demanded.

"How would I dare desert, sir?" retorted Hsiao Ho. "I ran after a deserter."

"Who was that?"

"Han Hsin."

Liu Pang swore another oath. "Dozens of officers have deserted, but you did not run after them. You must be lying."

"Other officers are easy to come by, but Han Hsin has not his equal in the country. If you are satisfied with ruling Hanchung, then you do not need him. But if you want to win the empire, Han Hsin is the only man who can help you to do it. All depends on your aims."

"Of course I want to march east. How can I stay cooped up here indefinitely?"

"If you plan to march east eventually and can use him, he will stay. Otherwise he will end up by deserting again."

"To please you, I'll make him a general."

"A general's rank will not hold him."

"Then I'll make him the chief marshal."

"Very good!"

Liu Pang was about to summon Han Hsin to confer this appointment on him, when Hsiao Ho said, "You are too off-hand and lacking in politeness, sir, appointing a chief marshal as if you were calling for a child. That is why Han Hsin left. If you mean to appoint him, choose an auspicious day and prepare an altar after fasting and purification: that will do."

To this Liu Pang agreed. His generals were pleased by the news that a chief marshal was to be appointed, each fancying that he was to be the man. The whole army was astounded when the title was conferred on Han Hsin.

After the ceremony, Han Hsin took his seat and Liu Pang said, "The prime minister has spoken of you many times. What do you advise me to do?"

Han Hsin first expressed his gratitude, then asked, "Are you not contending in the east with Hsiang Yu for the empire?"

"I am," replied Liu Pang.

"How do you compare with Hsiang Yu in courage and magnanimity?"

After a thoughtful silence Liu Pang answered, "I am not his equal."

Han Hsin bowed approvingly and said, "I agree, sir. But having served under him, I can tell you what Hsiang Yu is like. When Hsiang Yu bellows with rage a thousand men are rooted to the ground, but since he cannot appoint worthy commanders all he has is the courage of a single man. He is polite, kindly and an amiable talker. If a man falls ill he will shed tears and share his meal with him; but when a man renders such services that he deserves a fief, Hsiang Yu plays with the seal till its corners are rubbed off before he can bring himself to part with it. This is what is called womanly kindness.

"Although Hsiang Yu is overlord of all the states, he would

not stay within the Pass but has made his capital at Pengcheng. He has broken faith with the Righteous Emperor and made his own favourites princes, so that all the hereditary princes are discontented. When they saw that he banished the Righteous Emperor to the south, they in turn drove away their own rulers to make themselves kings in the best regions. Moreover, since Hsiang Yu spreads ruin wherever he goes, he is detested by most of the world and the common people do not follow him out of affection but because they must submit to his might. Although he has the title of overlord, he has lost the hearts of the people. Hence his power can easily be undermined.

"If you, sir, follow a different course, relying on brave men from every state, you will carry all before you. If you reward those who have served you well with different cities, everyone will submit to you. If you lead troops who fight for justice and are eager to return to the east, all your enemies must scatter before you.

"In the years when they commanded the sons of Chin as Chin generals the three princes ruling over the land of Chin slaughtered more men than we can count; but they tricked their men into surrendering to Hsiang Yu, and at Hsin-an by a dastardly trick he massacred more than two hundred thousand of those who had surrendered, sparing only the three generals Chang Han, Szuma Hsin and Tung Yi. So the elders of Chin hate these three to the very marrow of their bones! Chu has set them up by force as kings, and the people of Chin have no love for them.

"When you entered the Wu Pass, you did not touch a single plant but repealed the harsh laws and only laid down three rules to bind the men of Chin, so that all of them want you to be their ruler. According to the agreement reached by the feudal lords, it is you, Great King, who should rule within the Passes, and all the people there know it. When you were deprived of your rightful throne and went to Hanchung, everyone in Chin was sorry. Now if you lead your forces east, you can conquer the land of Chin simply by issuing a proclamation."

Liu Pang was overjoyed and wished he had consulted Han

Hsin earlier. Acting on his advice, he assigned tasks to his commanders.

In the eighth month Liu Pang led his men east from Chentsang and conquered the land of Chin. In the second year of Han* he advanced east from the Pass and took Wei south of the river. The kings of Hann and Yin surrendered, and he allied with Chi and Chao against Chu. In the fourth month he reached Pengcheng, but there his army was routed and he withdrew. Han Hsin mustered men to join him at Yingyang and defeated Hsiang Yu's army between Ching and Suo, so that the men of Chu could not go further west.

After Liu Pang's defeat at Pengcheng, the kings of Sai and Ti went over to Chu. Chi and Chao also wanted to turn against Han and make their peace with Chu. In the sixth month Pao, king of Wei, asked leave to go home because one of his parents was ill; but as soon as he reached his state he sealed off the ford across the Yellow River and rebelled against Han, making terms with Chu. Liu Pang sent Li Yi-chi to urge him to return, but he refused.

In the eighth month Han Hsin was appointed junior prime minister and attacked Wei, whose king gathered all his men at Pufan and blockaded Linchin. Han Hsin, resorting to a ruse, made ready boats as if to cross at Linchin but secretly led his troops to Hsiayang where they crossed on rafts to launch a surprise attack on Anyi. The king of Wei, taken by surprise, led his men out to give battle. Then Han Hsin captured him, conquered Wei and made it the province of Hotung.

Liu Pang sent Chang Erh and Han Hsin eastwards against Chao and Tai in the north. In the intercalary ninth month the army of Tai was defeated and Hsia Yueh was captured at Yuyu. As soon as Han Hsin had subjugated Wei and Tai, Liu Pang had his best troops brought to Yingyang to resist the armies of Chu.

Han Hsin and Chang Erh with a few tens of thousands of men planned to march east by way of Chinghsing against Chao.

---

* 205 B.C.

When the king of Chao and Chen Yu, lord of Chengan, heard of their approach, they sent an army, said to be two hundred thousand strong, to the Chinghsing Defile.

Li To-cheh, lord of Kuangwu, advised the lord of Chengan saying, "We know that General Han Hsin of Han crossed the river in the west, captured the king of Wei and General Hsia Yueh, then caused a blood bath at Yuyu. Now he means to conquer us with the support of Chang Erh. A force like this, coming from a distance and flushed with victory, should not be met head-on. They say, 'When supplies must be shipped a thousand *li*, the soldiers will go hungry. When fuel must be gathered before a meal is cooked, the troops will sleep on empty stomachs.' Now the Chinghsing Defile is so narrow that two chariots cannot drive abreast nor cavalry ride in formation. After advancing for several hundred *li*, they must have outdistanced their supplies. Let me take thirty thousand men by a different route to cut off their baggage train, while you heighten your ramparts, deepen your trenches, and stand firm without giving battle.

"When they can neither advance to fight nor withdraw, my troops will cut off their rear so that they get no provisions from the countryside. In less than ten days I shall send the heads of their two generals to your army headquarters. I hope you will consider my proposal. Otherwise you are bound to be taken captive by them."

But the lord of Chengan was a Confucian scholar who believed that soldiers fighting in a just cause should resort to neither stratagems nor deceit. He said, "I have read in books of military strategy that 'if you outnumber the enemy ten to one you should surround him, whereas if you have twice his number you should give battle'. Now although Han Hsin's troops are said to number tens of thousands, their fighting strength is a few thousand only. After marching a thousand *li*, they will be worn out. If we were to avoid a fight, what should we do if greater forces came later? Other states, thinking us cowards, would attack us too." He rejected the plan proposed by the lord of Kuangwu.

When the spies sent out by Han Hsin reported the rejection of the lord of Kuangwu's plan, Han Hsin was overjoyed for now he dared to advance. He made his men pitch camp thirty *li* from the mouth of the defile. At midnight he ordered a picked force of two thousand light cavalry, each man with a red flag, to proceed along a small path hidden in the hills where they could keep Chao's army under observation.

"When the men of Chao see us in flight, they will leave their ramparts to pursue us," Han Hsin told them. "You must storm their position at once, tear down the banners of Chao and put up the red flags of Han." He also ordered his lieutenants to distribute light rations, saying, "We shall feast together today after routing Chao's army." His officers pretended to agree to this although they had misgivings.

Then he told his aide-de-camp, "Chao's men have constructed their fortifications in a strategic position. If they do not see our commander's flag they may not attack our vanguard, lest we withdraw rather than tackle such difficult terrain." He sent ten thousand men to form ranks in front of the river. When the men of Chao saw this, they laughed heartily.

As soon as the sun rose, Han Hsin had his commander's flag borne out and advanced with sounding drums through the defile. The troops of Chao left their ramparts to attack, and a fierce battle raged, until Han Hsin and Chang Erh made a feint of abandoning their drums and flags and fled back to the troops drawn up before the river. These ranks opened to receive them and joined battle with the attackers. Then, sure enough, all Chao's troops abandoned their ramparts to capture the Han flags and pursue the two generals. But once Han Hsin and Chang Erh had joined them, the Han forces by the river fought stubbornly and could not be defeated.

Meanwhile Han Hsin's surprise force of two thousand cavalry, who had waited till all Chao's troops had left their ramparts, galloped to the fortifications, tore down the banners and set up the two thousand red flags of Han. The men of Chao, unable to defeat their opponents or capture Han Hsin and Chang Erh, were about to return to their ramparts when they saw the walls lined with red flags. Frightened and believing that the soldiers of Han had seized their king and commander, they fled in confusion. Their general cut some down as they ran away, but could not halt the stampede. Then the men of Han closed in from both sides and completely routed them, taking many captive. The lord of Chengan was put to death beside the River Chih and King Hsieh of Chao was taken prisoner.

Han Hsin ordered his troops not to kill the lord of Kuangwu, and offered a reward of a thousand gold pieces to anyone who captured him alive. Some soldiers caught him and brought him to headquarters. Han Hsin untied his bonds and made him take the seat of honour facing east while he himself faced west, treating the lord of Kuangwu with the respect due to a teacher.

The officers presented their captives and the heads of the slain, and congratulated Han Hsin on the victory. "According to *The Art of War*," they said, "an army should keep hills to its rear or right, and a river in front or to the left. When you ordered us to form ranks before the river and promised us a feast after Chao's defeat, we could hardly believe our ears. Yet we won after all. What strategy was this?"

"This is in *The Art of War* too, if you only knew it," answered Han Hsin. "Does it not say, 'Put them in a death trap and they will come out alive; send them to destruction and they will survive'? Besides, I had no well-trained officers and men but only street rabble rounded up to fight. Circumstances compelled me to put them in a death trap and force them to fight for their lives. Had I left them in a safe place, they would all have run away. What use would that have been to me?"

"Quite right!" agreed the officers. "This was beyond us."

Then Han Hsin said to the lord of Kuangwu, "I want to attack Yen in the north and Chi in the east. What would be the most effective way to go about it?"

The lord of Kuangwu declined to advise him, saying, "I have heard that the general of a defeated army cannot talk about courage, the minister of a ruined state should not seek to survive. It is not for me, a defeated captive, to consider affairs of such moment."

Han Hsin replied, "I understand that when Poli Hsi was in the state of Yu, Yu was overthrown; but when he went to Chin, Chin became powerful. This is not because he was foolish when in Yu and wise when in Chin. It was a question of whether his advice was taken or not. Had the lord of Chengan adopted your plan, I should have been captured. It was because he ignored your advice that I have the honour of waiting on you now." He urged him again, assuring him, "I shall listen most earnestly to your proposals. I beg you not to decline, sir!"

Then the lord of Kuangwu said, " 'The wisest man, in a thousand schemes, must make at least one mistake; and the greatest fool must hit once on the truth.' That is why 'a sage weighs even the words of a madman'. I fear my advice will be useless, but I shall do my humble best.

"The lord of Chengan had tactics which appeared invincible yet failed him overnight, for his army was routed before the city of Ho and he himself met death by the River Chih. You, sir, have crossed the Yellow River in the west, captured the king of Wei, defeated Hsia Yueh at Yuyu, taken Chinghsing in one stroke, routed Chao's army of two hundred thousand in less than a day, and executed the lord of Chengan. Your fame spreads far and wide, your might awes the whole world. Even farmers have laid down their ploughs and hoes and, dressed in their best and feasting, are waiting attentively for further commands from you. This is your strength.

"But your men are exhausted, your troops tired out and of no great use at present. If you lead these weary, exhausted troops against the strongholds of Yen, you will fail to take them however long you fight. Conditions will worsen as the days drag on and you run short of supplies; for Yen, although weak, will not submit, while Chi will strengthen herself and defend her frontiers. And so long as these two states hold out, the contest between Liu Pang and Hsiang Yu will remain

274

deadlocked. This is your weakness. In my humble opinion, you are attempting too much. A good fighter does not attack strength with weakness, but attacks weakness with strength."

"What course should I take?" asked Han Hsin.

"If I were you," replied the lord of Kuangwu, "I would call a halt, rest your troops, settle the unrest in Chao and care for the orphans. Treat your officers and men with beef and wine brought in every day from a hundred *li* around, and make ready to advance north towards Yen. Then dispatch an orator with a letter setting forth your strength, and Yen will not dare to defy you. Once Yen has submitted, send a spokesman east to Chi to spread the news, and Chi will feel constrained to submit as well, for even the wisest man could devise no other course. Then you can go on to do whatever you please. This is one of those times in warfare when you should make a big noise before doing anything."

Han Hsin approved and took his advice. He sent an envoy to Yen and Yen submitted readily. Then he sent a man to report this to Liu Pang, asking to have Chang Erh made king of Chao to pacify the country. Liu Pang agreed, and Chang Erh was set up as king of Chao.

Hsiang Yu launched a series of surprise attacks across the Yellow River against Chao. Chang Erh and Han Hsin travelled up and down strengthening different points, pacifying cities and sending troops to the aid of Liu Pang, then besieged by Hsiang Yu at Yingyang.

Liu Pang went south to the district between Wan and Sheh, and Ying Pu came over to his side. He defended the city of Chengkao, but was at once surrounded by the Chu army. In the sixth month he headed east from Chengkao accompanied only by Lord Teng, and crossed the river to join Chang Erh's army at Hsiuwu. Upon his arrival he put up in the hostel and at dawn the next day galloped to Chang Erh's headquarters, announcing himself as an envoy of the king of Han. While Chang Erh and Han Hsin were still asleep he took the seals and tallies from their rooms, summoned their officers and assigned them to new posts. When the two generals woke, they were astounded to find Liu Pang there. After he had taken over their armies, he ordered Chang Erh to defend Chao and appointed Han Hsin his state chancellor, giving him the troops of Chao not then engaged in combat to attack Chi.

Han Hsin led his troops east, but before he crossed the river at Pingyuan he heard that Liu Pang had sent Li Yi-chi to Chi, and that he had talked Chi into surrendering. Han Hsin was about to halt, when an orator from Fanyang named Kuai Tung advised him, "You were ordered to attack Chi and, although the king also sent a secret envoy to make Chi submit, no order has come telling you to halt. Why not press on, then? Li Yi-chi, a single orator, just by bowing from his carriage and wagging his tongue, has made the seventy-odd towns of Chi surrender, while it took you, with an army tens of thousands strong, more than a year to conquer the fifty-odd cities of Chao. Have you achieved less in several years as a general than one wretched orator?"

Han Hsin took his advice and crossed the river. The king of Chi, after accepting Li Yi-chi's proposal, was entertaining him with feasts and wine, neglecting the defences prepared against Han. So Han Hsin attacked the forces of Chi at Lihsia and pressed on to Lintzu. King Tien Kuang of Chi, who thought Li Yi-chi had betrayed him, had him thrown into the cauldron and then fled to Kaomi, sending an envoy to Chu to beg for help.

After conquering Lintzu, Han Hsin marched east and pursued Tien Kuang to west of Kaomi. Hsiang Yu dispatched General Lung Chu with an army given out to be two hundred thousand strong to rescue Chi. Before their joint forces engaged Han Hsin, someone warned Lung Chu, "The men of Han, battling far from home, will fight so fiercely that they must not be met head-on. Chi and Chu are fighting on their own ground and their men can easily disperse if defeated. It would be better to strengthen your defences and ask the king of Chi to send trusted ministers to rally the towns he has lost; for when they know that the king is still alive and that Chu has come to Chi's rescue, they will revolt against Han. The Han soldiers are two thousand *li* from home. If all the towns of Chi rise against them, they will have no way to get food and will surrender without a fight."

"I know Han Hsin well," replied Lung Chu. "He is easy to deal with. Besides, I have come to save Chi, but what glory should I win by forcing him to surrender without a fight? If I defeat him, half Chi may be mine. Why should I stop?"

He prepared to give battle and drew up his army confronting Han Hsin across the River Wei. That night Han Hsin made his men block the upper stream with more than ten thousand sandbags. He led his army to the attack but turned back half way, as if fearing defeat.

"I knew he was a coward!" exulted Lung Chu and pursued Han Hsin across the river. Then Han Hsin sent men to break the dam of sandbags, and the water came rushing down so that the bulk of Lung Chu's army could not cross. Swiftly closing in, Han Hsin killed Lung Chu, while the men of Chu on the east bank scattered and ran. King Tien Kuang of Chi also fled. Han Hsin pursued the enemy north to Chengyang, and captured the whole Chu force.

In the fourth year of Han, having completed the conquest of Chi, Han Hsin sent an envoy to report to Liu Pang, "Chi is deceitful, unreliable and fickle, and it borders Chu on the south. Without an acting king to control the land, there can be no stability here. It would help if you appointed me the acting king."

This envoy arrived at a time when Chu was besieging Liu Pang at Yingyang and the situation was desperate. Liu Pang read the letter and swore, "I am tied down here, waiting day and night for him to come to my aid, and he wants to make himself king!"

Chang Liang and Chen Ping both trod on his feet and whispered in his ear, "Hard-pressed as we are, how can we stop Han Hsin from making himself king? You may as well appoint him and treat him well, encouraging him to defend his territory. Otherwise there will be trouble."

Liu Pang realized his mistake and said with another oath,

"One who conquers a state should be a full king, not an acting king." He sent Chang Liang to make Han Hsin the king of Chi and bring back some of his troops to attack Chu.

After Chu lost its general Lung Chu, Hsiang Yu grew alarmed and sent Wu Sheh of Hsuyi to urge Han Hsin, then king of Chi, saying, "The world suffered long under Chin till all the states joined forces to attack it. After Chin was overthrown, the land was distributed according to merit and kings appointed so that the troops might rest. Now the king of Han has taken up arms again and marched east, invading and occupying the territory of others. He has conquered the three states of Chin, led his troops out of the Passes and mustered men from other states to attack Chu in the east. He will not stop till he has swallowed up the whole world — nothing else will satisfy him.

"Besides, there is no trusting the king of Han. We have had him in our power more than once, but each time our king took pity on him and spared him. As soon as he escaped, however, he always broke faith and attacked our king again. That shows how untrustworthy he is. Now you are fighting your best for him because you think him your good friend, but he will end up by seizing you. You have only had a moment's respite because our king still lives. It is you who hold the balance between these two kings. If you move to the right, the king of Han will win; if to the left, our king will win. Then why not turn against Han and live on friendly terms with Chu, dividing the land into three? To let slip this opportunity and insist on taking Han's side against us is not the action of a wise man."

But Han Hsin turned down this proposal, saying, "When I served under your king I was merely a guardsman, a common halberdier, and my advice and plans were never accepted. So I left him and went to the king of Han, who gave me the seal of a grand marshal with tens of thousands of men under my command. He shared his food and clothing with me and adopted all my proposals. That is how I reached my present position. It would be wrong to betray one who trusts me so deeply. I shall remain true to him to the death. Please make my apologies to your king for me."

After Wu Sheh left, an orator of Chi named Kuai Tung, who saw that Han Hsin held the balance of power, tried to win him over by a remarkable means. Speaking to him as a physiognomist, he said, "I have learned to tell a man's fortune from his face."

"How do you do that?" asked Han Hsin.

"High rank or low depend on the bone structure, good fortune or bad on the countenance, success or failure on the judgement. By taking these three factors into account, I have not been mistaken once in ten thousand predictions."

"Good. And how do you read my face?"

"May I speak to you in private?"

Han Hsin ordered his attendants to retire.

"Judging by your face," said Kuai Tung, "you can be no more than a feudal lord in a dangerous and insecure position. But on your back I see greatness defying description."

"What do you mean?"

"When the world first rose in arms and heroes with one voice issued a call, men flocked to them like gathering clouds or shoals of fish, like wildfire or a rising wind. Their one thought then was how to overthrow Chin. But now the kings of Chu and Han are contending together so that innocent men are butchered and the bones of countless fathers and sons are lying in the wilderness. The army of Chu set out from Peng-cheng and fought its way to Yingyang, advancing victoriously and aweing the world by its might; yet it has been halted between Ching and Suo and can go no further than the western mountains. This has been the case for three years now.

"The king of Han, on the other hand, at the head of hundreds of thousands of men, is defending Kung and Loyang, making use of the natural barriers of mountains and rivers. But although he fought several times a day he gained not an inch of land, nor did flight save him. He was routed at Yingyang, wounded at Chengkao, and forced to flee to the district between Wan and Sheh. Neither wisdom nor courage have been of any avail. His men's keenness has been blunted by frustrations, the grain in his granaries is dwindling away; the people are exhausted and seething with discontent, and have no means of support. To my mind, none but a wise leader can end this turmoil.

"Now the fate of these two kings depends on you. If you join Han, Han will win; if Chu, then Chu will win. I would like to lay bare my heart and frankly offer you a humble plan; only I am afraid you may not be able to use it. If you follow my plan, however, you can take advantage of both sides and divide the land into three with them like the three legs of a tripod, so that neither of the others dare make the first move.

"You are a brilliant commander and your forces are mighty. With powerful Chi as your base, you could advance from Yen and Chao to unoccupied areas and control the king of Han's rear. Then if in accordance with the popular wish you turn west to plead for peace for the common people, the whole world will respond as swiftly as wind or an echo. No one will dare to defy you. You can weaken strong states by setting up feudal rulers, so that the whole world follows you and turns towards Chi. You can control the old land of Chi with the Chiao and Szu river valleys, influence the states with virtue and rule with courtesy, so that all the feudal lords pay homage to you. The proverb says, 'A man who does not take what Heaven offers will come to harm; a man who misses his chance will get into trouble.' I implore you to think this over carefully!"

But Han Hsin said, "The king of Han treats me well and shares his carriage, clothing and food with me. I have heard that he who rides in another man's carriage should share his burden, he who wears another man's clothing should share his worries, he who eats another man's food should serve him to the death. How can I, for the sake of personal gain, betray him?"

"You consider yourself his friend," replied Kuai Tung, "and want to found a dynasty that will endure for ever, but I believe you are mistaken. When Chang Erh and the lord of Chengan were common citizens, they were sworn friends. But when they fell out because of the affair of Chang Yen and Chen Tse, Chang Erh left Hsiang Yu and fled with the head of his envoy Hsiang Ying to Han. Then the king of Han sent him east with troops to kill the lord of Chengan south of the River Chih. Thus the lord lost his head and became an object of scorn to all the states. These men were two of the best friends in the world. Why then did they turn against each other? Because excessive ambition leads to trouble and the heart of man is hard to fathom.

"Now you want to keep faith with the king of Han, but your friendship can hardly be stronger than that between those two lords while more is at stake than the affair of Chang Yen and Chen Tse. These are my grounds for believing you mistaken in trusting the king of Han implicitly. When Chung and Fan Li saved Yueh from destruction and made King Kouchien a great conqueror, yet despite their achievements and their fame they perished. When no wild beasts are left, the hounds are tossed into the cauldron! If you talk of friendship, yours cannot compare with that of Chang Erh and Chen Yu. If you talk of loyalty, yours cannot surpass that of Wen Chung and Fan Li to Kou-chien. These two examples should suffice. I hope you will ponder this deeply!

"Furthermore, I have heard that a man whose courage and wisdom make his own sovereign tremble lives in danger, while superlative services are never rewarded. Let me enumerate your achievements, great king. You crossed the Yellow River in the west, captured the king of Wei, took Hsia Yueh prisoner, led your troops through Chinghsing, executed the lord of Chengan, subdued Chao, forced Yen to surrender, pacified Chi, crushed two hundred thousand men of Chu in the south, killed Lung Chu in the east and reported what you had done to the king in the west. Truly your achievements are unsurpassed in the world, your wisdom unparalleled in this generation. Your prestige dismays the king and your services are too great for any reward. Should you go over to Chu, the men of Chu would not trust you. Should you remain with Han, the men of Han must fear you. Then which way should you turn? You rank as a subject, yet your prestige makes rulers tremble and your fame is the greatest in the land. I am concerned for your safety."

Han Hsin thanked him, saying, "Enough! I shall think it over."

Some days later Kuai Tung broached the subject again. "When listening to advice one should show discrimination, for planning is the root of success," he said. "Few men prosper if they listen to bad advice or make the wrong plans. But a man who can take advice, make plans, grasp essentials and keep his sense of proportion, will not be misled by words. He who contents himself with a menial task will never have authority over ten thousand chariots, he who clings to a salary of one or two bushels of grain will never become a high minister. Wisdom means action, whereas doubt means failure. If you see a small part but forget the greater, know what is right but cannot determine how to act, you are simply courting disaster. That is why they say, 'Better an angry hornet than a hesitant tiger, better a poor horse that canters than a lame thoroughbred, better an ordinary fellow determined to act than a brave man who vacillates. A man with the wisdom of Shun or Yu who mumbles or keeps silent is less effective than a deaf mute who can make gestures.' So it is important to be able to act. Distinction is hard to achieve, easy to mar. Opportunities are hard to find, easy to let slip. The same chance never comes twice. I beg you to consider this carefully."

Still Han Hsin hesitated, unwilling to betray Liu Pang and confident that after all he had achieved the king would never take Chi away from him. So finally he rejected Kuai Tung's advice. When the latter saw this, he feigned madness and became a witch-doctor.

When Liu Pang was hard-pressed at Kuling, he adopted a plan proposed by Chang Liang to summon Han Hsin, and they joined forces at Kaihsia. But after Hsiang Yu's defeat, the emperor took Han Hsin's army from him. In the first month of the fifth year of Han, Han Hsin was transferred from Chi to be king of Chu with his capital at Hsiapei.

When Han Hsin reached his state, he summoned the wash-erwoman who had fed him and gave her a thousand gold pieces. To the constable of Nanchang he gave one hundred coins, saying, "You are a mean fellow, doing a kindness by halves."

He sent for the young man who had insulted him by making him crawl between his legs, and made him the military commander of the capital of Chu. "He is a brave man," Han Hsin told his ministers. "When he insulted me, I could easily have killed him, but what glory was there in that? So I put up with it, and reached my present position."

One of Hsiang Yu's former generals, Chungli Mo, came from Yilu and was an old friend of Han Hsin. After Hsiang Yu's death he took refuge with Han Hsin. When the Han emperor, who bore him a grudge, heard that he was in Chu, he issued an order for his arrest. On arriving in his state Han Hsin made a tour of inspection of the different districts and was accompanied everywhere by troops.

In the sixth year someone reported that he was plotting revolt. So the emperor, on Chen Ping's advice, announced that he would make an imperial tour and meet the feudal lords on his way to the Yunmeng Marshes in the south. Messengers were sent to summon the lords to Chen, through which the emperor would pass on his way to Yunmeng. Han Hsin did not realize that the emperor meant to catch him off his guard. When the emperor was just approaching Chu, Han Hsin was tempted to raise troops and rebel but reminded himself that he was innocent. He decided to see the emperor, though afraid he might be arrested.

Someone advised him, saying, "If you cut off Chungli Mo's head before your audience with the emperor, he will be pleased and you will have no trouble."

Han Hsin repeated this to Chungli Mo, who said, "The only reason he has not attacked you is because I am here. If you arrest me to curry favour, I may die today but you will be the next to perish!" Then he cursed Han Hsin for an evil man and cut his own throat. Han Hsin carried his head when he went to meet the emperor. But the emperor ordered guards to bind him and place him in the rear carriage.

"So it is true what they say!" cried Han Hsin. "When the cunning hares are killed, the good hound is thrown into the cauldron; when the soaring birds have been caught, the good bow is put away; when enemy states are overthrown, the wise minister is killed. Now that the empire is won, it is natural that I should be put to death."

"I have information that you are plotting revolt," said the emperor.

Han Hsin was taken in chains to Loyang, but there he was pardoned and made the marquis of Huaiyin.

Han Hsin, knowing that the emperor feared his ability, often stayed away from court on the pretext of illness. He nursed a grievance day and night and remained sullenly at home, humiliated at holding the same rank as Chou Po and Kuan Ying.

One day he called on General Fan Kuai, who knelt down to welcome him, referring to himself as Han Hsin's subject and saying, "Your Highness does me a great honour by this visit."

As Han Hsin left he laughed and said, "So I have come down to the level of men like Fan Kuai."

Once the emperor was casually discussing with Han Hsin the relative abilities and shortcomings of his generals.

"How many troops would you say I could command?" asked the emperor.

"Not more than a hundred thousand," was Han Hsin's reply.

"How about yourself?"

"In my case, the more the better."

"The more the better!" The emperor laughed, "Then how is it that you let me capture you?"

"You are not a good general, sir, but a good commander of generals. That is why you captured me. Besides, you are one of those favoured by Heaven, with more than human power."

When Chen Hsi was appointed governor of Chulu he went

to take his leave of Han Hsin, who took his hand and, dismissing his attendants, strolled with him through the courtyard. Presently Han Hsin looked up and said with a sigh, "Can you keep a secret? There is something I want to tell you."

"I am yours to command, general!" was Chen Hsi's reply.

"The post you are going to has the best troops in the empire," said Han Hsin. "And you are a minister whom the emperor favours and trusts. If someone accused you of plotting revolt, the emperor would not believe it. But a second impeachment would arouse his suspicions, while a third would so enrage him that he would march against you with an army. Then, if I raised troops to support you in the capital, between us we could win the empire."

Since Chen Hsi admired and trusted Han Hsin he replied, "I shall remember your instructions."

In the eleventh year of Han, Chen Hsi did indeed revolt. The emperor himself led an army against him, but Han Hsin, pleading illness, did not accompany the troops. He sent a man in secret to tell Chen Hsi, "Rise in arms and revolt! I shall assist you from here."

Han Hsin plotted with his followers at night to forge an edict freeing all public slaves, intending to use them to attack Empress Lu and the crown prince. All his dispositions had been made and he was waiting for word from Chen Hsi. Then the brother of a steward who had been imprisoned and sentenced to death by Han Hsin for some offence, informed Empress Lu of the plot. The empress wanted to summon Han Hsin to court, but feared he and his followers might not come. She consulted the prime minister, Hsiao Ho, and they spread word that men had come from the emperor with news that Chen Hsi had been killed. Then nobles and ministers flocked to court to offer congratulations, and Hsiao Ho tricked Han Hsin, saying, "Although you are unwell, you should make an effort to go to the palace to offer congratulations."

When Han Hsin arrived, Empress Lu ordered guards to bind him and behead him in the bell chamber of Changlo Palace.

As he was led to his death, Han Hsin exclaimed. "Too bad I did not take Kuai Tung's advice! Now I have been tricked by a woman and a boy. This is surely fate." Han Hsin's three classes of relatives were wiped out.

The emperor, returning from his expedition against Chen Hsi, was both pleased and distressed by the news of Han Hsin's death.

"Did he say anything before he died?" he asked.

"He said he was sorry not to have taken Kuai Tung's advice," answered Empress Lu.

"That man is an orator of Chi," said the emperor and ordered Kuai Tung's arrest.

When Kuai Tung was brought before him, Emperor Kao-tsu asked, "Did you advise the marquis of Huaiyin to rebel?"

"I did," said Kuai Tung. "The fool would not do as I urged, so now he has been killed. If the fool had taken my advice, how could you have destroyed him?"

"Throw him into the cauldron!" roared the emperor in a fury.

"Ah!" cried Kuai Tung. "How unjust!"

"Unjust? When you advised Han Hsin to rebel!"

"When Chin's rule was weakened and confusion reigned in the east, various clans raised armies and brave men gathered together. Chin had lost the stag — the imperial power — and all the world was chasing after it. The prize would go to the ablest and the swiftest. Brigand Chih's dog barked at Emperor Yao not because Yao was wicked but because dogs bark at all but their own masters. At that time I knew only Han Hsin, not Your Majesty. Besides, there were many men who sharpened their weapons and took up arms, eager to do as you did. But their strength was not equal to yours. Do you intend to throw them all into the cauldron?"

"Let him go!" said the emperor and pardoned Kuai Tung.

The Grand Historian comments: When I visited Huaiyin, the local people told me that even while a common citizen Han Hsin was not like ordinary people. At the time of his mother's death he could not afford to give her a funeral, yet he found a high burial ground with room enough for ten thousand households to settle. I visited his mother's grave and confirmed that this was true.

Had Han Hsin followed the Way and been more modest instead of boasting of his achievements and glorying in his ability, all would have been well. For his services to the House of Han he might have been compared with the duke of Chou, the duke of Shao or the Patriarch Lu Shang, and sacrifices would have been made to him by later generations. But instead he attempted to revolt when the empire was united. To have his family wiped out was no more than he deserved.

CHI PU AND LUAN PU

Chi Pu was a man of Chu, where he was well-known for his gallantry and spirit. Made a general by Hsiang Yu, he worsted the king of Han on several occasions. After Hsiang Yu perished, the emperor offered a reward of a thousand gold pieces for his capture, threatening anyone who dared to shelter him with the destruction of three classes of their relatives.

Chi Pu took refuge in Puyang with a man named Chou, who told him, "The emperor is searching hard for you, general, and will soon trace you here. If you are willing to take my advice, I shall venture to propose a plan. If not, I had better kill myself."

Chi Pu agreed to his plan and let himself be shaved and dressed in coarse clothes, with an iron chain round his neck. Then he was sent in a covered wagon with several dozen slaves to be sold to Chu Chia in Lu.

Chu Chia, knowing that this was Chi Pu, bought him and set him to work on his farm. He instructed his son, "You must farm as this slave says and share your meals with him." Then he went by a one-horse carriage to Loyang to see Hsiahou Ying, marquis of Juyin and Lord Teng. The latter entertained him for several days, and Chu Chia found an opportunity to ask, "What is Chi Pu's great crime that the emperor is searching so hard for him?"

"Chi Pu often had him on the spot when he was fighting for Hsiang Yu," replied Lord Teng. "The emperor bears him such a grudge that he has set his heart on capturing him."

"What is your opinion of Chi Pu?"

"An able man."

"Every subject serves his own master. Chi Pu, serving Hsiang Yu, was doing no more than his duty. Does the emperor mean to kill all Hsiang Yu's followers? The empire is newly won and if the emperor hounds one man on account of a private grudge, how narrow-minded the world is going to think him! Besides, if Chi Pu is an able man and the emperor hounds him like this, he will escape north to the Huns or south to the Yuehs. Goading a good man into helping an enemy state was what made Wu Tzu-hsu whip the grave of the king of Chu. Might you mention this to the emperor if an occasion arises?"

Lord Teng knew that Chu Chia was noble-minded and guessed that Chi Pu was hiding with him, so he agreed. Later he found occasion to speak to the emperor as Chu Chia had suggested, and Chi Pu was pardoned.

Chi Pu won general approval at the time for the way he adapted himself to circumstances, while Chu Chia made a name for himself on this account too. Chi Pu was summoned to court, where he apologized to the emperor and was appointed an imperial guardsman.

During the reign of Emperor Hui, while Chi Pu was captain of the imperial guards, the Hunnish khan sent a coarse and insulting letter to Empress Lu. In a rage, she summoned the generals for a consultation.

Fan Kuai the high marshal said, "Give me a hundred thousand men and the Huns will scatter before me."

Other generals, to please the empress, expressed approval.

But Chi Pu said, "Fan Kuai deserves to lose his head. The First Emperor, with more than four hundred thousand men, was nevertheless surrounded at Pingcheng. Now Fan Kuai with a hundred thousand will make the Huns scatter before him. A bare-faced lie! Besides, it was Chin's campaigns against the Huns that enabled Chen Sheh and the rest to start a rebellion. The country has not yet recovered from the ravages of war, but Fan Kuai is flattering you to stir up fresh trouble for the empire."

The whole court was aghast. Empress Lu dismissed the generals, and no more was said about attacking the Huns.

In the reign of Emperor Wen, when Chi Pu was governor

of Hotung, someone recommended him to the emperor, who summoned him to the capital with the intention of making him a chief counsellor. Then, however, it was reported that he was reckless, headstrong when in his cups, and hard to deal with. So after his arrival he was lodged in a government hostel for a month and then dismissed.

When he went to take his leave of the emperor, he said, "For no merit of mine, I was favoured with the governorship of Hotung, then received an unexpected summons to court, due no doubt to an unwarranted recommendation. Since my arrival, however, I have been given no new appointment but dismissed, due no doubt to some detractor. Apparently Your Majesty summoned me on one man's recommendation and dismissed me because another spoke ill of me. I fear that all intelligent men who hear this will know how to judge you, sir."

After a long, embarrassed silence the emperor said, "Hotung is a vital province in my eyes. That is why I sent for you." Then Chi Pu returned to his post.

An orator of Chu known as Master Tsaochiu relied on influential connections to make money. He undertook certain tasks for Chao Tan and other high officials, and was on good terms with Empress Ching's uncle, Tou Chang-chun. When Chi Pu knew this he wrote to warn Lord Tou, "I hear bad reports of Tsaochiu Sheng. Better have nothing to do with the man!"

As Tsaochiu Sheng was about to return to Chu, he asked Lord Tou for a letter of introduction to Chi Pu.

"General Chi has taken a dislike to you," said Lord Tou. "I advise you to steer clear of him."

But Tsaochiu insisted on going. The letter of introduction was sent on ahead and, sure enough, Chi Pu was very angry as he waited for the orator.

Tsaochiu, arriving, bowed to Chi Pu and said, "The men of Chu have a saying, 'A promise from Chi Pu is worth more than a hundred catties of gold.' How did you make such a name for yourself in Liang and Chu? I am a native of Chu and so are you. Have I not done much to spread your fame through the world? Why should you be so prejudiced against me?"

Chi Pu was very pleased. He invited Tsaochiu in and kept him for several months as his honoured guest, loading him with rich gifts when he left. It was indeed Tsaochiu who helped to spread Chi Pu's fame.

Chi Pu's younger brother Chi Hsin was so renowned within the Pass for his courtesy and chivalry that gentlemen for a thousand *li* around would risk their lives for him. Once he killed a man and fled to Wu to take refuge with Yuan Ang. He treated Yuan Ang as his senior and men like Kuan Fu and Chi Fu as his juniors. When he served as major to the metropolitan commander Chih Tu, the latter had to show him respect. Many young men went about doing things in his name. For at that time Chi Hsin's courage and Chi Pu's integrity were famed throughout the area within the Pass.

Chi Pu's maternal uncle, Lord Ting, was a general of Chu who had served under Hsiang Yu and driven the Han emperor west of Pengcheng, where the two of them crossed swords. The emperor in desperation had turned to ask him, "Why should two good men harass each other like this?" Then Lord Ting led his forces back, allowing the emperor to escape. After Hsiang Yu had been destroyed Lord Ting went to see the emperor, who denounced him publicly before the army.

"Lord Ting was disloyal to Hsiang Yu," he said. "It was he who lost Hsiang Yu his empire." He had him beheaded and warned, "Let no subject henceforward follow Lord Ting's example!"

Luan Pu was a man of Liang who befriended Peng Yueh, king of Liang, when he was still a common citizen. Being hard pressed for money, they worked as hired hands in Chi and as waiters in a tavern. Some years later Peng Yueh became a brigand in the Chuyeh Marshes, but Luan Pu was captured and sold as a slave in Yen. Subsequently he avenged his master's death and General Tsang Tu of Yen made him a commander. After Tsang Tu became king of Yen, he made

Luan Pu a general. When Tsang Tu revolted, the army of Han attacked Yen and Luan Pu was captured. News of this reached Peng Yueh, then king of Liang, who interceded with the emperor for Luan Pu's release and made him one of his ministers.

Luan Pu was sent as an envoy to Chi, but before his return the emperor summoned Peng Yueh to court, accused him of treason and wiped out all his kinsmen. Peng Yueh's head was displayed on the gate of Loyang with the warning: "The watch shall arrest any man who dares remove this head!"

When Luan Pu came back from Chi, he reported on his mission to Peng Yueh's head, sacrificed to it and mourned. The officers arrested him and reported the matter to the emperor, who sent for Luan Pu and swore at him, "Were you involved in Peng Yueh's revolt? I gave orders that his head was not to be taken down, yet you sacrificed to it and mourned him. It is obvious that you plotted treason with him. Throw this fellow into the cauldron!"

As Luan Pu was being dragged to the cauldron, he looked over his shoulder and called, "I beg to say one word before I die!"

"What is it?" demanded the emperor.

"When Your Majesty was hard pressed at Pengcheng and lost a battle between Hsiangyang and Chengkao, Hsiang Yu could not advance further west because Peng Yueh was harassing him for you in Liang. All depended on Peng Yueh then. Had he gone over to Chu, Han would have been beaten. By aiding Han, he brought about Chu's defeat. If not for his help at Kaihsia, you could not have destroyed Hsiang Yu.

"After the empire was secure, Peng Yueh received a tally and a fief, and expected to hand them down to his heirs for countless generations. Then you summoned his army from Liang and, just because he was too ill to come, suspected that he had rebelled. With no real evidence, you executed him on a flimsy pretext. All your other worthy subjects must fear for their lives. Now that he has been killed, I would rather die than live. Lead me to the cauldron!"

The emperor pardoned him and made him a commander.

During the reign of Emperor Wen, Luan Pu served as prime minister of Yen and then as a general. He said, "One who cannot humble himself and curb his ambitions in poverty is no true man. One who cannot enjoy wealth and rank does not amount to much either." He heaped rich rewards on all who had done him a service, but invoked the law to kill those who offended him.

During the revolt of the prince of Wu he distinguished himself in battle and was enfeoffed as marquis of Yu, after which he served as Yen's prime minister again. The people of Yen and Chi instituted temple sacrifices for him, calling him Lord Luan. He died in the fifth year of the middle era of Emperor Ching.* His son Fen who succeeded to his title was a master of ceremony, but he was deprived of his fief for sacrificing in a way contrary to government orders.

The Grand Historian comments: Thanks to Hsiang Yu, Chi Pu became known for his courage in Chu. On several occasions at the head of his troops he captured the enemy flag. He was a brave warrior. Yet when humiliated and sold as a slave he suffered meekly and did not kill himself. He must have had such confidence in his own ability that he endured disgrace without shame, determined to fulfil his ambitions later. So finally he became a great general of Han. A great man will not die in vain. When slave girls and concubines kill themselves in a passion, this is not because they are brave but because they have no way out.

Luan Pu mourned for Peng Yueh and courted death in the cauldron because he knew where he stood, and therefore did not set great store on his life. Even the heroes of old could have done no more.

* 145 B.C.

LIU PI, PRINCE OF WU

Liu Pi, prince of Wu, was the son of Emperor Kao-tsu's elder brother Liu Chung.

In the seventh year of the reign of the First Emperor,* after he had pacified the empire he made Liu Chung prince of Tai. Then the Huns attacked Tai and Liu Chung, unable to defend it, abandoned his principality and fled to Loyang to throw himself on the mercy of the emperor. Since they were the same flesh and blood, the emperor could not bring himself to exact the full legal penalty but merely deposed Liu Chung and made him marquis of Hoyang.

In the autumn of the eleventh year of the First Emperor, Ying Pu, prince of Huainan, rebelled, annexed Ching in the east, seized its troops and crossed west over the River Huai to attack Chu. Emperor Kao-tsu himself led the army to suppress the revolt.

Liu Chung's son Liu Pi, marquis of Pei, was twenty at this time and a brave fighter. He joined the expedition as a cavalry officer and helped to defeat Ying Pu's army at Kuaichui west of Chi, putting Ying Pu to flight.

Liu Chia, the prince of Ching, had been killed by Ying Pu and left no heir. The men of Wu and Kuaichi were reckless and given to violence and the emperor was concerned that they had no strong prince to control them. Since his own sons were too young, while in Pei he made Liu Pi the prince of Wu to govern its three provinces and fifty-three cities.

After Liu Pi had accepted the official seal, Emperor Kao-tsu sent for him and examined his features. "This man has the face of a rebel!" he exclaimed and regretted his decision. But

---

* 200 B.C.

294

since the appointment was already made he patted Liu Pi on the back and said, "Within fifty years there will be a rising in the southeast — will that be your doing? Now the empire belongs to our clan, we are all one family. Mind you do not rebel!"

Liu Pi bowed and answered, "How would I dare do such a thing?"

During the reigns of Emperor Hui and Empress Lu,* order was newly restored to the empire and the princes were busy pacifying their people. Wu had mountains rich in copper at Yuchang, and Liu Pi gathered fugitives from justice and brigands from all sides to mint money and boil sea water to extract salt. Since no taxes were imposed on these occupations, his principality soon became rich.

During the reign of Emperor Wen,** Liu Pi's son went to court, where he drank and played checkers with the crown prince. The prince of Wu's tutors, all of whom came from Chu, were reckless arrogant men, and one day he disputed so rudely over the score that the crown prince struck him with the checker-board and killed him. His body was sent home for burial to Wu.

"The whole empire belongs to the clan of Liu!" declared Liu Pi angrily. "Since he died in Changan, why not bury him in Changan? Why must he be buried here?" He sent the body back to the capital for burial.

After this, Liu Pi gradually stopped showing the respect due from a vassal and, pleading illness, absented himself from court. The authorities knew this was because of the death of his son. Having ascertained that he was not ill at all, they arrested and cross-examined all envoys from Wu. Then the prince of Wu, in his alarm, started plotting seriously.

Later he sent someone else to pay the autumn homage in his place. The envoy from Wu, questioned by the emperor, confessed, "The prince is not actually ill but is pleading sick-

---

* 194-180 B.C.
** 179-157 B.C.

ness because so many of his envoys have been arrested and tried. Peering too closely at fish in deep waters will only lead to trouble. The prince began by feigning illness, but since that was discovered and pressure applied he is growing more and more desperate. Fear of punishment may lead him to some folly. But if you will overlook the past, he can make a fresh start."

Then the emperor pardoned the envoy and sent him back with a low table and a walking-stick as gifts for the prince of Wu, implying that he was too old to come to court. And thanks to this lenient treatment, the prince abandoned his schemes. At the same time, because his principality produced salt and copper, the people were exempt from taxes. Compulsory labour exemptions were sold at a fair price, while at certain times each year the prince recruited able men and rewarded deserving villages. And when other provinces or principalities sent men to arrest fugitives there, he refused to hand them over. So it went on for forty years and more, and the people of Wu were devoted to their prince.

Chao Tso, the imperial crown prince's favoured chamberlain, several times pointed out the faults of the prince of Wu and urged that his territory be reduced. He presented memorials on this subject to Emperor Wen, but the emperor was too lenient to punish the prince, who as a result became more insubordinate every day.

When Emperor Ching ascended the throne,* Chao Tso was made grand secretary. He advised the new emperor saying, "When Emperor Kao-tsu first restored peace to the empire he gave large fiefs to his kinsmen because he had few brothers and his sons were still children. Thus Prince Tao-hui of Chi, his son by a concubine, ruled over seventy cities; Prince Yuan of Chu, a half brother, had over forty cities; Liu Pi, his elder brother's son, had over fifty. These three sons of concubines had half the empire between them.

"The prince of Wu, embittered by his son's death, absented

_____

* 156 B.C.

himself from court on the pretext of illness, and according to established law he should have been punished. But Emperor Wen in his clemency gave him a low table and walking-stick instead. Such good treatment should have made him mend his ways, yet he is growing more insubordinate. He mints money in the mountains, boils sea water to extract salt, and has gathered fugitives from all parts of the land to plot treason. He will revolt whether you cut down his fief or not. If you do, his revolt will come sooner and cause less damage. If you do not, his revolt will come later and the damage will be much greater."

In the winter of the third year of Emperor Ching, the prince of Chu came to court and Chao Tso urged that he be executed because previously, when mourning for Empress Po, he had been guilty of illicit intercourse while living in mourning quarters. The emperor commuted his punishment into confiscation of the province of Tunghai. At the same time he deprived the prince of Wu of the provinces of Yuchang and Kuaichi. Two years previously the prince of Chao had lost the province of Hochien for some offence, while Prince Ang of Chiaohsi had been deprived of six counties on account of his illegal sale of ranks.

While the ministers at court were discussing the diminution of Wu's territory, the prince of Wu, fearing that he would soon have no fief left, began to make plans for revolt. He could think of no worthy confederate among the feudal lords, but having heard that the prince of Chiaohsi was bold, spirited, warlike and feared by all the other principalities of Chi, he sent his minister Ying Kao to win him over. Ying Kao took nothing in writing but delivered a verbal message.

"The prince of Wu, unworthy as he is, has long been worried," he said. "He dares not leave his territory but has sent me to convey his greetings to you."

"What are his instructions?" asked the prince of Chiaohsi.

"Our present emperor favours wicked men and is surrounded by evil ministers," said Ying Kao. "He thinks only of trifles and gives ear to slander. Laws are arbitrarily rescinded, land is seized from the feudal lords, more demands are made every day and more innocent citizens punished. Country folk have a saying, 'Once the husk is licked away it is the turn of the rice. The princes of Wu and Chiaohsi are famed throughout the land, but once an investigation begins you will lose your freedom of action. For more than twenty years the prince of Wu has not been well enough to pay homage at court. He fears suspicion may fall on him and he will be unable to clear himself. Even cringing and cowering may not procure him a pardon. It is said that Your Highness has had some trouble over the sale of ranks, while other nobles have been deprived of territory for even less than that. And loss of territory may not be the end."

"That is so," said the prince of Chiaohsi. "What would you advise?"

"Those who hate the same things help each other, those who love the same things hold together," said Ying Kao. "Those with common sympathies co-operate, those with common desires seek the same goal, and those with common interests die for each other. The prince of Wu believes that he has the same cause for anxiety as Your Highness. The time has come, he thinks, to stand up for the right and risk your lives to rid the empire of calamity. Do you approve of this plan?"

"How dare I contemplate such a thing?" exclaimed the prince taken aback. "If the emperor presses me hard, all I can do is to die. How can I withdraw my allegiance?"

"The chief counsellor Chao Tso is deceiving the emperor, depriving princes of their rights and debarring the loyal and good from government posts. Feeling is running high at court and all the princes have rebellion in their hearts. Matters have come to a head now. Comets have appeared and there have been plagues of locusts. This is a time which comes only once in ten thousand generations: it is in troubled days like these that sages arise. The prince of Wu means to rid the court of Chao Tso and then journey in your train through the provinces. Wherever you go men will surrender to you, and every city you want to take will fall, for no one in the empire will dare to resist. Your Majesty has only to give the word and the prince of Wu, leading the prince of Chu, will seize the Hanku Pass, guard the granaries of Yingyang and Aotsang, hold back the soldiers of Han and prepare quarters in readiness for you and your guard. If you will honour us by taking part, sir, the whole empire can be conquered and divided between you and the prince of Wu. Is this not feasible?"

"Very well," said the prince of Chiaohsi.

After Ying Kao returned to report this, the prince of Wu, still afraid that the other might not join him, went in person to reach an agreement with the prince of Chiaohsi.

Some ministers of the prince of Chiaohsi learned of this plot and advised against it, saying, "Allegiance to one emperor is best of all. Now you mean to march west with the prince of Wu but, even if you succeed, trouble will follow when you both contend for power. The lands of the princes make up less than one-fifth of the empire. It would not be wise to revolt and cause anxiety to the empress dowager."

Instead of listening to them, however, the prince sent envoys to enlist the support of the princes of Chi, Tzuchuan, Chiaotung, Chinan and Chipei, all of whom consented to join the conspiracy. "Prince Ching of Chengyang showed his loyalty in the overthrow of the Lu clan," they said. "He would not take part. When all is done we shall share the empire with him."

The princes lived in fear because of recent punishments or the confiscation of their land, and greatly hated Chao Tso. When the order came that the provinces of Kuaichi and Yuchang were to be taken from Wu, the prince of Wu took the lead in calling out his troops. In the first month all Han officers from the two thousand piculs rank downwards were killed in Wu and Chiaohsi. The same was done in Chiaotung, Tzuchuan, Chinan, Chu and Chao, after which the rebels marched west.

The prince of Chi, repenting, went back on his word and took his own life by drinking poison. The wall of the prince of Chipei's capital was under repair, and the chief of his palace guard forcibly restrained him from sending out his troops.

With the prince of Chiaohsi in command, the forces of Chiaotung, Tzuchuan and Chinan besieged Lintzu. The prince of Chao also rebelled and secretly sent for the Huns to join his forces.

As soon as the seven princes rose in revolt, the prince of Wu mobilized his troops and issued this proclamation: "I am sixty-two, yet I shall lead the troops in person. My youngest son is fourteen but he too will march in the vanguard. Let all men no older than myself and no younger than my son take up arms!" He raised an army of more than two hundred thousand and sent envoys south to the Minyueh and Tungyueh tribes,* and Tungyueh dispatched troops to join him.

The rebellion broke out at Kuangling in the first month of the third year of Emperor Ching. The prince of Wu crossed the River Huai to the west and joined the army of Chu. He sent envoys to the other princes bearing this letter:

> Liu Pi, prince of Wu, sends his greetings to the princes of Chiaohsi, Chiaotung, Tzuchuan, Chinan, Chao, Chu, Huainan, Hengshan and Luchiang, and the two sons of the late prince of Changsha. Han has evil ministers who do not serve the empire but seize the lands of the princes and arrest and try their envoys, not showing the respect due to kinsmen of the imperial clan of Liu. The good ministers of the last reign are thrust aside while scoundrels are given posts, causing confusion throughout the land and endangering the state. Since the emperor, in bad health and infirm of purpose, is unable to see the true state of affairs, I am raising troops to destroy the evil-doers. I hope for guidance from you.
>
> Although my principality is small, it covers three thousand square *li* of land. Although my people are few, I can gather half a million picked troops. The chieftains of Nanyueh, whom I have aided for thirty years and more, have acceded to my request and placed their troops under my command, giving me an additional three hundred thousand

---

* Present-day Chekiang and Fukien in southeastern China.

men. Unworthy as I am, I would like to follow the lead of the other princes.

Since Nanyueh lies next to Changsha, the sons of the late prince of Changsha should pacify the land to their north, then march west to Hanchung and Shu. The chieftains of Tungyueh, the prince of Chu and the three princes of Huai-nan, Hengshan and Luchiang, should march west with me. The princes of Chi and Chao should pacify Hochien and Honei, then proceed through the Linchin Pass or join my forces at Loyang. Since the princes of Yen and Chao have an alliance with the Hunnish chief, let the prince of Yen advance north to conquer Tai and Yunchung, then lead the Hunnish hordes through the Hsiao Pass. We shall enter Changan to rectify the emperor's mistakes and preserve the ancestral temples of the founder of the dynasty. I trust all these princes will take action!

The son of Prince Yuan of Chu and the three princes of Huainan, Hengshan and Luchiang have not bathed for ten years and more, so deep is their hatred and longing for revenge! I have not ventured to agree to their wish without first obtaining the other princes' consent. But if the princes will preserve the descendants of the dead, protect the weak and fight against tyranny to safeguard the Liu clan, this will satisfy the longing of the people.

Although my principality is poor, I have dressed and eaten frugally to lay by money, prepare arms and accumulate grain for thirty years and more without a break. I hope the other princes will make use of this.

The reward for killing or capturing a marshal shall be five thousand catties of gold and a fief of ten thousand households; for a general, three thousand catties of gold and five thousand households; for a lieutenant-general, two thousand catties and two thousand households; for an officer of the two thousand piculs rank, a thousand catties and a thousand households; for an officer of the one thousand piculs rank, five hundred catties and five hundred households. And all these men will receive the title of marquis.

The reward for coming over to our side with an army of ten thousand men or a city of ten thousand households shall be the same as for the capture of a marshal; for five thousand men or five thousand households, the same as for the capture of a general; for three thousand men or three thousand households, the same as for the capture of a lieutenant-general; for a thousand men or a thousand households, the same as for the capture of an officer of the two thousand piculs rank. Junior officers who come over shall receive gold and rank according to their merit. Other rewards shall be double the conventional standard, and those already awarded ranks and fiefs shall receive new rewards over and above what they have. I hope the princes will announce this to their officers, for I shall not go back on my word. I have funds not only in Wu but all over the empire, an inexhaustible supply even if the princes draw on it day and night. If anyone deserves a reward, you have only to let me know and I shall send it. I proclaim this respectfully.

When this letter announcing the seven princes' rebellion reached the emperor, he sent the Grand Marshal Chou Ya-fu, marquis of Tiao, at the head of thirty-six generals to attack Wu and Chu. Li Chi, marquis of Chuchou, was sent to attack Chao, General Luan Pu to attack Chi, and Marshal Tou Ying to station troops at Yingyang to await the armies of Chi and Chao.

The report of the rebellion had arrived but troops had not yet been dispatched when Tou Ying, before setting out, recommended Yuan Ang, the former prime minister to the prince of Wu who was then living in retirement. The emperor sent for Yuan Ang, who arrived as Emperor Ching and Chao Tso were discussing the disposition of troops and the army supplies.

"You were once the prime minister of Wu," said the emperor to Yuan Ang. "What do you know of their marshal Tien Lu-po? And what do you think of this revolt of Wu and Chu?"

"There is no need to worry," Yuan Ang replied. "They will soon be defeated."

"The prince of Wu has minted money in the mountains, extracted salt from the sea and attracted useful men from all over the land," said the emperor. "Would a white-haired old man have started this revolt unless he had a foolproof plan? How can you dismiss it as nothing?"

"True, Wu makes a lot of money out of copper and salt," said Yuan Ang. "But what good men has the prince been able to attract? If he had any, they would have advised him to do what is right, not to rebel. He has simply assembled some scoundrels, fugitives from justice and criminals who coin counterfeit money. That is why they have encouraged him to revolt."

"Let Yuan Ang draw up a plan for us," said Chao Tso.

"What plan do you suggest?" asked the emperor.

"I would like to speak with you in private," replied Yuan Ang.

The emperor dismissed his attendants, leaving only Chao Tso.

"What I have to say is for Your Majesty's ears alone," said Yuan Ang.

Then the emperor dismissed Chao Tso, who retired to the east chamber in a rage.

Asked his opinion again, Yuan Ang replied, "This letter from the princes of Wu and Chu says that all Emperor Kaotsu's sons and younger brothers had fiefs until the traitor Chao Tso accused them falsely and seized their territory. They claim that they have risen in revolt to march west and punish Chao Tso, and that once their lands are restored they will call a halt. So the best plan now would be to execute Chao Tso and send envoys to pardon the seven princes, returning the provinces which were taken from them. Then their troops will be called off without any bloodshed."

The emperor was silent for some time. "If that is true," he said, "I should not grudge sacrificing a single man for the sake of the whole empire."

"Dull as I am, I have no better plan," said Yuan Ang. "I hope you will consider it carefully."

The emperor appointed Yuan Ang as officer in charge of sacrifices, and Marquis Teh, the son of the prince of Wu's younger brother, as officer of the imperial clan. Yuan Ang made ready to set out on a journey. After more than ten days, the emperor ordered the military commander of the capital to summon Chao Tso; but instead of being driven to the palace he was taken to the east market. There he was executed still wearing his court robes. Then Yuan Ang as the warden of the ancestral temples and the officer of the imperial clan with orders for the imperial kinsmen were dispatched to the prince of Wu in accordance with Yuan Ang's plan.

When they reached Wu, the troops of Wu and Chu were attacking the ramparts of Liang. Marquis Teh, as a kinsman, was received first by the prince of Wu. He told him the emperor's decision and ordered him to bow to receive the imperial decree.

But the prince of Wu, who knew that Yuan Ang had also come to persuade him, laughed and replied, "I am already the emperor of the east. Why should I bow to anyone's decree?" He refused to see Yuan Ang, but detained him in his camp and tried to force him to become his general. When Yuan Ang refused, the king had him surrounded and watched, meaning to kill him. But Yuan Ang contrived to slip out by night and escape on foot to the army of Liang, after which he went back to report to the emperor.

The marquis of Tiao, driving swiftly by six stages to the garrison at Yingyang, was delighted to meet Chu Meng at Loyang. "When the seven princes revolted, I hurried here by relay carriages, not expecting this place to have held out," he said. "I feared the feudal lords had got hold of you, but I find you have not moved. With Yingyang in my hands, we have nothing to fear from the east."

He proceeded to Huaiyang and asked an army tribune named Teng, a former protégé of his father, the marquis of Chiang, what strategy he advised.

304

"The army of Wu has a striking force hard to resist, that of Chu is lightly equipped with small staying power," said Teng. "Your best plan is to lead your men northeast to defend Changyi, abandoning Liang to Wu, for then the prince of Wu is bound to attack it with all his might. Meanwhile from behind deep trenches and high ramparts, you can send a light detachment to block the junction of the Huai and Szu Rivers, cutting Wu's supply route. When the forces of Wu and Liang have worn each other out and the rebels' grain is finished, you can attack the exhausted enemy in full strength and Wu's defeat is certain."

"Very good," said the marquis of Tiao and adopted this plan, building strong defences south of Changyi and sending a light detachment to cut Wu's supply route.

When the prince of Wu rose in revolt he appointed his minister Tien Lu-po as grand marshal. "If we advance west with our whole body of troops without making any surprise attacks, it will be hard to succeed," said Tien Lu-po. "Let me lead fifty thousand men along the Yangtse and Huai Rivers to conquer Huainan and Changsha, and then proceed through the Wu Pass to rejoin your forces. Then we could take the enemy by surprise."

The prince of Wu's son objected, however, saying, "Now that you have revolted openly, sir, it would be unwise to entrust your troops to others lest they in turn rise against you. Besides, when a man goes off at the head of troops, all sorts of things, either good or bad, may happen. Meanwhile our strength would be weakened." So the prince of Wu rejected Tien Lu-po's plan.

A young general of Wu named Huan advised the prince, saying, "Our army is mainly infantry, well suited to mountainous terrain, while the army of Han with all its war chariots and cavalry fights better on the plain. I suggest that when cities on the way prove hard to take, we simply abandon the attack and march swiftly west to seize the arsenals of Loyang and feed our men with grain from Aotsang, blocking the mountain passes by the river while you command the other princes. Then you will have the empire in your hands without even entering the Pass. But if you advance slowly, stopping to take cities, the war chariots and cavalry of Han will charge across the plains of Chu and Liang, and all will be lost."

The prince consulted older generals, who said, "This is the hare-brained scheme of a young man who does not think seriously." So the prince did not take General Huan's advice.

The prince of Wu took command of all his forces. Before crossing the River Huai he made all his protégés except Chou Chiu generals, colonels, captains and provincial governors. Chou Chiu was a native of Hsiapi who had gone to Wu as a fugitive from justice and was often drunk and disorderly. Hence the prince of Wu thought little of him and gave him no post.

Chou Chiu asked to see the prince and said, "I am not able enough to serve in this campaign and would not presume to ask for a command; but if you will give me one of the credentials used by the Han envoys, I swear to repay the gratitude I owe you."

The prince gave him the credential and Chou Chiu rode off that same night to Hsiapi. News of the revolt had reached Hsiapi and its cities were being defended. He went to the government hostel and summoned the magistrate. As soon as the magistrate arrived, he charged him with some crime and ordered his followers to kill him.

Then Chou Chiu sent for his brothers and the chief officers whom he knew, and told them, "The rebel troops of Wu are on their way here and, once they arrive, they will butcher the people of Hsiapi in the time it takes for a meal. By surrendering now, you can save your families and men of ability will be ennobled." These men went to spread the word, and Hsiapi surrendered.

In one night Chou Chiu had won over thirty thousand men. Sending a messenger to report this to the prince, he led his troops north to conquer other cities. By the time he reached Chengyang he had over a hundred thousand men and with these he routed the army of the commander of Chengyang. Then word came that the prince of Wu had been defeated and fled and, knowing that he could not go on alone, Chou Chiu led his troops back towards Hsiapi. Before he reached it, however, an ulcer developed on his back and he died.

In the middle of the second month, when the prince of Wu's army was routed and put to flight, the emperor issued this order to his generals:

We have heard that Heaven blesses those who do good but visits calamity upon wrong-doers. Emperor Kao-tsu himself honoured achievement and virtue and set up the princes. When Prince Yu and Prince Tao-hui had no heirs, Emperor Wu took pity on them and made Prince Yu's son Siu and Prince Tao-hui's son Ang princes, so that they might care for their ancestral temples as the vassals of Han. He was as virtuous as heaven and earth, and as discerning as the sun and moon.

But Liu Pi, the prince of Wu, flouted virtue and justice by attracting fugitives and evil-doers from all parts of the empire, debasing the currency and, on the pretext of illness, absenting himself from court for more than twenty years. The authorities urged more than once that he should be punished, but Emperor Wen pardoned him, hoping that he would mend his ways and do what was right. Now he has rebelled with Prince Wu of Chu, Prince Sui of Chao, Prince Ang of Chiaohsi, Prince Pi-kuang of Chinan, Prince Hsien of Tzuchuan and Prince Hsiung-chu of Chiaotung, lawlessly plotting treason. He has raised arms to endanger the imperial house, killed ministers and Han envoys, oppressed the people, murdered the innocent, burned and destroyed men's houses, razed their graves and resorted to violence of every description. Ang and others have committed yet more heinous crimes, burning the ancestral temples and looting the ceremonial costumes and vessels. We are deeply grieved. Dressed in plain clothes we have withdrawn from the main court while our generals urge their officers to attack these rebels. Those who strike deep into rebel territory and kill or capture many foes will be performing meritorious services. As for the captives, all rebel officers above the three hundred piculs rank must be put to death without mercy. Any man who dares to question this decree or fails to carry it out shall be cut in two at the waist.

When the prince of Wu had first crossed the River Huai, he stormed Chipi in the west with the prince of Chu and, flushed with victory, their army swept irresistibly forward, so that Prince Hsiao of Liang was afraid. He sent six generals out to intercept them, but two of these were defeated and their men fled back to Liang. The prince of Liang sent envoys to the marquis of Tiao with repeated requests for help, but the marquis made no response. Finally the prince sent an envoy to condemn the marquis to the emperor, who ordered him to go to the aid of Liang. Still the marquis, acting on expediency, did not dispatch his forces. The prince of Liang gave the command to Han An-kuo and Chang Yu, the younger brother of the minister of Chu who died after remonstrating with his prince, and they inflicted several defeats on Wu.

The troops of Wu wanted to proceed west, but in face of Liang's stubborn resistance they dared not do so. Instead they marched against the marquis of Tiao at Hsiayi, but his army remained behind the ramparts and would not give battle, till Wu's supplies ran out and its men were hungry. They challenged the enemy time and again and one night made a feint of attacking from the southeast. The marquis promptly prepared for an attack on the northwest, and when the Wu troops did attack from that direction they were routed. Many of them died of starvation, others mutinied and scattered.

The prince of Wu with a few thousand of his best fighters escaped at night and crossed the Yangtse River, fleeing to Tantu in the land of Tungyueh. Tungyueh had more than ten thousand troops, and he meant to rally his scattered forces there. But the court sent envoys with gifts to persuade the chieftain of Tungyueh to trick the prince of Wu. When he came out to review his troops, spearsmen set on him and killed him. His head was put in a casket and sent by post carriage to court. His two sons, Tzu-hua and Tzu-chu, fled to Minyueh. After the prince of Wu abandoned his army and fled, his men were dispersed and little by little surrendered to the prince of Liang and the grand marshal. The forces of Prince Wu of Chu were also defeated and he committed suicide.

The three princes of Chiaohsi, Chiaotung and Tzuchuan besieged Lintzu in Chi for three months but failed to take it. When government reinforcements arrived, they withdrew to their own principalities.

The prince of Chiaohsi bared his left arm, sat on a straw mat and drank nothing but water to apologize to the queen dowager.

His son Te said, "Han's army has come a long way and seems exhausted. Why not launch a surprise attack? Let me rally all our remaining troops to fight them. If we lose, we can still escape by way of the sea."

"My troops are too demoralized to be of any use," replied the prince and he ignored this proposal.

Han Tui-tang, the marquis of Kungkao and a Han general, sent this letter to the prince: "The emperor has ordered me to punish malefactors. Those who submit will be pardoned and their rank restored; those who refuse to surrender will be destroyed. What does Your Highness intend to do? I am waiting for your decision."

The prince bared his left arm and kowtowed before the Han ramparts to beg for an interview. "I have been remiss in observing the law and alarmed the people, putting you to the trouble of coming all this way to my poor principality," he said. "I beg to be punished by being cut into small pieces."

The marquis, holding a drum and gong, received him. "Your Highness is averse to fighting," he said. "May I ask why you rose in arms?"

The prince bowed his head and, advancing on his knees, replied, "We thought it unjust that Chao Tso, who was trusted by the emperor, should alter Emperor Kao-tsu's laws and seize the lands of the princes. We seven princes were afraid that he would destroy the empire, so we rose in arms to punish him. Now that we hear Chao Tso has been executed, we have withdrawn our troops."

"If you thought that Chao Tso was wrong, why did you not report it to the emperor?" the general asked. "Instead you mobilized troops with your tiger tally and attacked a loyal prince without the emperor's order. Judging by your actions, your aim was not to punish Chao Tso." He took out the imperial decree, read it to the prince and said, "You must decide for yourself what action to take."

"Even death cannot atone for my crime," said the prince of Chiaohsi. He committed suicide, and so did the queen dowager and the crown prince.

The princes of Chiaotung, Tzuchuan and Chinan all took their own lives. Their principalities were abolished and came under central government jurisdiction.

After a siege of ten months, General Li Chi took the capital of Chao and the prince of Chao committed suicide. Since the prince of Chipei had been forced by the other princes to join the revolt, his life was spared but he was removed to be the prince of Tzuchuan.

The prince of Wu had been the first to rebel, he had commanded the army of Chu as well as his own and had made the agreement with the princes of Chi and Chao. The rebellion broke out in the first month, but by the third all rebel forces were suppressed except for those of Chao, which were defeated later. Li, marquis of Pinglu and the youngest son of Prince Yuan of Chu, was made the king of Chu to carry on the royal line. Prince Fei of Junan was removed to rule over the former principality of Wu with the title of prince of Chiangtu.

The Grand Historian comments: The prince of Wu became prince as a result of his father's loss of territory. He succeeded in lowering taxes and winning the hearts of his people by his monopoly of copper and salt. His son's death was the root of his disaffection, and that quarrel over a game score ended in his utter ruin. He allied with the tribesmen of Yueh against his own clan, and came to an evil end. Chao Tso showed foresight in affairs of state but met with personal calamity. Yuan Ang was trusted thanks to his eloquence, but the favour he first enjoyed ended in disgrace. So we see why no feudal lord of old could have a fief exceeding a hundred *li* or possession of mountains and coastland. And it was said, "Do not make friends with the barbarians while keeping at a distance from kinsmen." This applies, surely, to the prince of Wu. "Do not try to rise above others, or you will suffer for it." This applies, does it not, to Chao Tso and Yuan Ang?

THE PRINCES OF HUAINAN AND HENGSHAN

Liu Chang, Prince Li of Huainan, was one of Emperor Kao-tsu's younger sons. His mother had been a court lady of Chang Ao, the former prince of Chao. In the eighth year of his reign,* when Emperor Kao-tsu went from Tungyuan to Chao, the prince of Chao presented her to him. She was favoured by the emperor and conceived. The prince of Chao did not dare to keep her in his palace, but built another palace for her.

When Kuan Kao and others plotted treason at Pojen and were discovered, the prince of Chao was also seized and tried, while his mother, brothers and court ladies, including Liu Chang's mother, were imprisoned at Honei. She told the officers that she was carrying the emperor's child, but when they reported this Emperor Kao-tsu was so enraged with the prince of Chao that he ignored the matter. Her brother Chao Chien sent word by the marquis of Piyang to Empress Lu, but the jealous empress would not speak up for her and the marquis did not insist.

As soon as Liu Chang was born, his mother killed herself in anger. The officers took the child to the emperor, who, filled with remorse, ordered Empress Lu to rear it and had the mother buried in Chenting where her family had lived for generations.

In the tenth month of the eleventh year of Emperor Kao-tsu, Ying Pu the prince of Huainan rebelled, and Liu Chang was made prince in his place to rule the four provinces which had belonged to him. His rule began after Emperor Kao-tsu led troops in person to wipe out the rebels. Since Liu Chang had lost his mother and was close to Empress Lu, he was fa-

---

* 199 B. C.

voured and came to no harm during the reigns of Emperor Hui and Empress Lu. Resentment rankled in his heart against the marquis of Piyang, but he dared not disclose his feelings.

When Emperor Wen first came to the throne, the prince of Huainan behaved in a proud, overbearing manner because he was next of kin, often breaking the law. But since they were brothers the emperor pardoned him.

In the third year he came to court and conducted himself in the most presumptuous manner. Hunting with the emperor in the imperial park, he rode in the same carriage and addressed him as "Elder Brother".

The prince was a powerful man, strong enough to lift a bronze cauldron. He went to call on the marquis of Piyang and, when the latter came out to see him, struck him with an iron hammer which he had concealed in his sleeve, then ordered his follower Wei Ching to cut off his head. The prince then rode to court and, baring his left arm, apologized.

"My mother was not involved in Chao's conspiracy, and the marquis of Piyang could have interceded successfully for her with the empress, but he let the matter slide. That was his first crime. Prince Ju-yi of Chao and his mother were innocent, but Empress Lu had them killed and the marquis did nothing to save them. That was his second crime. When Empress Lu endangered the imperial house of Liu by making her kinsmen princes, the marquis did not protest. That was his third crime. Now I have killed this traitor for the state and avenged my mother. I bow before the court and beg to be punished."

Because he had his reasons and they were brothers, the emperor pardoned him.

At this time Empress Po, the crown prince and all the chief ministers went in fear of the prince of Huainan. After his return to his principality he grew even more high-handed. He ignored the laws of the land, usurped the imperial prerogatives when he entered or left the palace, and issued his own decrees, all as if he were the emperor.

In the sixth year, he sent Tan and seventy other men to

plot rebellion with Chi, the son of Chai Wu, the marquis of Chipu. They drove in forty large carriages to Kukou. Envoys were also sent to approach the tribes of Minyueh and the Huns. The plot was discovered and investigated, and the prince was summoned to the capital.

When the prince reached Changan, the prime minister Chang Tsang, the master of ceremony Feng Ching, the clan officer and acting chief counsellor Yi, the chief justice Ho, and Fu the metropolitan commander in charge of suppressing rebels, presented this memorial to the throne:

Liu Chang, the prince of Huainan, has broken the laws of the late emperor and disobeyed Your Majesty's orders. His whole way of life is completely unrestrained, for he has adopted a yellow canopy and imperial equipage and goes about as if he were the emperor. He has issued his own decrees, ignoring the laws of the land, and has out-stepped his station by appointing his palace guard Chun as prime minister. He has gathered together men from the various fiefs of Han as well as fugitives from justice, and is giving them shelter, supplying them with houses, granting them money, goods, ranks, salaries and landed property, even enfeoffing some of them as marquises with a two thousand piculs stipend. He has done all these wrong things with a definite purpose.

His minister Tan with seventy others including Kai Chang, a retired officer, plotted rebellion with Chi, heir of the marquis of Chipu, to endanger our state. Kai Chang was sent in secret to report this to the prince of Huainan, that he might join in the conspiracy and send envoys to the Minyueh tribes and the Huns to enlist their support. When Kai Chang reached Huainan, the prince granted him several audiences, feasted him and gave him a house, a wife and a salary of two thousand piculs. Then Kai Chang sent to tell Tan that he had spoken to the prince. And prime minister Chun dispatched messengers to Tan and the others.

The authorities, discovering this plot, sent Chi the military tribune of Changan and others to arrest Kai Chang. But the prince concealed him and would not hand him over. He arranged with his former military tribune Chien Chi to murder Kai Chang in order to stop him from talking. A coffin and grave clothes were supplied and the corpse was buried at Feiling, while the prince denied all knowledge of Kai Chang's whereabouts. Then, to trick the authorities, he made a grave mound bearing the inscription: Here Kai Chang is buried.

Liu Chang has also killed an innocent man, ordered his officers to condemn six others to death, and arrested men to take the place of fugitives from justice who deserved death, letting those felons go free. He has condemned men without the court's permission, sentencing fourteen men to hard labour and other punishments. He has pardoned criminals, including eighteen who deserved death and fifty-eight who had been sentenced to hard labour, pounding rice and other punishments. He has bestowed titles up to the rank of a marquis on ninety-four men.

Not long ago when Liu Chang was ill, Your Majesty in concern sent an envoy to him with a letter and some preserved jujubes. But Liu Chang refused the gift and would not receive the envoy.

When the officers and men of Huainan quelled the revolt of the people of Nanhai who had been moved to Luchiang, Your Majesty out of compassion for their poverty sent an envoy to the prince with five thousand rolls of silk to recompense the officers and men for their exertions. But again Liu Chang refused the gift and lied, "No one here has suffered any hardships."

When Wang Chih of Nanhai sent a jade disc and a letter to the emperor, Chien Chi the metropolitan tribune burned the letter and did not report the matter. The authorities asked for Chien Chi to put him on trial, but the prince would not hand him over, making out that he was ill.

When his prime minister Chun asked permission to come

to court, the prince stormed at him, "Do you want to leave me and go over to Han?"

Liu Chang should be executed in the market-place. We beg that this be done according to the law.

The emperor decreed, "We cannot bear to punish the prince according to the law. Discuss the matter further with the feudal lords and ministers of the two thousand piculs rank."

They presented another memorial:

Your subjects Tsang, Chin, Yi, Fu and Ho, make this report at the risk of death. We have discussed the matter with the feudal lords and ministers of the two thousand piculs rank, including Marquis Hsiaho Ying and others, forty-three in all. They agree that the prince of Huainan has broken the law and disobeyed Your Majesty's orders. He has secretly gathered followers and conspirators, he has used his wealth to keep fugitives from justice and to plot treason. We recommend that he be punished according to the law.

The emperor decreed, "We cannot bear to punish the prince according to the law. Let him be spared the death penalty but deprived of his rank as a prince."

Then the ministers replied:

Your subjects Tsang and the others make this report at the risk of death. The prince of Huainan deserves the death penalty, but unwilling to enforce the rigour of the law Your Majesty has pardoned him, depriving him only of his rank as a prince. We suggest that he be exiled to Chiung Station in Yentao in the province of Shu, accompanied by his children and their mothers. The district authorities can build him a house and supply him with food, providing him with firewood, vegetables, salted beans, cooking utensils, mats and bedding. Deserving death for our presumption, we beg that this be announced throughout the empire!

The emperor decreed, "Regarding food for Liu Chang, let

him be given five catties of meat a day and two measures of wine. Let ten ladies who have won his favour also join him. For the rest, it shall be as you propose. Let all the conspirators be executed."

Then the prince of Huainan was sent off in a covered carriage, and the district authorities were ordered to pass him on from one station to another.

Yuan Ang remonstrated with the emperor, saying, "Your Majesty has always spoilt the prince of Huainan, not appointing strict tutors and ministers for him. That is how this came about. Moreover, the prince is proud and stubborn. Now that you have suddenly crushed him, I am afraid he may die on this difficult journey. What if you are accused of fratricide?"

"I am doing this to teach him a lesson," replied the emperor. "I shall soon reinstate him."

The district authorities through whose hands the prince passed were too afraid to open up the sealed carriage.

"Who calls me a brave fellow?" the prince of Huainan asked his attendants. "What courage can I show now? In my pride, I never realized the extent of my fault. What man could bear to live on wretchedly like this?" He refused all food and died.

When his carriage reached Yung, the local magistrate broke open the seals and reported the prince's death.

The emperor wept bitterly. "By ignoring your advice I have lost the prince of Huainan," he told Yuan Ang.

"It cannot be helped now," replied Yuan Ang. "Your Majesty must not take it too much to heart."

"What should I do now?" asked the emperor.

"The only way to propitiate the empire is to execute the prime minister and chief counsellor."

But the emperor ordered the prime minister and chief counsellor to punish all the local officials along the way who had failed to open the prince's carriage or supply him with food and attendants, and all of them were publicly executed. The prince of Huainan was buried at Yung with the funeral rites

317

of a marquis, and thirty households were appointed to take charge of his tomb.

In the eighth year of his reign Emperor Wen, still grieving over the prince of Huainan, ennobled his four sons who were all about seven or eight years old at that time. Liu An was enfeoffed as marquis of Fuling, Liu Po as marquis of Anyang, Liu Tzu as marquis of Chouyang, and Liu Liang as marquis of Tungcheng.

In the twelfth year of Emperor Wen, the people made up this song about the prince of Huainan:

> A single foot of cloth can be sewn,
> A single peck of millet hulled;
> But an elder and younger brother
> Can never abide each other.

The emperor sighed when he heard this and said, "When Yao and Shun exiled their own flesh and blood and the duke of Chou killed Kuan and Tsai,* the whole world called them sages. For they would not let private sentiment interfere with the public good. Does the world really believe that I coveted the land of the prince of Huainan?" He made the prince of Chengyang take over the former kingdom of Huainan and gave the prince of Huainan the posthumous title of Li, laying out a walled garden round his tomb as befitted a prince.

In the sixteenth year, Emperor Wen moved the new prince of Huainan back to be prince of Chengyang. Still grieved because Prince Li had lost his kingdom and met an untimely death on account of his lawless and unprincipled behaviour, the emperor divided the old territory of Huainan into three parts and made Liu Chang's son An, the marquis of Fuling, prince of Huainan; Po, the marquis of Anyang, prince of Hengshan; and Tzu, the marquis of Chouyang, prince of Luchiang. Liang, the marquis of Tungcheng, had died leaving no heir.

In the third year of Emperor Ching, the princes of Wu, Chu and five other kingdoms rebelled. The prince of Wu

---

* Kuan and Tsai were brothers of the duke of Chou.

sent an envoy to the prince of Huainan and the latter wanted to send troops to join them. His chief minister said, "If you mean to raise an army to aid Wu, let me serve as commander." But when the prince gave him command of the army he defended the city, ignoring the prince's orders, and remained loyal to Han. The emperor also sent the marquis of Chucheng with troops to save Huainan. Thus it was kept out of the war.

When the prince of Wu's envoy reached Luchiang, the prince of Luchiang did not join the rebels but remained in touch with the Yueh tribesmen. When the prince of Wu's envoy reached Hengshan, the prince of Hengshan remained steadfast and loyal too.

In the fourth year of Emperor Ching, after the defeat of Wu and Chu, the prince of Hengshan came to court and the emperor commended his loyalty. "The south is low and swampy," he declared. "Let the prince of Hengshan rule over Chipei instead." When the prince died he was given the posthumous title of Chen.

Since the prince of Luchiang's territory bordered on that of Yueh and he had often exchanged envoys with the tribesmen, he was moved to Hengshan north of the Yangtse River. The prince of Huainan retained his former territory.

Liu An, prince of Huainan, was fond of reading and playing the lyre, but took no pleasure in hunting with hounds and horses. He tried to win the people by acts of kindness so that his fame might spread through all the land. Long embittered by the death of his father, Prince Li, he intended to revolt at the first opportunity.

In the second year of the reign period *Chienyuan*,* the prince of Huainan went to pay homage at court. An old friend of his, the marquis of Wu-an, who was then the grand marshal, came to meet him at Pashang and told him, "Now the emperor has no heir. Your Highness is the grandson of Emperor Kao-tsu, and your deeds of kindness and

---

* 139 B.C.

justice are known to all. Should the emperor die, who would be a more fitting successor?"

The prince in high delight gave the marquis of Wu-an rich gifts and gold. In secret he set about gathering followers and winning the hearts of the people in preparation for a revolt.

In the sixth year of *Chienyuan* a comet appeared. The prince thought it a strange omen and someone told him, "At the start of the prince of Wu's rebellion, a comet only a few feet long appeared, yet blood flowed for a thousand *li*. This comet has filled the whole sky. It must portend fierce fighting in the empire."

The prince believed that as the emperor had no heir there would be trouble and the princes would contend for supremacy. So he got weapons and laid up a store of money to win over the other princes, wandering scholars and men of outstanding ability. Then orators and strategists made wild, fantastic predictions to please the prince who showered gold on them in his delight, and plotted rebellion even more eagerly.

The prince had a daughter, Ling, an intelligent girl who had a ready tongue. She was his favourite and he kept her well supplied with money to act as his spy in the capital and get on good terms with the emperor's attendants.

In the third year of *Yuanshuo** the emperor gave the prince of Huainan a stool and walking-stick and exempted him from paying homage at court.

The prince was much attached to his consort Tu, the mother of the crown prince Tsien, who had married Lord Hsiucheng's daughter, a grand-daughter of Empress Dowager Wang. Fearing lest the crown prince's wife learn of his plot and disclose it, the prince secretly instructed his son to treat her coldly and refuse to sit on the same mat with her for three months. Then the prince, pretending to be angry with his son, confined him in the same room as his wife for three months, but still Tsien never went near her. At that she asked to leave him, and the prince of Huainan sent her back with a letter of apology to the emperor. Queen Tu, the crown prince Tsien and Princess Ling were favoured by the prince of Huainan. They wielded absolute power within the principality, seizing land and houses from the people or arresting men at will.

The crown prince Tsien had studied swordsmanship and fancied himself unsurpassed in all the land. In the fifth year of *Yuanshuo*, having heard that the palace guardsman Lei Pei was a good swordsman, he summoned him to a contest. Lei Pei repeatedly refused to strike but then by accident wounded the prince, who was so angry that Lei Pei feared reprisals. At this time anyone who asked to join the army was sent straight to the capital, so Lei Pei volunteered to go and fight the Huns. But the crown prince had spoken ill of him to the prince, who ordered the chief of the palace guards to dismiss Lei Pei from his post as a warning to others. Then Lei Pei fled to Changan and reported the matter.

The emperor ordered an investigation by the chief justice and the governor of Honan, who sent to arrest the crown prince. The prince of Huainan and his consort were tempted not to hand Tsien over but to raise a revolt. They hesitated for more than ten days, however, and could not make up their mind. Meanwhile there came another decree ordering Tsien's trial on the spot.

By now the chief minister of Huainan, angry with the local chief justice for holding back the order for the crown prince's arrest, charged him with insubordination and insisted on sending in this charge despite the prince of Huainan's protests. Then the prince sent someone to court to inform against the minister. The matter was investigated by the chief justice, and the prince of Huainan was found to be involved. Some of his men who were spying on high government officials learned that they had asked for his arrest and trial, and he was afraid that his whole plot would come out.

The crown prince said, "When the envoy of Han comes to arrest you, sir, post halberdiers dressed as bodyguards in the court. In the event of trouble, they can kill the envoy while

I send men to kill the government's military tribune of Huainan. It will not be too late then to rise in arms."

The emperor did not agree to his ministers' proposal, however, but sent the tribune Hung to question the prince and verify the facts. When the prince of Huainan heard that the court envoy had come, he did as his son had suggested. But so mild and affable did the tribune prove, simply asking how Lei Pei had come to be dismissed, that the prince assumed he had no cause for alarm and did not carry out his plan.

The tribune returned to make his report, and the ministers in charge of the case said, "Liu An the prince of Huainan detained Lei Pei and others who had volunteered to go and fight the Huns. For defying a government decree, he deserves public execution." To this the emperor would not agree, and when the ministers asked that the prince be deposed, the emperor again refused his consent. Then they suggested that Liu An be deprived of five counties. The emperor deprived the prince of two counties and sent Hung to inform him that his offence was pardoned but that some of his land was to be confiscated.

The tribune crossed the border into Huainan to announce the pardon. The prince, who knew that the ministers had proposed his execution but not that he would simply be deprived of some territory, feared that the government envoy was coming to arrest him. He therefore plotted with his son, as before, to kill the envoy. When the tribune arrived, however, he congratulated the king on his pardon, and so the king did not carry out his plan.

Later he regretted this and said, "I act with humanity and justice and yet am deprived of territory. How shameful!" After this he stepped up his plans for revolt. If his envoys came back from the capital with wild rumours and declared that the emperor had no son or the country was badly governed, the prince exulted. If anyone said the country was well governed or a son had been born to the emperor, he raged and considered these as vicious lies.

Day and night the prince, Wu Pei, Tso Wu and others

pored over maps and discussed where to station troops for the attack on Han.

"The emperor has no heir," said the prince. "When he dies, the ministers at court will summon the prince of Chiao-tung or the prince of Changshan. Then all the princes will contend for the throne. I must be prepared. I am Emperor Kao-tsu's grandson, known for my kindness and justice. Since His Majesty has treated me well, I can bide my time. But after his death you need not expect me to swear allegiance to some silly boy."

One day, sitting in his East Palace, the prince summoned Wu Pei to consult him.

"Come here, general!" he cried.

"The emperor has pardoned Your Highness," said Wu Pei gravely. "Why should you still plot to overthrow the state? I have heard that after Wu Tzu-hsu's advice was ignored by the king of Wu, he said, 'I foresee the day when wild deer will roam the terraces of Kusu.' And I can foresee the day when brambles will grow over your palace and the dew will wet men's clothes."

In a rage the prince had him and his parents imprisoned for three months, at the end of which time he summoned him again.

"Do you agree with me now, general?" he asked.

"No!" said Wu Pei. "But let me offer Your Highness some advice. I have heard that a man with good ears can hear what has not yet made a sound, a man with good eyes can see what has not yet taken form. That is why a sage succeeds in all he does. King Wen of old made but one move, yet he has been honoured for a thousand generations as the founder of one of the three great dynasties. For he carried out the will of Heaven and all men followed him of their own accord. This is a case from a thousand years ago, whereas the Chin Dynasty of a hundred years ago and Wu and Chu in recent times are examples of how kingdoms fall. I am not afraid to share the fate of Wu Tzu-hsu, but I hope Your Highness will not listen to wrong advice like the king of Wu.

323

"Chin abandoned the ways of the former kings, killed scholars, burnt the ancient songs and documents, gave up ceremony and justice, advocated treachery and force, relied on punishments and shipped grain from the coast to Hsiho. In those days, although men wore themselves out in the fields, they had not even enough chaff or husks to eat. Although women wove and spun, they had not clothes enough to cover themselves. The emperor sent Meng Tien to build the Great Wall extending thousands of *li* from east to west. He kept hundreds of thousands of troops deployed in the field, and the dead were past counting. Corpses lay strewn for a thousand *li*, hundreds of *mou* flowed with blood, and the people were so exhausted that five households out of ten longed to revolt.

"Then Hsu Fu was sent out to sea in search of supernatural beings, and on his return he lied to the emperor, saying, 'I have seen the great god of the ocean, who asked whether I was the envoy from the Emperor of the West. When I signified that I was, he asked me my business. I told him I was looking for an elixir to prolong life. He replied that since the king of Chin's gifts were so poor, I could see what I wished but might take nothing away. Then he let me go southeast to Mount Penglai, where I saw palaces built of sacred fungus. There was a god the colour of bronze and shaped like a dragon, whose light blazed up to illuminate the sky. I bowed and asked what presents I should bring, and the god replied that the elixir could be had by anyone who brought young boys and girls and crafts of every kind.'

"The First Emperor of Chin in high delight sent him back with three thousand boys and girls, the five types of grain and a hundred different craftsmen. But when Hsu Fu reached a plain with a broad expanse of water, he set himself up as king there and never returned. Then the people grieved over their bitter loss, and six households out of ten longed to revolt.

"Then the emperor dispatched Chao To south across the mountains to attack the Yueh tribes. Knowing that the people were at the end of their tether, Chao To set himself up as king there and did not go back but sent to ask for thirty thousand unmarried women to mend his troops' uniforms and the emperor sent him fifteen thousand women. That was when the people became further demoralized and seven households out of ten wanted to revolt.

"Someone advised Emperor Kao-tsu, 'Now is the time!' But he answered, 'Wait. Wise men are going to rise in the south-east.' Before a year had passed, Chen Sheh and Wu Kuang started their revolt, and when Emperor Kao-tsu issued a call from Feng and Pei countless multitudes throughout the land responded spontaneously. That was a case of waiting for the right occasion and striking as Chin was about to fall, when the people longed for its overthrow as men in time of drought long for rain. Thus he rose from the ranks to become the emperor, his achievement surpassed that of the three sage kings and his virtuous influence will be handed down for ever.

"Now Your Highness has seen how easily Emperor Kao-tsu won his empire. But consider the case of Wu and Chu in recent times. The prince of Wu was entitled the chief of the imperial clan and did not have to go to court to pay homage. He ruled the multitudes of four provinces with a territory of several thousand square *li*. He minted money from copper and boiled sea water on the east coast to extract salt. To the west he felled timber at Chiangling to make boats, each able to carry as much as several dozen waggons of the central states. His land was wealthy and populous and he sent jewels, gold and silk to bribe the princes, members of the imperial clan and high ministers. All but the Tou family were in his plot.

"After his preparations were complete, he led his army westward. Defeated at Taliang and routed at Hufu, he fled eastward to Tantu where he was captured by the Yueh tribes-men. So he perished and his clan was wiped out, becoming the world's laughing-stock. The reason why he failed despite the size of his forces was that he flouted Heaven's law and did not choose the right time.

"Now your troops are less than one-tenth of those of Wu and Chu, while the empire is infinitely more stable than it was then. I beg Your Highness to take my advice. If you refuse I foresee you are bound to fail. News of your plan will leak out in advance.

"I have heard that when Wei-tzu saw the ruins of the former kingdom of Shang, he made the *Song of the Millet* in his grief to lament that King Chow had not listened to Prince Pi-kan. And that is why Mencius said, 'Although Chow was exalted as the Son of Heaven, his death was worse than that of a common man.' For King Chow had long cut himself off from the people, it was not that they left him in the hour of his death.

"Dismayed to see Your Highness cast away your position as lord of ten thousand chariots, I beg to be allowed to kill myself, that I may die here in the East Palace before all your ministers perish."

The prince sank into gloom too deep to dispel, so that tears welled up in his eyes. He rose, walked down the steps and went away.

Now the prince had a son named Pu-hai whose mother was a concubine. Although he was the eldest son, the prince had no love for him and neither the prince, the queen, nor the crown prince treated him as one of their family.

Pu-hai's son Chien was talented and ambitious. He resented the crown prince's coldness to his father and the fact that the sons of all the other princes were ennobled while the son of the prince of Huainan who was not the heir was not even a marquis. He therefore formed secret connections, hoping to inform against the crown prince and overthrow him so that his father could become the heir instead. The crown prince, learning of this, had Chien arrested and flogged several times. When in the sixth year of *Yuanshuo* Chien discovered the crown prince's plot to kill the central tribune he made his friend Chuang Chih, a native of Shouchun, present this report to the emperor:

> Harsh medicine is bitter to taste but cures disease, loyal words offend the ear but benefit conduct. Now Chien the grandson of the prince of Huainan has abilities of a high order but is persecuted by Queen Tu and her son the

crown prince Tsien. Chien's father Pu-hai has done no wrong yet he has been arrested several times and they mean to do away with him. Chien is ready to be summoned and questioned. He knows all the secrets of the prince of Huainan.

Having read this report, the emperor referred it to the chief justice, who referred it to the governor of Honan.

At this time Shen Ching, grandson of the former marquis of Piyang, was a good friend of the prime minister Kungsun Hung, and he had never forgiven Prince Li of Huainan for killing his grandfather. He painted the situation in Huainan so black that the prime minister began to suspect that the prince was plotting rebellion and determined to make a thorough investigation. The governor of Honan interrogated Chien, who incriminated the crown prince of Huainan and his followers.

The prince of Huainan was alarmed and decided to rebel. He asked Wu Pei, "Does the Han court rule well or badly?"

"The empire is well governed," answered Wu Pei.

The prince, displeased with this reply, demanded, "Why do you say that?"

"I have observed that the court administration, the relationships between sovereign and subjects, father and son, husband and wife, senior and junior are all properly regulated," said Wu Pei. "The emperor administers the realm in accordance with the ancient way and there is no breach of conventions or discipline. Wealthy merchants with heavy loads travel the length and breadth of the empire, for all the roads are open; hence trade is flourishing. The southern Yueh tribes acknowledge our suzerainty, the men of Chiang and Po in the west send tribute, the eastern tribes have surrendered, the northern frontier at Changyu has been extended, and the new province of Shuofang has been opened up. The Huns, their wings clipped and torn, are cut off from their allies and cannot stir against us. Although this cannot compare with the great peace of antiquity, it is nevertheless a time of good government."

The prince was furious, and Wu Pei apologized for his presumption.

Then the prince questioned him again. "If fighting breaks out in the east, the Han court is bound to send Grand Marshal Wei Ching with an army to subdue the land east of the Pass. What is your estimate of the grand marshal?"

"A friend of mine, Huang Yi, served under Wei Ching in a campaign against the Huns," said Wu Pei. "On his return he told me, 'The grand marshal is courteous to his officers and good to his men, so that all of them like to serve under him. He gallops up and down the hills as if he had wings and is of outstanding ability.' To my mind, a seasoned campaigner of such ability would prove hard to resist. When the imperial herald Tsao Liang came from Changan, he described the marshal as a brilliant commander, fearless in the face of the enemy, and as one who always fights in the forefront of the battle. When the army encamps and wells are dug, he drinks only after all his men have drunk. When the army is in retreat, he crosses a river only after all his men have crossed. When the empress dowager gives him gold and silk, he presents them all to his officers. Even celebrated generals of old were no better."

The prince was silent.

Now that Chien was being cross-examined, the prince feared his plot might come to light and was eager to rebel, but Wu Pei still opposed it. So once more the prince asked him, "Do you think the prince of Wu was right or wrong in starting his rebellion?"

"I think he was wrong," said Wu Pei. "The prince of Wu enjoyed great wealth and the highest rank, but because he did wrong he perished at Tantu, his head was severed from his body, and all his sons and grandsons were wiped out. I have heard that he repented bitterly. I hope Your Highness will weigh the matter well rather than have to regret the same fate as the prince of Wu."

"A brave man must be ready to die for a mere word," retorted the prince of Huainan. "Besides, what did the prince of Wu know about rebellion? In one day he let over forty Han generals pass Chengkao! If I send Lou Huan to block the pass at Chengkao, send Chou Pei from Yingchuan to block the passes of Huanyuan and Yichueh, and Chen Ting at the head of the troops of Nanyang to hold the Wu Pass, the governor of Honan will have nothing left but Loyang and we need not worry about him. Further north, of course, there are still the Linchin Pass, Hotung, Shangtang, Honei and Chao. But there is a saying, 'Block Chengkao and you have nothing to fear from the rest of the empire.' Then I can seize the strongholds of Sanchuan and raise troops east of the Pass. What do you think of this plan?"

"No good can come of it, nothing but disaster."

"Tso Wu, Chao Hsien and Chu Chiao-ju think it good and almost bound to succeed. Why are you the only one to see no good in it, nothing but disaster?"

"All your ministers and the officers you could trust to command troops have been imprisoned by the emperor. You have no good generals left."

"Chen Sheh and Wu Kuang had not even a pin-point of land when they rose in the marshes with a thousand men. They raised their arms and with a great call the whole empire responded. By the time they reached Hsi in the west, they had rallied one million two hundred thousand men. My kingdom may be small, but I have more than a hundred thousand fighting men. This is much better than a bunch of conscripts with scythes, picks and wooden spears. Why do you say nothing but disaster can come of it?"

"In time past the emperor of Chin defied what was right, oppressing and injuring the people. He had a retinue of ten thousand carriages, built Apang Palace, took away over half his subjects' income in taxes, and conscripted those who should have been exempt from service. Fathers were unable to support their sons, elder brothers to help their younger brothers. Harsh administration and cruel punishments made the whole country groan in distress. The people craned their necks to look for salvation and inclined their ears to listen, crying out to Heaven and beating their breasts in hatred of the emperor. That is why the whole empire responded to Chen Sheh's call.

"Now our emperor rules over a united empire, his love extends to all, his virtue and liberality are manifest. His lips do not move, yet his voice travels with the speed of a thunderbolt. He issues no order, yet his influence spreads like magic. When he wishes for something, his might is felt ten thousand *li* away and his subjects respond like a shadow or an echo. Furthermore, Grand Marshal Wei Ching is abler than either Chang Han or Yang Hsiung. And so I think Your Highness is mistaken to compare yourself with Chen Sheh and Wu Kuang."

"If that is true," said the prince, "is there no chance at all?"

Wu Pei replied, "I have a humble plan."

"What is that?"

"The feudal lords have no treason in their hearts, the people no dissatisfaction. But the province of Shuofang has extensive pasture lands and is well-watered, and not enough migrants have moved there yet to populate it fully. My humble plan is to forge a petition from the prime minister and chief counsellor asking to move powerful men and gallant citizens from the provinces, to pardon prisoners serving light sentences, and to settle these in Shuofang along with men who possess more than half a million cash, and all their families, dispatching soldiers to hasten their departure. Warrants issued by the law officers of the imperial clan should also be forged to arrest the sons and favourite ministers of the nobles. Then the people will murmur, the nobles will take fright, and if you send orators to incite them, you have one chance in ten of succeeding."

"That could be done," said the prince. "Although I think it hardly necessary."

The prince summoned slaves to his palace to forge an imperial seal and the seals of the prime minister, the chief counsellor, the grand marshal, officials of the two thousand piculs rank, officials in the capital, magistrates and assistant magistrates, as well as governors and army commanders of nearby provinces. Government credentials and official caps were also made, to carry out Wu Pei's plan. The prince in addition sent men, supposedly fugitives from justice, to serve Grand Marshal Wei Ching and the prime minister. For in this way, once he called out his troops, he thought the marshal could be assassinated and the prime minister forced to surrender as easily as lifting the cover off a pot.

The prince wanted to rise in revolt, but feared his chief minister and officers of the two thousand piculs rank might not agree. So he made plans with Wu Pei to kill them first. They would pretend that the palace was on fire, and when the chief minister and other high officials came to put out the fire, they would kill them. Before putting this plan into action, the prince decided to dress some men as constables and have them arrive from the east carrying emergency orders and crying, "The southern Yueh tribesmen have crossed the border!" Then he would call out his troops. But before these "constables" set out to Luchiang and Kuaichi, the prince consulted Wu Pei again.

"When I lead my troops west, some other princes should certainly join me," he said. "But what if some refuse to answer my call?"

"You must seize Hengshan to attack Luchiang," said Wu Pei. "Take the Hsunyang fleet, defend the city of Hsiachih, hold the river at Chiuchiang and block the Yuchang Pass, using strong bowmen to defend the Yangtse and keep Nanchun from falling into enemy hands. Then you can seize Chiangtu and Kuaichi in the east and ally with the Yueh fighters in the south. Strongly entrenched between the Yangtse and the Huai Rivers, you should be able to hold out for a long time."

"That is my best course," agreed the king. "If the worst comes to the worst, I can always flee to Yueh."

Meanwhile the chief justice had reported that the crown prince of Huainan was incriminated by the prince's grandson Chien. The emperor appointed the chief justice's lieutenant as military tribune of Huainan and sent him there to arrest the crown prince. When the prince of Huainan heard that he was coming, he took counsel with his son and decided to summon the chief minister and the officials of the two thousand piculs rank to kill them before starting the revolt. The chief minister came at their summons, but the city prefect made some excuse not to appear, while the military tribune said that he had orders from the emperor not to see the prince. The prince realized that it was useless to kill the chief minister alone, in the absence of the city prefect and the military tribune, and therefore he let him go.

While the prince vacillated and could not reach a decision, the crown prince reflected that since he was the one charged with plotting to kill Han's military tribune, if he were dead there would be no witnesses left. So he said to his father, "All those officers of any use to us have been arrested. There is no one we can rely on in our cause, and an untimely rising might result in failure. I am willing to give myself up."

The prince, anxious to find some way out, consented to this. And the crown prince tried to cut his own throat, but only wounded himself.

Wu Pei went of his own accord to the authorities and made a full confession of how he had plotted revolt with the prince of Huainan, as has been related above. Then the authorities arrested the crown prince and his mother and besieged the palace, while they searched for and arrested all those protégés of the prince who had plotted with him and were still in his kingdom. When all their findings were reported to the emperor, he ordered his ministers to investigate the matter. Several thousand men were involved in the plot, including princes, officers of the two thousand piculs rank and prominent citizens. They were punished according to the gravity of their offences.

Liu Tzu, the prince of Hengshan and younger brother of the prince of Huainan, was one of those involved. But when the authorities asked permission to arrest him, the emperor replied, "All the princes should be judged according to their behaviour in their own territory, not held responsible for each other's actions. Let the princes and marquises discuss the matter with the prime minister."

Then forty-three nobles including Prince Peng-tsu of Chao

and Marquis Jang declared, "Liu An, the prince of Huainan, is guilty of high treason. There is clear evidence of his plot to revolt. He should suffer the extreme penalty."

Prince Tuan of Chiaohsi also said, "The prince of Huainan has broken the laws and done evil, conspiring in secret to plunge the land into chaos, deceive the people, betray the ancestral temples and spread false rumours. In the *Spring and Autumn Annals* we read, 'A subject must not even contemplate rebellion; if he does, he must die.' The prince's crime is worse than contemplating rebellion, for his rebellion has taken visible form. Judging by the evidence I saw, his letters, credentials, seals, maps and other proofs of his guilt, it is very clear that he committed high treason and should suffer the full penalty of the law. With regard to his principality, all the officers above the two hundred piculs rank or those of equivalent ranks, as well as his kinsmen and favourites, even if they had no part in the plot, should be stripped of their titles and posts, reduced to the rank of commoners and debarred from holding official posts, because they failed to remonstrate with the prince. Those of them with no official post should pay a fine of two catties and eight taels of gold. This would make manifest Liu An's guilt so that everyone in the empire understands the duty of a subject and ceases to harbour wicked and rebellious thoughts."

When the prime minister Kungsun Hung and the chief justice Chang Tang reported this, the emperor sent the officer of the imperial clan with the imperial tally and credentials to arrest the prince. Before the officer reached Huainan, the prince killed himself. His consort Tu, his son Tsien and the other conspirators were executed with all their families.

Since Wu Pei had spoken eloquently of the virtues of the Han Dynasty, the emperor wished to pardon him. But the chief justice said, "Wu Pei was the first to plot rebellion for the prince. His crime is unpardonable."

So Wu Pei was killed. The principality of Huainan was abolished, becoming the province of Chiuchiang.

333

Liu Tzu, the prince of Hengshan, and his consort Cheng-shu had three children: an elder son Shuang, the heir; a second son, Hsiao; and a daughter named Wu-tsai. The prince had four more children by his concubine Hsu-lai, and another two by Lady Chueh-chi.

The princes of Hengshan and Huainan although brothers were not on good terms, each accusing the other of discourtesy. When the prince of Hengshan heard that the prince of Huainan was plotting rebellion, he started gathering protégés as a counter-measure, to prevent the seizure of his territory.

In the sixth year of *Yuankuang,* the prince of Hengshan went to court to pay homage. His herald Uei Ching, who had some knowledge of magic arts, asked to present a memorial to the throne offering his services to the emperor. The prince in a rage accused him of a capital crime and tortured him in order to obtain a confession. The city prefect of Hengshan did not believe the charge, however, and refused to prosecute. Then the prince impeached the city prefect. During his interrogation, the city prefect spoke of the prince's injustice, how more than once he had seized land from his subjects and destroyed graveyards to enlarge his estate. The authorities asked to have the prince arrested and tried, but the emperor withheld his consent, simply decreeing that all officers above the two hundred piculs rank should be appointed for him by the court. The prince of Hengshan, resenting this, began to plot with Hsi Tzu and Chang Kuang-chang and search for strategists and astrologers. Day and night they met in secret to plot rebellion.

When the consort Cheng-shu died Hsu-lai became the queen, but Lady Chueh-chi remained a favourite too. Lady Chueh-chi slandered her rival to Shuang, the crown prince, saying, "Hsu-lai had a maid cast a spell on your mother to kill her." Because of this Shuang hated Queen Hsu-lai, and when her brother came to Hengshan Shuang drew his sword and wounded him while drinking. Then the queen in her fury kept speaking ill of the crown prince to the prince of Hengshan.

The prince's daughter Wu-tsai, who had left her husband and returned home, had illicit relations with a slave and a protégé.

The heir apparent Shuang rebuked her for this several times, till she lost her temper and would have no more to do with him. When Queen Hsu-lai knew this, she treated Wu-tsai well. Since Wu-tsai and her second brother Hsiao had lost their mother early, they attached themselves to Hsu-lai, who treated them kindly so that they would help her to slander the crown prince. As a result of such slander, the prince had Shuang beaten several times.

In the fourth year of *Yuanshuo* someone attacked and injured Queen Hsu-lai's nurse, and the prince, suspecting that Shuang was behind this, beat him again. Later the prince fell ill but Shuang did not wait upon him, pleading illness himself. Then the queen, Wu-tsai and Hsiao denounced the crown prince, saying, "He is not really ill, only shamming. In fact, he looks very pleased." The prince in his rage decided to disinherit Shuang and make his younger brother Hsiao the heir.

When the queen knew of this decision, she schemed to have Hsiao repudiated as well. One of her ladies in waiting was a good dancer who enjoyed the prince's favour, and the queen told her to seduce Hsiao in order to discredit him, hoping that both brothers would be disinherited and her own son Kuang become crown prince instead.

Shuang came to know of this plot and reflected that the only way to stop the queen's mouth was by becoming her lover. Advancing during a feast to offer a toast, he pressed her thigh and begged her to sleep with him. The queen flew into a rage and told the prince, who sent for the crown prince. He was about to have him bound and beaten when Shuang, who knew that his father had decided to disinherit him in favour of Hsiao, said, "Hsiao is the lover of your favourite dancer, and Wu-tsai has been sleeping with a slave. This is true, whether you like it or not. I am going to report it to the emperor." With that he turned and left. The prince sent a man to stop him but in vain. Then he drove off himself in pursuit and arrested him. He put him in chains and imprisoned him in the palace because of his slanderous and reckless talk.

Then Hsiao rose daily in favour. The prince thought so

highly of his ability that he gave him a royal seal and the title of general, let him set up a separate establishment and supplied him with plenty of money to collect followers. The protégés that came to him knew that the princes of Huainan and Hengshan were plotting rebellion, so they urged him day and night to take action. The prince told two of them, Chiu Heh and Chen Hsi, both citizens of Chiangtu, to prepare war chariots and arrows and forge imperial seals as well as the seals of generals, ministers and army officers. Day and night the prince searched for strong men like Chou Chiu, who discussed the plans of the rebels of Wu and Chu and urged him to do likewise. The prince did not aspire to the imperial throne like the prince of Huainan, but was afraid his brother, starting a revolt, might seize his territory. All he meant to do, should the prince of Huainan march west, was to send troops to hold the region between the Yangtse and the Huai Rivers.

In the autumn of the fifth year of *Yuanshuo*, the prince of Hengshan was due to go to court. But in the sixth year he visited Huainan, cleared up past misunderstandings with his brother and agreed to join his revolt. Then the prince of Hengshan sent a letter to court pleading illness, and the emperor wrote him a letter exempting him from paying homage at court.

In the sixth year of *Yuanshuo* the prince of Hengshan sent a petition to the emperor asking permission to disinherit Shuang and make Hsiao crown prince in his place. Shuang, hearing of this, got a friend named Pai Ying to go to Changan and present a report to the emperor accusing Hsiao of preparing war chariots and arrows and having an affair with one of the prince's dancing girls. He hoped in this way to finish Hsiao. Pai Ying reached Changan but for his part in the Huainan plot was arrested before he could present this report.

The prince of Hengshan, learning of Pai Ying's mission and dreading exposure, sent a letter to the emperor accusing Shuang of wicked deeds for which he deserved execution in the marketplace. This matter was referred to the governor of Pei.

In the winter of the seventh year of *Yuanshuo*, the government ordered the governor of Pei to round up and arrest all those who had conspired with the prince of Huainan. Then Chen Hsi was apprehended in the house of the prince's son Hsiao, and Hsiao was charged with harbouring a felon. Hsiao knew how often Chen Hsi had plotted rebellion with the prince and was afraid the whole affair might come out. He had heard that according to the law an informer would be pardoned and, since he suspected that the report Pai Ying had taken for the crown prince laid bare the conspiracy, he came forward to inform against Chiu Heh, Chen Hsi and the other conspirators.

The chief justice examined the case and found the charges true. Then the high ministers asked to have the prince of Hengshan arrested and brought to trial. The emperor would not permit this, however, but sent the metropolitan tribune Szuma An and the imperial herald Li Hsi to question the prince, who made a full confession. The authorities set a watch upon his palace, while the metropolitan tribune and imperial herald went back to report to the court. The high ministers asked to have the imperial clan officer, the imperial herald and the governor of Pei sent to try the prince together. And when the prince heard this, he took his own life. Since Hsiao had volunteered information, he was pardoned for his part in the plot to rebel but was executed in the market-place for his illicit relations with the prince's maid. Queen Hsu-lai was charged with murdering Queen Cheng-shu, Shuang with the unfilial behaviour of which his father had accused him. They too were executed in the market-place. All the conspirators were killed along with their families. The principality was abolished, becoming the province of Hengshan.

The Grand Historian comments: Well does the *Book of Songs* say: "The northern barbarians should be punished, and those of Ching and Shu chastised." The princes of Huainan and Hengshan were the emperor's kinsmen and ruled as princes over a thousand *li* of territory. Yet instead of assisting their sovereign as good vassals, they took to evil courses and plotted high treason. Thus both fathers and sons lost their land and perished themselves, becoming a laughing-stock throughout the empire. The fault lay not solely with the kings, however, for the local traditions were bad and their ministers led them into evil ways. The men of Ching and Chu are reckless, foolhardy and quick to revolt, as has been recorded since ancient times.

CHANG SHIH-CHIH AND FENG TANG

The chief justice Chang Shih-chih, whose courtesy name was Chang Chi, was a man of Tuyang and lived with his elder brother Chang Chung. He bought the post of a cavalry guard under Emperor Wen, but served for ten years without winning promotion, remaining unknown.

"I have served all this time and been a considerable expense to my brother, without getting anywhere," he said and offered to resign and go home.

But Yuan An, the captain of the palace guards, knew his ability and thought it would be a pity if he left. He therefore had him transferred to the post of an imperial herald.

After his presentation at court, Chang Shih-chih stepped forward to propose reforms.

"Let's have no high-flown schemes," said Emperor Wen, "but modest proposals which can be put into practice."

Then Chang Shih-chih spoke at some length of the Chin and Han Dynasties, the reason for Chin's downfall and Han's rise to power. The emperor, approving his views, made him the chief herald.

Once he went with Emperor Wen to see the Tiger Enclosure in Shanglin Park. The emperor asked the warden more than ten questions about the animals and birds listed in the park records, but the warden looked this way and that and could not reply. Then the tiger-keeper, standing near by, answered for him, going into great detail to display his knowledge, reeling off the answers and hardly stopping for breath.

"That's how the warden should be," said Emperor Wen. "The other fellow is no good." He told Chang Shih-chih to have the keeper made warden of the park.

After a little reflection, Chang Shih-chih stepped forward

and asked, "What is your opinion, sir, of Chou Po the marquis of Chiang?"

"An excellent man."

"What of Chang Hsiang-ju the marquis of Tungyang?"

"Another excellent man."

"You call both of them excellent men, yet when it comes to making reports they can hardly get a word out. They are not as glib and fluent as this keeper. The emperor of Chin employed scribes who tried to outdo each other in harshness and severity. Their fault was that they enforced the letter of the law, untempered by mercy. And as the emperor never realized his mistakes, things went from bad to worse until, in the reign of the Second Emperor, the empire fell to pieces. If you promote this keeper for his eloquence, sir, I fear others will follow his example and aim at eloquence instead of solid worth. Those below respond to the influence of those above as swiftly as shadows or echoes. Appointments and dismissals should be carefully considered."

The emperor approved and did not promote the keeper. Mounting his carriage, he asked Chang Shih-chih to take the reins, and as they drove slowly back questioned him about the mistakes of the Chin government. And he received practical, realistic answers. Upon their return to the palace, the emperor made him keeper of the palace gate.

Some time later the crown prince and prince of Liang drove together to the palace, but did not stop at the outer gate. Chang Shih-chih ran after them, stopped them, and would not let them enter the inner gate. He reported them to the throne for their disrespect in failing to alight at the palace gate, and the matter was referred to Empress Dowager Po. Emperor Wen uncovered his head to apologize to her, saying, "I have not brought my sons up well," after which she sent a messenger to order that the princes be pardoned, and then at last they were admitted. Much impressed by this, Emperor Wen appointed Chang Shih-chih a court adviser. And later on he became captain of the palace guards.

Chang Shih-chih once accompanied Emperor Wen to the imperial tomb at Paling. Looking down from the north side of the hill, the emperor turned to Lady Shen, who was also in attendance, and pointed out the Hsinfeng highway. "That's the road to Hantan," he told her. He asked her to play the cithern and sang to her accompaniment. Then gazing sadly at his courtiers he said, "Ah, if we used stone from the north hill for the outer coffin, filled the cracks with hemp and silk floss and covered the whole with lacquer, no thief could break in."

All agreed but Chang Shih-chih, who stepped forward and said, "If there is something men covet inside the coffin, even if it is sealed up under the south hill thieves will find a way in. If there is nothing men covet, even without a stone coffin there is no need to worry." The emperor approved, and later made him chief justice.

Some time after this, Emperor Wen was crossing the Middle Wei Bridge when a man ran out from under the bridge, frightening the horses of the imperial carriage. Cavalrymen were sent to seize this man and take him to the chief justice. Chang Shih-chih tried the fellow, who said he came from the country; when he heard the order 'Clear the way for the emperor!' he hid himself for a long time under the bridge, coming out when he thought the retinue had passed; then, at sight of the imperial carriage and riders, he ran. The chief justice recommended that he be fined for violating the order to clear the way.

"That fellow frightened my horses!" protested Emperor Wen indignantly. "It's a good thing that team is so docile. Had they been any other horses, I should have been hurt. Yet the chief justice simply fines him."

"The law should be observed by the Son of Heaven and the people alike," replied Chang. "This is the law and, were I to impose a heavier punishment, the people would lose faith in the law. If Your Majesty had ordered the man to be executed on the spot, no one would have objected. But the matter was referred to the chief justice who should administer justice impartially to all. If I show bias all officers will apply the law with a bias, and the people will not know what to do. I beg Your Majesty to consider this."

The emperor thought it over and said, "The sentence proposed by the chief justice is right."

Later a jade ring was stolen from the shrine of Emperor Kao-tsu's temple. The thief was caught and the emperor in a passion sent him to the chief justice for trial. Chang Shih-chih ruled that, since this was a case of stealing from an ancestral temple, the culprit should be publicly executed.

The emperor protested in a rage, "This fellow had the effrontery to rob Emperor Kao-tsu's temple! I sent him to you expecting to have him and his relatives executed, but you simply passed sentence according to the law. This is not my idea of respect to ancestral temples."

Chang Shih-chih bared his head and bowed to apologize, saying, "That is all the law demands. Besides, there are different degrees in the same crime. If you wiped out this man's relatives because he robbed the temple, how would you punish some fool — if we can imagine such a case — who dug up Emperor Kao-tsu's tomb?"

Emperor Wen discussed this later with the empress dowager and they agreed that Chang Shih-chih was right. At that time the metropolitan tribune Chou Ya-fu, marquis of Tiao, and Wang Tien-kai, marquis of Shantu and prime minister of Liang, were so struck by Chang Shih-chih's fair administration of justice that they allied themselves with him by marriage. Then the fame of Chief Justice Chang spread through all the land.

When Emperor Wen died and Emperor Ching came to the throne,* Chang Shih-chih was afraid and pretended to be unwell. He wanted to resign but feared that might result in his execution. He wished to apologize, but did not know how the emperor would take it. Finally on the advice of Wang Sheng he apologized to Emperor Ching, who did not punish him.

Wang Sheng lived in retirement and was well versed in the teachings of the Yellow Emperor and Lao Tzu. Once he was

* 157 B.C.

summoned to court and allowed to sit down while all the chief ministers were standing around.

The old man exclaimed, "My leggings are coming down!" And turning to Chang Shih-chih he said, "Tie them up for me, will you?"

Chang Shih-chih knelt down and did as he was told.

Later Wang Sheng was asked, "Why did you insult the chief justice in public by making him kneel down and tie up your leggings?"

"I am an old man in a humble position," replied Wang Sheng. "What can I do to help the chief justice who is known throughout the land? I put him to the indignity of kneeling to tie up my leggings so that men might respect him even more."

Word of this increased men's regard for Wang Sheng as well as their respect for Chang Shih-chih.

Chang Shih-chih served as chief justice under Emperor Ching for more than a year, after which he was transferred to be chief minister to the prince of Huainan. Evidently this was because of his former fault. He died some time afterwards. His son Chang Chih, whose courtesy name was Chang-kung, served as a high official but was dismissed. Because he could not follow the fashion, he never again held an official post.

Feng Tang's grandfather came from Chao. His father moved first to Tai and then, at the beginning of the Han Dynasty, to Anling. Because of his reputation for filial piety Feng Tang served as a lieutenant to the chief of the palace guard under Emperor Wen.

Once the emperor, passing in his sedan-chair, asked, "How did you become a palace guard? Where are you from?" When Feng Tang had explained his background the emperor said, "When I was in Tai, the imperial steward Kao Chu often told me what a fine general Li Chi of Chao was, and how he fought that battle at Chulu. Now I hardly ever sit down to a meal without thinking of the Battle of Chulu. Did you know Li Chi?"

"He was not such a great general as Lien Po and Li Mu," said Feng Tang.

"Why do you say that?"

"When my grandfather served in Chao as a centurion, he knew Li Mu well. And my father as chief minister of Tai was friendly with General Li Chi. So I know what sort of men they were."

Delighted to hear about Lien Po and Li Mu, the emperor slapped his thigh and exclaimed, "Ah, if I had generals like them, I need not worry about the Huns!"

"Excuse my presumption, sir," said Feng Tang. "But even if you had Lien Po or Li Mu, you would not be able to use them."

The emperor sprang up angrily and went back to the inner palace. After some time he summoned Feng Tang and reproached him. "Why did you insult me in public?" he asked. "Couldn't you have waited till we were alone?"

"I am a fool," apologized Feng Tang. "I should have held my tongue."

Now the Huns had just invaded Chaono in force, killing Sun Ang the army commander of Peiti, and the emperor was worried about their incursions. So he finally asked Feng Tang, "How do you know that I couldn't make good use of men like Lien Po or Li Mu?"

Feng Tang answered, "I have heard that when a king of ancient times saw a general off to war, he would kneel to push the chariot wheels and say, 'I shall see to things at home, general, while you see to things outside.' All military distinctions and awards were decided by the general, who simply reported them after his return from the campaign. I am not making this up.

"My grandfather told me that when Li Mu served as a general at Chao's frontier he spent all the revenue from the camp markets on his men, and decided awards with no interference from the court. This meant that he could bring all his wisdom and ability into full play. With a picked force of thirteen hundred chariots, thirteen thousand mounted archers and a hundred thousand of the best fighters, he was able to drive away the Hunnish khan in the north, rout the Tungus, destroy the Tanlins, halt the advance of powerful Chin in the west and support Hann and Wei in the south, so that Chao very nearly became the leader of the states.

"But later King Chien, son of a dancing girl, came to the throne. He listened to the slanders of Kuo Kai and had Li Mu killed, appointing Yen Chu in his place. As a result his army was defeated, his men fled and he was captured by Chin.

"I hear that when Wei Shang was governor of Yunchung, he used all the revenue from his camp markets to feast his troops and drew on his own purse to kill an ox every five days for his protégés, officers and stewards. And the Huns kept their distance, not daring to approach the ramparts at Yunchung. Once they crossed the frontier, Wei Shang attacked with his chariots and cavalry and inflicted heavy casualties on them.

"Soldiers are simple peasants who join the army straight from the fields, knowing nothing of official documents and forms. At the end of a hard day of fighting they report to headquarters the number of enemies they have killed or captured, and if there is any inconsistency in their reports the civil officers punish them according to the law. Rewards are not given but the law is always enforced.

"In my humble opinion, sir, your laws are too strict, your rewards too small and your penalties too heavy. Because Wei Shang, the governor of Yunchung, was accused of reporting six more enemy heads than there were, you had him tried, degraded and punished with penal servitude. Judging by this, even if you had Lien Po and Li Mu you would not be able to use them. I am a simpleton, unable to hold my tongue. I deserve death for my presumption."

Emperor Wen was pleased and that same day he sent Feng Tang with the imperial credentials to pardon Wei Shang and reinstate him as governor of Yunchung. Feng Tang was made

345

a tribune of chariots and cavalry in charge of the chariots and horsemen of the capital and the principalities.

Seven years later Emperor Ching came to the throne and appointed Feng Tang chief minister of Chu, but later dismissed him. After Emperor Wu ascended the throne,* he made a search for able and worthy men and Feng Tang was recommended. He was then over ninety, however, and could not serve as an official, so his son Feng Sui was made a palace guard. Feng Sui's courtesy name was Wang-sun. He, too, was a remarkable man and a good friend of mine.

The Grand Historian comments: Chang Shih-chih knew what constitutes a superior man and he upheld the law regardless of the emperor's wishes, while Feng Tang's comments on what makes a good general are well worth pondering too. The proverb says, "You can know a man by his friends." The sayings of these two men deserve to be preserved in the court archives. The *Book of Documents* says, "No prejudice, no bias, how broad is the Kingly Way! No bias, no prejudice, how smooth is the Kingly Way!" Both Chang Shih-chih and Feng Tang came close to this.

* 140 B.C.

CHI AN AND CHENG TANG-SHIH

Chi An, whose courtesy name was Chang-ju, was a man of Puyang. One of his ancestors had been favoured by a former prince of Uei, since when seven generations of the family down to Chi An had served as ministers. On his father's recommendation, Chi An became one of the crown prince's outriders in the reign of Emperor Ching, and his impressive bearing commanded respect. Upon Emperor Ching's death and the crown prince's accession to the throne, Chi An was appointed imperial herald.

When the tribes of Tungyueh started fighting among themselves, the emperor sent Chi An to make an investigation. He went no further than Wu, returning to report, "The men of Yueh make a practice of fighting each other. The Son of Heaven need not stoop to send an envoy."

When a fire in Honei burned down more than a thousand houses, the emperor sent him again to investigate. On his return Chi An reported, "The houses were so close together that the fire breaking out in one spread to the rest. There is no reason to worry. But on my way through Honan I found more than ten thousand poor families reduced to such desperation by floods and drought that sons and fathers were eating one another. I took the liberty of using my credentials to order grain to be distributed from the public granaries there to relieve them. Allow me to return my credentials and ask to be punished for overstepping my authority."

But Emperor Wu approved and pardoned him, transferring him to the magistracy of Yingyang. Chi An scorned the post, however, and went home on the pretext of illness. When the emperor came to know this, he summoned him and appointed him a court adviser. But his constant remonstrances made it impossible to keep him at court and he was transferred to the governorship of Tunghai.

Chi An studied the teachings of the Yellow Emperor and Lao Tzu, and his administration was easy-going. He entrusted affairs to specially selected assistants, concerning himself with the main issues only and not troubling with trifles. He was often ill and confined to his room, yet after a year or more Tunghai was so well governed that the people praised him. As soon as the emperor knew this, he summoned him to court to be the officer in charge of the principalities, one of the nine chief ministers. Again he pursued a laissez-faire policy, dealing only with great matters and disregarding the letter of the law.

Chi An was by nature arrogant and offhanded. He denounced men to their faces and could not tolerate any shortcomings. Those whom he found congenial he treated well; the uncongenial he could not even bear to see. Thus he had few friends among the literati. He stood up for the right, however, had great moral courage, and was scrupulously honest. He liked to speak his mind and often offended the emperor by his remonstrances. He admired men like Fu Po and Yuan Ang, and was on friendly terms with Kuan Fu, Cheng Tang-shih and Liu Chi, the officer of the imperial clan. Owing to his outspoken criticisms, he could never remain in one position for long.

That was the time when the empress dowager's younger brother Tien Fen, marquis of Wu-an, was prime minister. Officials of the two thousand piculs rank who bowed to him would receive no return of courtesy, but Chi An never bowed to him, merely raising clasped hands in salute.

The emperor had summoned various scholars and Confucians to court and was telling them of certain wishes he had.

Chi An said to him, "Your Majesty's heart is full of desires, yet you make a show of benevolence and justice. How can you hope to imitate Yao and Shun?"

The emperor was silent. Scowling angrily he left the court, while all the ministers trembled for Chi An. Once out of the court the emperor told his attendants, "Chi An is too confoundedly blunt!"

But when some officials cautioned Chi An he said, "The Son of Heaven appoints ministers to assist his rule. Are we to flatter him and agree to his wishes till we encourage him to take a dangerous course? In our position we must not try to save our own necks at the cost of disgracing the court."

Chi An was often ill for more than the three months allowed. The emperor several times extended his leave, but he never wholly recovered.

Once Chuang Chu came to request sick leave for him.

"What do you think of Chi An?" asked Emperor Wu.

"In discharging ordinary official duties he is not outstanding," said Chuang Chu. "But if called on to help a young ruler or defend a city, he could not be won over or frightened away. Even brave men like Meng Pen and Hsia Yu* could not shake him."

"True," said the emperor. "In the old days they spoke of ministers who would die for the state. Chi An seems a man of that sort."

When the grand marshal Wei Ching came to court, the emperor would not rise to greet him. When the prime minister Kungsun Hung saw him in private, the emperor did not always cover his head. But for Chi An he invariably put a hat on. Once Emperor Wu was seated on his curtained throne surrounded by guards when Chi An came to present a memorial. Since the emperor's head was bare, at Chi An's approach he hid himself behind the curtain, telling someone else to accept the memorial. This illustrates Emperor Wu's respect for him.

Chang Tang had just been made chief justice for his work in revising the legal code, yet Chi An often denounced him in the presence of the emperor saying, "You are a high minister, but what have you done to carry forward the former emperor's achievements, curb men's evil desires, pacify the state, enrich the people, or empty the prisons of criminals? You have done

---

* Famous strong men in the Chou Dynasty.

none of these things, yet you make a point of finding fault with others. You would stoop to anything to win some credit. How dare you tamper with the rules laid down by Emperor Kao-tsu? For this you and your family should be wiped out!"

Whenever Chi An argued with Chang Tang, the chief justice split hairs about the law, whereas Chi An kept stubbornly to principles and refused to compromise. He would fume, "How right people are to say that pen-pushers should never be made high officials! If Chang Tang had his way, no one would dare take a step forward or look men straight in the eye."

At that time the Han court had sent out expeditions against the Huns and was trying to win over all the frontier tribes. Chi An, who believed in not making trouble, seized every chance to urge the emperor to make peace with the Huns and stop raising armies. But the emperor then leaned towards Confucianism and thought highly of Kungsun Hung, and as the administration became more complex the people grew cunning at evading the law. Emperor Wu was well versed in the legal code and Chang Tang and others courted his favour by proposing measures which met with his approval. But Chi An spoke up against the Confucians, attacking Kungsun Hung and others to their faces for trying to ingratiate themselves by flattery and cunning. He declared that these pettifoggers twisted the law to ruin men, obscuring the truth to win credit for themselves at the expense of the people. The emperor, however, valued Kungsun Hung and Chang Tang more and more. These two, for their part, loathed and detested Chi An. Even the emperor was displeased with him and would have been glad of some excuse to kill him.

Kungsun Hung the prime minister told the emperor, "The area under the jurisdiction of the senior city prefect of the capital contains so many nobles and members of the imperial clan that it is difficult to administer. Only a most prominent official is up to the task. I suggest that Chi An be appointed senior city prefect." So for several years Chi An served in this capacity and affairs were well administered.

The grand marshal Wei Ching was becoming more and more exalted now that his elder sister was the empress, yet Chi An continued to treat him as an equal.

Someone said to Chi An, "The emperor wants all other ministers to defer to the grand marshal, that is why he is heaping all these honours on him. You really should bow to him, sir."

But Chi An replied, "If the grand marshal lets a visitor simply raise clasped hands in greeting, will that not make men respect him even more?"

When the grand marshal heard this, Chi An rose in his estimation. He frequently consulted him on state and court affairs and treated him with special consideration.

When the prince of Huainan was plotting rebellion he was afraid of Chi An. "A man who speaks out frankly and would die for his principles is hard to corrupt," he said. "As for winning over Kungsun Hung, that is as easy as lifting off a cover or shaking down withered leaves."

By now several successful campaigns against the Huns made Emperor Wu pay even less attention to Chi An's advice. Chi An had been one of the nine chief ministers when Kungsun Hung and Chang Tang held only minor posts. Now they had risen in importance to rank equal with him, yet Chi An continued to point out their mistakes. Kungsun Hung was the prime minister, enfeoffed as a marquis, while Chang Tang was the grand secretary. These men who had been clerks when Chi An was prime minister now ranked as high as he did, or even higher. Chi An was too narrow-minded to tolerate this, and going to see the emperor he said, "Your Majesty appoints ministers in the way men stack firewood: the latest to arrive are piled on top."

The emperor said nothing till Chi An had withdrawn, when he exclaimed, "A man really needs to study! Look at Chi An. He is talking more outrageously every day."

Soon after this the Hunnish chief of Hunyeh surrendered with his men, and the government decided to send twenty thousand chariots to bring them to Changan. Since the administration was short of funds, horses had to be requisitioned from the people, but so many hid their horses that the necessary number was not forthcoming. The emperor was angry and wanted to execute the magistrate of Changan.

"The magistrate is not to blame. Just cut off my head," said Chi An, "then the people may produce their horses. In any case, those Huns rebelled against their khan to surrender to us. Why not have them sent here by stages from county to county instead of turning the whole empire upside down and exhausting the Middle Kingdom for the sake of barbarians?"

The emperor was silent.

After the arrival of the chief of Hunyeh, more than five hundred merchants in the capital were condemned to death for trading with the Huns. Then Chi An asked for a private interview with the emperor in Kaomen Hall.

"The Huns attacked our frontier posts and broke off friendly relations," he said. "So we raised armies to subdue them. Countless men have been killed or wounded and millions of cash spent. In my humble opinion, all captured Huns should be given as slaves to the families of those who fell in the wars, along with all the booty, to atone to the people for their pains and comfort their hearts. Instead of this, however, when the chief of Hunyeh surrenders with his horde we empty our treasury to offer them gifts and make loyal subjects serve them as if they were favourite children. How are the people in their ignorance to know that trading with the Huns in Changan counts as shipping contraband goods outside the frontier? You are not making use of the Huns to placate the empire but using some trifling legal clause to kill five hundred and more simple people. This is known as 'protecting the leaves but harming the bough'. I think, sir, you have made the wrong decision."

The emperor listened in silence, then rejected Chi An's advice. "It is some time since I heard from Chi An," he said. "Now he is raving again."

Some months later Chi An was charged with some trifling

offence and his sentence was commuted to loss of office. He therefore retired to the country.

Several years after this, when the new *wu-chu* coins were issued, a great deal of counterfeit money was minted, especially in Chu. Considering Huaiyang as a focal point in Chu, the emperor summoned Chi An to court and appointed him governor of Huaiyang. Chi An kowtowed and declined the seal, but Emperor Wu insisted until he had to accept.

When summoned to an audience Chi An shed tears and said, "I expected to die and be thrown into a ditch without setting eyes on Your Majesty again, yet now you have recalled me. But this miserable illness of mine has left me too weak to administer a prefecture. All I ask is to serve as a palace guard always at Your Majesty's side, able to remind you of shortcomings that may have escaped your attention."

"Do you despise the post at Huaiyang?" asked the emperor. "I shall recall you very soon, but at present the officers and people of Huaiyang are at odds. I thought, with your prestige, you could set things in order quite comfortably from your couch."

After Chi An withdrew he met the imperial herald Li Hsi and told him, "I am being packed off to the provinces and shall not be able to join in discussions at court. The grand secretary Chang Tang is clever enough to refute criticisms and cunning enough to gloss over his faults. He uses artful flattery and specious arguments not to profit the empire but simply to please his master. Whatever the emperor disapproves of, he condemns; whatever the emperor wants, he praises. He loves to stir up trouble and manipulate the law. He is ingratiating himself with the emperor and relying on harsh officials to increase his power. You are one of the nine chief ministers. Unless you speak out against him in good time, you will end up by sharing his punishment."

But Li Hsi was too afraid of Chang Tang to speak against him. Chi An went to his post and governed as before, so that Huaiyang was well administered. Later Chang Tang did get into trouble and the emperor, hearing of Chi An's advice to

Li Hsi, had Li Hsi punished too. Chi An remained in Huaiyang with the rank of a chief minister to a prince until his death seven years later.

After Chi An's death, in recognition of his services, Emperor Wu made his younger brother Chi Jen a high minister and his son Chi Yen chief minister of a principality. Chi An's cousin Szuma An, who had served in his youth as one of the crown prince's outriders with Chi An, was intelligent and knew how to get on as an official. Four times he was made a high minister, and he died governor of Honan. At one time ten members of his family were officers of the two thousand piculs rank, thanks to Szuma An's influence. Another native of Puyang, Tuan Hung, worked under Wang Hsin the marquis of Kai and became a high minister twice on his recommendation. But all the men of Wei who served as officials had a great respect for Chi An and looked up to him.

Cheng Tang-shih, whose courtesy name was Chuang, was a man of Chen. An ancestor of his was a general under Hsiang Yu and after Hsiang Yu's death came over to Han, but when Emperor Kao-tsu ordered Hsiang Yu's former officers to register, this man alone refused to do so. Emperor Kao-tsu made all the others high officials but dismissed Cheng, who died during the reign of Emperor Wen.

Cheng Tang-shih liked to perform deeds of gallantry, and after he rescued Chang Yu when in distress his fame spread through Liang and Chu. During the reign of Emperor Ching he was steward to the crown prince. On his leave, which came on every fifth day, he had post horses ready in the suburbs of the capital to call on old friends and protégés, or invited them home and entertained them all through the night until dawn. His only worry was that he might miss someone out. He liked the teachings of the Yellow Emperor and Lao Tzu, admired his seniors and never lost a chance of meeting one. Although he was young and held such a humble post, the friends he sought out were men of his grandfather's generation whose names were known throughout the land.

After Emperor Wu came to the throne, Cheng Tang-shih was appointed army commander of the principality of Lu, then governor of Tsinan, chief minister of Chiangtu and finally senior prefect of the capital, one of the nine chief ministers. At the time of the dispute between the marquises of Weichi and Wu-an, he was reduced in status and made the crown prince's steward, then he was transferred to become minister of revenue.

During Cheng Tang-shih's term as city prefect he told his servants, "When visitors come, whether high or low, never keep them waiting at the gate." He treated all guests with deference in spite of his eminence. Incorruptible and indifferent to his own estate, he depended on his official salary to entertain his friends, and his gifts to others were never more than food served in bamboo vessels.

At court he took every opportunity of recommending worthy men to the emperor. He spoke with genuine enthusiasm of ordinary scholars and his subordinates, as if they were all better men than he. He never called officials by their familiar names and took great care in conversation not to hurt the feelings of his subordinates. When he heard of some good proposal, he made haste to report it to the emperor. As a result, all the gentlemen of the east spoke well of him.

When he was sent to investigate a flood of the Yellow River, he asked for five days to get ready for the journey. The emperor said, "I heard that you could travel a thousand *li* without taking any grain.* What do you have to prepare for this journey?"

At court Cheng Tang-shih generally spoke mildly and fell in with the emperor's wishes, rarely venturing to express decided opinions. By the time he was old, the costly campaigns against the Huns and other barbarian tribes were draining the resources of the empire. Certain transport officers in the ministry of revenue, who had been recommended by Cheng Tang-shih or were his protégés, defaulted. Szuma An, the governor of

---

* He had friends everywhere glad to entertain him.

Huaiyang, reported this and Cheng Tang-shih was implicated. On payment of a fine he was pardoned but struck off the list of officials. Later he was made a senior secretary in the prime minister's office, but in view of his age the emperor appointed him as governor of Junan instead. He died in that office several years later.

Cheng Tang-shih and Chi An both ranked among the nine chief ministers, were incorruptible and scrupulously honest. Later both were degraded, their families became poor and their protégés gradually deserted them. Both died in the provinces leaving no property for their heirs. However, six or seven of Cheng Tang-shih's brothers and descendants became officers of the two thousand piculs rank because of him.

The Grand Historian comments: If worthy men like Chi An and Cheng Tang-shih had friends by the score when they were in power and none when they fell from power, how must it be with ordinary men! Lord Chai of Hsiakuei said that when he was chief justice guests thronged his gate, when he was dismissed you could have trapped birds at his door, but when he became chief justice again, his old protégés hoped to come back. Then he wrote in large characters on his gate:

> When a lifelong friend is dead,
> Friendship has fled;
> When a rich man becomes poor,
> Friendship is no more;
> When a noble is brought low,
> Friendship must go.

Chi An and Cheng Tang-shih might have said the same, alas!

THE MARQUISES OF WEICHI AND WU-AN

Tou Ying, the marquis of Weichi, was the son of a cousin of Empress Tou. Until his father's time his family had lived in Kuanchin. He had many protégés.

In the reign of Emperor Wen, Tou Ying served as chief minister of Wu but had to give up this post because of illness. When Emperor Ching came to the throne, he served as steward in the household of the empress.

Prince Hsiao of Liang was Emperor Ching's younger brother and the favourite of Empress Dowager Tou. When he came to court the emperor entertained him as a brother. Emperor Ching had not yet designated his heir and while drinking one day he remarked casually, "When I die I shall pass on the crown to the prince of Liang."

Empress Dowager Tou was delighted, but Tou Ying presented a cup of wine to the emperor, protesting, "The empire was won by Emperor Kao-tsu and the rule of the House of Han is that the throne must pass from father to son. How can you make the prince of Liang your heir, sir?"

Empress Dowager Tou hated Tou Ying for this, and since he did not think much of his post he retired on the pretext of illness. Then the empress dowager struck his name off the palace list so that he could no longer go to court.

When the princes of Wu and Chu rebelled in the third year of Emperor Ching,* the emperor sent for Tou Ying, having decided that he was abler than anyone else in the imperial house or the Tou family. Tou Ying came to the palace, to the embarrassment of the empress dowager, but insisted that he was too ill to take up a command.

---

* 154 B.C.

357

"At a time of crisis how can you refuse?" demanded the emperor. He made Tou Ying grand marshal and presented him with a thousand catties of gold. Then Tou Ying recommended Yuan Ang, Luan Pu and other good army officers or scholars who were living in retirement. He stacked the gold in his corridor and gatehouse so that officers who needed it could help themselves. None of it went to his own family.

Tou Ying defended Yingyang and kept a watch over the forces of Chi and Chao. After the suppression of the revolt he was enfeoffed as marquis of Weichi. Then wandering scholars and protégés flocked to him eagerly to offer their services. During the reign of Emperor Ching, no other nobles dared claim equality with the marquis of Tiao and the marquis of Weichi in any important deliberations at court.

In the fourth year of Emperor Ching, his son by Lady Li was made crown prince and Tou Ying was appointed as his tutor. In the seventh year the crown prince was deposed although Tou Ying interceded for him several times. Pleading illness he retired for several months to Lantien in the south hills, nor could any of his orators or protégés prevail on him to return.

Then Kao Sui of Liang reasoned with him saying, "The emperor has conferred rank and wealth on you, the empress dowager has befriended you. You were the crown prince's tutor, yet you failed to prevent his being deposed and failed to die for him. You simply retired here on the pretext of illness to fondle beauties from Chao and voice opinions at variance with those of the court. This means you are casting aspersions on your sovereign. Should the emperor and empress dowager turn against you, your whole family must perish."

Convinced by this argument Tou Ying went back and started attending court as before.

When the marquis of Tao was dismissed from his post as prime minister, Empress Dowager Tou several times recommended Tou Ying.

"Don't think, madam, that I begrudge him the post," said the emperor. "But Tou Ying has too good an opinion of himself and takes life too easily. He is not fit for a responsible post like that of prime minister." He appointed Wei Wan the marquis of Chienling instead.

Tien Fen, the marquis of Wu-an and younger brother of Empress Wang, was born in Changling. When Tou Ying was grand marshal and at the height of his power, Tien Fen was still a palace guard, not yet ennobled. He used to go to Tou Ying's house and wait on him as a cup-bearer as humbly as his son. Towards the end of Emperor Ching's reign, however, Tien Fen had risen to become grand counsellor.

Tien Fen was eloquent, he had studied the ancient precepts inscribed on bronze vessels, and his sister, Empress Wang, thought highly of him. The day that Emperor Ching died, the crown prince ascended the throne with the empress dowager as regent, and many of the security measures she took were proposed by Tien Fen's followers. Because they were the empress dowager's brothers, Tien Fen and his younger brother Tien Sheng were enfeoffed in the last year of Emperor Ching's reign as the marquises of Wu-an and Chouyang.

Since Tien Fen wanted to take power and become prime minister he was good to his guests and honoured noted scholars living in retirement, hoping in this way to undermine Tou Ying and his powerful party.

In the first year of the *Chienyuan* period,* the prime minister Wei Wan was relieved of his duties because of ill health and Emperor Wu consulted his ministers about the appointment of a new prime minister and grand marshal.

Chi Fu advised Tien Fen, saying, "Tou Ying has been prominent for a long time and worthy men from all over the land have flocked to him. Since you have just come to power and are not as influential as Tou Ying, if the emperor offers to make you prime minister you should decline in favour of Tou Ying. If he becomes prime minister you are sure to be

---

* 140 B.C.

made grand marshal. These two posts rank equal. And you will win praise for your modesty and wisdom."

Tien Fen proposed this to the empress dowager, asking her to suggest it to the emperor. Then Tou Ying was made prime minister and Tien Fen grand marshal.

When Chi Fu congratulated Tou Ying he warned him, "I know, sir, that you naturally appreciate good men and hate evil men. Now thanks to the praise of good men you have become prime minister. But because you hate evil men and they are many, they are bound to attack you. The more tolerance you can show, the longer you will enjoy your present position. Otherwise their slander will lead to your dismissal." But Tou Ying ignored his advice.

Both Tou Ying and Tien Fen admired the teachings of Confucius. Hence they recommended Chao Wan for the post of chief counsellor and Wang Tsang for that of chief of the palace guard. They invited Master Shen of Lu to the capital and wanted to set up an Audience Hall, send the marquises back to their fiefs, abolish travel restrictions, change the funeral customs to accord with the ancient practice, and bring about a reign of peace. They denounced the members of the imperial clan and kinsmen of Empress Dowager Tou who were guilty of immoral conduct and had their names struck off the list of nobles.

At that time most of the men of the Tou family had become marquises and married imperial princesses, and none of them wanted to return to their territories. So every day they slandered these two ministers to Empress Dowager Tou. And because she liked the teachings of the Yellow Emperor and Lao Tzu, while Tou Ying, Tien Fen, Chao Wan and Wang Tsang wanted to propagate Confucianism and suppress Taoism, her dislike for these men increased.

In the second year of the *Chienyuan* period, the grand secretary Chao Wan proposed that memoranda and reports should not be submitted to Empress Dowager Tou. In a great rage she dismissed him and three others and appointed Hsu Chang the marquis of Pochih as prime minister and Chuang Ching-ti the marquis of Wuchiang as grand secretary. Tou Ying and Tien Fen retired from the government but retained their titles.

Although Tien Fen was now out of office, he was still a favourite because of Empress Dowager Wang, and his advice was often taken. And so all those officers and gentlemen who were eager for power or profit left Tou Ying and flocked to Tien Fen, who grew daily more high-handed.

In the sixth year of *Chienyuan*, Empress Dowager Tou died. The prime minister Hsu Chang and the grand secretary Chuang Ching-ti were accused of mismanaging the funeral and dismissed. Tien Fen was made prime minister with Han An-kuo, the minister of revenue, as grand secretary. Thereupon the gentlemen of the empire and the marquises of the principalities rallied even more closely round him.

Tien Fen was undistinguished in appearance but he attained great distinction. At that time most of the princes were old while Emperor Wu was young when he ascended the throne. Tien Fen felt that as prime minister and a relative of the imperial house, he must force others to submit humbly to him or he would not be respected through the land.

When he went to the palace to make his reports as prime minister, he would sit talking for hours, and all his proposals were accepted. When recommending men for office, he sometimes had commoners appointed as officials of the two thousand piculs rank. He became the dominant force behind the throne.

Once the emperor asked, "Have you finished appointing officials? If you have, I should like to select some myself."

Another time Tien Fen asked for some land belonging to a government workshop to enlarge his estate, and the emperor retorted angrily, "Why don't you simply take over the armoury?" After that he was a little more circumspect.

One day Tien Fen invited guests to a drinking party and made his elder brother, the marquis of Kai, sit facing south while he took the place of honour facing east. He explained that family etiquette must not be allowed to detract from the prime minister's dignity.

As time went on he became more and more overbearing.

His mansions were the finest in the land. He owned the most fertile fields, and the roads were thronged with merchants bringing him goods from all parts of the empire. In the front hall he had a display of bronze bells, drums and pennants on curved flagstaffs, while in the inner quarters were hundreds of women. As for the dogs, horses, jewels and other articles of amusement and adornment presented to him by various nobles, these were past counting.

Tou Ying had lost power since the death of Empress Dowager Tou and one by one all his protégés left him in contempt except General Kuan Fu. Thus Tou Ying, in his bitterness and frustration, treated General Kuan Fu as his only friend.

General Kuan Fu was a man of Yingyin. His father Chang Meng had been a favourite steward of Kuan Ying, the marquis of Yingyin, who raised him to be an official of the two thousand piculs rank. Out of gratitude he took Kuan's name, becoming Kuan Meng.

During the rebellion of Wu and Chu, Kuan Ho, the second marquis of Yingyin, served as a general under the grand marshal and Kuan Meng was made a general. Kuan Fu accompanied his father to the war at the head of a thousand men. By this time Kuan Meng was an old man, but the marquis of Yingyin insisted that he should accept the command; so in his resentment he kept charging the enemy's strong points until he was cut down by the troops of Wu.

According to the military regulations, when both father and son serve in the army and one is killed, the other may ask leave to attend to the funeral. But instead of doing this, Kuan Fu hotly vowed, "I shall avenge my father by cutting off the head of the prince of Wu or one of his generals."

He buckled on his armour, seized his halberd, and called for a few dozen volunteers to go with him. Once outside their ramparts, however, the others dared not charge the enemy. Only two men and about a dozen attendants galloped with him through the ranks of Wu. They fought their way up to one of the enemy flags and killed or wounded several dozen men, but could advance no further. By the time Kuan Fu galloped back to the Han ramparts, all his attendants were dead and only one man returned with him. Kuan Fu himself had received more than ten serious wounds, but his life was saved with a precious salve.

When he had somewhat recovered, he asked permission to try again now that he had a better idea of Wu's defences. His general admired his spirit but did not want to lose him, so he reported the matter to the grand marshal who forbade Kuan Fu to make the attempt.

After the prince of Wu's defeat, Kuan Fu's fame spread throughout the land. The marquis of Yingyin reported this to the emperor, who made Kuan Fu general of the palace guard. A few months later, however, he was dismissed for some offence. He made his home in the capital and everyone in Changan spoke highly of him. During the reign of Emperor Ching he was appointed as chief minister of the principality of Tai.

After Emperor Ching died and the present emperor had just come to the throne, Kuan Fu was appointed as governor of Huaiyang because that was a centre of communications and a military stronghold. In the first year of *Chienyuan,* he served as minister of the imperial equipage.

The next year while drinking one day with Tou Fu, commander of the Changlo Palace guard, Kuan Fu quarrelled with him and, being in his cups, struck him. Tou Fu was the younger brother of Empress Dowager Tou. Afraid the empress dowager might have Kuan Fu killed, the emperor transferred him to be the chief minister of the principality of Yen. Several years later he was dismissed for some offence and returned to the capital to live in retirement.

Kuan Fu was strong-willed, outspoken and boisterous when drunk. He never flattered anybody. He behaved in a cavalier and insulting way to nobles and all who were more powerful than himself, but treated those below him as his equals — the poorer they were, the more respect he showed. In a large group he always singled out his inferiors for attention, and gentlemen admired him for this trait.

He had no taste for literature but admired gallant deeds

of daring and kept his word without fail. All his friends were prominent citizens or men of great resourcefulness. His property ran into tens of millions of cash, and he daily entertained tens and hundreds of guests. His estates were large, including hills, lakes and fields, and he had a host of kinsmen and protégés. His power went unchallenged in Yingchuan, where the children used to sing:

> When the River Ying runs clear,
> The Kuans have nothing to fear;
> When the River Ying runs muddy,
> The Kuans' end will be bloody!

But although Kuan Fu was wealthy, his power declined once he was out of office and the ministers, courtiers and protégés who had associated with him stayed away.

So when Tou Ying also lost power, he was eager to join forces with Kuan Fu and sever relations with those former admirers who had now deserted him. Kuan Fu for his part hoped with the help of Tou Ying to make friends with other nobles and imperial clansmen and so increase his reputation. The mutual attraction and admiration they felt made the two men as close as father and son. They got on capitally together, never tiring of each other's company; they only regretted that they had not met earlier.

One day when Kuan Fu was in mourning he called on Tien Fen the prime minister, who remarked casually, "I would like to go with you to see Tou Ying the marquis of Weichi. It is a pity that you are in mourning."

"If Your Excellency means to do him that honour, I certainly cannot let my mourning stand in the way," said Kuan Fu. "May I tell him to prepare for a visit from you early tomorrow?"

Tien Fen agreed.

Kuan Fu told Tou Ying what he had said to Tien Fen. Then Tou Ying and his wife bought plenty of beef and wine and spent the whole night cleaning and sweeping their house to have all ready for the feast. Early the next morning they posted attendants outside the gate to keep a look-out for the prime minister, but though they waited till noon he did not come.

Tou Ying asked Kuan Fu, "Could the prime minister have forgotten?"

"I invited him in spite of my mourning," replied Kuan Fu sullenly. "He ought to have come." And he took a carriage to fetch Tien Fen.

Tien Fen had been joking the previous day as it happened, and had no intention of going. When Kuan Fu reached his gate he was still in bed.

Kuan Fu strode in and said, "Yesterday Your Excellency promised to call on the marquis of Weichi. He and his wife have prepared a feast and been waiting since early morning, not venturing to take a bite."

Tien Fen was taken aback and apologized, saying, "I must have had too much to drink yesterday. It completely slipped my mind." He set off in his carriage but drove so slowly that Kuan Fu grew even angrier than before.

At the height of the feast Kuan Fu rose to dance, after which he urged Tien Fen to perform a dance, but the latter refused to move. Then Kuan Fu sat there making cutting remarks till Tou Ying dragged him out and apologized for him to the prime minister. Tien Fen stayed and drank till nightfall, when he went cheerfully away.

Later on, Tien Fen sent Chi Fu to ask Tou Ying for some fields south of the city which he owned. Tou Ying refused, indignantly exclaiming, "I may be an old man who has been pushed aside while he holds the high rank of prime minister, but he has no right to seize my land."

When Kuan Fu heard this he cursed Chi Fu roundly. Anxious to avoid a quarrel between Tien Fen and Tou Ying, Chi Fu made some excuses to the prime minister to smooth the matter over. "Tou Ying is old and won't live much longer," he said. "Just be patient and wait."

But when Tien Fen learned that Tou Ying and Kuan Fu had angrily refused to give up the fields, he flew into a passion. "I saved Tou Ying's son after he killed a man," he fumed.

"I have treated him handsomely in every respect. Why should he grudge me a few plots of land? In any case, what has this to do with Kuan Fu? Well, I shall not ask again." From that day on, Tien Fen bore a deep grudge against Kuan Fu and Tou Ying.

In the spring of the fourth year of *Yuankuang*, Tien Fen reported to the emperor, "Kuan Fu's family in Yingchuan is so overbearing that the people are suffering. I ask for an investigation."

"This is within your jurisdiction as prime minister," replied the emperor. "Why ask my permission?"

Kuan Fu for his part knew something of Tien Fen's dark deeds and corruption, and was aware that he was in communication with the prince of Huainan and had accepted bribes from him. But friends intervened to patch things up between them.

That summer Tien Fen married the daughter of the prince of Yen, and the empress dowager decreed that all the nobles and members of the imperial house should go to offer their congratulations. Tou Ying called to ask Kuan Fu to accompany him, but Kuan Fu declined.

"I have offended the prime minister several times when in my cups," he said. "And now he has another grudge against me."

"But all that has been settled," said Tou Ying, and prevailed upon Kuan Fu to go with him.

When the drinking was at its height Tien Fen rose to propose a toast, at which all his guests left their mats and bowed low. But when Tou Ying proposed a toast only his friends left their mats, all the other guests simply kneeling where they were. Kuan Fu took umbrage at this and rose to urge the rest to drink. When he came to Tien Fen, the prime minister merely knelt on his mat and said, "I cannot drink a whole cup."

Kuan Fu was furious but he forced a smile. "A great man like Your Excellency must drink up!" he cried. Still Tien Fen refused to drink.

Next Kuan Fu went to the marquis of Linju, who was whispering to Cheng Pu-shih and did not leave his mat either. To vent his anger, Kuan Fu swore at him, "You usually run down Cheng Pu-shih as if he were not worth a cent; yet today when one of your elders offers you a toast, you are whispering into his ear like a girl!"

Tien Fen drew him aside and warned him, "Cheng Pu-shih and Li Kuang are commanders of the guard at the East and West Palaces. If you insult General Cheng in public like this, what must General Li feel?"

"I am ready to have my head cut off or my chest ripped open," retorted Kuan Fu. "What do I care about either Cheng or Li?"

One by one the guests went off to the lavatory and then slipped away, and Tou Ying signed to Kuan Fu to go with him. But Tien Fen exclaimed angrily, "That was my own fault — I let Kuan Fu go too far!" He ordered his horsemen to detain Kuan Fu, so that he could not leave. Chi Fu rose to apologize for him, putting a hand on the back of his neck to force him to bow. But Kuan Fu, more angry than ever, refused to apologize. Then Tien Fen ordered his horsemen to bind him and hold him prisoner.

Summoning his chief officer, he said, "Today I invited members of the imperial house at the order of the empress dowager. Because Kuan Fu swore at my guests and showed no respect, I have detained him in my house." Then he brought up the old charges against Kuan Fu and sent officers to arrest his entire clan, accusing them of capital offences.

Tou Ying, bitterly repenting his part in this, laid out money and sent men to beg for Kuan Fu's release, but all to no avail. With Tien Fen's officers hot on their track, all the Kuans went into hiding; and since Kuan Fu himself was under arrest he could not report Tien Fen's misdeeds to the emperor.

Tou Ying made every effort to save Kuan Fu, although his wife warned him, "General Kuan has offended the prime minister and annoyed the empress dowager and her family. How can you save him?"

"I won the title of marquis for myself and can give it up without regret," replied her husband. "I cannot let Kuan Fu die while I am alive."

Unknown to his family, he slipped out and presented a memorial to the throne. He was immediately summoned to the palace, where he explained that Kuan Fu had been drunk during the feast and that this offence should not be punished by death. The emperor agreed and kept him to a meal, then said, "Go and argue your case now in the East Empress Dowager's Court."

So Tou Ying went to the East Court. There he stressed Kuan Fu's good qualities, admitted that he had drunk too much, but declared that the prime minister was now bringing false charges against him. Thereupon Tien Fen expatiated at length on Kuan Fu's arrogance and lawlessness, declaring him guilty of treason. Since Tou Ying feared he could not refute these charges, he started enumerating the prime minister's own faults.

Tien Fen replied, "Fortunately the world is at peace now so that I, as a relative of the imperial house, can enjoy music, horses, hounds and my estate. I am fond of musicians, actors and craftsmen, unlike Tou Ying and Kuan Fu who day and night gather adventurers and powerful men from all parts of the land to plot together, taunting and slandering others behind their backs, searching the heavens for omens and sketching their plans of campaign on the ground, manoeuvring between the emperor and empress dowager, and hoping for unrest so that they can achieve great deeds. I cannot tell what Tou Ying and that crew are up to."

The emperor asked his ministers, "Which of these two is right?"

The grand secretary Han An-kuo said, "Tou Ying, the marquis of Weichi, has told us how Kuan Fu after his father's death seized his spear and, blind to danger, charged the ranks of Wu. He received a dozen wounds and his fame spread throughout the army as one of the bravest fighters in all the land. Now he has committed no serious crime in simply brawling over a cup of wine, and we should not execute him for other faults. In this respect, the marquis of Weichi is right.

"The prime minister, however, tells us that Kuan Fu is in league with evil men, has oppressed the common people, amassed millions, tyrannized over Yingchuan, and even insulted members of the imperial house, encroaching upon their rights. When the branch is larger than the trunk, it will destroy the tree unless it is broken off. Thus the prime minister is also right. Only our sagacious sovereign can decide between them."

Chi An, the officer in charge of principalities, spoke in favour of Tou Ying. The city prefect, Cheng Tang-shih, spoke up for him too but dared not make out a strong case. All the others were afraid to speak at all.

The emperor was angry and swore at Cheng Tang-shih, "You usually have plenty to say about the good points and bad of Tou Ying and Tien Fen. Yet in a debate at court you are like a pony caught between shafts. I should have the lot of you beheaded."

Emperor Wu dismissed the court and went to the inner apartments to offer food to the empress dowager. But her spies had already told her about the debate and she was too angry to eat.

"Even while I am alive they are trampling on my younger brother!" she scolded. "As soon as I am dead they will swallow him up! And do you expect to last as long as a stone statue? If you give way so meekly in your lifetime, after your death which one of these men can be trusted?"

The emperor apologized and said, "It is because they are both related to the imperial house that I had this debate in court. Otherwise such matters could be decided by any law officer."

Then Shih Chien, chief of the palace guards, analysed the two men's cases for the emperor.

When the court was dismissed Tien Fen went to find his carriage at the gate and made the grand secretary Han An-kuo ride with him.

"What made you dither like a mouse poking his head out

of his hole when dealing with that old bald pate?" he demanded angrily.

After a considerable silence Han An-kuo replied, "Why couldn't you keep your temper? When Tou Ying attacked you, you should have taken off your official cap and seal and handed in your resignation, saying, 'As a relative of the imperial family I have had the privilege of serving Your Majesty but proved unworthy of my post. The marquis of Weichi is right.' The emperor would have admired your modesty so much that he would not have accepted your resignation, while Tou Ying would have been so ashamed that he would have locked himself up, bitten out his tongue and taken his own life. Instead, you hurled back abuse when he abused you as if this were a squabble between hawkers or women. It was most undignified."

Tien Fen excused himself, saying, "In the heat of the moment that never occurred to me."

The emperor ordered the censorate to verify Tou Ying's statements about Kuan Fu, and when these were found to be untrue he was impeached and imprisoned by the gaoler of the imperial clan.

During the reign of Emperor Ching, Tou Ying had received an imperial decree saying that any serious offence he might have committed should be dealt with leniently when tried. Now that he was in prison and Kuan Fu had been arrested and condemned to death with his whole family, the situation was growing daily more ominous, yet nobody dared to intercede with the emperor. So Tou Ying made his brother's son mention the decree he had received, thus hoping to have an audience with the emperor. But the imperial secretariat could find no such decree left by the previous emperor at the time of his death. The only copy was that in the possession of Tou Ying, sealed by his family steward. Accordingly he was charged with forging an imperial decree, a capital offence.

In the tenth month of the fifth year of *Yuankuang*, Kuan Fu and all his family were executed. When Tou Ying subsequently learned of this, he was so enraged that he had an epileptic fit and tried to starve himself to death. But hearing that Emperor Wu did not mean to kill him, he started eating and taking medicine again. It had been decided that his life should be spared, but then a rumour reached the emperor to the effect that Tou Ying was slandering him. He was therefore condemned to be executed at the end of the twelfth month in Weicheng.

The following spring Tien Fen fell ill and kept crying out to beg forgiveness for his crimes. A sorcerer who could see spirits was sent for, and he saw the ghosts of Tou Ying and Kuan Fu watching over Tien Fen and waiting for a chance to kill him. And so he died.

His son Tien Tien succeeded to his title. In the winter of the third year of *Yuanshuo*, this second marquis of Wu-an was found guilty of disrespect to the throne because he wore a short tunic to the palace. Thereupon the fief was abolished.

After the prince of Huainan's plot to rebel was discovered and investigated it emerged that previously, when he had come to court, Tien Fen, then grand marshal, had welcomed him at Pashang. "The emperor has no heir and Your Highness is the ablest of the First Emperor's grandsons," said Tien Feng. "When the emperor dies, you should naturally succeed him." The prince was so pleased that he presented Tien Fen with much gold and other gifts.

Emperor Wu had been prejudiced against Tien Fen ever since he destroyed Tou Ying and had only put up with him for the sake of the empress dowager. When he heard about these gifts from the prince of Huainan, he declared, "If Tien Fen were still alive today I should have executed him and all his family."

The Grand Historian comments: Both Tou Ying and Tien Fen rose to power because they were related to an empress. Kuan Fu won fame for a single daring exploit, Tou Ying was promoted after the rebellion of Wu and Chu, and Tien Fen became prominent at a time when the emperor was young and the empress dowager wielded power.

But Tou Ying did not know how to change with the times, while Kuan Fu was overbearing and tactless. Each, by aiding the other, brought calamity on himself. Tien Fen took advantage of his high position to display his power, destroying two good men because of a quarrel over a cup of wine. The pity of it!

One who vents his anger on an innocent party will not long survive. Those who lack popular support must fall prey to slander. Alas, disaster never strikes without cause!

LI KUANG

General Li Kuang, a man of Chengchi in Lunghsi, was descended from Li Hsin, the general of Chin who pursued and captured Tan, the crown prince of Yen. His family originated in Huaili but later moved to Chengchi, and the men of each generation were trained in archery.

In the fourteenth year of Emperor Wen,* a strong force of Huns rode through the Hsiao Pass. Then Li Kuang, as the son of a good family, joined the army to resist the enemy. A brilliant mounted archer, he killed and captured many Huns and was made a palace guard. He and his cousin Li Tsai, another palace guard, served as mounted guards with a stipend of eight hundred piculs of grain.

Li Kuang often accompanied the emperor on his trips, and his skill in attack and defence or in grappling with wild beasts made Emperor Wen remark, "What a pity you weren't born at a different time! Had you lived during Emperor Kao-tsu's reign, you would easily have won a fief with ten thousand households."

When Emperor Ching ascended the throne, Li Kuang was appointed as commander of Lunghsi and soon promoted to the rank of a general of the mounted guard. During the campaign against Wu and Chu he served as commander of the Valiant Cavalry under Grand Marshal Chou Ya-fu and distinguished himself by capturing the rebels' flag at Changyi. But because he accepted an appointment as a general from the prince of Liang without imperial sanction, he was not rewarded on the return of the army. Instead he was made the governor of Shangku, a district constantly harried by the Huns.

---

* 166 B.C.

The director of dependent states, Kungsun Kunyeh, pleaded with the emperor, "There is no braver or more brilliant officer in the empire than Li Kuang, but trusting to his own ability he never loses a chance of engaging the Huns. I am afraid we may lose him."

Li Kuang was therefore transferred to the governorship of Shangchun. He was later transferred to govern various frontier provinces and then made the governor of Shangchun again. He also held posts at Lunghsi, Peiti, Yenmen, Taichun and Yunchung. And wherever he went he won fame for his hard fighting.

When the Huns invaded Shangchun in force, Emperor Ching ordered one of his favourite eunuchs to join Li Kuang in order to gain experience in fighting the Huns. One day this eunuch at the head of several dozen horsemen met with three Hunnish riders and engaged them in a fight. The Huns turned in their saddles and drew their bows, wounding the eunuch and killing most of his men. The eunuch fled back to Li Kuang.

"These must be their best sharp-shooters known as the 'eagle-hunters'," said Li Kuang, and rode out with a hundred horsemen in pursuit. The three Huns had lost their horses and covered several dozen *li* on foot. Li Kuang ordered his men to fan out to the left and the right while he shot at the enemy and, after killing two of them and taking the third alive, he found that these were indeed "eagle-hunters".

Li Kuang had barely bound the captive on his horse when several thousand Hunnish horsemen came in sight, but the smallness of the Chinese force made them suspect a trap and they took to the hills in defensive formation. The hundred horsemen with Li Kuang were so alarmed that they wanted to gallop straight back.

"We are dozens of *li* from our main force," said Li Kuang. "If the hundred of us make a dash for it, the Huns will give chase and shoot us down in no time; whereas if we stay here they will think we are acting as a decoy for a great army behind, and will not dare to attack."

374

He gave the order, "Advance!" When they were about two *li* from the enemy, he halted and ordered, "Dismount and undo your saddles."

"This horde of Huns is almost on top of us," protested his men. "What shall we do if they attack?"

"They expect us to withdraw," replied Li Kuang. "But when they see us unsaddle our horses to stop here, they will be surer than ever that this is a trick."

The Huns dared not attack, but one of their chieftains galloped out on a white horse to reconnoitre. Li Kuang remounted and charged with a dozen riders to shoot down the Hun. This done, he returned to his troops, unsaddled his mount and ordered his men to turn loose their horses and lie down to sleep. It was now dusk and the Huns were too bewildered to attack. Suspecting that an ambushing Han force might fall on them in the dark, they withdrew by night. At dawn Li Kuang rejoined the main army, which had not come to his rescue because it had no idea where he had gone.

When Emperor Ching died and Emperor Wu succeeded to the throne, Li Kuang's fame as a general won him promotion from his post at Shangchun to the command of the guard of Weiyang Palace. At this time Cheng Pu-shih was commander of the guard of Changlo Palace. He, like Li Kuang, had served as a governor of frontier provinces, defending the border and leading expeditions against the Huns.

Li Kuang paid little attention to military formation on the march, but would make camp wherever he found water and grass and let his men do as they pleased. He appointed no one to sound the watch and kept dispatch-writing and clerical work down to a minimum at his headquarters. But his scouts always reconnoitred deep into enemy territory, and he had never come to any harm.

Cheng Pu-shih, on the other hand, laid great stress on military formation and discipline. Sentries sounded the watch in his camp, and his officers had to sit up all night writing records and reports. But he had never come to grief either.

"Li Kuang's army routine is certainly simple," said Cheng

Pu-shih once. "But if the enemy launches a sudden attack, he will be at their mercy. Still, his troops have such an easy time of it that they would gladly die for him. Our army routine may be irksome, but the enemy will never catch us napping."

Although both these men were famous generals of the frontier provinces, the Huns feared Li Kuang's tactics and soldiers preferred to serve under him rather than under Cheng, who had a reputation for harshness. During Emperor Ching's time, Cheng Pu-shih had been made a grand counsellor because of the frank advice he gave on several occasions. He was scrupulously honest and a stickler for regulations and discipline.

Some time later an attempt was made to entice the Huns into the town of Mayi, and a large Han force was concealed in a neighbouring valley. Li Kuang was appointed as General of the Valiant Cavalry under the command of Han An-kuo, General of the Protecting Army. But the Hunnish khan discovered the trap and withdrew so that the Han troops had no chance to distinguish themselves.

Four years later Li Kuang, then still a captain of the palace guard, was made a general and sent to attack the Huns beyond Yenmen. His army was outnumbered and routed but he was captured, for the khan, who had heard of his ability, had given orders that he must be taken alive.

When the Hunnish cavalry caught him he was wounded, so they laid him on a litter between two horses. They had covered more than ten *li* when Li Kuang, who had shammed dead, saw through half-closed eyelids that a young Hun mounted on a fine horse was beside him. He leapt suddenly on to this horse, throwing down its young rider and snatching away his bow. Then he galloped south for several dozen *li* until he found what was left of his troops and led them back inside the frontier. Several hundred Hunnish horsemen had galloped after him, but shooting with the Hun's bow as he rode he killed many of his pursuers and made good his escape.

Upon his return to the capital, he was tried. As he had lost many men and let himself be captured alive by the Huns, he was sentenced to death; but he was permitted to ransom himself and become a commoner.

He lived in retirement for a few years near the grandson of the former marquis of Yingyin in Lantien among the southern hills, where he devoted most of his time to hunting. One day he went out with an attendant and accepted an invitation to drink in a farm house, not returning to Paling watch station till it was dark. The constable guarding the station was drunk and yelled at him to halt.

"This is the former General Li," said Li Kuang's man.

"Even an accredited general cannot wander about after dark," retorted the constable. "Much less a former general!" He detained Li Kuang there.

Later the Huns crossed the border again, killed the governor of Liaohsi and defeated General Han An-kuo, who withdrew to Yupeiping. Then the emperor made Li Kuang the governor of Yupeiping. Li Kuang asked to have the constable of Paling Station sent with him, and as soon as the man arrived he cut off his head.

The Huns called Li Kuang the "Winged General" of Han, and as long as he was governor they dared not invade Yupeiping.

Once when out hunting Li Kuang shot a boulder in the grass which he mistook for a tiger, and the entire tip of his arrow was embedded in the rock. But when he realized what it was and shot again, he could not pierce the boulder. Whenever he heard of a tiger in the province where he was living, he would hunt it. In Yupeiping a tiger leapt at him and mauled him, but he finally succeeded in killing the beast.

Li Kuang was open-handed. He divided all his rewards among his officers and ate the same food as his men. For over forty years his stipend was two thousand piculs a year, but he saved no money and never talked about property. He was tall and long-armed like an ape. His skill in archery can only be attributed to natural aptitude, for none of his descendants or others who learned bowmanship from him could equal him. He was a poor talker who had little to say. To pass the time with others he would draw military formations on the ground and compete in shooting at them: the losers had to drink. Indeed, up to the end of his life shooting was his sole recreation.

When Li Kuang's troops were short of water and food, he would not drink until all his men had drunk, nor eat until they had eaten. And since he was lenient and generous to his troops, they served him loyally. In battle, he would not shoot until his adversary was within a few dozen paces and he could be sure of hitting him. Then as soon as his bowstring twanged the enemy fell. Because of this, he and his men were often worsted, just as he was often wounded by beasts in the chase.

When Shih Chien the captain of the palace guard died, the emperor appointed Li Kuang in his place. In the sixth year of *Yuanshuo* he served again as rear general under Grand Marshal Wei Ching, advancing from Tinghsiang to attack the Huns. Most of the other generals killed and captured enough foes to be made marquises for their services, but Li Kuang's army met with no success.

Three years later Li Kuang, still captain of the palace guard, advanced at the head of four thousand horsemen from Yupei-ping, while Chang Chien, the marquis of Powang, led ten thousand cavalry by a different route. Li Kuang had advanced several hundred *li* when he was surrounded by the Eastern Prince of the Huns with forty thousand horsemen. Seeing that his men were afraid, Li Kuang ordered his son Li Kan to break through the enemy's ranks. Li Kan and a few dozen men galloped through the left and right flanks of the enemy lines, then returned to report, "These Huns are easy to handle!" At this the other soldiers took heart again.

Li Kuang drew up his troops in a circle, the men facing outwards. The Huns attacked in force, arrows rained down; soon more than half of the Han soldiers had fallen, and their supply of arrows was nearly exhausted. Then Li Kuang ordered his men to fit arrows to their bows but not to shoot. Meanwhile he aimed with his large yellow crossbow at the Hunnish leaders and killed several of them. After this the Huns attacked less fiercely. Night was falling and his officers and men were deathly pale but Li Kuang remained calm and confident as he regrouped his forces. Ever after, he was a byword for courage in the army.

The next day they again fought desperately until Chang Chien brought up reinforcements and the Huns retreated. The Han troops were too weary to give chase. Since Li Kuang's men had nearly been wiped out, he gave up the fight and returned. According to the law, Chang Chien should have been sentenced to death for arriving late; but he was permitted to ransom himself and become a commoner. Li Kuang's achievement was cancelled out by his losses; hence he went unrewarded.

Li Kuang's cousin Li Tsai, who had also served as a palace guard in Emperor Wen's time, accumulated enough merit during the reign of Emperor Ching to rise to a post worth two thousand piculs a year, and under Emperor Wu he became the chief minister of Tai. In the fifth year of *Yuanshuo,* he served under Grand Marshal Wei Ching as General of the Light Chariots in an expedition against the Western Prince of the Huns. His services in this campaign entitled him to be ennobled as the marquis of Lo-an. In the second year of *Yuanshou,* he succeeded Kungsun Hung as prime minister. Li Tsai had slightly less than average ability and was far less famous than his cousin, yet Li Kuang was never awarded a fief nor promoted above the rank of a high minister, while Li Tsai became a marquis and one of the three highest officials in the land. Even some of Li Kuang's own officers and men became marquises.

Once Li Kuang remarked in a casual conversation with the astrologer Wang Shuo, "I have been in every campaign waged against the Huns, yet while several dozen officers of no more than average ability have been made marquises for their services I have neither been cited for merit nor granted a fief, although I am not inferior to them. Why is this? Have I got the wrong face for a marquis? Or is this a matter of fate?"

"Can you remember doing anything you later regretted?" asked Wang Shuo.

"When I was governing Lunghsi and the Chiang tribes revolted, I tricked them into giving themselves up. But when more than eight hundred surrendered, I broke my promise to spare them and massacred them that same day. This is the one thing I really have on my conscience."

"Nothing can be worse than killing those who have surrendered," replied Wang Shuo. "That must be why you have never been made a marquis."

Two years later Grand Marshal Wei Ching and Huo Chu-ping, General of the Swift Cavalry, led a great expedition against the Huns. Li Kuang begged several times to be sent with them, but the emperor considered him too old and only consented after a long time, appointing him as general of the vanguard. This took place in the fourth year of *Yuanshou*.

Li Kuang was under Grand Marshal Wei Ching's command. After crossing the frontier they learned the whereabouts of the khan from some Hunnish captives, and Wei Ching decided to lead his best troops there directly, ordering Li Kuang to join forces with Chao Yi-chi, the general of the right, and advance by the eastern route. This route was slightly longer and, since little water or grass was to be had there, the army could not pass that way in force.

"My post is in the vanguard," protested Li Kuang, "yet you are ordering me to take the eastern route. Though I have been fighting the Huns since I was a lad, this is the first time I have had a chance to encounter the khan himself. I beg to be allowed to ride in the vanguard and be the first to attack him."

But Wei Ching had received secret orders from the emperor not to let Li Kuang engage the khan, because he was old, and his luck had always been bad, and therefore he might easily fail again. Moreover Kungsun Ao, who had just lost his marquisate, was serving as the general of the centre and Wei Ching wanted him to have this chance to fight the khan. That was why he had removed Li Kuang from his post. Knowing this, Li Kuang begged Wei Ching to reconsider the matter, but the grand marshal dispatched his chief officer to him with a sealed note ordering him to report to Chao Yi-chi without delay.

Li Kuang stormed off without even taking leave of the grand marshal. He led his troops to join the general of the right and they set out by the eastern route. But having no guide, they lost the way and failed to meet the main force at the time appointed. When Wei Ching joined battle with the Huns, the khan fled, and they had to return without having captured him. Riding southward across the desert, Wei Ching met the troops of Li Kuang and Chao Yi-chi; and Li Kuang, seeing the grand marshal, rejoined the main force.

Presently Wei Ching sent an officer with a gift of dried rice and wine to Li Kuang. The man asked how he and Chao Yi-chi had come to lose their way, as Wei Ching must send a detailed report of their misadventure to the emperor. Before Li Kuang had time to explain, however, Wei Ching sent his chief officer to summon him to headquarters at once to stand trial.

"My lieutenants were not to blame," declared Li Kuang. "I am the one responsible for losing the way. I shall answer for this myself before the tribunal."

When he reached headquarters he turned to his officers. "Since I was old enough to wear my hair bound up, I have fought more than seventy battles, great and small, against the Huns," he said. "This time I was fortunate enough to set out under Grand Marshal Wei Ching to fight the khan; but the grand marshal transferred me to another post and sent me by a longer route. And then I lost my way. This must be fate. I am over sixty now, too old to face up to the questions of these clerks." With that he drew his sword and cut his throat.

All the officers and men of his army wept. And everyone in the land, old and young alike, those who had known him and those who had not, shed tears when they heard of his death. Chao Yi-chi, the general of the right, was court-martialed and sentenced to death but permitted to ransom himself and become a commoner.

Li Kuang had three sons, Li Tang-hu, Li Chiao and Li Kan, all of whom served as palace guards. One day when Emperor Wu was joking with his favourite, young Han Yen, the lad took such liberties that Li Tang-hu struck him and made him take to his heels. The emperor was impressed by his courage, but

Li Tang-hu died early. Li Chiao became the governor of Tai-chun, but he also died before his father. A son named Li Ling was born to Li Tang-hu after his death. Li Kan was serving under Huo Chu-ping, General of Swift Cavalry, when Li Kuang killed himself at the front.

The year after Li Kuang's death Li Tsai, then prime minister, was accused of encroaching upon the grounds of Emperor Ching's tomb. He committed suicide rather than suffer the indignity of a trial, and his fief was abolished.

Li Kan served as a colonel under General Huo in a campaign against the Eastern Prince of the Huns. He fought bravely, capturing the prince's drum and flag and killing many of the enemy. For these services he was made a marquis within the Pass, with the revenue of two hundred households, and succeeded Li Kuang as captain of the palace guards.

Later Li Kan struck and injured Grand Marshal Wei Ching, whom he hated because of the wrong he had done his father, but Wei Ching hushed the matter up. Some time after this Li Kan accompanied the emperor to Yung and, while they were hunting in the grounds of Kanchuan Palace, Wei Ching's nephew Huo Chu-ping shot and killed Li Kan. But since General Huo was a favourite with the emperor, the matter was kept quiet and it was given out that Li Kan had been gored to death by a stag. A year or so later General Huo Chu-ping died.

Li Kan had a daughter who was the crown prince's favourite lady in waiting. His son Li Yu also enjoyed the prince's patronage, but he was a greedy, grasping man. Thus by degrees the house of Li declined.

When Li Ling grew up he was appointed superintendent of Chienchang Palace, in charge of the cavalry. An excellent archer, he was good to his men. Since his forbears for several generations had been military officers, Emperor Wu put Li Ling at the head of eight hundred horsemen. Once he led his troops over two thousand *li* into Hunnish territory, passed Lake Chuyen and observed the lie of the land, but came back without having encountered any Huns. On his return he was appointed a cavalry commander at the head of five thousand men of

Tanyang in Chu; and for several years he trained them in archery and settled them in Chiuchuan and Changyeh to defend the border against the Huns.

In the autumn of the second year of *Tienban,** Li Kuang-li conqueror of Osrouchana led thirty thousand cavalry against the Western Prince of the Huns in the Chilien and Tienshan Mountains. Li Ling was ordered to advance over a thousand *li* north of Chuyen with five thousand archers and infantrymen to divert the Huns and prevent them from concentrating their forces against General Li Kuang-li.

Li Ling reached his objective, but as he was returning his troops were surrounded by eighty thousand Huns. He had only five thousand men, and soon their arrows were exhausted and more than half of them had fallen; yet they killed and wounded over ten thousand of the enemy, fighting a running battle for eight days as they withdrew.

About a hundred *li* from Chuyen, their road was cut by the Huns in a narrow glen. All their food was gone, there was no help at hand, and the enemy pressed their attack, calling upon them to surrender. "I could never face the emperor to report this!" cried Li Ling. And he surrendered to the Huns. His army was destroyed, only four hundred or so surviving to return.

The Hunnish khan, who had always admired Li Ling's family and had been impressed by the fight he put up, married his daughter to him and made him a noble. But when the emperor knew of this, Li Ling's mother, wife and son were executed. After this the whole family was disgraced, and the gentlemen of Lunghsi who had been Li Ling's protégés bowed their heads in shame.

The Grand Historian comments: We read in the classics, "If a man is straight, others will follow him without being told. If he is not, no amount of orders will make them follow him." This applies to General Li Kuang.

---

* 99 B.C.

I found him as unassuming as a simple farmer, hardly able to get a word out. Yet the day that he died his sincerity and honesty had so impressed men that, whether they knew him or not, all mourned deeply for him. The proverb says, "The peach and plum trees cannot speak, yet a path is trodden out to them." This simple saying conveys a wealth of meaning.

THE ASSASSINS

Tsao Mo, a native of Lu, was powerfully built and brave and served Duke Chuang of Lu,* who admired physical strength. As a general of Lu, Tsao Mo fought Chi and was put to flight three times. Then Duke Chuang in alarm gave Suiyi to Chi to make peace, keeping Tsao Mo, however, as his general.

Duke Huan of Chi agreed to conclude a treaty with Lu at Ko. After the two dukes had taken their oath at the altar, Tsao Mo produced a dagger and seized Duke Huan, whose followers dared make no move.

"What do you want?" asked Duke Huan.

"Chi is strong, Lu weak," replied Tsao Mo, "and your state has overrun so much of our land that if any city of Lu is taken by the enemy it will mean a direct menace to Chi. Think this over well, sir."

As soon as Duke Huan agreed to return all the territory wrested from Lu, Tsao Mo tossed aside his dagger and descended from the altar to join the other attendants respectfully facing the rulers north. He had not changed colour or spoken less suavely than usual.

Duke Huan was angry and did not mean to keep faith.

"No!" said Kuan Chung. "If you break your promise to another state in order to enjoy some petty gain, you will lose the trust of the world. Better let them have it."

So Duke Huan returned the land he had seized from Lu, restoring all that Tsao Mo had lost in three battles.

One hundred and sixty-seven years after this there was the case of Chuan Chu in Wu.

Chuan Chu was a citizen of Tangyi in Wu. When Wu Tzu-

---

* 693-662 B.C.

hsu fled from Chu to Wu he discovered Chuan Chu's ability. When he saw King Liao of Wu he urged the advantages of attacking Chu, but Lord Kuang said, "His father and elder brother were killed by the king of Chu: hence his advice to attack. He is out for private revenge, not to assist us." So the king did not take his advice.

Knowing that Lord Kuang meant to kill the king, Wu Tzu-hsu said, "This fellow wants to seize power inside the state; it is useless to speak to him now about matters outside." He recommended Chuan Chu to Lord Kuang.

Lord Kuang's father, the late King Chu-fan, had three younger brothers, Yu-chai, Yi-mo and Cha. Aware that of these Cha was the worthiest, the king had not appointed an heir but had decreed that his three brothers should succeed him by turns, hoping that Cha would eventually become king. After his death he was succeeded by Yu-chai, who in turn was succeeded by Yi-mo; but when Yi-mo died and Cha should have succeeded, he fled and would not ascend the throne. Then the men of Wu made Yi-mo's son Liao their king.

Lord Kuang protested, "If the succession goes by brothers, Cha should be king; if by sons, I am the rightful heir and should rule." So he secretly kept advisers to help him win the throne. And he treated Chuan Chu well as his protégé.

Nine years later, King Ping of Chu died. That spring, King Liao took advantage of his death to send his younger brothers Kai-yu and Chu-yung with an army against Chu to besiege Chien. He also sent his uncle Cha to Tsin to observe the reactions of the other states. Then Chu dispatched troops to cut off Kai-yu and Chu-yung, with the result that Wu's army could not return.

At this Lord Kuang said to Chuan Chu, "Here is an opportunity not to be missed. Nothing venture, nothing gain! I am the rightful heir. Even if Cha returns, he cannot depose me."

Chuan Chu replied, "Yes, King Liao should be killed. His mother is old, his son a mere child, and his two younger brothers gone with the troops to Chu have their way of retreat cut off. Wu is beset outside by Chu, while at home there is no one, no strong minister. King Liao is helpless against us."

Lord Kuang bowed and said, "Your fate shall be my fate."

One day in the fourth month, Lord Kuang hid armed men in his cellar and invited King Liao to a feast. Troops escorted the king from his palace to Lord Kuang's residence, all the attendants at the gates and on the steps were his relations, and he was flanked by halberdiers. In the middle of the feast Lord Kuang, pleading a pain in the leg, went down to the cellar and sent Chuan Chu up with a dagger hidden in a fish. When he reached King Liao, Chuan Chu broke open the fish and stabbed the king with the dagger, dispatching him in an instant. The attendants killed Chuan Chu, but the king's men were thrown into such confusion when Lord Kuang sent his hidden men up to attack that they were all wiped out. He then set himself up as King Ho-lu, making Chuan Chu's son a high minister.

More than seventy years after this there was the case of Yu Jang in Tsin.

Yu Jang was a native of Tsin, who served the noble clans of Fan and Chunghang but whose talents went unrecognized. When he took service under the House of Chih, however, Lord Chih showed him high respect and favour. Later Lord Chih attacked the House of Chao and Lord Hsiang of Chao allied with Hann and Wei to defeat him, wiping out his clan and dividing his land into three. Because of the deep hatred he bore Lord Chih, Lord Hsiang lacquered his skull and used it as a wine vessel.

Yu Jang, escaping to the mountains, lamented, "Alas! A woman adorns herself for her lover, and a true man dies for one who appreciates him. Lord Chih appreciated me, so I must die to avenge him. Then my ghost need feel no shame."

He changed his name and went, disguised as a convict, to mend the palace privy, carrying a dagger to assassinate Lord Hsiang. But as Lord Hsiang was entering the privy he acted on a premonition and had him seized. And Yu Jang, a weapon in his hand, admitted, "I meant to avenge Lord Chih."

The attendants wanted to kill him but Lord Hsiang said,

"This is a man of honour. I shall just keep out of his way. Lord Chih died without heirs, yet this follower tried to avenge him. He must be a most worthy man." With that he released him.

Later Yu Jang lacquered his skin to cause scabies and swallowed charcoal to hoarsen his voice, changing himself out of all recognition. He begged in the market and even his wife did not know him. But he met a friend who saw through his disguise and asked, "Are you not Yu Jang?"

He admitted that he was.

The friend with tears pleaded with him, "A man of your talent should seek Lord Hsiang's patronage. You would soon stand high in his favour and could then easily carry out your plan. Why should you mutilate yourself and inflict so much suffering on yourself to take revenge? This is too hard a way."

Yu Jang answered, "If I entered his service to assassinate him, I should be guilty of disloyalty to him as my lord. This way is very hard, but my aim is to shame all those who in future are guilty of disloyalty to their lords."

He went off then, for soon Lord Hsiang was to come out, and Yu Jang hid under the bridge which he had to cross. When Lord Hsiang reached the bridge his horse shied and he said, "Yu Jang must be here!" He sent men to investigate and it was so. Then Lord Hsiang reproached Yu Jang saying, "Formerly you served the Houses of Fan and Chunghang, yet when Lord Chih destroyed them instead of avenging them you took service under him. Why are you so determined now to avenge Lord Chih's death?"

Yu Jang answered, "When I served the Houses of Fan and Chunghang, they treated me as an ordinary man and I treated them as ordinary men in return. But Lord Chih treated me as the finest man in the state, and that is how I must treat him."

"Ah, Yu Jang," cried Lord Hsiang, sighing and shedding tears. "You have made a name by your loyalty to Lord Chih, and I have given you quite enough quarter. Now settle this

388

business yourself. I am not letting you off again." He ordered his troops to surround him.

Yu Jang said, "I have heard that a wise master does not conceal men's qualities, while a loyal subject will die for fame. Already the whole world is praising the generosity with which you spared me. Now I am ready to take my punishment, but first give me your coat to run through as a token of revenge, and I shall die content. Presumptuous as it is, please grant my request."

Greatly moved by his loyalty, Lord Hsiang ordered his coat to be given to Yu Jang, who unsheathing his sword leapt and ran it through three times. "Now I can go down to report to Lord Chih!" he cried. With that he fell upon his sword and died. News of his death made all true men of Chao shed tears.

More than forty years after this there was the case of Nieh Cheng of Chih.

Nieh Cheng was a native of Shenching Village in the district of Chih. Having killed a man, he escaped with his mother and elder sister to Chi where he set up as a butcher. Later Yen Sui of Puyang, who owed allegiance to Marquis Ai of Hann, offended the chief minister Hsia Lui and fled to escape punishment, searching everywhere for a man who would kill Hsia Lui for him. When he reached Chi, he heard that Nieh Cheng was a brave man who was living as a butcher to avoid vengeance. Yen Sui called on him several times, then prepared a feast in honour of Nieh Cheng's mother at which he presented her with a hundred pieces of gold. Amazed by such munificence, Nieh Cheng declined the gift. When Yen Sui insisted he said, "I am blessed with an aged mother. Though I am but a poor stranger in these parts, I am able to supply her daily food and clothing by selling dog meat. Since I can provide for her, I dare not accept your gift."

Yen Sui sent the others away and told Nieh Cheng, "I have an enemy. Reaching Chi after travelling through many states, I heard that you, sir, were a man with a high sense of honour.

So I am offering you a hundred gold pieces to supply food and clothing for your mother and to win your friendship. I want no other return."

Nieh Cheng replied, "I have lowered my ambitions and humbled myself to sell meat in the market solely for my mother's sake. While she lives, I cannot promise my services to anyone." He could not be prevailed upon to accept, whereupon Yen Sui took a courteous leave of him.

In due time Nieh Cheng's mother died. After she was buried and the mourning over, Nieh Cheng said, "I am a poor stall-keeper wielding a butcher's cleaver, while Yen Sui is a state minister; yet he came a thousand *li* in his carriage to seek my friendship. I did very little for him, performed no great services to deserve his favour, yet he offered my mother a hundred pieces of gold; and though I did not accept, this shows how well he appreciated me. His longing for revenge made this worthy gentleman place his faith in one so humble and obscure. How, then, can I remain silent? Previously I ignored his overtures for my mother's sake. Now that my mother has died of old age, I must serve this man who appreciates me."

So he went west to Puyang to see Yen Sui and told him, "I refused you before because my mother was still alive, but now she has died of old age. Who is the man on whom you want to take vengeance? I am at your service."

Then Yen Sui told him the whole story, saying, "My enemy is Hsia Lui, chief minister of Hann and uncle of the marquis of Hann. He has many clansmen and his residence is closely guarded. All my attempts to assassinate him have failed. Since you are good enough to help me, I can supply you with chariots, cavalry and men."

"Hann is not far from Uei, and we are going to kill the chief minister who is also the ruler's uncle," said Nieh Cheng. "In these circumstances, too many men would make for trouble and word might get out. Then the whole of Hann would become your enemy and that would be disastrous."

So refusing all assistance, he bid farewell and carrying his sword went alone to the capital of Hann. Hsia Lui, seated in his office, was surrounded by a host of guards and armed attendants; but Nieh Cheng marching straight in and up the steps stabbed the minister to death. The attendants, in utter confusion, were set upon with loud cries by Nieh Cheng, till several dozen of them were laid low. Then he gashed his face, gouged out his eyes and stabbed himself so that his guts spilled out and he died.

Nieh Cheng's corpse was exposed in the market-place in Hann and inquiries were made but no one knew who he was. A reward of a thousand gold pieces was offered for identifying the assassin, but time passed without any news. Then Nieh Cheng's sister Jung heard of Hsia Lui's assassination and the large reward offered for the identification of his unknown assassin, whose corpse had been exposed. "Can this be my brother?" she sobbed. "Ah, how well Yen Sui understood him!"

She went to the market-place in Hann and found that it was indeed he. Falling on the corpse she wept bitterly and cried, "This is Nieh Cheng from Shenching Village in Chih!"

The people in the market warned her, "This man savagely murdered our chief minister and the king has offered a thousand gold pieces for his name. Did you not know this? Why do you come to identify him?"

"I knew this," she replied. "But he humbled himself to live as a tradesman in the market because our mother was living and I had no husband. After our mother died and I was married, Yen Sui raised him from his squalor to be his friend. How else could he repay Yen Sui's great kindness? A man should die for a friend who knows his worth. Because I was still alive, he mutilated himself to hide his identity. But how can I, for fear of death, let my noble brother perish unknown?"

This greatly astounded the people in the market. Having called aloud on heaven three times, she wailed in anguish and died beside her brother.

Word of this reached Tsin, Chu, Chi and Wei, and everyone commented, "Not only was Nieh Cheng able, but his sister was a remarkable woman too." Nieh Cheng might never have given his life for Yen Sui had he known that his sister, with her strong resolution, would not balk at his corpse exposed in the market-place and take the long difficult journey to make his name known and perish by his side. Yen Sui certainly was a good judge of character able to find loyal helpers!

More than two hundred and twenty years after this, and there was the case of Ching Ko in Chin.

Ching Ko was a native of Uei, whose ancestors had migrated to that state from Chi. The people of Uei called him Master Ch'ing, but when he went to Yen he was known as Master Ching. He loved reading and swordsmanship and advised Prince Yuan of Uei on the art of government; but the prince did not take his advice. Later, when Chin attacked Wei and annexed some territory as its Eastern Province, the prince's family was moved to Yehwang.

Ching Ko once went to Yutzu to discuss swordsmanship with Kai Nieh, but walked out when Kai Nieh lost his temper and glared at him. Someone suggested that he be recalled.

"No," said Kai Nieh. "Just now, when we were talking about swords, he said something foolish for which I glared at him. He was right to leave. He will not stay here now."

A messenger sent to Ching Ko's lodging reported that he had indeed already driven away from Yutzu.

"Naturally," said Kai Nieh. "I overawed him with a look."

Later Ching Ko went to Hantan, where he fell out with Lu Kou-chien while gambling; and when Lu shouted angrily at him he left without a word, never going to seek Lu again.

On arriving in Yen, Ching Ko made friends with a dog-flesh vender and a guitar player named Kao Chien-li. Ching Ko was fond of wine, and he spent his days drinking with these men in the market-place. When they had drunk themselves tipsy, Kao would play the guitar while Ching Ko sang in the middle of the market; they were now merry, now sad, shedding tears as if no one else were near.

Though Ching Ko spent much time with drinking companions, he was serious and studious too and made friends wherever he went with the worthy men and elders. In Yen, for instance, he was well received by a retired scholar named Tien Kuang, who understood that he was no ordinary man.

About this time Tan, crown prince of Yen, escaped from Chin where he had been a hostage and returned to his own state. This prince had previously been a hostage in Chao, and as King Cheng of Chin was born in that state they had been playmates together. After Cheng ascended the throne of Chin, Prince Tan went there as a hostage; but being shabbily treated he fled in disgust. He longed for revenge, but because his state was small he was powerless. Later the king of Chin launched repeated campaigns against Chi, Chu and the three successor states of Tsin in the east, annexing their territory and drawing ever nearer to Yen. The king of Yen and his ministers trembled at this impending danger, and Prince Tan in his anxiety consulted his tutor, Chu Wu.

"Chin has extended its borders on every side and is now threatening Hann, Chao and Wei," said Chu Wu. "In the north it has the strongholds of Kanchuan and Kukou, in the south the fertile valleys of the Ching and Wei Rivers. It controls the wealth of Pa and Han, has the mountains of Lung and Shu to its west, and the Hanku Pass and Yao Mountains to its east. Its population is large, its soldiers brave, and it possesses weapons and to spare for its troops. If it is bent on mischief, there is no telling what may befall the land south of the Great Wall and north of the River Yi. Then why risk rubbing him the wrong way just because he once slighted you?"

"What then can I do?" asked the prince.

"Allow me to go back and think of a plan," said Chu Wu.

Some time after this, General Fan Yu-chi of Chin offended his king and fled to Yen, where Prince Tan took him in.

"You cannot do this!" protested Chu Wu. "If a tyrant like the king of Chin centres all his rage on Yen that would be enough to strike terror into our hearts — especially should he learn that General Fan is here. This is setting meat before a hungry tiger: disaster must surely follow! Not even Kuan Chung or Yen Ying could save you then. I advise you to lose no time in sending General Fan to the Huns in order to clear yourself; then ally with the three successor states of Tsin in the west, with Chi and Chu in the south, and with the khan in the north. This done, you can start making plans."

"Yours is a long-term scheme, sir," objected the prince, "and I am too frantic to wait. And that is not all. General Fan threw himself on my mercy because he was desperate, and I am certainly not going to let myself be intimidated by a powerful Chin into abandoning a friend with whom I sympathize and handing him over to the Huns. I would rather die than do such a thing. Please think again, sir."

Chu Wu said, "Risking danger in the hope of winning safety, courting disaster to obtain good fortune, devising shallow schemes to redress a great wrong, and binding yourself in friendship to one man with no regard for the great harm to the state — this is 'building up enmity and inviting disaster'. When wild duck feathers are dropped into a charcoal stove, their fate is a foregone conclusion; and when Chin swoops down like a vulture in all its fury, you do not need me to tell you what will happen. There is an old gentleman in our state named Tien Kuang, who has great wisdom and courage. You might consult him."

"Will you introduce me to him, sir?" asked the prince.

Chu Wu assented and went to inform Tien Kuang that Prince Tan wished to consult him on state policy. Tien Kuang agreed and went to call on the prince.

Prince Tan welcomed and led him in, then knelt to dust the mat for him. As soon as Tien Kuang was seated and they were alone, the prince rose to his feet.

"It is Chin or us!" he said. "What are we to do?"

"I have heard that a good steed in its prime can gallop a thousand *li* in one day," said Tien Kuang. "But when it grows weak and old, the poorest nag can outstrip it. Your Highness has heard about me as I was in my prime, not knowing that my strength is already spent. But though I dare not advise on affairs of state, my friend Ching Ko would be of service to you."

"Will you introduce me to him, sir?" asked the prince.

Tien Kuang agreed and stood up to leave. Prince Tan saw him to the gate.

"What I have just told you and what you have said are of vital consequence to our state," the prince cautioned him. "I must beg you not to disclose this."

Tien Kuang nodded and smiled as he said, "Certainly not!" then went quickly to see Ching Ko.

"Everyone in Yen knows that we are on good terms," he said. "The prince had heard of my fame during my youth and, not knowing that I am past my prime, favoured me with an audience during which he said, 'It is Chin or us. What are we to do?' I made so bold as to recommend you to him, and hope you will go to the crown prince's palace."

To this Ching Ko agreed.

"I have heard that the actions of a man of honour should be above suspicion," continued Tien Kuang. "But by warning me that our talk was of vital consequence to the state and asking me not to disclose it, the prince showed that he doubts me. To give rise to suspicion is a slur upon a man's honour." Making up his mind to kill himself to spur Ching Ko on, he proceeded, "Please go at once to the crown prince and tell him I am dead, to show that I will not talk." With this, he cut his throat and died.

Then Ching Ko went to see Prince Tan, told him of Tien Kuang's death and what he had said. The prince bowed twice and knelt down, advancing on his knees as he shed tears. "I warned Master Tien not to speak to ensure the success of a great enterprise," he said after a long silence. "I did not mean him to die to prove his discretion."

After Ching Ko had taken his seat the prince moved off his mat, bowed his head to the floor and said, "Not knowing my unworthiness, sir, Master Tien asked you here so that I could consult you. This shows that Heaven has pity on our state and will not abandon us. Now Chin is insatiable in its greed and will not rest satisfied until it has seized all the lands in the world and made all princes its subjects. It has already captured the king of Hann, annexed his kingdom and raised troops to attack Chu in the south and threaten Chao in the north. Wang Chien is leading several hundred thousand men against Chang and Yeh, while Li Hsin is advancing from Taiyuan and Yunchung. Chao cannot resist Chin but must become its vassal. Once that happens, disaster will overtake Yen.

"Ours is a small, weak state, exhausted by constant warfare, so that even if we mobilize the whole country we cannot hold Chin at bay; and the other states are too cowed to ally with us against our common enemy. This, then, is my plan: if we can find a man of outstanding courage to go as our envoy to Chin and offer a large enough bait, that greedy king is sure to rise to it. If he can be forced to return all the land he has seized, in the way Tsao Mo forced Duke Huan of Chi, well and good. If not, he can be stabbed to death. Then with generals commanding armies outside their borders and trouble at home, the ruler of Chin and his subjects will fall out; and we can seize this opportunity to form an alliance of states which will certainly defeat Chin. This is the great desire of my heart, but I do not know to whom to entrust this task. I hope you will consider my plan."

Ching Ko was silent for a time.

"Our kingdom depends upon this," he said at last. "But my ability is of the meanest. I fear I am not fit for such a mission."

But when the prince came up to him and bowed, begging him not to refuse, Ching Ko accepted. Then Prince Tan honoured him as a high minister and lodged him in a fine mansion. He called on Ching Ko every day and presented him with delicacies, precious objects, carriages and beautiful girls, to satisfy his every wish and give him pleasure. This state of affairs went on for quite a while, yet Ching Ko made no move to leave for Chin. Then General Wang Chien of Chin defeated Chao, captured the king of Chao, annexed the whole state, and marched north to occupy all the land up to Yen's southern border. Prince Tan was thoroughly alarmed.

"The army of Chin may cross the River Yi any day now," he told Ching Ko. "Then I shall no longer be able to entertain you, much as I would like to."

"I was thinking of going to see you about this, but now you have mentioned it first," replied Ching Ko. "Unless I take some proof of goodwill, the king of Chin will not let me approach him. He has offered a thousand catties of gold and a fief of ten thousand families for the capture of General Fan. If I can have General Fan's head and the map of Tukang,* the king will welcome me and I shall be able to carry out your plan."

"General Fan came to me to take refuge," said Prince Tan. "I do not want to go counter to your wishes, but would like you to consider the matter again."

Knowing that the prince was too soft-hearted to take his advice, Ching Ko went privately to Fan Yu-chi.

"The king of Chin has abused you cruelly," he said. "Your parents and kinsmen have been put to the sword, and now I hear a reward of a thousand catties of gold and a fief of ten thousand families has been offered for your head. What do you mean to do?"

General Fan gazed up at the sky and sighed, then shed tears.

"The thought of this makes me burn with hatred to the very marrow of my bones!" he cried. "But I cannot think of any way to take vengeance."

"I have a plan to avert danger from Yen and to avenge you," said Ching Ko. "Would you care to hear it?"

General Fan stepped forward.

"Tell me what it is," he begged.

"If I could have your head to present to the king of Chin,

---

* A rich district in Yen.

he would receive me with pleasure; then with my left hand I should seize his sleeve, and with my right hand stab him through the heart. You would be avenged and our prince would pay off an old score. Are you willing to help me?"

General Fan bared one arm and advanced clasping his wrists.

"This is the chance for which I have been waiting day and night, gnashing my teeth and burning with rage!" he cried. "Now you have pointed out the way."

Thereupon he killed himself.

When the prince knew of this, he hurried there to lament bitterly over the corpse; then, since there was nothing he could do, he had Fan's head placed in a sealed casket. He had been searching for a fine dagger and found one made by Hsu Fu-jen of Chao, which cost a hundred pieces of gold. Now he made his artisans temper this dagger in poison, and upon testing it found that if it drew blood — be it only a drop sufficient to stain a thread — the result was instant death. Then Prince Tan helped Ching Ko to prepare for his journey. In Yen there lived a bold youth of thirteen named Chin Wu-yang, a killer from whose angry glance everyone shrank. He was chosen as Ching Ko's assistant.

But Ching Ko was waiting for another assistant of his own choice who lived some distance away, and while making arrangements for this man to come he delayed his departure. Then Prince Tan lost patience, suspecting that Ching Ko had repented of his promise.

"Time is running out," he said. "Do you want to change your mind? Maybe I had better send Chin Wu-yang first?"

"Why send a boy to certain death?" roared Ching Ko in a rage. "I am going to powerful Chin armed only with a dagger. I was waiting for a friend to go with me on this desperate mission. But if you are so impatient, I will leave now."

So he set out. The prince and those who knew of the plan, dressed in white mourning clothes, escorted him to the River Yi where they sacrificed to the god of the roads before he began his journey. Kao Chien-li played the guitar and Ching

Ko sang a plaintive air which moved all who heard it to tears. Then he stepped forward and chanted:

> The wind is wailing, cold the River Yi,
> And a hero sets forth, never to return.

After this he sang a stirrring, martial air, which made their eyes bulge with anger and their hair stand on end. Then he mounted his carriage and drove off without further ado.

Upon reaching Chin, Ching Ko bribed the king's favourite, the chamberlain Meng Chia, with money and gifts worth a thousand pieces of gold. And Meng Chia explained his mission to the king.

"The king of Yen trembles before your might and dares not oppose your troops," he said. "He begs to become your subject like the other princes and send tribute like your provinces, in order to continue his ancestral sacrifices. He was afraid to come in person to announce this, but he has cut off Fan Yu-chi's head to present to you in a sealed casket with the map of Tukang in Yen. The envoy who brought these here is awaiting Your Majesty's orders."

Very pleased at this, the king of Chin prepared a grand reception in Hsienyang Palace to receive the envoy from Yen. Ching Ko entered first with the sealed casket containing Fan Yu-chi's head, followed by Chin Wu-yang with the map case. When they reached the steps to the dais, the ministers were surprised to see Chin Wu-yang change colour and tremble; but Ching Ko stepped forward with a laugh to apologize, saying, "He is a rough country fellow from the barbarous north who is overawed by his first sight of Your Majesty. Please excuse him so that we can carry out our mission."

The king bade Ching Ko hand him the map which Chin Wu-yang was holding, and he unrolled it to reveal the dagger. Ching Ko seized the king's sleeve with his left hand, snatching up the dagger to stab him with his right. Before he could strike, however, the king leapt up in alarm and his sleeve tore off. He tried to draw his long sword but it stuck in the scabbard, and in his panic he could not pull it out. The king fled behind a pillar with Ching Ko in hot pursuit, while the ministers, taken by surprise, were thrown into confusion.

According to the law of Chin, ministers were forbidden to bear arms in the audience hall and the royal guards in the courtyard could not enter without orders from their sovereign; but the king in his panic did not call for them. So while Ching Ko pursued the king, the panic-stricken ministers, having no weapons, tried to ward him off with their bare hands; and the king's physician, Hsia Wu-chu, used his bag of herbs to beat the assassin off. Too terrified to know what to do, the king was running round the pillar when some attendants shouted:

"Put the sword over your shoulder, Your Majesty!"

He did so and, drawing his sword, struck Ching Ko a blow that shattered his left leg. Unable to move, Ching Ko hurled his dagger at the king, but missed him and hit the bronze pillar instead. The king struck again and again, inflicting eight wounds. Then, knowing that all was up with him, Ching Ko squatted against the pillar with a scornful smile.

"I failed through trying to take you alive," he swore. "And because I was determined to force you to agree to our prince's demands!"

At that, attendants ran forward and finished him off. The king brooded in silence for a while, then rewarded those who had been of service and punished others. His physician, Hsia Wu-chu, received two hundred pieces of gold for his loyalty.

And now the king of Chin, roused to fury, dispatched more troops to the east and ordered Wang Chien to advance from Chao upon Yen. After ten months Chi, the capital of Yen, fell; and King Hsi of Yen and Prince Tan withdrew eastwards with their best troops to Liaotung. General Li Hsin of Chin was pressing them hard when King Chia of Tai* wrote to the king of Yen, "Chin is pursuing you hotly because of Prince Tan. If you present the prince's head to the king of Chin, he

---

* Tai was a small state annexed by Chao but reinstated after the annexation of Chao by Chin.

will surely make terms with you and your state sacrifices will not be ended."

Li Hsin pursued Prince Tan to the River Yen, and the king of Yen had the prince killed by an assassin and presented his head to Chin; but Chin continued to attack. Five years later Yen was finally destroyed and King Hsi taken prisoner. By the following year the king of Chin had conquered all the states and styled himself emperor, but he did not cease to persecute the friends of Prince Tan and Ching Ko, all of whom went into hiding.

Kao Chien-li changed his name and became a waiter, living incognito in Sungtzu. He worked hard for his master until one day, hearing a guitar played in the hall, he could not tear himself away but lingered to comment on the music. The other servants reported this to their master.

"That fellow understands music," they told him. "He is secretly commenting on what is good and bad in the playing."

Then his master ordered him to come forward to strum the guitar, and all the guests marvelled at his skill and offered him wine. Kao Chien-li decided that he had been in hiding long enough and could not continue indefinitely in this way, so he fetched his guitar and good clothes from his baggage, and when he reappeared richly dressed all the guests bowed to him in amazement. They made him sit in the seat of honour to play the guitar and sing, and were moved to tears before they left.

Subsequently all the chief citizens of Sungtzu invited him to their houses, and news of this reached the First Emperor of Chin, who summoned him to court. Someone recognizing him turned informer; but the emperor thought so highly of his playing that instead of killing him he put out his eyes and made him perform at court. And the emperor enjoyed his music so much that little by little he let the blind man approach him. Then Kao Chien-li weighted his guitar with lead and when he was close enough raised it to strike, but he missed his enemy. He was immediately put to death, and never again did the emperor allow followers of the former princes to approach him.

When Lu Kou-chien heard of Ching Ko's attempt on the king of Chin, he said to his friends, "What a pity he did not make a better study of swordsmanship, and that I failed to recognize his greatness! After I shouted at him that day, he must have thought me beneath contempt."

The Grand Historian comments: In the popular story about Ching Ko, the statements about grain falling from heaven and horses growing horns are simply wild talk. Another tradition, which maintains that Ching Ko succeeded in wounding the king of Chin, is equally untrue. Kungsun Chi-kung and the scholar Tung, who were friends at one time with the king of Chin's physician Hsia Wu-chu, knew what happened and I have reported what they told me.

Of the five men from Tsao Mo to Ching Ko, some succeeded in their mission while others failed; but all were equally determined and loyal to their cause. Not for nothing have their names been known to later generations.

THE JESTERS

Confucius said, "All Six Arts help to govern. The *Book of Rites* helps to regulate men, the *Book of Music* brings about harmony, the *Book of Documents* records incidents, the *Book of Songs* expresses emotions, the *Book of Change* reveals supernatural influence, and the *Spring and Autumn Annals* shows what is right."

The Grand Historian comments: How infinitely great are the ways of Heaven! Even words spoken in jest may hit on the truth and serve to settle disputes.

Chunyu Kun was a man of Chi who lived with his wife's family. He was less than five feet tall. Thanks to his wit and ready tongue he was sent several times as an envoy to other states and was never worsted in argument.

King Wei of Chi liked riddles and was so given up to pleasure that he often spent the whole night drinking, neglecting the government in his carousals and entrusting affairs of state to his ministers. Disorder reigned in the government offices and the land was invaded by other states with the result that Chi was in imminent danger of destruction. Yet none of his followers dared to remonstrate.

Then Chunyu Kun asked him a riddle. "A great bird has alighted in our royal court, but for three years has neither spread its wings nor cried out. Can you guess what bird this is?"

"The bird may not have flown yet," replied the king. "Once it does, it will soar to the sky. It may not have cried out yet, but once it does it will startle everyone."

Then he summoned his seventy-two magistrates to court, rewarded one, punished another, and led out his army. The other states were alarmed and returned to Chi the land they had overrun. King Wei ruled in state for thirty-six years, as has been related in the life of Tien Wan.

In the eighth year of King Wei,* Chu sent a great force against Chi. The king gave Chunyu Kun a hundred catties of gold and ten four-horse carriages, bidding him go to Chao to ask for aid. Chunyu Kun threw back his head and laughed so hard that the cord of his hat snapped.

"Do you think it too little, sir?" demanded the king.

"How dare I!" was the reply.

"Then why are you laughing?"

"As I came here today from the east," answered Chunyu Kun, "I saw on the road a man praying for a good harvest and offering one pig's trotter and one cup of wine. 'May the crops from the highland fill whole crates!' he prayed. 'May the crops from the lowland fill whole carts! May grain harvested in abundance fill my house!' He offered so little but expected so much in return. That is why I laughed."

Then King Wei gave him one thousand *yi* of gold, ten pairs of white jade discs and a hundred four-horse carriages. Chunyu Kun left and made his way to Chao, whose king provided him with a hundred thousand picked troops and a thousand war-chariots. Once the army of Chu knew this, it withdrew by night.

King Wei in high delight summoned Chunyu Kun to a feast in his inner palace and offered him wine.

"How much does it take to make you drunk?" he asked.

"Anything from one to ten measures."

"If one measure makes you drunk, how can you drink ten? Kindly explain!"

"When I am offered wine in Your Majesty's presence, with the law officer beside me and the censor behind, I bow and drink in fear and trembling and less than one measure makes me drunk," said Chunyu Kun. "When my family entertains respected guests and I kneel with rolled-up sleeves to offer

---

* 371 B.C.

404

wine, if they give me the dregs to drink their health and keep me jumping up all the time, less than two measures makes me drunk.

"When I run into some friend or acquaintance whom I haven't seen for years and we gossip cheerfully over old times together, and are able to say just what we think, I can take five or six measures before getting drunk.

"In country fairs where both sexes sit together and the wine goes round and round, we play a game of checkers or cottabus, choosing our own partners, and there is no taboo on holding hands or looking into each other's eyes, while the women's earrings and hairpins drop right and left. . . . Why then, secretly rejoicing, I can drink eight measures and be barely one-third tipsy.

"At dusk towards the end of a feast we cuddle together mixing our drinks, men and women sharing one mat, shoes and slippers intermingled, cups and dishes everywhere. Then as the candles in the hall flicker out, the other guests are seen off but my hostess keeps me, and as her silk blouse parts I inhale her fragrance! In that instant there is such joy in my heart that I can drink ten measures. As the old saying goes, 'Too much wine leads to licence and too much joy to sorrow.' This is true of everything." This talk of the ill effects of all excess was a joking form of remonstrance.

"You are right," said the king and gave up his nightly drinking. He put Chunyu Kun in charge of entertaining envoys from other states, and the jester was invited to all feasts given by members of the royal clan.

More than a hundred years after this lived another jester of Chu named Meng who started life as a musician. Six feet tall, with a ready tongue, he often made the king see reason by means of jests.

King Chuang of Chu had a favourite horse which he caparisoned in rich brocade, housed in magnificent quarters with a couch to sleep on and fed upon dried jujubes. When the horse grew too fat and died, the king ordered his ministers to mourn for it and decided to have it buried in a double coffin with all the rites befitting a high official. So many of his courtiers advised against this that the king decreed, "The next man to remonstrate on the subject of the horse will be put to death."

When word of this reached Meng, he went to the palace and raising his eyes to heaven wept bitterly. The king in astonishment asked him the reason.

"That horse was Your Majesty's favourite," said Meng. "A great state like Chu can surely meet all your wishes. Burial with the rites befitting a high official is too shabby. Why don't you bury it with royal rites?"

"What do you mean?" asked King Chuang.

"I suggest that the coffin be carved of jade and the outer coffin made of the finest catalpa ornamented with cedar, camphor and other precious wood. Send men at arms to build the tomb while the old and weak carry earth; and let envoys from Chi and Chao lead the funeral cortège with envoys of Hann and Wei following behind. Build a temple, sacrifice oxen, and put ten thousand households in charge of the upkeep of the mausoleum. Then the other states, hearing of this, will know that Your Majesty thinks little of men but very highly of horses."

"How wrong I have been!" exclaimed the king. "What can I do to remedy matters?"

"Why not bury it like other livestock?" suggested Meng. "Use the hearth and a bronze cauldron as its double coffin, adding ginger, jujubes and spices. Offer a sacrifice of rice, enfold it in flames and bury it in men's bellies!"

Then the king gave the horse to his cook and had the matter hushed up.

Sunshu Ao, prime minister of Chu, knew Meng's ability and respected him. When he lay dying he told his son, "After my death you will be poor. But go to Meng and tell him you are my son."

A few years later, when the young man was reduced by poverty to carrying firewood, he met Meng and said to him,

"I am Sunshu Ao's son. My father told me on his deathbed to come to you if ever I was in difficulties."

"Stay in this neighbourhood," was Meng's advice. He practised wearing Sunshu Ao's clothes and imitating his talk and behaviour. In a year or so, the resemblance was so close that neither the king nor his courtiers would be able to tell the difference. One day then, when the king was giving a feast, Meng entered to offer a toast. The king was amazed, imagining that this was Sunshu Ao returned to life. He wanted to appoint him as prime minister, but Meng said, "Let me go and talk it over with my wife. I shall give you my answer three days from now." To this the king agreed.

Three days later Meng came back.

"Well, what does your wife say?" asked the king.

"My wife advises me not to accept. It is no good being prime minister of Chu, she says. Just look at Sunshu Ao! He worked loyally and honestly to make Chu a powerful state, yet now that he is dead his son is so poor that he owns not an inch of land. He is reduced to carrying firewood for a living. Suicide is preferable to such a fate."

Then he chanted:

> It is rough work farming the hills,
> Hard to get food.
> One who becomes an official may grasp at wealth,
> And, dead to shame, leave his family well-off;
> Or for taking bribes and breaking the law
> He may be put to death and his clan wiped out.
> Do not be a rapacious official!
> What then of a good official
> Who abides by the law, does his duty,
> And makes no wrong move all his life?
> His case is no better.
> For Sunshu Ao was honest to the end,
> But his wife and son are left destitute,
> Forced to subsist by carrying firewood.
> Why follow his example?

Then King Chuang, having thanked Meng, summoned Sunshu Ao's son and enfeoffed him with four hundred households in Chinchiu, so that he might sacrifice to his ancestors. And his line continued for ten generations. This was surely a timely use of wit!

More than two hundred years later there was Chan of the Chin Dynasty. Chan was a dwarf, who made jokes which contained profound truths. Once the First Emperor of Chin held a feast while it was raining, and the guards by the steps were all soaked and shivering with cold.

Chan was sorry for them and asked, "Would you like a rest?"

"We certainly would!" they replied.

"All right. When I call you, answer quickly."

Then a toast was offered to the emperor, and during the cheering Chan walked to the balustrade. He called down to the guards, who promptly responded.

"You may be tall, but what good does that do you?" he asked. "You have to stand in the rain. I may be short, but I can enjoy myself here." Upon that, the emperor ordered the guards to serve in two shifts.

When the First Emperor of Chin wanted to extend his imperial park to the Hanku Pass in the east and to Yung and Chentsang in the west, Chan commented, "A good idea! And fill it with animals. If invaders come from the east, the stags can gore them." Thereupon the emperor abandoned his plan.

When the Second Emperor came to the throne, he decided to lacquer the walls of his capital. "Splendid!" said Chan. "If you had not ordered this, I should have proposed it. It may cost the people dear, but what a fine thing it will be! No invaders will be able to climb such smooth, handsome walls. And lacquering is easy, too. The only difficulty will be building a shelter large enough to dry it." Then the emperor laughed and gave up the idea.

Soon afterwards the Second Emperor was killed and Chan went over to Han. A few years later he died.

The Grand Historian comments: When Chunyu Kun leaned back and laughed, King Wei of Chi became a mighty monarch. When Meng shook his head and sang, a firewood vender was enfeoffed. When Chan called down from the balustrade, the guard was reduced by half. Isn't that splendid!

THE MONEY-MAKERS

Lao Tzu said, "When perfect government prevailed, although neighbouring states within sight of each other could hear the crowing of each other's cocks and the barking of each other's dogs, the people of each enjoyed their own food, admired their own clothing, were content with their ways and happy in their work, and would grow old and die without having any dealings with each other." Yet if we tried to set the world right today by stopping up the eyes and ears of the people, it would prove well-nigh impossible.

The Grand Historian comments: What it was like before the time of Shen Nung* I do not know, but, judging by the *Book of Songs* and *Book of Documents*, ever since the time of Emperor Shun and the Hsia Dynasty men have desired to feast their eyes on beautiful women, their ears on music; their mouths have delighted in meat, their bodies in pleasure and comfort, and their hearts in power and glory. Even if you went from door to door reasoning with them, such deep-rooted habits as these could never be changed. The best thing, then, is to let matters take their own course; the next is to lead people through benefiting them; the next to use exhortations; the next, restrictions; and the worst way of all is to fight against these instincts.

Roughly speaking, the region west of the mountains has an abundance of timber, bamboo, grain, mulberry, hemp, yak hide and jade; the region east of the mountains is rich in fish, salt, lacquer, silk, musicians and beautiful women. South of the Yangtse are catalpa, cedars, ginger, cassia, gold, tin, lead, cinnabar, rhinoceros horns, tortoise shell, pearls, ivory and hides;

---

* Legendary emperor of ancient China.

north of Lungmen and Chiehshih are horses, cattle, sheep, felt, furs, tendons and horns in plenty. As for copper and iron, the mountains stretching thousands of *li* are scattered with mines. This is the general outline. All these commodities are valued by the people of China, who use them for food and clothing, to supply the living and to bury the dead.

There must be farmers to produce food, men to extract the wealth of mountains and marshes, artisans to process these things and merchants to circulate them. There is no need to wait for government orders: each man will play his part, doing his best to get what he desires. So cheap goods will go where they fetch more, while expensive goods will make men search for cheap ones. When all work willingly at their trades, just as water flows ceaselessly downhill day and night, things will appear unsought and people will produce them without being asked. For clearly this accords with the Way and is in keeping with nature.

The *Book of Chou* says, "Without farmers, food will be scarce; without artisans, goods will be scarce; without merchants, the three precious things will disappear; without men to open up the mountains and marshes, there will be a shortage of wealth." Here we have the four sources of men's food and clothing. When these sources are large there is prosperity; when small, there is scarcity. Above, they enrich a state; below, they enrich a family. The laws governing poverty and wealth are immutable, and the shrewd have plenty while the stupid go short.

When the Patriarch Lu Shang was given Yingchiu as his fief, the land was swampy and brackish and sparsely inhabited; but he encouraged the women to work, developed skilled occupations and opened up trade in fish and salt, so that men and goods poured in from every side. Soon the state of Chi was supplying the whole world with caps, belts, clothes and shoes, and the states between the Eastern Sea and Mount Tai paid respectful homage to it.

Later, Chi's power declined, but Kuan Chung restored it by setting up a new currency and nine treasuries. As a result,

Duke Huan of Chi became an overlord and nine times summoned the other feudal lords to conferences, bringing order to the whole empire. Kuan Chung was rewarded with the fief of Sankuei, and although his rank was only that of a servant's servant, he amassed greater wealth than the princes of other states. So Chi remained rich and powerful through the reigns of King Wei and King Hsuan.

Thus it is said, "When the granaries are full, men learn propriety. When food and clothing are enough, men have a sense of honour and shame. Ceremony is born of sufficiency and disappears in time of want." That is why when a gentleman is rich he delights in cultivating virtue, but when an inferior man is rich he will display his power. Just as fish multiply in deep lakes and wild beasts flock to deep mountains, humanity and justice follow riches. A wealthy man's influence is greater while he has power, but once he loses power his protégés have nowhere to go and there is an end of pleasure. This is even more true of the barbarians.

As the proverb justly says, "A man with a thousand pieces of gold will not die in the market-place." So it is said,

> How quickly after gain
>   The whole world races!
> How madly after gain
>   The whole world chases!

Even the king of a land with a thousand chariots, a marquis with a fief of ten thousand households, or a lord with a hundred households dreads poverty, much more so, then, the common citizens on the state register.

When King Kou-chien of Yueh was in desperate straits on Mount Kuaichi, he followed the advice of Fan Li and Chi Jan. Chi Jan said, "One who knows how to compete prepares in advance; one who understands seasonal needs knows commodities; and a grasp of these two things enables him to understand the whole market. Each year is dominated by an element. Metal means a good harvest, water a flood, wood a

412

crop failure, and fire a drought. In time of drought, invest in boats; in time of flood, invest in carriages. This is the principle to follow. Every six years there will be a good harvest, every six years a drought, every twelve years a great famine. When the price of grain is too low, the farmers suffer; when it is too high, the merchants and artisans suffer. When the merchants and artisans suffer, wealth is not forthcoming; when the farmers suffer, they stop weeding the fields. If the price of grain is neither too high nor too low, farmers and merchants and artisans will all profit. The right way to govern is to keep the price of grain steady so that there is no lack of goods and no shortage of taxes.

"The way to accumulate wealth is to produce goods and not let money stay idle. Let there be an exchange of goods. Do not store up perishable commodities, or go in for those which are costly. By noting surpluses and shortages, you can tell what will be expensive and what cheap. When prices rise too high, they must fall again; when prices fall too low, they will rise again. When things are expensive, sell them off as if they were dirt, and buy up cheap goods as though they were jewels. Money should circulate like flowing water."

After King Kou-chien had observed these rules for ten years, his kingdom was so rich and his soldiers so well rewarded that they charged against arrows and stones like thirsty men rushing to drink. Then he took his revenge on the powerful state of Wu, demonstrated the might of his arms throughout the land and became one of the Five Overlords.

After the disgrace of Kuaichi was wiped out, Fan Li sighed and said, "By using five of Chi Jan's seven precepts, Yueh gained its ends. They have been applied in our state, and now I shall try them out for the benefit of my own family."

He sailed in a small boat down rivers and across lakes and, having changed his name, went to Chi, where he was known as Chih-yi Tzu-pi, the Old Wine-skin. Then he went to Tao, where he was known as Lord Chu.

Observing that Tao, at the hub of the realm, was a centre of communications and of barter, he acquired land property there, stored up commodities, and made a profit by biding his time without much exertion. He was a good manager, a sound judge of men, able to take advantage of the times. Three times in nineteen years he accumulated a thousand pieces of gold, and twice divided these between distant relatives and those in want. He was, in fact, a rich philanthropist. Later, when he grew old and infirm, he turned over his affairs to his sons and grandsons, who carried on and developed his business until they had millions. Thus Lord Chu of Tao became a byword for a rich man.

Tzu-kung, after studying with Confucius, went to hold office in Uei. He made money by buying cheap and selling dear in the region of Tsao and Lu. Of the seventy disciples of Confucius, he was the richest. While Yuan Hsien had not even husks enough to fill his belly and lived hidden in a wretched lane, Tzu-kung travelled in a carriage drawn by four horses with an escort of riders bearing rolls of silk to present to the rulers of states. And wherever he went, the ruler received him as an equal. Indeed, it was thanks to Tzu-kung that the fame of Confucius spread — a clear case of power increasing reputation.

Pai Kuei, a native of Chou, lived during the time of Marquis Wen of Wei, when Li Ke was utilizing the land to the full. Pai Kuei, however, enjoyed looking out for seasonal changes. What others spurned he took, what others sought he supplied. At harvest time he bought in grain and sold silk and lacquer, when cocoons came on the market he bought in raw silk and sold grain.

When the Primal Female Principle is in the sign of Cancer there will be a good harvest, but a bad one the following year. When it is in the sign of Libra there will be a drought, but a good harvest the next year. When it is in the sign of Capricorn, a good harvest will be followed by a failure the next year. When it is in the sign of Aries, there will be a serious drought followed by a good crop but also a flood the next year. When it returns to the sign of Cancer, the yearly store of grain will be doubled.

When he wanted more money, Pai Kuei bought inferior grain; when he wanted to increase his stock, he bought good seeds. He spent little on food and drink, curbing his appetite and sharing the hardships and pleasures of his slaves, but seizing on any chance of gain as fiercely as some wild beast or bird of prey.

He said, "I do business in the same way that Yi Yin and Lu Shang planned their policies, Sun Tzu and Wu Chi made war, and Lord Shang applied the law. If men lack the intelligence to change with the times, the courage to make quick decisions, the magnanimity to give things away and the strength to hold what they have, though they want to learn my art I will not teach them."

So all the world knows Pai Kuei as the father of business management. He set a standard for those who wanted to learn from him, and accepted only those who came up to this standard. He did not teach everyone.

Yi Tun prospered because of his salt ponds and Kuo Tsung of Hantan made a fortune in iron smelting. Both were as wealthy as any prince.

Then there was Luo of Wuchih who raised livestock. When his herd had multiplied, he sold it to buy rare objects and coloured silk as presents for the king of the western tribes, who repaid him tenfold, giving him so many herds that he reckoned his cattle and horses by the valleyful. The First Emperor of Chin made him equal in status to a prince and allowed him to pay homage at court in spring and autumn with the ministers.

There was also the widow named Ching in the region of Pa and Shu, whose family owned a cinnabar mine and had monopolized the profit for several generations, so that her wealth was past counting. Although only a widow, she knew how to hold on to her property and used her wealth to protect herself so that nobody could molest her. The First Emperor of Chin treated her as a protégée and built the Tower of Nu-huai-ching to honour her chastity.

Luo was only a rustic herdsman and Ching a widow in a

poor district, yet both were treated with as much respect as the rulers of a state with ten thousand chariots, while their fame spread throughout the empire. Was this not on account of their wealth?

After the rise of the Han Dynasty, the whole country was united, passes and bridges were opened, and restrictions on the exploitation of mountains and marshes were abolished. The result was that rich traders and influential merchants travelled all over the empire and goods of every kind circulated wherever men desired, while prominent citizens, nobles and powerful clans were moved to the capital.

Within the Hanku Pass, from the Chien and Yung Rivers east to the Yellow River and Mount Huashan, are a thousand *li* of rich and fertile fields, recognized as excellent land since the times of Emperor Shun and the Hsia Dynasty. Kung Liu moved to Pin, Tai-wang and Wang-chi resided in Chi, King Wen built the city of Feng and King Wu ruled from Hao. Thus the people of that region still show traces of the influence of the former kings. They are fond of agriculture, grow the five crops, value their land, and oppose evil practices.

Later, Duke Wen, Duke Hsiao and Duke Mu of Chin had their capital at Yung, which became a centre of commerce for all the products of Lung and Shu. When Duke Hsien and Duke Hsiao moved the capital to Yoyi, which was safe from the tribesmen of the north and had communications with Han, Wei and Chao, this too became a great centre of commerce. Since Duke Wu and King Chao had their capital at Hsienyang, while the Han Dynasty capital with its mausoleums was at Changan, goods from all directions converged here. Because this region is small and populous, the people here are more ingenious and make a living by secondary occupations.

To the south are Pa and Shu, another fertile region, rich in safflower, ginger, cinnabar, stone, copper, iron and utensils of bamboo and wood. In the south Pa and Shu control Tien and Po, the latter known for its slaves. To their west lie Chiung and Tse, the latter noted for its horses and yaks. Pa and Shu have natural barriers on four sides, but plank roads extend a thousand *li* through the mountains, communicating with all parts of the country, while they all meet at the Paoyeh Defile where men can barter surplus goods for what they lack.

The provinces of Tienshui, Lunghsi, Peiti and Shangchun follow the same customs as the area within the Passes; but with the resources of the Chiang tribesmen in the west and the cattle of the Jung and Ti tribes in the north, these provinces have more herds than any other part of the empire. This region is mountainous and inaccessible, in communication with the capital only.

Thus the area within the Pass makes up one-third of the territory of the empire, with three-tenths of the population; yet its wealth amounts to three-fifths of the whole.

In the old days, Emperor Yao had his capital east of the Yellow River; the Shang capital was north of the river bend; and the Chou capital was south of the Yellow River. These three parts of the empire are like the three feet of a tripod; many kings have established states and capitals there which lasted for centuries. Since these small regions have large populations and the nobles have congregated there, the people are petty-minded, thrifty and worldly.

Yang and Pingyang trade with Chin and Ti in the west and with Chung and Tai in the north, further north than Shih. They lie next to the Huns, who often attack them. So the people here are bold, stubborn, adventurous and unruly, not given to farming or trading. Because these districts are so close to the northern barbarians, troops have often been sent there and goods from the interior have been taken there in large quantities. The strain is very mixed, and even before Tsin was divided into three parts the people were known for their boldness. King Wu-ling of Chao encouraged this, and the local customs today still smack of those times. The merchants of Yang and Pingyang do business with them and can get what they want from them.

Wen and Chih trade with Shangtang in the west and with Chao and Chungshan in the north. Chungshan has poor soil and a large population. Some of the inhabitants of Shachiu are descended from families already there in the time of wicked King Chow.* The people are hot-tempered and live by their wits. Bands of able-bodied men roister together or sing melancholy songs, setting out openly to kill and steal, or secretly robbing graves and minting counterfeit money. They have many fine possessions and can sing and mime. The women play clear-sounding lyres, wear pointed slippers and try to bewitch the rich and noble, in the hope of being taken into the palaces of the noble lords all over the country.

Hantan, between the Chang and the Yellow Rivers, is another important centre, communicating with Yen and Chao in the north, with Cheng and Uei in the south. The customs of Cheng and Uei are like those of Chao, except that their proximity to Liang and Lu makes the people more sedate and circumspect. Since the capital of Uei was moved from Puyang to Yehwang, the men there are bold and adventurous in the tradition of Uei.

Yen, between Pohai and Chiehshih, is a major centre communicating with Chi and Chao in the south and bordering on the Huns in the northeast. The vast, thinly populated highlands between Shangku and Liaotung are often raided by tribesmen. The customs resemble those of Chao and Tai. The people are bold and reckless. Fish, salt, jujubes and chestnuts abound here. On the north the region adjoins the Wuhuan and Fuyu tribes; on the east it does a profitable trade with Huimo, Chaohsien and Chenpan.

Loyang does business in the east with Chi and Lu, in the south with Liang and Chu.

South of Mount Tai is Lu, and north is Chi. Chi, bounded by mountains and the sea, has fertile fields stretching a thousand *li*, where mulberries and hemp thrive. The people have an abundance of coloured silk, cloth, plain silk, fish and salt.

Lintzu is an important centre between the sea and Mount Tai. The local people are easy-going, open-minded and intelligent, fond of discussion, stable and not easily shaken. They

---

* Last king of the Shang Dynasty.

show cowardice if fighting in a body but courage in single combat, and so there are many brigands. Theirs are the ways of a great kingdom. Here all five categories of men are to be found.

Tsou and Lu on the banks of the rivers Chu and Szu have kept up the tradition of the duke of Chou. The people favour the Confucian school, have an elaborate code of etiquette, and are therefore punctilious in their behaviour. Mulberries and hemp are widely cultivated, but they have no forests or marshes. Land is scarce and the population dense. Frugal, cautious and afraid of trouble, the people steer clear of evil. Since the decline of their state they have taken to trading and become more grasping than the men of Chou.

East of Hungkou and extending to Chuyeh north of the Mang and Tang Mountains lie the regions of Liang and Sung. Tao and Suiyang are important centres here. In ancient times, Emperor Yao travelled to Chengyang, Emperor Shun fished at Leitse and King Tang stayed at Po; hence the tradition of these former rulers is maintained. The people are generous, gentlemen are numerous, and farming is their favourite occupation. Although they lack rich mountains and rivers, the people accumulate wealth by spending little on their food and clothing.

Three different traditions prevail in Yueh and Chu. From the River Huai north to Pei, Chen, Junan and Nanchun, is the western Chu region. Its people are impetuous and easily moved to anger. The land is poor with little store of wealth. Chiangling, on the site of the old Chu capital Ying, communicates with Wu and Pa in the west while to its east are the rich Yunmeng marshes. Chen, between Chu and Hsia, trades in fish and salt, and most of its people are merchants. The men of Hsu, Tung and Chiulu are honest and keep their word.

From Pengcheng east to Tunghai, Wu and Kuangling is the region of eastern Chu with customs similar to those of Hsu and Tung. The people north of Chü and Tseng follow the customs of Chi. South of the River Che the customs resemble those of ancient Yueh. Ever since King Ho-lu, Lord Chunshen

and Prince Pi of Wu invited wandering scholars from all parts
to Wu, this region with salt from the sea in the east, the
copper mines of Mount Chang and the advantages of three
rivers and five lakes, has become an important centre in the
east Yangtse Valley.

Southern Chu comprises Hengshan, Chiuchiang, Chiangnan,
Yuchang and Changsha, and the customs are similar to those
of western Chu. Shouchun, where the Chu capital was moved
from Ying, is also an important centre. The district of Hofei
has waterways in the south and north and is a centre for the
shipping of hides and leather, salted fish and timber. It shares
some of the customs of Minchung and Yuyueh. The men of
southern Chu are eloquent speakers but not too reliable. Chiangnan is low and damp and men die early there, but bamboo
and wood abound. Yuchang produces gold, Changsha tin and
lead. The output is too little, however, to cover the cost of
mining.

From Chiuyi and Tsangwu south to Chan-erh, the customs
are similar to those of Chiangnan, particularly as regards the
people of Yangyueh. Panyu is an important centre with its
pearls, rhinoceros horn, tortoise shell, fruit and cloth.

Yingchuan and Nanyang were the home of the Hsia Dynasty,
and the people are known for their honesty and simplicity,
a relic of the old Hsia tradition. The men of Yingchuan are
honest and law-abiding. Towards the end of the Chin Dynasty
law-breakers were sent to Nanyang, which communicates with
the Wu and Yun Passes and with the Han, Yangtse and Huai
Rivers in the southeast. Wan is another important city. Its
customs are mixed. The people are enterprising and among
them are many merchants and gallant men; there are direct
communications with Yingchuan. The people of this district
have always been known as men of Hsia.

That is a general picture of the distribution of products and
the local customs in different parts of the empire. The people
east of the mountains use salt extracted from the sea, those
west of the mountains use rock salt, while south of the Five

Mountain Ranges and north of the desert they produce some salt as well.

To sum up, the extensive region of Chu and Yueh is sparsely inhabited. The people eat rice and fish, prepare the land for ploughing by burning, cultivate paddy-fields, and have a sufficiency of fruit, gourds and shellfish so that they need not resort to trade. Since there is an abundance of food and no fear of famine, the people are indolent and easy-going. They do not store up wealth and many of them are poor. As a result, south of the Huai and Yangtse Rivers no one suffers from cold or hunger, but neither are there very wealthy families.

North of the Yi and Szu Rivers, the land is suitable for grain, mulberries, hemp and livestock. The area is not large but densely populated and, owing to the frequency of floods and drought, the people store up provisions. Hence in Chin, Hsia, Liang and Lu attention is paid to agriculture and most of the people are farmers. The same is true of Sanho, Wan and Chen, although the people also engage in trade. The people of Chi and Chao are shrewd and resourceful and live by their wits, while those of Yen and Tai make a living by farming, cattle-breeding and sericulture.

From this one thing becomes clear. For what purpose do able men try to plan ahead in affairs of state, dispute with each other at court, abide by their word and die for their principles? For what purpose do hermits in mountain caves try by every means to win fame? Their aim is wealth and comfort. So honest officials, remaining long at their posts, get rich in the end. Honest merchants, too, become wealthy.

Wealth is something all men desire instinctively without having to be taught. Brave soldiers scale a city wall ahead of their fellows, break through enemy lines, throw back the foe, kill his general, capture his flag and brave arrows, stones, boiling water and flames, all because of the prospect of a rich reward.

Young men from the byways set on passers-by and rob them, murder men and bury their bodies, kidnap people and plunder them, rob graves, coin counterfeit money, become local despots, seize property, carry out personal vendettas and do dark and secret deeds, defying all laws and prohibitions and rushing headlong into danger — they do all this for the sake of money too.

The girls of Chao and Cheng paint their faces, play clear lyres, flutter their long sleeves, mince about in pointed slippers, make eyes at men, flirt, and will gladly go a thousand *li* to find a lover regardless of his age, because they are after wealth and comfort too.

Idle young nobles wear splendid hats and swords and keep carriages and retinues of riders, to flaunt their riches and rank. Some go hunting, shooting or fishing morning and night, braving frost and snow and riding through valleys where wild beasts may spring out at them, so eager are they to get game. Gamblers and those who bet on horses, cock-fights and hounds grow angry or boastful and insist on winning, so reluctant are they to lose their wagers. Men who devote all their skill and energy to medicine, cooking or other arts, do so for the sake of handsome payment. Clerks who juggle with phrases twist the law, fake seals and forge signatures at the risk of decapitation or being sawn asunder, do so because they have been bribed.

In the same way, peasants, artisans, merchants and cattle-breeders seek wealth and an increase of their possessions. Men of any intelligence spare no effort and will stop at nothing to achieve this, never letting slip a chance to make money.

There is a maxim: "Don't go a hundred *li* to sell firewood. Don't go a thousand *li* to deal in grain." If you are to be in a place for one year, sow grain; if for ten years, plant trees; if for a hundred years, rely on virtue — in other words on personal prestige. There are men with no government stipends, no revenue from fiefs, who live as well as if they had these things and are called "nobles without titles". An enfeoffed noble lives off taxes and levies an average of two hundred cash a year from each household. Thus the lord of a thousand households has an annual income of two hundred thousand cash, out of which he has to cover the expenses of his visits to court to pay homage, his gifts to other nobles and his sacrifices.

Common people such as farmers, artisans and merchants, who have ten thousand cash, can get a yearly interest of two thousand. This means that families with a million cash will also have an income of two hundred thousand, enough to buy themselves off conscript service, pay taxes and duties and still get all the fine clothes and food they want.

Thus it is said that a man's income equals that of a marquis with a fief of a thousand households if he has any of the following: pastures with fifty horses or a hundred and sixty-seven oxen, or two hundred and fifty sheep; swamps with two hundred and fifty pigs; ponds stocked with a thousand piculs of fish; hills bearing a thousand timber trees; a thousand jujube trees in Anyi; a thousand chestnut trees in Yen or Chin; a thousand tangerine trees in Shu, Han or Chiangling; a thousand catalpas north of the Huai River, south of Changshan, or between the Yellow and Chi Rivers; a thousand *mou* of lacquer trees in Chen or Hsia; a thousand *mou* of mulberries or hemp in Chi and Lu; a thousand *mou* of bamboos in Weichuan; a thousand *mou* of land producing sixty-four pecks a *mou* in the vicinity of cities with ten thousand households in big provinces; a thousand *mou* of safflower; a thousand plots of ginger or scallion. Such men do not have to go to market or travel to other districts, but can sit at home waiting for the harvest, living as private gentlemen of means.

As for those paupers with old parents and an ailing wife and children who are not ashamed of being unable to sacrifice at the right season or to provide entertainment, food, drink, clothing and bedding, such men have no social standing. That is why, as a general rule, a man with no money works hard, one with a little money uses his wits, and one who is well off seizes every chance to better himself.

A good man should exert himself to make a living without waiting till he is in desperate straits. The best kind of wealth comes from farming, the next best from trade and handicrafts, the worst from evil practices. When, in spite of poverty and lowliness, one who is no hero or gentleman of talent still talks about virtue and justice, he ought to be thoroughly ashamed of himself.

The ordinary citizen will abase himself before one ten times richer than he, fear one a hundred times richer, serve one a thousand times richer, and be the slave of one ten thousand times richer. This is the nature of things.

If a poor man wants to become rich, it is better to be an artisan than a farmer, better to be a merchant than an artisan, better to be a vender than work at embroidery. In other words, trade and handicrafts are the best way for a poor man to make money.

In centres of communications and large cities a man can live like the lord of a thousand chariots if each year he produces a thousand jars of wine, a thousand jars of vinegar or a thousand pots of sauce; if he slaughters a thousand oxen, sheep or pigs; if he sells a thousand *chung** of grain or a thousand cartloads of firewood; if he owns boats ten thousand feet long if set in a line, a thousand logs of timber, ten thousand bamboo poles, a hundred small carriages, a thousand ox-carts, a thousand varnished wood utensils, thirty thousand catties of bronze, a thousand piculs of safflower, plain wooden vessels and iron implements, two hundred horses, two hundred and fifty oxen, two thousand sheep and swine, a hundred slaves, a thousand catties of tendons, horns and cinnabar, thirty thousand catties of silk floss, a thousand bolts of patterned silk, a thousand piculs of coarse cloth, skin or hide, a thousand *tou*** of lacquer, a thousand *ta**** of yeast, salt and salted beans; a thousand catties of large sea fish, a thousand piculs of small fish, thirty thousand catties of salted fish, three thousand piculs of jujubes and chestnuts, a thousand fox or squirrel furs, a thousand piculs of sheep skins, a thousand carpets, or a thousand *chung* of fruit and vegetables; or if he lends out a thousand strings of cash, demanding an interest of thirty per

---

* One *chung* is equal to sixty-four pecks.

** About a peck.

*** One *ta* is equal to 1.6 *tou*.

cent from merchants who are greedy and fifty per cent from those who are scrupulous. This is the general rule. Various other trades which bring in a profit of less than twenty per cent are not worth pursuing.

Now let me speak briefly of how able men in recent times have made fortunes in different parts, so that later generations may profit by their example.

The ancestor of the Chos of Shu came from Chao, where he made a fortune by smelting iron. When Chin conquered Chao, the family was moved away and Cho and his wife as captives had to push a cart to the place assigned to them. Other captives who had little money asked the officers not to send them too far away, and were allowed to settle in Chiameng.

But Cho said, "That is a circumscribed and barren region. I have heard that at the foot of Mount Wen there is fertile land where taros grow so well that no one need ever go hungry; and trade is easy in the local market."

So he asked to be sent far away and was assigned to Linchiung, to his great delight. Then he smelted iron ore from the mountain, contriving to have workers sent there from Tien and Shu. He became so rich that he had a thousand slaves and could live like a lord, hunting and shooting among the fields and lakes.

Cheng Cheng, who was taken captive east of the mountains and forced to resettle, smelted iron too and traded with the people who wear their hair in cone-shaped knots. He became as wealthy as Cho and also lived in Linchiung.

The ancestors of the Kung family of Wan came from Wei where they had made a living by smelting iron. When Chin conquered Wei, the family was moved to Nanyang and carried on iron smelting on a large scale till Kung owned hills and lakes and a retinue of carriages and horses. He travelled through various states making money by trading, but had the name of a gentleman of leisure while he was making fabulous profits, far exceeding those of other tight-fisted merchants. His family came to have thousands of piece of gold, and all

425

the travelling merchants of Nanyang imitated his easy manner.

The men of Lu are frugal and close-fisted, and the Ping family of Tsao was more so than most. Although they made tens of thousands by smelting iron, the whole family from the grandparents to the grandchildren by common accord seized every chance to make money. They engaged in usury as well as trade in all the provinces and principalities. Indeed, it was owing to this family that so many people in Tsou and Lu gave up the pursuit of learning to seek profit.

The men of Chi despise slaves, but Tiao Chien treated his well. And whereas other men mistrusted cunning slaves, he specially looked out for them and set them to trade in fish and salt to make a profit for him. Some of his slaves travelled about in carriages with mounted retainers and made friends with provincial governors and ministers, but Tiao Chien only trusted them the more, with the result that they helped him make tens of millions. Hence the saying, "An official title is not as good as working for Tiao Chien." This was because he let his slaves become rich and powerful while utilizing their abilities to the full.

The men of Chou are canny, and Shih Shih more than most. With a few hundred cartloads of goods, he traded in every single province and principality. Loyang lies at the centre of Chi, Chin, Chu and Chao, and the poor people in the city imitated the rich, priding themselves on making long business trips and passing their houses without time to cross the threshold. By employing such men, Shih Shih succeeded in making seventy million.

The ancestor of the Jen family of Hsuanchu was a granary officer at Tutao. When the Chin empire was overthrown and the chief citizens were scrambling for gold and jade, Jen's was the only family to store up grain. Soon the armies of Chu and Han were locked in combat at Yingyang, the peasants could not farm and the price of a picul of rice rose to ten thousand. Then gold and jade flowed from the others to the Jens, who made a fortune. Most rich men rival each other in extravagance, but the Jens lived simply and frugally, farming and raising cattle. Most farmers and cattle-breeders look out for bargains, but they bought only the best and most valuable. That is why they have remained rich for generations. The elder Jen has a rule that the family must not eat or wear anything not produced from their own fields and pastures, and must not drink wine or eat meat till their business is finished. As a result, they are an example to the whole district, rich and highly regarded by the emperor.

After the extension of the northern frontier, Chiao Yao alone seized the opportunity to acquire a thousand horses, two thousand head of cattle, ten thousand sheep and ten thousand *chung* of grain.

When Wu, Chu and the five other states revolted, the nobles in Changan joined the imperial army and tried to raise money for the expedition. But because their principalities lay east of the Pass and the outcome of the fighting there was uncertain, most of the money-lenders refused to make loans. Only the Wuyen family lent them a thousand pieces of gold at an interest of nine hundred per cent. When three months later the rebellion was crushed, Wuyen received a tenfold return on his money, becoming one of the richest men within the Passes.

Most of the wealthiest merchants within the Passes belong to the Tien family, such as Tien Seh and Tien Lan. The Li family of Weichia and the Tu families of Anling and Tu are also worth millions.

These are some of the most outstanding examples. None of these men had fiefs or government stipends, nor did they make money by evading the law or by sharp practice. They simply acted intelligently and kept up with the times. They made their fortunes in trade and handicrafts but preserved them through agriculture, seized their wealth in war but retained it by peaceful means. There was method in their rise to fortune which is worth studying.

Countless other cases might be cited of men who made money by working hard at farming, cattle-breeding, handicrafts, lumbering or trade, the greatest of them dominating provinces, the next counties, and the lesser ones villages.

Thrift and hard work are the proper way to make a living, yet men always owe their wealth to some special gift. Farming is rough work, yet by it Chin Yang became predominant in his province. Grave-robbing is evil, yet this gave Chu Shu a start in his career. Gambling is bad, yet that is how Huan Fa made his money. Pedding is a low occupation, yet Lo Cheng of Yung became wealthy in this way. Selling animal fat is degrading, yet by so doing Yung Po made a thousand gold pieces. Hawking drinks is a poor trade, yet that is how the Chang family made ten million. Sharpening knives requires little skill, yet it enabled the Chih family to live like lords with food served in tripods. Selling preserved tripe is lowly enough, yet in this way the Cho family had a mounted retinue. A horse doctor is held cheap, yet Chang Li had bronze bells to make music. All these men achieved wealth through single-mindedness.

From this we can see that there is no fixed road to wealth, and goods do not stay with the same master for ever. Wealth flows to those with ability as the spokes of a wheel converge upon the axle, but it slips like a smashed tile through the hands of incompetent men. A family with a thousand pieces of gold is comparable to the lord of a city; a man with millions can live like a king. Not for nothing are such men called "nobles without fiefs".

THE GALLANT CITIZENS

Han Fei Tzu has said, "Confucian scholars with their writings confuse the law, gallant citizens with their weapons infringe the rules." But although Han Fei Tzu ridicules both, Confucian scholars often win praise in the world.

We need not speak of those who through their arts rise to become prime ministers or high officials assisting their sovereigns, those whose feats and fame are recorded in the annals of the state. But men like Chi Tzu and Yuan Hsien were ordinary citizens engaged in studying the classics, who held aloof from the world and practised the virtues of a gentleman. Too upright to pander to the age, they were laughed at in their day. They lived all their lives in bare rooms with matting doors, content with coarse garments and the simplest fare. Now more than four hundred years have passed since their death, yet their disciples still commemorate them.

As for the gallant citizens, although they do not always do what is right, their word can be trusted. They keep all their promises, honour all their pledges, and hasten to rescue those in distress regardless of their own safety. They risk their lives without boasting, not stooping to speak of their good deeds. So there is much to be said for them, especially as anyone may find himself in trouble sooner or later!

The Grand Historian comments: In days gone by, Emperor Shun was trapped in a well and caught in a granary; Yi Yin toiled as a scullion; Fu Yueh worked as a convict at Fuhsien; Lu Shang sold food at Chichin; Kuan Chung was shackled; Poli Hsi herded cattle; Confucius was threatened by the men of Kuang and grew pale from hunger in Chen and Tsai. If such hardships befell these men so esteemed by scholars for their moral character, there must be no end to the sufferings

429

of men of lesser stature who live in decadent and troubled times.

The common people say, "Don't talk about humanity and justice. Whoever does you a good turn is a good man." So although Po Yi so hated the Chou Dynasty that he starved to death on Shouyang Mountain, people thought none the worse of King Wen and King Wu. Although Cheh and Chiao were cruel brigand chiefs, their followers extolled their merits. This illustrates the truth of the saying, "The man who steals a knife is killed but the man who steals a kingdom is ennobled, and virtue and justice are on the side of the nobles."

Scrupulous, punctilious scholars isolate themselves from the world, when they could win glory and fame by lowering themselves to the level of the vulgar and pandering to the fashions of the time. But when common citizens pledge themselves to a just cause and will travel a thousand *li* to die for it, not caring what the world thinks, this has its merits too. Such men have not lived for nothing. That is why people who are hard pressed entrust their fate to them, for these are worthy and outstanding men. Indeed, if we compare the power and influence of these gallant citizens with Chi Tzu and Yuan Hsien's, they render society a much greater service. The main thing is that they do all they promise, proving as good as their word. How can the world belittle such men?

The names of gallant citizens of ancient times are lost. In recent ages there have been men like Lord Yen Ling, Lord Mengchang, Lord Chunshen, Lord Pingyuan and Lord Hsinling, all related to royal houses or high ministers with rich fiefs, who used their wealth to gather men of talent from all parts of the empire to spread their fame through the states. These were certainly worthy men, but their winning themselves fame was like calling down the wind: even if the sound itself was not loud, the wind carried it a long way.

It was much more difficult for the common citizens to practise virtue till their fame spread everywhere and their praise was on all lips. These men were brushed aside, moreover, by both Confucians and Mohists, who scorned to record their actions. That is why these gallant citizens who lived before the Chin Dynasty are lost in oblivion — much to my regret.

From what I have heard, men like Chu Chia, Tien Chung, Wang Meng, Chu Meng and Kuo Hsieh at the beginning of the Han Dynasty were admirably honest, scrupulous and modest in their private lives although they often broke the law of their time. Their fame was well deserved and it was not for nothing that others sought their protection.

As for those gangs and powerful families who band together and use their wealth to enslave the poor and bully the weak and helpless, with no thought of anything but their own pleasure, such men are also despised by the gallant citizens. I consider it a pity that no distinction is generally made between the two, and that men class Chu Chia and Kuo Hsieh with those local bullies and sneer at both groups.

Chu Chia of Lu lived during the region of Emperor Kao-tsu, but while most men of Lu observe the teachings of Confucius Chu Chia made a name as a gallant man. He protected and saved several hundred eminent men, to say nothing of ordinary people. Yet he never boasted of his ability or made much of his kindness. He tried, indeed, to avoid those whom he had helped. In aiding those in distress he started with the poor and humble. There was no spare money in his home, his clothes were shabby and faded, he ate no more than one dish at each meal and travelled in a small ox-cart. He secretly aided General Chi Pu when he was in trouble, but after Chi Pu became a great nobleman Chu Chia never went to see him. All who lived east of the Hanku Pass craned their necks in their eagerness to get to know him.

Tien Chung of Chu, who made a name as a gallant man and loved swordsmanship, looked up to Chu Chia as to his father and regarded himself as much inferior.

After Tien Chung's death there was Chu Meng of Loyang.

431

Most of the men of Chou were traders, but Chu Meng won fame among the feudal lords by his gallant deeds of daring. When the princes of Wu and Chu rebelled, Chou Ya-fu the marquis of Tiao was made the grand marshal. As he was approaching Honan by relay carriages he was delighted to meet Chu Meng and said, "The princes of Wu and Chu have raised a rebellion without seeking out Chu Meng. Now I know they will not accomplish anything." For in those unsettled times a prime minister considered Chu Meng's help as equivalent to the conquest of an enemy state. Chu Meng behaved like Chu Chia, except that he was fond of gambling and other young men's amusements. When his mother died, about a thousand carriages came from distant parts to the funeral. When Chu Meng himself died, his family was left without so much as ten pieces of gold.

Wang Meng of Fuli was also famed as a gallant citizen between the Yangtse and the Huai Rivers. Men of the Chien family of Tsinan and Chou Yung of Chen were also known at that time for their gallant deeds. When Emperor Ching learned of this, he sent and had them killed. They were followed later by others like the Pai family in Tai, Tan Wu-pi of Liang, Hsueh Kuang of Yangti and Han Ju of Shan.

Kuo Hsieh of Chih, whose courtesy name was Weng-po, was the grandson on his mother's side of the successful physiognomist Hsu Fu. His father was executed for his daring deeds in the reign of Emperor Wen.

Kuo Hsieh was short but agile and intrepid. He never drank wine. In his youth he was sullen and vindictive. He killed many men when his anger was aroused but would risk his life to avenge friends. He sheltered outlaws, conspired against the authorities, was always going in for armed robbery, and was guilty time and again of counterfeiting money and robbing tombs. As luck would have it, however, he always contrived to extricate himself from trouble or to be pardoned by an amnesty.

As Kuo Hsieh grew older he became more humble and repaid evil with kindness, giving much and asking little in return. He grew fonder than ever of noble deeds of daring. But although he no longer boasted of the lives he had saved, he remained vindictive and prone to sudden bursts of anger over trivial humiliations. The young men who admired him would often avenge his wrongs without his knowledge.

Kuo Hsieh's elder sister had a son who took advantage of his uncle's influence. One day while drinking, this lad insisted that his companion should drain his cup, and although the other declared himself unable to do so he forced the wine down his throat. In a fury the man drew his dagger and stabbed the boy to death, after which he fled.

Kuo Hsieh's sister flew into a passion. "Who says my brother is an honourable man?" she exclaimed. "He lets my son's murderer go free!" She left the corpse unburied on the road in order to shame her brother.

Kuo Hsieh sent men to find out the whereabouts of the murderer. And the latter, knowing that he could not escape, came to Kuo Hsieh of his own accord and told him what had happened.

"You were right to kill him," said Kuo Hsieh. "The boy was in the wrong," So he let the man go, declaring that his nephew was to blame, and gave the dead body burial. When this became known, men were so impressed by his sense of justice that more admirers flocked to him.

Whenever Kuo Hsieh went out, people usually kept out of his way. One day, however, a man squatted insolently by the roadside to stare at him, and Kuo Hsieh sent to inquire this stranger's name. His followers wanted to kill the man but Kuo Hsieh said, "If someone in my own district treats me rudely, it must mean that I am lacking in virtue. Why do you blame him?" And he secretly told the local officers, "I have a high regard for this man. When his turn comes for conscription, let him off."

So every time men were conscripted, this fellow was surprised to find that the officers passed him by. When he discovered to whom he owed his exemption, he went with bared shoulders to apologize to Kuo Hsieh. And the young men, hearing of this, admired Kuo more than ever.

Two men in Loyang were carrying on a feud, and although a dozen or more of the chief citizens had tried to act as peacemakers they refused to be reconciled. When the matter was taken to Kuo Hsieh he went by night to see the two enemies, and they brought themselves to accept his mediation.

"I hear that many citizens of Loyang have interceded with you, yet you did not listen to them," said Kuo Hsieh. "I am glad that you are willing to take my advice. But it is not right for a stranger from another district to outshine your own worthies and detract from their prestige." He left under cover of darkness so that no one might know of his visit. "Go ahead without me," he told the two men. "Once I have gone and the chief citizens of Loyang come again to reason with you, do as they say."

Kuo Hsieh was a stickler for etiquette and would never ride into the district court in his carriage. When he went to neighbouring districts at his friends' request, if he could solve their problems, well and good; if not, he made a point of satisfying them in different ways before tasting food and wine. Thus he was highly respected and many people were only too eager to serve him. Often ten or more carriages came to his gate in one night, bringing young men of his district or prominent citizens from neighbouring provinces who offered to take away some of his protégés and look after them.

When it was decided to move the wealthiest and most powerful citizens of the empire to Maoling, Kuo Hsieh's family was not rich enough to be included, but the officer in charge dared not leave him out. General Wei Ching spoke up for him, saying that he was a poor man and should not be moved. But the emperor retorted, "If a private citizen is influential enough to prevail on the grand marshal to speak for him, he cannot be very poor!" So his family was finally forced to move, and the people who saw him off presented him with more than ten million cash.

The district officer who had recommended Kuo Hsieh's removal was the son of Yang Chi-chu, a native of Chih. His head was cut off by Kuo Hsieh's nephew, and after that the two families were enemies.

The chief citizens west of the Hanku Pass, whether they knew Kuo Hsieh or not, soon heard of his fame and vied with one another to befriend him.

Some time later, Yang Chi-chu was murdered. His family wrote a memorial to the throne, but their messenger was killed outside the palace. When news of this came to the ears of Emperor Wu, he sent officers to arrest Kuo Hsieh, who fled to Lintsin, leaving his mother and family in Hsiayang. Since Chi Shao-kuang, the officer at Lintsin, did not know him and Kuo Hsieh had assumed a false name, he was able to escape through the Pass and make his way east to Taiyuan. Because Kuo Hsieh told his hosts each night where he was heading, the authorities were able to trace him as far as Chi Shao-kung; but as the latter had committed suicide the trail was lost and it was some time before Kuo Hsieh was captured.

During Kuo Hsieh's trial, it was found that he had committed no murders since the last amnesty. A Confucian scholar from Chih was sitting with the officers during the investigation. When one of Kuo Hsieh's admirers praised him, this scholar said, "Kuo Hsieh has done nothing but break the law and commit crimes. What good can there be in such a man?"

One of Kuo's followers killed this scholar and cut out his tongue. The officers laid the blame for this on Kuo Hsieh, although in fact he did not know the murderer, who was never found.

The officers reported that Kuo Hsieh was not guilty of the charges against him. Kungsun Hung the chief counsellor protested, "Kuo Hsieh is a common citizen who sets himself up as the arbiter of justice and kills men for the most trivial offences. The fact that he does not know the murderer makes the case more serious than if he had killed the scholar himself. He is guilty of high treason." So Kuo Hsieh and his clan were put to death.

There have since been many gallant citizens, too arrogant in their behaviour to be worth mentioning. But there was Fan Chung-tzu of Changan, Chao Wang-sun of Huaili, Kao Kung-tzu of Changling, Kuo Kung-chung of Hsiho, Lu Kung-ju of Taiyuan, Ni Chang-ching of Linhuai and Tien Chun-ju of Tungyang. Although these men acted in a daring way, they were courteous and unassuming gentlemen.

The Yao family in the north, the Tu family in the west, Chiu Ching in the south, Chao Ta-yu or Chao Kung-tzu in the east, and Chao Tiao in Nanyang were virtually brigands quite beneath our notice and utterly unfit to be compared with Chu Chia of earlier times.

The Grand Historian comments: When I saw Kuo Hsieh, his appearance was in no way striking, neither was his conversation memorable. Yet everybody in the empire, high or low, whether he knew him or not, admires him and cites him as an example of gallant daring. "Fame sheds lustre on beauty," says the proverb. "It is fame that endures." Alas, that he came to such an end!

THE HARSH OFFICIALS

Confucius said, "If you govern the people by laws and control them with punishments, they will try to keep out of trouble but will have no sense of shame. If you govern them with virtue and control them with ceremony, they will have a sense of shame and correct themselves."

Lao Tzu said, "The man of superior virtue does not lay stress on virtue and so he has virtue. The man of inferior virtue clings to virtue and so he has no virtue." Again, "The more laws are promulgated, the more brigands and thieves there will be."

The Grand Historian comments: How true this is! Laws and codes are instruments of government, but not the cause of good government.

In former times the empire was hemmed in by legal restrictions, yet evil and deception grew so rife that those above and those below concealed the truth from each other, until the situation became hopeless. Then the officials' attempt to maintain order was like trying to put out a fire or prevent boiling water from bubbling over. Only the most ruthless and harshest could carry out this task satisfactorily. To have spoken of virtue would have been shirking their duty. That is why Confucius said, "I am no better than others in dealing with lawsuits. The thing is to do away with them." And Lao Tzu said, "When men of low understanding hear about the Way, they laugh out loud at it." These are true words.

At the start of the Han Dynasty, smoothness was preferred to sharp angles, simplicity to ornamentation. A whale could have slipped through the net of the law! Yet the law officers were honest and uncorrupted, while the people lived in peace. We can see that this did not come about through harshness.

In the time of Empress Lu, the only harsh official was Hou Feng, who harried members of the imperial clan and humiliated worthy ministers. But after the Lu clan was overthrown, Hou Feng's family was destroyed.

In the reign of Emperor Ching, Chao Tso was an exacting official who achieved his end partly by cunning. And the seven princes revolted because of their resentment against Chao Tso, who was finally executed for causing this trouble. After him there were men like Chih Tu and Ning Cheng.

Chih Tu was a native of Yang. He served under Emperor Wen as a palace guard and Emperor Ching made him captain of the palace guard. He had no scruples about speaking bluntly and would contradict high officials to their faces at court.

Once while he was accompanying the emperor to Shanglin Park, Lady Chia went to the privy and a wild boar charged after her. The emperor looked at Chih Tu, who did not move. Then the emperor took a weapon to go to her rescue, but Chih Tu prostrated himself and cried, "If one lady in waiting dies, another can be found. The empire has no lack of Lady Chias! Your Majesty may think lightly of your own safety, but what of the temples of your ancestors? What of the empress dowager?"

Then the emperor turned back and the wild boar made off. When this came to the ears of the empress dowager, she gave Chih Tu a hundred catties of gold, and from that time on he was very highly regarded.

Now the clan of Chien in Chinan consisted of more than three hundred families and was so powerful and lawless that not even officials of the two thousand piculs rank could control it. So Emperor Ching appointed Chih Tu as governor of Chinan. Upon his arrival there, he wiped out the ringleaders of the clan together with their relatives, making the rest tremble with fear. In his year and more of office, no one in the province dared to pick up anything that had been dropped in the road, and the dozen or so governors of neighbouring provinces feared him as if he were a chief minister.

Chih Tu was a courageous and powerful man, so scrupulously honest in the conduct of public affairs that he carried on no private correspondence, accepted no gifts and listened to no special requests. He used to say, "Since I left my family and took office, I must do my duty and be ready to die at my post, with no thought of wife and children."

When Chih Tu was transferred to be the metropolitan tribune, the prime minister, the marquis of Tiao, was most powerful and arrogant, yet Chih Tu greeted him as an equal.

In those days the common people were simple and honest. Afraid to do anything wrong, they kept out of harm's way. It was Chih Tu who laid stress on severity and applied the full rigour of the law even to relations of the emperor. The feudal lords and members of the imperial clan dared not look him in the face but nicknamed him the Grey Falcon.

When the prince of Linchiang was summoned for trial in Chih Tu's office, he asked for a knife and stylus to write a letter to the emperor, but Chih Tu would not let the officers grant his request. The marquis of Weichi sent them to him in secret, however, and after writing the letter the prince took his own life. Empress Dowager Tou was so angry when she learned of this that she found some legal pretext to indict Chih Tu, who was dismissed from office and went home. Emperor Ching sent an envoy with credentials to appoint him as governor of Yenmen, ordering him to proceed straight from home to his new post and act there as he thought fit.

Since the Huns had long heard that Chih Tu was incorruptible, while he was at the frontier they withdrew their troops, never invading Yenmen so long as he lived. They even carved an effigy of him and made their mounted archers use it as a target, but such was the awe in which they held him that none of them could hit it. He was, indeed, a thorn in the side of the Huns.

When Empress Dowager Tou brought another charge against him, the emperor said, "Chih Tu is a loyal subject." He would have released him, but the empress dowager retorted, "And the king of Linchiang, was he not a loyal subject?" So in the end Chih Tu was executed.

Ning Cheng of Jang served Emperor Ching first as a palace guard and then as a herald. He was an irascible man. As a subordinate he was rude to his superiors, while he tied down those under him as tightly as a bundle of wet twigs. Through cunning and ruthlessness he was gradually promoted to the post of the military tribune of Chinan, when Chih Tu happened to be the governor there.

Former tribunes, such was their fear of Chih Tu, had gone on foot to his office to pay their respects as if they were mere magistrates. Ning Cheng, however, behaved even more arrogantly than Chih Tu. And since the latter knew his reputation, he treated him well and they became good friends.

Some years later, after Chih Tu's execution, so many of the emperor's attendants and members of the imperial clan in Changan started resorting to violence and breaking the law that the emperor summoned Ning Cheng to be metropolitan tribune. His administration was like that of Chih Tu, except that he was not so incorruptible. However, members of the imperial clan and prominent citizens all feared him to a man.

When Emperor Wu came to the throne, Ning Cheng was transferred to the prefectship of the capital. Then the relatives of the empress brought a false charge against him. His head was shaved and a chain put round his neck. In those days it was usual for high ministers guilty of capital offences to commit suicide rather than submit to punishment. But Ning Cheng put up with this disgrace and, confident that he would not be arrested again, got rid of his chains, forged a permit to get through the Pass, and returned home.

"An official who cannot reach the two thousand piculs rank or a merchant who cannot make ten million cash is no true man," he said. So he borrowed money to purchase a hundred thousand *mou* and more of hilly land, and got several thousand poor families to work for him. By the time an amnesty was declared a few years later, he was worth several thousand pieces of gold. He took the law into his own hands, bending the local officials to his will. He had a retinue of several dozen horsemen and could order the people about with more authority than the provincial governor.

Chouyang Yu's father, originally called Chao Chien, took the surname Chouyang because as an uncle of the prince of Huainan he was made the marquis of Chouyang. And owing to this connection he served in the palace guard in the reigns of Emperor Wen and Emperor Ching. Under Emperor Ching he became a provincial governor.

When Emperor Wu came to the throne, the local officials exercised their jurisdiction with great moderation. Chouyang Yu alone of the officers of the two thousand piculs rank went to extremes in his savage repression and arrogance. If he liked a man he would stretch the law to save his life; if he hated a man he would twist the law to kill him. Whatever province he administered, he invariably killed off its chief citizens. Serving as governor, he treated the military tribune as a county magistrate; serving as a military tribune himself, he insulted the governor and usurped his authority. He was as harsh as Chi An, and as skilful as Szuma An in manipulating the law to ruin men; but although both of them belonged to the two thousand piculs rank they never presumed to act as Chouyang Yu's equal when riding in the same carriage.

When later Chouyang Yu became military tribune of Hotung, he fought for power with the local governor Lord Shentu, and each impeached the other. Lord Shentu was found guilty but committed suicide rather than suffer the punishment. Chouyang Yu was executed in the market-place.

After the time of Ning Cheng and Chouyang Yu there was an increase in litigation, the law became more involved, and most officials were men of their type.

Chao Yu was a native of T'ai. He served first as a district clerk, then as an officer in the capital, where for his scrupulous conduct he was appointed as a secretary under Grand Marshal

441

Chou Ya-fu. When Chou Ya-fu became prime minister Chao Yu was his secretary, known to all his colleagues for his integrity and justice. But Chou Ya-fu did not trust him. "I know very well that Yu is competent," he said. "But he is too harsh to hold a high position."

During the present reign, he so distinguished himself as a secretary that step by step he was promoted to the post of censor. The emperor, struck by his ability, made him grand counsellor. With Chang Tang he revised the legal codes, drawing up laws dealing with failure to report a crime and the system of mutual surveillance. Since then the laws have been more strictly enforced.

Chang Tang of Tu was the son of the assistant magistrate of Changan. One day when he was a child his father left him to mind the house, only to find on his return that a rat had stolen a piece of meat. In anger he beat his son. Then Chang Tang dug out the rat hole, found the guilty rat and what remained of the meat, tried the rat, recorded its confession and decided on its punishment. He then took the rat and meat into the yard, where he passed sentence and executed the culprit. His father, observing this, was amazed to find that the records read like those drawn up by an experienced scrivener. So he set the lad to writing legal documents. After his father's death, Chang Tang served for many years as an officer in the capital.

While the marquis of Chouyang was still only a minister he was involved in trouble in Changan, and Chang Tang did his utmost to help him. When he was released and ennobled he proved a good friend to Chang Tang, introducing him to all the important people. Chang Tang worked in the city prefect's office under Ning Cheng, who recommended him to the court for his outstanding ability, with the result that he was transferred to be military tribune of Maoling in charge of the construction of the imperial mausoleum.

When the marquis of Wu-an became prime minister, he chose Chang Tang as his secretary and recommended him several times to the emperor, who appointed him a censor. He investigated the charge of witchcraft brought against Empress Chen and made a thorough round up of all her clique. Then the emperor, impressed by his ability, promoted him by degrees to the rank of grand counsellor. He and Chao Yu together revised the legal code, drawing up strict regulations to control all government officials. Later Chao Yu was promoted to be metropolitan tribune, then transferred to the post of privy treasurer while Chang Tang became chief justice. The two men were good friends, Chang Tang treating Chao Yu like an elder brother.

Chao Yu was both close-fisted and overbearing. During the whole of his official career he did no entertaining. When other ministers called on him, he never returned their calls. He made every effort to forestall requests from friends and visitors and took an independent stand, doing whatever he pleased. He based all his decisions on the legal code, would never reopen a case, and was on the look-out for secret malpractices among his subordinates.

Chang Tang was a hypocrite who resorted to cunning to get the better of others. Starting out as a minor official, he engaged in speculation and made friends with Tien Chia, Yu Weng-shu and other rich merchants in the capital. When he became one of the nine chief ministers he befriended the most noted scholars and gentlemen of the empire, making a show of admiring even those he disliked.

At that time the emperor took a great interest in literature. So when Chang Tang was dealing with important cases he tried to find support for his views in the classics. He asked students of the court scholars who were familiar with the *Book of Documents* and *Spring and Autumn Annals* to serve as secretaries in the office of the chief justice and help settle dubious points of law. Before presenting a decision on controversial cases, he would analyse them for the emperor, then bring in a verdict according to the emperor's instructions and pay open tribute to his sagacity.

If he was criticized for some report, he would apologize and fall in with the emperor's wishes. Then he made a point of mentioning one of his more capable subordinates, saying, "So-and-so's advice coincided with Your Majesty's instructions; but I failed to take it and made this stupid mistake." As a result, the fault was always condoned.

If the emperor approved of some report, Chang Tang would say, "This was not originally my idea, but proposed by so-and-so in my office." This was how he recommended his officials, bringing forward their good points and hiding their faults.

When it came to trials, those whom the emperor wished to condemn Chang Tang handed over to his most implacable secretaries, while those whom the emperor wanted to have pardoned he assigned to more lenient men. When trying someone wealthy and influential, he would manipulate the law to prove his guilt. But he always took the side of the weak and poor, and even if the man was guilty according to the law Chang Tang would often speak well of him in front of the emperor. Thus when the case came to the attention of the emperor he would remember what Chang Tang had said and pardon the man.

Chang Tang's behaviour was exemplary after he became a high official. He supplied all his protégés with food and drink, showing special regard for those officers who were the sons and younger brothers of old friends, as well as for poor relations. He called on other officials regardless of the cold or heat. So in spite of his harshness in applying the law, in spite of his cunning, prejudices and bias, he won fame. Many ruthless officials came to work for him, as well as men of letters, and on several occasions the prime minister Kungsun Hung commended his virtue.

When investigating the rebellion of the princes of Huainan, Hengshan and Chiangtu, Chang Tang went to the root of the matter and opposed the emperor's wish to pardon Yen Chu and Wu Pei. "It was Wu Pei who drew up the plan for revolt," he said. "As for Yen Chu, he enjoyed your favour and was a trusted official with access to the inner palace, yet he had private dealings with the princes. If men like these are not executed, things will get out of hand." Then the emperor accepted his recommendation. This is only one example of the way in which Chang Tang utilized prosecutions to sweep aside other high officials and win credit himself. So he was appointed to more important posts and finally promoted to be grand secretary.

When the Hunyeh and other Hunnish tribes surrendered, the Han government sent out great armies against the Huns. There were flood and drought in the eastern provinces and the destitute were roaming the country, depending upon relief from the local authorities, whose resources were soon exhausted. Then Chang Tang, at the wish of the emperor, proposed minting *wu-chu* and silver coins, setting up a state monopoly of salt and iron, and restricting the great merchants. He drew up a law promising a reward for information about tax-evasion, attacked the powerful families which were annexing land, and twisted the law to make its enforcement even stricter.

When Chang Tang went to court to report on affairs of state, the emperor would forget to eat till sunset. The prime minister was no more than a figurehead, for all affairs in the empire were decided by Chang Tang. Then the people, dissatisfied with their life, grew restive, and the government derived no profit from the new measures, for corrupt officials appropriated the gains. So such offences were more severely punished. Chang Tang was hated by everyone from the high officials down to the common people. Yet when he fell ill the emperor went in person to see him, so greatly did he favour and respect him.

Now the Huns made overtures for peace and the ministers discussed their request in the emperor's presence. A court scholar named Ti Shan said, "To make peace is best."

Asked by the emperor for his reasons, he said, "Arms are weapons of destruction which should not be resorted to lightly or too often. When Emperor Kao-tsu wanted to attack the Huns he got into serious difficulties at Pingcheng, after which he made peace with them. In the time of Emperor Hui and the empress dowager the empire enjoyed peace. Then Emperor

Wen decided to deal with the Huns, and the northern borders were laid waste by war. During the reign of Emperor Ching, when the princes of Wu, Chu and five other states rebelled, the emperor was constantly going from his own palace to that of the empress dowager to consult her during those anxious months, and once the revolt was suppressed he never again spoke of war and the empire prospered. Now since Your Majesty sent out expeditions against the Huns, the empire has become exhausted while the people at the borders are in desperate straits. For these reasons I say it would be best to make peace."

The emperor then asked Chang Tang's opinion.

"This Confucian is an ignorant fool," said Chang Tang.

"My loyalty may be foolish," retorted Ti Shan. "But the loyalty of the chief counsellor Chang Tang is spurious. Take the way he handled the case of the princes of Huainan and Chiangtu. He prosecuted them with the utmost rigour of the law, estranging those of one flesh and blood and spreading unrest among the princes. So I know that his loyalty is nothing but an outward show."

The emperor's face darkened and he demanded, "If I gave you a province to govern, could you keep the barbarians from invading it?"

"No, I could not," admitted Ti Shan.

"How about a county?"

"No."

"One frontier post, then?"

Fearful of being put on trial if his answer was found wanting, Ti Shan replied, "Yes, I could manage that."

Then the emperor sent him to hold a frontier post, but in little more than a month Hunnish raiders cut off his head. After that all the other officials were thoroughly cowed.

One of Chang Tang's protégés, Tien Chia, was a merchant but a man of good character. When Chang Tang was a minor official he had certain transactions with him, but after Chang Tang became a high official Tien Chia used to criticize him for his faults like a man of honour. Chang Tang served as grand secretary for seven years before his downfall.

Li Wen of Hotung bore Chang Tang a grudge. After he became an assistant to the grand secretary, his resentment rankled and he searched the files for incriminating documents, but could find none. One of Chang Tang's favourite secretaries, Lu Yeh-chu, knew that the grand secretary was uneasy on this score and persuaded someone to impeach Li Wen. The case was referred to Chang Tang, who had Li Wen sentenced to death. Chang Tang knew quite well that Lu Yeh-chu was behind this, but when the emperor asked, "Who brought this charge of sedition?" he put on a look of surprise and replied, "I suppose it was some old acquaintance who disliked Li Wen."

When Lu Yeh-chu fell ill and was lying in bed in the house of a neighbour, Chang Tang went in person to ask after him and massaged his feet for him.

The main industry in the principality of Chao is iron smelting, and the prince of Chao repeatedly went to law with the government officer in charge of this industry, but Chang Tang always took the latter's side. So the prince was eager to catch Chang Tang out. And he also hated Lu Yeh-chu, who had once filed charges against him. He therefore addressed a memorial to the throne saying that Chang Tang was a high minister, yet when his secretary Lu Yeh-chu fell ill he had gone so far as to massage his feet for him. He suspected that they must be plotting treason together.

By the time the matter was referred to the chief justice Lu Yeh-chu had died of illness, but the case involved his younger brother, who was detained in the retainers' office. Chang Tang happened to be investigating a case in that office and, noticing Lu Yeh-chu's brother, he was eager to help him; but wanting to do so in secret, he pretended not to know him. The young man, not realizing this, was highly indignant and got someone to write a memorial to the throne accusing Chang Tang of plotting with Lu Yeh-chu to charge Li Wen with sedition. The matter was investigated by Chien Hsuan, and as he had a grudge against Chang Tang he went into the case very thoroughly.

Before Chien Hsuan submitted a report, Emperor Wen's sepulchre was opened and coins stolen from it. The prime minister Chuang Ching-ti and Chang Tang agreed to go to court together to apologize for this. Before they reached the court, however, Chang Tang decided that since it was the prime minister's duty to make seasonal inspections of the burial grounds, he himself was in no way responsible and need not apologize. After the prime minister made his apologies, the emperor ordered Chang Tang to investigate the case. Chang Tang wanted to prove that the prime minister was to blame, and Chuang Ching-ti was seriously alarmed.

At this time the three chief secretaries of the prime minister's office hated Chang Tang and were eager to ruin him. One of them, Chu Mai-chen of Kuaichi, had made a study of the *Spring and Autumn Annals*. Chuang Chu induced someone to recommend him to the emperor and both he and Chuang Chu won the imperial favour. Chu Mai-chen was favoured because of his knowledge of the *Literature of Chu*. They were serving in the palace as grand counsellors while Chang Tang was still a minor officer who had to kneel before them. After Chang Tang became chief justice and investigated the case of the prince of Huainan, he vented his dislike of Chuang Chu and Chu Mai-chen by denouncing them. Later Chang Tang became grand secretary while Chu Mai-chen served as governor of Kuaichi and then as the officer in charge of the principalities, ranking as one of the nine chief ministers. A few years later, being charged with some offence, he was removed from his post and made a secretary. When he called on Chang Tang, the latter did not rise from his couch but treated him as unceremoniously as if he were a petty clerk. Chu Mai-chen, a true man of Chu, was consumed with indignation and cast about for means to kill Chang Tang.

Then there was Wang Chao of Chi, who became senior city prefect through his knowledge of the classics. And Pien Tung, a man of a stubborn, violent temper, who had studied oratory and twice served as the minister of Chinan. All three of these men ranked above Chang Tang till they lost their posts and became secretaries of the prime minister, lower in position than Chang Tang. On several occasions when he was acting prime minister, knowing that these three men had held high positions, he went out of his way to insult them.

Accordingly these three secretaries plotted together and told the prime minister, "Chang Tang went with you, sir, to apologize to the emperor, but then let you down. Now he intends to impeach you over the desecration of the ancestral temple so that he can take your place. But we know his guilty secrets."

They sent officers to arrest Chang Tang's friend Tien Hsin and other merchants on the charge that Tien Hsin knew in advance whatever memorial Chang Tang was going to present, and that he shared the wealth made in this way with Chang Tang. There were other charges too.

When the emperor learned of this he said to Chang Tang, "The merchants know all my decisions in advance and hoard certain commodities. Someone must be disclosing my plans to them."

Instead of apologizing, Chang Tang put on an air of surprise and said, "Yes, it certainly looks like that."

Chien Hsuan also submitted his report on Lu Yeh-chu and others. Then the emperor realized that Chang Tang had deceived him and sent eight officers to check up on his records. But Chang Tang denied all guilt and would not confess. The emperor ordered Chao Yu to reprove him.

Chao Yu went to Chang Tang and said scathingly, "Can't you understand the position you are in? Not even after all the men you have condemned to death with their whole families? All the charges against you are backed by written evidence. The emperor has ordered an investigation because he wants you to choose your own way to die. What good would a long trial do?"

Then Chang Tang wrote an apology, saying, "Although with no vestige of merit, I was raised by Your Majesty's favour

449

from the position of a clerk with knife and stylus to become one of the three highest ministers. It is true I have failed in my duty, but I am the victim of a plot by the three secretaries of the prime minister." Then he committed suicide.

After his death his property was found to amount to no more than five hundred pieces of gold, and these had been a gift from the emperor. He had no other estate. His younger brothers and sons would have given him a fine funeral had not his mother objected.

"He was a high minister serving the Son of Heaven, yet he got a name for corruption and took his own life," she said. "Why should he have a fine funeral?" So they had his coffin loaded on to an ox-cart and gave him no outer coffin.

When this came to the ears of the emperor he remarked, "Only such a mother could have had such a son!" He had the three secretaries tried and executed. The prime minister committed suicide and Tien Hsin was released. Because the emperor regretted Chang Tang's death, he promoted his son Chang An-shih.

Chao Yu was once dismissed from office but later became chief justice. The marquis of Tiao had given him no appointment because he considered him too ruthless, and when Chao Yu later became privy treasurer with the rank of a high minister he did indeed prove extremely harsh. In his later years, when there was more litigation and most officials applied the utmost rigour of the law, Chao Yu became more lenient and won a name for fairness. Law officers after him like Wang Wen-shu were much harsher than Chao Yu. In his old age he was transferred to be chief minister of Yen. A few years later he was dismissed on a charge of improper conduct, and he died of old age at home more than ten years after Chang Tang's death.

Yi Tsung was a native of Hotung. As a young man he and Chang Tzu-kung lived as brigands. His elder sister Chu found favour with Empress Dowager Wang thanks to her knowledge of medicine.

"Have you any sons or brothers in official posts?" the empress dowager asked her.

"I have a younger brother, but he is not fit for any post," she replied.

However, the empress dowager persuaded the emperor to make Yi Tsung a palace guard and a magistrate in the province of Shangtang. He proved a firm, enterprising administrator and there was no tax evasion in his county, so that he was held up as an example to others. Promoted to be magistrate of Changling and then of Changan, he governed justly according to the law, not shrinking from clashes with nobles. His arrest and trial of Chung, the son of Lady Hsiucheng who was the empress dowager's grand-daughter, so impressed the emperor that he promoted Yi Tsung to be military tribune of Honei. There he wiped out the powerful clan of Jang, and soon the people of Honei dared not pick up anything dropped in the road.

Chang Tzu-kung also served as a palace guard. Being a fearless man he joined the army, advanced boldly into enemy territory and so distinguished himself that he was enfeoffed as marquis of Antou.

Ning Cheng was then living in retirement and the emperor wanted to make him the governor of a province, but the grand secretary Kungsun Hung objected. "When I served as a minor official east of the mountains, Ning Cheng was the military tribune of Chinan," he said. "He harried the people as a wolf harasses sheep. It would never do to let him govern a province." So the emperor made Ning Cheng military tribune of the Hanku Pass. And a year or so later officers who had come through the Pass from provinces to the east declared, "Better to meet a tigress with cubs than face an angry Ning Cheng!"

After Yi Tsung was transferred from his post in Honei to be governor of Nanyang, he heard that Ning Cheng was living there in retirement. Ning Cheng came to welcome him humbly at the Pass, but Yi Tsung behaved insolently and did not greet him. Upon reaching his post he put Ning Cheng on trial

451

and destroyed his family. After Ning Cheng was convicted and men of the Kung and Pao families fled, the officers and citizens of Nanyang all took care to keep in step. Moreover Yi Tsung used Chu Chiang of Pingshih and Tu Chou of Tuyen as his claws and teeth in applying the law, and appointed them as secretaries in the office of the chief justice.

After several expeditions had marched through Tinghsiang, the provincial authorities and the people there were demoralized, and Yi Tsung was transferred to govern the province. His first act upon arrival was to seize two hundred and more prisoners who were in the provincial gaol for heavy and light offences, along with more than two hundred friends and relatives who had slipped in without permission to see them. Accusing them all of conniving at the escape of criminals charged with capital offences, he had all four hundred and more of them executed that same day. Then the men of that province trembled and those who were cunning began to help the officers in their tasks.

By this time Chao Yu and Chang Tang had become high officials through their harsh application of the law, yet they were lenient compared with Yi Tsung and they acted in accordance with the law, whereas he enforced his rule like a hawk swooping down on its prey.

Later the debasing of the coinage gave rise to malpractices among the people, particularly in the capital. So Yi Tsung was appointed the senior prefect of the capital with Wang Wen-shu as metropolitan tribune. Wang Wen-shu was quite merciless. But if he took action without first consulting Yi Tsung, the latter would abuse and discredit him. Yi Tsung in his term of office executed a whole host of people yet failed to establish good order, for lawlessness only increased and special constables had to be appointed. Their main task was to carry out executions and arrests, and Yen Feng was employed because of his cruel nature.

Yi Tsung was incorruptible, modelling his administration on that of Chih Tu.

The emperor fell ill while visiting Tinghu and remained

there for some time. When at last he recovered and made a trip to Kanchuan, he was angry to find the road in poor repair and exclaimed indignantly, "Yi Tsung must have thought I would never pass this way again!"

That winter Yang Ko was given the task of collecting evidence of tax evasion and, fearing this would lead to public unrest, Yi Tsung told his officers to arrest Yang Ko's agents. When the emperor heard of this he ordered Tu Shih to investigate the matter. Yi Tsung was convicted of obstructing state policy and executed in the market-place. Chang Tang died the following year.

Wang Wen-shu was a native of Yangling who in his youth robbed graves and broke the law. He was made a constable in his county and, although dismissed several times, subsequenly became an officer of the law and a secretary in the office of the chief justice under Chang Tang. Transferred to be a censor in charge of suppressing brigandage, he had a great number of people executed. Then he became military tribune of Kuangping and chose more than ten able men of that province as his henchmen, keeping them under his thumb with evidence of their secret crimes while he used them to control thieves and brigands. So long as they fell in with his wishes, Wang would not punish them even if they were guilty of a hundred crimes. But once a man went against his wishes, he charged him with his past crimes and had him executed with all his clan. As a result, no brigand in the region of Chi and Chao dared come near Kuangping, and it became known as a district in which no one picked up anything dropped in the road. When the emperor heard of this he promoted Wang to be governor of Honei.

While still in Kuangping Wang Wen-shu had learned which of the powerful families of Honei had committed crimes. When he reached his new post in the ninth month, he ordered the provincial office to requisition fifty horses to use as post horses between Honei and the capital and made his subordinates act just as in Kuangping, arresting all evil-doers of any prominence in the province. More than one thousand families were involved. He drew up a memorial to the throne asking that the major offenders should have their clans wiped out, and that the lesser offenders should be executed and have their property confiscated by the public treasury. Only two or three days after dispatching this memorial he received the emperor's approval. He took action at once, and more than ten *li* of land was drenched with blood. The whole of Honei marvelled at the speed with which this was done. By the twelfth month not a voice was raised in the province, not a man dared walk abroad at night, there was not a bandit in the countryside to set dogs barking. And the few who escaped to neighbouring provinces and principalities were hounded by his men.

When spring came, Wang Wen-shu stamped his foot and sighed. "If only the winter had lasted one month longer, I could have finished off the job," he said. Such was his delight in killing men and demonstrating his might and ruthlessness. The emperor, learning of this, considered Wang Wen-shu able and promoted him to be the metropolitan tribune where he acted as in Honei. He enlisted as his subordinates the officers noted for cruelty and cunning, men like Yang Chieh and Ma Wu of Honei and Yang Kan and Cheng Hsin of Kuanchung. So long as Yi Tsung was city prefect, Wang Wen-shu did not dare go too far. But after Yi Tsung's death and Chang Tang's fall, Wang Wen-shu was made chief justice with Yin Chi as the metropolitan tribune.

Yin Chi was a native of Shihping in Tungchun. He started his career as a clerk, then became a censor working under Chang Tang, who on several occasions commended his integrity and courage and put him in charge of suppressing brigands. In executing and punishing men, he did not spare nobles. Promoted to be military tribune within the Pass, he won greater fame than Ning Cheng. The emperor, impressed by his ability, appointed him as the metropolitan tribune. Then officers and citizens alike had an even harder time.

Yin Chi was blunt and lacking in refinement. Powerful and harsh officials tried to keep out of his way, while the good officials could not work with him. Thus he failed in many undertakings and was punished. The emperor transferred Wang Wen-shu back to the post of metropolitan tribune and made Yang Pu, known for his severity, the officer in charge of the principalities.

Yang Pu was a native of Yiyang who started his official career as an officer commanding a thousand men. The governor of Honan recommended him and he was promoted to the post of a censor in charge of bandit suppression east of the Pass. He adopted the bold, ruthless tactics of Yin Chi. Before long he was promoted to be the officer in charge of the principalities, ranking as one of the nine chief ministers. The emperor thought highly of his ability and, when the Nanyueh rebelled, made him General of the Tiered Galleys. He distinguished himself in this campaign and was enfeoffed as the marquis of Chiangliang. But he was subsequently arrested by Hsun Chih, and some time later he died of illness.

Then Wang Wen-shu again served as metropolitan tribune. Lacking refinement, at court he appeared dull and stupid, but as military tribune he was in his element. He suppressed brigands and thieves, understood the way of the people within the Pass, knew which were the ablest and most cunning and employed them as his officers to keep a close watch for robbers, thieves and young men of bad character. He offered rewards for informing on evil-doers through special letter boxes, and posted officers in the villages to look out for brigands.

Wang Wen-shu was a sycophant who flattered those with power and treated the lowly like slaves. A powerful family might be guilty of a host of crimes, yet he would do nothing, whereas he would bully a family without influence even if it was a noble one. He skilfully manipulated the law to destroy petty rogues so as to bring pressure to bear on great families. This was his way as military tribune of the capital.

He carried out such exhaustive investigations that most of those accused died in prison; few were released. His henchmen were tigers in uniform. So all the lesser rogues in the region under his jurisdiction were subdued, while the powerful spread his fame as an able administrator. After several years of his administration most of his subordinates had grown rich by taking advantage of their position.

After Wang Wen-shu's return from the expedition against Tungyueh, the emperor was displeased with something he said and punished and dismissed him for some trifling offence.

The emperor at this time was planning to build the Tower Reaching to Heaven, but no workmen were available. Wang Wen-shu suggested using all the men who had evaded conscript duty under the jurisdiction of the metropolitan tribune, and by this means succeeded in getting several tens of thousands of workers. The emperor was pleased and made him privy treasurer and later senior metropolitan prefect. By employing his previous methods, he was able to put a certain check to crime. Subsequently he lost this post for some offence, but was later made the prefect of West Changan with the powers of a metropolitan tribune. He carried out his duties in this post as before.

A year or so later, just before the dispatch of the expedition to Ferghana, some powerful officers were summoned to take part in the campaign but Wang Wen-shu concealed his lieutenant Hua Cheng. Later someone informed against him, accusing him of taking bribes and making illegal profits. Condemned to execution with his clan, he committed suicide. At the same time the families of his two brothers and brothers-in-law were also exterminated for other crimes.

The superintendent of the imperial household Hsu Tzu-wei remarked, "Alas! In ancient times three classes of relatives were sometimes wiped out, but now Wang Wen-shu has been punished by the destruction of five."

At the time of Wang Wen-shu's death his family had a thousand pieces of gold. A few years later, when Yin Chi died while military tribune of Huaiyang, his estate was less than fifty pieces of gold. He had killed so many citizens of Huaiyang that his enemies wanted to burn his corpse, but it was taken secretly to his old home and buried.

Since Wang Wen-shu and these others governed with such cruelty, most provincial governors, local tribunes and officers of the two thousand piculs rank who wanted to govern effectively copied their ways. Then officers and citizens alike thought nothing of breaking the law, while the number of brigands increased — men like Mei Mien and Pai Cheng in Nanyang, Yin Chung and Tu Shao in Chu, Hsu Po in Chi, and Chien Lu and Fan Sheng in the region between Yen and Chao. The larger bands, numbering several thousand men, assumed titles, attacked cities and towns, seized weapons from the arsenals, released condemned prisoners, bound and insulted provincial governors and local tribunes, killed high officials of the two thousand piculs rank, and ordered the counties to supply them with food. The smaller bands of several hundred men which plundered innumerable villages were past counting.

The emperor ordered the chief officers under the prime minister and the censor to restore order, but they could not put an end to brigandage. Then the emperor sent out Fan Kun, superintendent of the imperial household, the prefects of the capital, the former minister Chang Teh and others. Clad in embroidered robes, bearing the imperial credentials and tiger tallies, they mobilized forces to attack the bandits and killed large numbers of them, sometimes more than ten thousand at a time. Those who had supplied them with food were also punished, and in some cases this involved thousands of people in the provinces.

After several years most of the chief bandits had been caught and the rest had scattered and fled. But they gathered behind the defences of mountains and rivers, and the authorities were powerless against them. Then a law against harbouring outlaws was promulgated. This decreed that if any officer failed to discover an outbreak of banditry, or having discovered one failed to arrest the chief culprits, everyone responsible would be put to death from officers of the two thousand piculs rank down to petty clerks. This so intimidated the lesser officials that they dared not report the presence of brigands for fear they might be unable to capture them. And as high officials were held responsible for the lower, they instructed the latter to hush up such cases. So although the country swarmed with more and more brigands, officials high and low concealed this fact, sending in false reports to keep out of trouble.

Chien Hsuan was a native of Yang. Known for his competence as a clerk, he was employed by the governor of Hotung. And when Marshal Wei Ching was sent to Hotung to buy horses he was so struck by Chien Hsuan's ability that he recommended him to the emperor, who appointed him officer of the imperial stables. Proving competent, he was promoted to the post of law officer and that of censor. And he was in charge of the prosecution of Chufu Yen and those who had rebelled with the prince of Huainan. He kept to the letter of the law, brought serious charges, was responsible for many executions, and won a name for his bold handling of difficult cases. He was dismissed several times but always reinstated, and he served as law officer and censor for nearly twenty years.

After Wang Wen-shu's dismissal from the post of military tribune of the capital, Chien Hsuan became the junior metropolitan prefect. A meticulous administrator, he kept all matters, large and small, in his own hands and personally supervised all the officers in the counties and stores under his jurisdiction. No official might modify his orders on pain of severe punishment. After he had held office for several years, all the affairs in that region were well ordered; but his insistence on looking into every detail taxed his strength, and he could not keep this up indefinitely. He was later demoted to be prefect of the western district of the capital.

Chien Hsuan hated Cheng Hsin, who fled to Shanglin Park, and he ordered the magistrate of Mei to pursue and kill him. While the magistrate's troops were attacking Cheng Hsin, one of their arrows struck the gate of the imperial park and Chien Hsuan was charged with this offence, which ranked as high treason, and sentenced to execution with all his clan. He committed suicide and Tu Chou succeeded to his post.

Tu Chou was a native of Tuyen in Nanyang. When Yi Tsung was governor of Nanyang Tu Chou was a henchman of his. He was then promoted to be a secretary of the chief justice, Chang Tang, who gave such good reports of him to the emperor that he was made a censor. Ordered to investigate cases of flight from border districts, he had a great many people condemned to death. Since his memorials pleased the emperor, he was trusted as much as Chien Hsuan. For more than ten years he served as the law officer in the censor's office.

Tu Chou's administration was like that of Chien Hsuan, but while outwardly lenient he was in fact quite ruthless. When Chien Hsuan was the junior city prefect, Tu Chou served as chief justice. He pursued a policy similar to that of Chang Tang, and was also skilled in anticipating the emperor's wishes. If the emperor wanted to get rid of someone, Tu Chou would ruin the man; if the emperor wanted to spare someone, Tu Chou would use delaying tactics and try to prove that the charge was unfounded.

One of his guests reproached him for this, saying, "You are dispensing justice for the Son of Heaven, but instead of following the legal statutes you pass sentence according to your sovereign's wishes. Is this proper behaviour for a judge?"

"Where did those statutes originate?" Tu Chou retorted. "The legal codes were laid down by earlier sovereigns, the enacting clauses by their successors. Anything that suits the present time is right — what need have we for ancient laws?"

While Tu Chou was chief justice even more officials were condemned to imprisonment by the emperor, and there were usually more than a hundred officials of the two thousand piculs rank in prison. Every year more than a thousand indictments were referred to the chief justice from governors and high officials of the provinces, the graver cases involving several hundred men, the minor ones several dozens. Accused men came to the capital from several hundred or several thousand *li* away. When a case was tried, those who denied the charges brought against them were beaten until they confessed. So all who heard that they might be arrested immediately went into hiding, sometimes for ten years, even though several amnesties were meanwhile pronounced. Most of the indictments were for immoral conduct or more serious crimes. Those arrested and imprisoned by imperial decree numbered sixty or seventy thousand, those arrested and imprisoned by the officials more than a hundred thousand.

Later Tu Chou was dismissed from the post of chief justice and appointed as military tribune of the capital. He arrested and dealt with brigands and investigated the cases of Sang Hung-yang and the brothers of Empress Wei. He was severe in his judgements and the emperor, impressed by his energy and impartiality, raised him to the position of grand secretary. His two sons served as provincial governors on both sides of the Yellow River and proved even harsher and more tyrannical than Wang Wen-shu and the rest.

When Tu Chou was first appointed as a secretary under the chief justice, he owned only one horse, and that not fully equipped. After holding office for many years, however, he rose to be one of the three chief ministers, all his sons and grandsons had become high officials and his family estate was worth millions of cash.

The Grand Historian comments: These ten men from Chih Tu to Tu Chou were all known for their harshness. Chih Tu was honest and upright, guided by principles in dealing with important questions. Chang Tang was always well informed and he and the emperor thought alike; many of his proposals were of benefit to the state. Chao Yu usually upheld justice and abided by the law. Tu Chou was eager to please the emperor and tried to win favour by speaking as little as possible. After Chang Tang's death the law became more involved and punishments more severe, so that the regular government work was gradually neglected. High ministers gave all their efforts to keeping their posts and tried so hard to avoid mistakes that they had no time to do more than obey the law.

The virtues of these ten men can be taken as models, their defects as a warning. Their measures and instructions were designed to curb evil and, taken in the aggregate, were of significance as regards both their civil and military aspects. Although cruel and harsh, these men did what their duty prescribed.

But when it comes to officials like Feng Tang, the governor of Shu, who savagely oppressed people; Li Chen, the governor of Kuanghan, who made mincemeat of men; Mi Pu, the governor of Tungchun, who sawed off people's heads; Lo Pi, the governor of Tienshui, who tortured people until they confessed; Chu Kuang, the governor of Hotung, who killed men wantonly; Wu-chi, the prefect of the capital, and Yin Chou of Fengyi who were as ruthless as vipers and vultures; and Yen Feng the privy treasurer who beat up men to extort money from them — their careers are not worth recording.

史 记 选

司马迁著

自　编

＊

外文出版社出版（北京）

1979年（28开）第一版

编号：（英）10050—603

00315（精）

00280（平）

10—E—1480